FINANCE AND ACCOUNTING FOR NONFINANCIAL MANAGERS

FINANCE AND ACCOUNTING FOR NONFINANCIAL MANAGERS

THE McGRAW-HILL
EXECUTIVE MBA SERIES

SAMUEL C. WEAVER
J. FRED WESTON

McGraw-Hill

New York   Chicago   San Francisco   Lisbon   London
Madrid   Mexico City   Milan   New Delhi   San Juan   Seoul
Singapore   Sydney   Toronto

Library of Congress Cataloging-in-Publication Data

Weaver, Samuel C.
    Finance and accounting for nonfinancial managers/by Samuel C. Weaver and J. Fred Weston.
      p. cm.
    Includes bibliographical references and index.
    ISBN 0-07-136433-1
    1. Finance. 2. Accounting. I. Title: Finance and accounting for non-financial
executives. II. Weston, J. Fred (John Fred) III. Title.

HG173.W448 2001
658.15—dc21   00-066447

McGraw-Hill

*A Division of The **McGraw·Hill** Companies*

1 2 3 4 5 6 7 8 9 0 AGM/AGM 0 9 8 7 6 5 4 3 2 1

ISBN 0-07-136433-1

This publication is designed to provide accurate and authoritative information in regard to the subject matter covered. It is sold with the understanding that neither the author nor the publisher is engaged in rendering legal, accounting, futures/securities trading, or other professional service. If legal advice or other expert assistance is required, the services of a competent professional person should be sought.
        —From a Declaration of Principles jointly adopted by a Committee of the American Bar Association and a Committee of Publishers.

This book was set in Cheltenham by Lisa Hernandez.

Printed and bound by Quebecor World/Martinsburg.

McGraw-Hill books are available at special quantity discounts to use as premiums and sales promotions, or for use in corporate training programs. For more information, please write to the Director of Special Sales, McGraw-Hill, Two Penn Plaza, New York, NY 10121-2298. Or contact your local bookstore.

This book is printed on recycled, acid-free paper containing a minimum of 50% recycled, de-inked fiber.

CONTENTS

PREFACE

This book shows how the principles of finance can be used by executives to enhance the value of their companies. Dr. Weaver had been a senior executive in finance at Hershey Foods for twenty years through 1998, when he joined the Finance Department at Lehigh University. For the past ten years as a director of the Financial Management Association, he has organized and directed a program linking financial principles to financial practices. These full-day sessions focused on the interaction between financial theories and real world practices. Papers on financial concepts important to financial executives were presented by academics. Executives from business firms presented papers on how financial concepts were used in their companies. Spirited discussions took place on how financial principles are related to financial practices. Dr. Weaver has brought these years of study and experience of relating finance theory and practice to the writing of this book.

In addition to his textbooks and articles published in academic journals, J. Fred Weston has decades of experience in testing the validity of financial concepts in his consulting activities. Industries represented in his consulting assignments have included pharmaceuticals, agricultural equipments, autos, steel, aluminum, power generating equipments, telecommunications, and e-commerce. Dr. Weston has applied finance theory to the practice of finance in a wide range of markets.

This book draws on our studies and experience to provide executives with a concise treatment of the principles and practices of finance. It is a user's manual for both financial executives and nonfinancial executives since finance permeates all aspects of business operations.

Two topics which space did not permit us to cover in this volume are share repurchases and all aspects of merger and restructuring activities. These will be covered in a companion book entitled *Mergers and Acquisitions*. Draft materials for this book are available on our websites.

Samuel C. Weaver
J. Fred Weston

PART ONE

ACCOUNTING AND FINANCE FUNDAMENTALS

CHAPTER 1

The Role and Functions of Accounting and Finance

In late June 2000 the financial press carried a summary of an analyst's report which stated that Amazon.com had financial problems. The report cited a combination of negative cash flow, inadequate working-capital management, and mounting debt. Amazon officials called the report hogwash. Raising such matters in a nervous market caused Amazon's stock price to decline from a December 1999 high of 133 to 33 by June 23, 2000. Regardless of whether the concerns had validity, the crucial role of financial management is highlighted.

FINANCE AND FIRM VALUE

Finance and accounting are exciting subjects as we enter the 21st century. The daily newspapers (not just the business press) as well as radio and television carry dramatic stories of growth and decline of firms, earnings surprises, corporate takeovers, and many types of corporate restructuring. To understand these developments and to participate in them effectively requires knowledge of the principles of finance. This book explains these principles and their applications in making decisions.

A fundamental question in the study of finance is whether financial executives can increase the value of a firm. Economic and financial theorists begin with models of an idealized world of no taxes, no transaction costs of issuing debt or equity securities, the managers of firms and its outside investors all having the same information about the firm's future cash flows, no cost of financial distress, and no cost of resolving conflicts of interest among different stakeholders of the firm. In such a world, financial structure does not matter, nor does dividend policy.

The pure idealized models of finance are useful in that they stress the importance of investment opportunities, current and future, on the value of the firm. In the actual world, however, taxes, bankruptcy costs, transactions costs, and the information content of cash flows and dividend or share repurchase policies cause financial policies to have an influence on the value of the firm. Also of great importance is the role of finance in developing information flows so that a firm can evaluate the effectiveness of alternative strategies, policies, decisions, operations, and outcomes. The objective is to create an information flow to provide rapid feedback as a basis for the revision of strategies and decisions to enlarge the growth opportunities of firms and to improve their performance. So there are important ways in which financial executives can contribute to the improved performance of a firm and therefore of its value. This is the central theme of this book, and we shall return to it repeatedly as we demonstrate how financial concepts can contribute to increasing the value of a firm and the returns to its stakeholders, as well as to society as a whole.

BASIC FINANCE ISSUES

The accounting and finance problems faced by all types of organizations are similar. Consider the Extrusion Plastics Company (EP) formed to manufacture a line of containers ranging from small holders of kitchen utensils to large, heavy-duty plastic boxes used to carry parts in manufacturing operations. EP requires a building to house the equipment to form the plastic from its basic ingredients. It must buy raw materials. It needs workers and salespeople. As it manufactures the products, it will have inventories of raw materials, work-in-process, and finished goods. It needs funds to obtain the use of the building and equipment, for raw materials, and for manufacturing operations. It will need to pay its employees. EP finds that it must wait before the sales it makes are actually paid for in cash; while it waits, EP has accounts receivable. The more it grows, the more funds it needs.

This real-life example suggests the two basic financial statements useful for any firm—a balance sheet and income statement. We supply some illustrative numbers.

Balance Sheet

Cash	$ 10		Accounts payable	$ 10	
Accounts receivable	20		Short-term debt	20	
Inventories	30		Total current liabilities		$ 30
Total current assets		$ 60	Long-term debt		$ 20
Property	$ 10				
Plant	10				
Equipment	20				
Total fixed assets		$ 40	Shareholders' equity		$ 50
Total assets		$100	Total claims on assets		$100

Income Statement	
Sales	$200
Costs	190
Net income	$ 10

From this brief example of the basic financing problems facing a representative operation, we can describe the major decision areas for the firm and the role of finance.

RESPONSIBILITIES OF FINANCIAL MANAGERS

Some key decision strategy areas of the firm include

1. Choice of the products and markets of the firm
2. Strategies for research, investment, production, marketing, and sales
3. Selection, training, organization, and motivation of executives and other employees
4. Obtaining funds at a low cost and efficiently
5. Adjustments to the above as environments and competition change

Financial managers must interact with these decisions. These areas are regarded as primarily finance functions in the firm:

1. Analysis of the accounting and financial aspects of all decisions.
2. How much investment will be required to generate the sales that the firm hopes to achieve. These decisions affect the left-hand side of the balance sheet—the investment decisions.
3. How to obtain funds and provide for financing of the assets that the firm requires to produce the products and services whose sales generate revenues. This area represents financing decisions or the capital structure decisions of the firm, affecting the right-hand side of the balance sheet.
4. Analysis of specific individual balance sheet accounts: cash for transactions, accounts receivables reflecting credit policies, inventory strategies, etc.
5. Analysis of individual income statement accounts: revenues and costs. In our highly condensed income statement for EP Company, sales minus all costs equals net income. There are many

kinds of costs—some involve large outlays in advance with costs assigned to operations in subsequent years. (These represent costs that are *fixed* in some sense.) Other costs, such as the materials used in making products, will rise or fall directly as the number of units produced is increased or decreased (direct or *variable* costs.) A major responsibility of financial officers is to control costs in relation to value produced, so that the firm can price its products competitively and profitably.

6. Analysis of operating cash flows of all types. This aspect has received increasing emphasis in recent years and has given rise to a third major financial statement, the *statement of cash flows*, which can be derived from the balance sheets and income statements.

With the background of this compact case study of the Extrusion Plastics Company, we have a basis for defining the finance function in general terms.

THE FINANCE FUNCTION

While the specifics vary among organizations, the *key finance functions are the investment, financing, and dividend decisions of an organization.* Funds are raised from internal operations and from external financial sources and allocated for different uses. The flow of funds within the enterprise is monitored. Benefits to financing sources take the form of returns, repayments, products, and services. These functions must be performed in business firms, government agencies, and nonprofit organizations alike. *The financial manager's goal is to plan for, obtain, and use funds to maximize the value of the organization.* Several activities are involved. First, in planning and forecasting, the financial manager interacts with the executives responsible for general strategic planning activities.

Second, the financial manager is concerned with investment and financing decisions and their interactions. A successful firm usually achieves a high rate of growth in sales, which requires the support of increased investment. Financial managers must determine a sound rate of sales growth and rank alternative investment opportunities. They help decide on the specific investments to be made and the alternative sources and forms of funds for financing these investments. Decision variables include internal versus external funds, debt versus owners' funds, and long-term versus short-term financing.

Third, the financial manager interacts with other functional managers to help the organization operate efficiently. All business decisions have financial implications. For example, marketing decisions affect sales growth and, consequently, change investment requirements;

hence the financial manager must consider their effects on (and how they are affected by) the availability of funds, inventory policies, plant capacity utilization, and so on.

Fourth, the financial manager links the firm to the money and capital markets in which funds are raised and in which the firm's securities are traded.

In sum, the central responsibilities of the financial manager relate to decisions on investments and how they are financed. In the performance of these functions, the financial manager's responsibilities have a direct bearing on the key decisions affecting the value of the firm.

FINANCE IN THE ORGANIZATIONAL STRUCTURE OF THE FIRM

How is the firm organized to carry out the finance functions? The chief financial officer is high in the organizational hierarchy of the firm because of the central role of finance in top-level decision making. Figure 1.1 depicts the typical organizational structure for large firms in the United States. The board of directors represents the shareholders. The president is often the chief executive officer (CEO) or operating officer. One of the key executives is the senior vice president of finance or chief financial officer (CFO), who is responsible for the formulation and implementation of major financial policies. The CFO interacts with senior officers in other functional areas, communicates the financial implications of major decisions, defines the duties of junior financial officers, and is held accountable for the analytical aspects of the treasurer's and controller's activities.

FIGURE 1.1

Finance in the Organizational Structure of a Large Firm

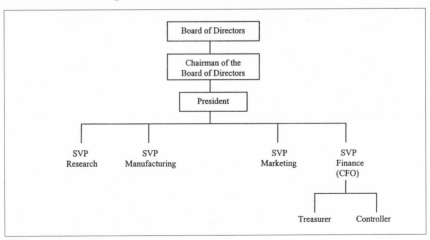

SVP is senior vice president

Specific finance functions are typically divided between two high-ranking financial officers—the treasurer and the controller. The *treasurer* handles the acquisition and custody of funds. The *controller's* function includes accounting, reporting, and control. The treasurer is typically responsible for cash acquisition and management. Although the controller has the main reporting responsibilities, the treasurer provides reports on the daily cash and working-capital position of the firm, formulates cash budgets, and generally reports on cash flows and cash conservation. As a part of this role, the treasurer maintains the firm's relationships with commercial banks and investment bankers. The treasurer is also usually responsible for credit management, insurance, and pension fund management.

The controller's core function is the recording and reporting of financial information. This typically includes the preparation of budgets and financial statements (except as noted above). Other duties include payroll, taxes, and internal auditing.

Some large firms include another corporate officer—the *corporate secretary*—whose activities are related to the finance function. The corporate secretary is responsible for communications relating to the company's financial instruments—record keeping in connection with the instruments of ownership and borrowing activities of the firm (e.g., stocks and bonds). The corporate secretary's duties may also encompass legal affairs and recording the minutes of top-level committee meetings.

Company history and the abilities of individual officers greatly influence the areas of responsibility of these four financial officers. CFOs take responsibility for information systems capable of providing a complete and current financial picture of the firm's operations and performance related to its business model and strategies. This capability is one of the strengths of Cisco Systems—it is able to run off a complete set of financial reports at any hour. With command of the total financial picture of the company, the CFO is likely to be involved in all top management policies and decisions. This kind of experience often results in CFOs becoming the chief executive in a firm.

In addition to individual financial officers, larger enterprises use finance committees. Ideally, a committee assembles persons of different backgrounds and abilities to formulate policies and decisions. Financing decisions require a wide scope of knowledge and balanced judgments. For example, to obtain outside funds is a major decision. A difference of 0.25 or 0.50 percent in interest rates may represent a large amount of money in absolute terms. When such firms as IBM, General Motors, or Kellogg borrow $600 million, a difference of 0.5 percent amounts to $3 million per year. Therefore, the judgments of senior managers with finance backgrounds are valuable in arriving at decisions with bankers on the timing and terms of a loan. Also, the finance committee, working closely with the board of directors, characteristically has major responsibility for administering the capital and operating budgets.

In larger firms, in addition to the general finance committee, there may be subcommittees. A *capital appropriations committee* is responsible primarily for capital budgeting and expenditures. A *budget committee* develops operating budgets, both short-term and long-term. A *pension committee* invests the large amounts of funds involved in employee pension plans. A *salary and profit-sharing committee* is responsible for salary administration as well as the classification and compensation of top-level executives. This committee seeks to set up a system of rewards and penalties that will provide the proper incentives to make the planning and control system of the firm work effectively.

All important episodes in the life of a corporation have major financial implications: adding a new product line or reducing participation in an old one; expanding or adding a plant or changing locations; selling additional new securities; entering into leasing arrangements; paying dividends and making share repurchases. These decisions have a lasting effect on long-run profitability and, therefore, require top management consideration. Hence, the finance function is typically close to the top of the organizational structure of the firm.

GOALS OF THE FIRM

Within the above framework, the *goal of financial management is to maximize the value of the firm,* subject to the constraints of responsibilities to stakeholders. However, there are potential conflicts between a firm's owners and its creditors. For example, consider a firm financed half from the owners' funds and half from debt borrowed at a fixed interest rate, such as 10 percent. No matter how high the firm's earnings, the bondholders still receive only their 10 percent return. Yet if the firm is highly successful, the market value of the ownership funds (the common stock of the company) is likely to rise greatly.

If the company does very well, the value of its common stock increases, while the value of the firm's debt is not likely to be greatly increased (but the equity cushion will be enhanced). On the other hand, if the firm does poorly, the claims of the debtholders will have to be honored first, and the value of the common stock will decline greatly. Thus, the value of the ownership shares provides a good index for measuring the degree of a company's effectiveness in performance. It is for this reason that the goal of financial management is generally expressed in terms of maximizing the value of the ownership shares of the firm—in short, maximizing the share price.

By formulating clear objectives in terms of stock price values, the discipline of the financial markets is implemented. Firms that perform better than others have higher stock prices and can raise additional funds (both debt and equity) under more favorable terms. When funds go to firms with favorable stock price trends, the economy's resources are directed to the most efficient uses. For this reason, the finance literature has generally adopted the basic objective of maximizing the price of the firm's common stock. The shareholder wealth maximization rule provides a basis for rational decision making with respect to a wide range of financial issues faced by the firm.

The goal of maximizing the share price does not imply that managers should seek to increase the value of common stock at the expense of bondholders. For example, managers should not substantially alter the riskiness of the firm's product-market investment activities. Riskier investments, if successful, will benefit shareholders. But risky investments that fail will reduce the security to bondholders, causing bond values to fall and the cost of debt financing to rise. As a practical matter, a firm must provide strong assurances to bondholders that investment policies will not be changed to their disadvantage, or it will have to pay interest rates high enough to compensate bondholders against the possibility of such adverse policy changes.

Social Responsibility

Another important aspect of the goals of the firm and of financial management is the consideration of social responsibility. Maximization of share price requires well-managed operations. Successful firms are at the forefront of efficiency and innovation, so that value maximization leads to new products, technologies, and greater employment; hence, the more successful the firm, the better the quality and quantity of the total "pie" to be distributed.

But in recent years, *externalities* (such as pollution, product safety, and job safety) have attained increased importance. Business firms must take into account the effects of their policies and actions on society as a whole. It has long been recognized that the external economic environment is important to a firm's decision making. Fluctuations in overall business activity and related changes in financial markets are also important aspects of the external environment. Also, firms must respond to the expectations of workers, consumers, other stakeholders, and interest groups to achieve a long-run wealth maximization. Indeed, responsiveness to these new and powerful constituencies may be required for the survival of the private enterprise system. This point of view argues that business firms must recognize a wider range of stakeholders and external influences. Throughout this book, we assume that managements operate in this way.

Business Ethics

Business ethics are the conduct and behavior of a firm toward its stockholders, employees, customers, and the community. Business ethics are measured by a firm's behavior in all aspects of its dealings with others in all areas including product quality, treatment of employees, fair market practices, and community responsibility.

The case for ethical behavior is based on widely accepted codes of conduct. Without integrity, a person cannot be psychologically healthy. If people cannot be trusted, the social system cannot function effectively. But in addition, a reputation for ethical behavior and fairness to all stakeholders is a source of considerable organizational value. A reputation for integrity enables a firm to attract employees who believe in and behave according to ethical principles. Customers will respond favorably to business firms who treat them honestly. Such behavior contributes to the health of the community where the firm operates.

Firms should have codes of ethical behavior in writing and conduct training programs to make clear to employees the standards to which the firms seek to achieve. This is an area in which the firm's board of directors and top management must provide leadership. They must demonstrate by their actions as well as by communications their strong commitment to ethical conduct. The company's promotion and compensation systems should reward ethical behavior and punish conduct that impairs the firm's reputation for integrity.

The behavior of top executives of a firm establishes the firm's reputation. If the behavior of the firm is not consistently ethical, other stakeholders—workers, consumers, suppliers, etc.—will begin to discount every action and decision of the firm. For example, the bonds and common stock of a firm with an uncertain reputation will be viewed with suspicion by the market. The securities will have to be sold at lower prices, which means that the returns to investors will have to be higher to take into account that the issuing firm may be selling a "lemon"—trying to put something over on investors.

Thus, a strong case can be made that executives and the firm establish a reputation for unquestioned ethical behavior. The psychological health of an individual is better, the reputation of the firm is a valuable asset, and the social and economic environment is more conductive to efficient and equitable economic activity. Indeed, the upheavals in the governments of eastern Europe in 1989–90 resulted from the perceptions that their rulers were self-serving at the expense of the general population.

VALUE MAXIMIZATION AS A GOAL

We have discussed some broad aspects of value maximization as a goal. Now we turn to a consideration of technical distinctions and implementation aspects of the role of financial management in value maximization.

Value maximization is broader than profit maximization. Maximizing value takes the time value of money into account. First, funds that are received this year have greater value than funds that may be received 10 years from now. Second, value maximization considers the riskiness of the income stream, for example, the rate of return required on an investment starting a new business is in the range of 25 to 35 percent, but 10 to 15 percent in established firms. Third, the *quality* and timing of expected future cash flows may vary. Profit figures can vary widely depending upon the accounting rules and conventions used. The financial markets have demonstrated that analysts see through differences in accounting procedures that affect "profit" measures and perceive underlying cash flows.

Thus, value maximization is broader and more general than profit maximization and is the unifying concept used throughout the book. Value maximization provides criteria for pricing the use of resources such as capital investments in plant and machinery. If limited resources are not allocated by efficiency criteria, production will be inefficient and perceived as unfair. Value maximization provides a solution to these kinds of problems. But value maximization must take into account the expectations of all categories of stakeholders—workers, consumers, and government. Thus, the rules for the sound pricing and allocation of economic resources are essential to a stable social order required for the existence of business firms.

Performance Measurement by the Financial Markets

The basic finance functions must be performed in all types of organizations and in all types of economic systems. What is unique about business organizations in a market economy is that they are directly subject to the discipline of the financial markets. These markets continuously value business firms' securities, thereby providing measures of the firms' performance. A consequence of this continuous assessment of a firm by the capital markets is the change in valuations (stock market prices). Thus, the capital markets stimulate efficiency and provide incentives to business managers to improve their performance.

The Risk-Return Tradeoff

Financial decisions affect the level of a firm's stock price by influencing the cash flow stream and the riskiness of the firm. These relationships are diagrammed in Fig. 1.2. Policy decisions, which are subject to government constraints, affect the levels of cash flows and their risks. These two factors jointly determine the value of the firm.

FIGURE 1.2

Valuation as the Central Focus of the Finance Function

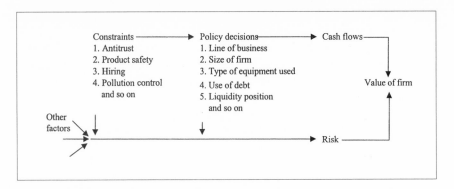

The primary policy decision is made in choosing the markets in which the firm operates. Profitability and risk are further influenced by decisions relating to the size of the firm, its growth rate, the types and amounts of equipment used, the extent to which debt is employed, the firm's liquidity position, and so on. An increase in the cash position reduces risk; however, since cash is not an earning asset, converting other assets to cash also reduces profitability. Similarly, the use of additional debt raises the rate of return, on the stockholders' equity; but more debt means more risk. The financial manager seeks to strike the balance between risk and profitability that will maximize stockholder wealth. Most financial decisions involve *risk-return tradeoffs.*

THE CHANGING ECONOMIC AND FINANCIAL ENVIRONMENTS

Major changes in the economic, political, and financial environments began to explode in the 1980s. These in turn had major impacts on the practice of finance.

International Competition

While the trends have been underway for decades, full recognition of the international economy took place in the 1980s, continuing to the present. In every major industry—automobiles, steel, pharmaceuticals, oil, computers, other electronic products, for example—the reality of global markets had to be taken into account. In addition to competition from western European and Japanese companies, even developing countries began to offer challenging competition in manufactured products. The pressures on prices and profit margins presented continued challenges. Investments had to be made wisely; the importance of capital budgeting increased. Profit margins were under pressure so that efficiency had to increase. Some argue that this is a major reason for the increased takeover and restructuring activity since the 1980s.

Financial Innovations and Financial Engineering

Many financial innovations have been made in recent years. These have been referred to as financial engineering, representing the creation of new forms of financial products. They include debt instruments with fluctuating (floating) interest rates, various forms of rights to convert debt to equity (or vice versa), the use of higher levels of leverage and lower-grade ("junk") bonds, the use of debt denominated for payment in variously designated foreign currencies, and the development of pools of funds available for investment in new firms or to take over existing firms. Option theory has made it possible to use observable data to calculate option values. Option pricing has also given rise to the field of real options in which the ability to modify investment programs alters the traditional net present value (NPV) calculations of business (versus financial) investments. Growth has taken place in the use of options, futures, and forward contracts, as well as the construction of various combinations to create new forms of derivative securities. These and other innovations are covered in the chapters that follow.

The Increased Availability of Computers

Increasingly, personal computers make available computational powers which in earlier decades could be obtained only from relatively large-scale systems. Thus, the ability to develop complex models and spreadsheet analysis has become widely available. It remains important, however, to have a clear understanding of the underlying principles involved. Otherwise, increased complexity will result in less clear understanding and lead to error rather than improved analysis.

Mergers, Takeovers, and Restructuring

The increased international competition has been one of the major factors causing U.S. companies to rethink their strategies to become competitive. Mergers, takeovers, and restructuring represent, in part, responses to pressures to increase efficiency to meet increased competition resulting from the new international and technological developments.

Ecommerce

The ecommerce and related telecommunications developments will have a major impact on business and investments. Their significance will be similar to that of previous revolutionary innovations such as steam engines, electricity, automobiles, radio, television, and computers in all their forms. Ecommerce was stimulated by the development of the Internet accompanied by transformations in computers and telecommunications.

In its initial stages, the major growth in ecommerce was seen in the business-to-consumer (B2C) market as a revolutionary distribution vehicle. Buyers could benefit from superior product selection, efficient processing, and lower prices. The business-to-business (B2B) markets are expected to become larger than the B2C. Value will be created by streamlining the supply chain as well as improving the information chain by managing complex business information online. By 1998 many traditional businesses began to awaken to the challenges and opportunities of ecommerce.

Since the Netscape initial public offering (IPO) in August 1995, more than several thousand Internet IPOs have been made. The early ecommerce companies used their stock with high price-earnings ratios to make acquisitions to beat competitors to name recognition, critical mass, and leadership. Ecommerce companies have demonstrated high volatility in their stock market prices. All firms are impacted, and financial managers must perform critical roles in the operating and financial dimensions of ecommerce activities.

In review, the environments of firms have changed dynamically in recent decades. This has affected all aspects of strategic planning in all types of organizations. Since financial markets are especially sensitive and responsive to turbulence in economic environments, financial decision making has become increasingly challenging. The following chapters seek to assist financial managers in meeting these new challenges and responsibilities.

ORGANIZATION OF THIS BOOK

The aim of this book is to explain the procedures, practices, and policies by which accounting and financial management can contribute to the successful performance of organizations. Our emphasis is on strategies involved in the tradeoffs between risk and return in seeking to make decisions that will maximize the value of the firm. Each subsequent topic is treated within this basic framework.

The three major parts of the book are:

- Part One: Accounting and Finance Fundamentals

- Part Two: Financial Planning and Control

- Part Three: Investment and Financing Strategies

Part One discusses financial statements, the nature of the finance function, and introduces fundamental concepts related to valuation, the basic theme of this book. Part One also discusses financial markets (both domestic and international), organizational forms, and taxation.

Part Two begins with financial performance metrics. This provides a basis for strategic financial planning. The use of ratio analysis in performance measurement provides a framework for cash, receivables, and inventory management.

Part Three begins with Chapter 9, which analyzes capital investment decisions under both certainty and uncertainty. This chapter emphasizes the net present value criterion, which is the basis for increasing the economic value of the firm. Chapter 10 deals with financing strategies. The subjects include financial structure, the cost of capital, and the use of hurdle rates. The concepts developed guide long-term financing strategies formulated in the concluding Chapter 11.

SUMMARY

Managerial finance involves the investment, financing, and dividend decisions of the firm. The main functions of financial managers are to plan for, acquire, and use funds to make the maximum contribution to the efficient operation of an organization. This requires familiarity with the financial markets from which funds are drawn as well as with the product markets in which the organization operates. All financial decisions involve alternative choices between internal and external funds, long-term and short-term projects, long-term and short-term financing, a higher growth rate, and a lower rate of growth. The basic financial statements, which encapsulate the effects of operating and financial decisions, are also explained.

For practical implementation in making financial decisions, stock price maximization is used as a proxy for value maximization. Decisions relating to value maximization involve a tradeoff between prospective risks and returns. Financial decisions must be made within the framework of socially responsible behavior as well as in relation to dynamic external environments, both domestic and international.

The criteria and rules that guide the acquisition and use of resources in a market system perform an important social role. Without decision rules developed from the value maximization principle, the allocation and use of a society's limited resources will be arbitrary and inefficient. This book on managerial finance seeks to implement, at the level of the firm, sound rules and strategies for a socially desirable allocation and use of resources—people, materials, and capital goods.

QUESTIONS AND PROBLEMS

1.1   What are the main functions of financial managers?

1.2   Why is shareholder wealth maximization a better operating goal than profit maximization?

1.3   What are the issues in the conflict of interest between stockholders and managers and how can they be resolved?

1.4   What are the potential conflicts of interest between shareholders and bondholders and how can they be resolved?

1.5   What is the nature of the risk-return tradeoff faced in financial decision making?

1.6   What opportunities and threats are created for financial managers by increased international competition?

SOLUTIONS TO QUESTIONS AND PROBLEMS

1.1   The main functions of financial managers are (1) to raise funds from external financial sources, (2) to allocate funds among different uses, (3) to manage the flow of funds involved in the operation of the enterprise, and (4) to provide for returns to investors and other sources of financing of the firm. In short, the main functions of financial managers are to plan for, acquire, and utilize funds to make the maximum contribution to the efficient operation of an organization.

1.2   Profit maximization would have to be from a long-run standpoint to be meaningful at all. However, it would still be deficient in not considering the risk of alternative income streams. Wealth maximization is a better goal because it takes into account both the stream of income, or cash flow, over a period of years and the appropriate capitalization factor which reflects the degree of risk involved.

1.3   The conflict of interest between the shareholders and managers has been referred to as the *agency problem*. Managers "control" the firm and may do things in their own self-interest at the expense of the owners. Four methods are used to solve the agency problem:

(1)   Establish outside audit committees to review and limit abuses.

(2)   Limit the authority of lower levels of management over potentially troublesome items. e.g., hiring of additional staff and use of company cars.

(3)   Provide managers with stock options, stock bonuses, and other forms of compensation that align their interest with those of shareholders.

(4)   The market for corporate control—tender offers and mergers—will lead to a takeover if managers abuse their responsibilities, with the new owners replacing the old managers.

1.4   Shareholders have limited liability, but receive all the returns after the fixed payments to the bondholders are made. After obtaining funds from bondholders, the shareholders may seek to make more risky investments because they can benefit without limit, but the bondholders are still limited to the returns that have already been fixed.

These conflicts are resolved in two ways. The contract for obtaining funds (called the bond indenture) will have written provisions (called covenants) restricting the ability of the shareholders (or managers) from taking actions that increase the risks to bondholders. The second protection to bondholders is that they may require a high rate of interest in advance because of the risk that the bond covenants may not fully anticipate all the ways that the shareholders may take actions adverse to the bondholders.

1.5   The choice of the industry or risk class of the firm influences both profitability opportunities and risk. When the choice of industry or risk class has been made, both profitability and risk are determined by decisions relating to the size of the firm, the types of equipment used, the extent to which debt is employed, the firm's liquidity position, etc. Such decisions generally affect both risk and profitability. An increase in the cash position reduces risk; however, since cash is not an earning asset, converting other assets to cash also reduces profitability. Similarly, the use of additional debt raises the rate of profitability on stockholders' net worth; but more debt usually means more risk. The financial liquidity and leverage policies should be chosen in such a way as to maximize the value of the firm. This is the basic risk-return tradeoff faced in financial decision making.

1.6   Opportunities created by international competition:

- Larger markets for U.S. products due to globalization
- Increased efficiency (including via mergers and restructuring) encouraged to compete effectively
- Access to international financial markets
- Opportunities to learn from foreign firms (e.g., GM-Toyota joint venture)

Threats created by international competition:

- Added uncertainty of fluctuating currency exchange rates
- Competition from lower-cost producers in developing countries
- Increased world capacity and conditions of supply that may create downward pressures on prices and profit margins
- New foreign industry started from scratch, avoids mistakes or need for modernizing plan and equipment (Japanese car plants more efficient than old U.S. plants)

CHAPTER 2

Financial Statements and Cash Flows

Financial statements report the historical performance of a company and provide a basis for assessing the firm's achievements as well as a foundation, along with business and economic performance, for projecting the firm's future. Financial statements are consistently prepared using U.S. generally accepted accounting principles, commonly called U.S. GAAP. For public corporations, financial statements are publicly disclosed annually, through an annual report and 10K (a Securities and Exchange requirement), and quarterly, through a more concise quarterly report and 10Q. Beyond the external reporting requirements, within most firms, financial statements are often prepared on a monthly basis to assist management. In some cases, key components of the financial statements (such as product sales and product costs) are available on a daily basis. Some firms have achieved the capability of producing all financial statements on a daily basis. The Internal Revenue Service and foreign governments (in the case of a multinational) have their own very specific guidelines for reporting financial data.

This chapter describes the basic financial statements that record an organization's activity, develops key accounting concepts that underlie the financial statements, demonstrates the interrelationships between the statements, and provides an overview of essential financial data that are contained in the accompanying notes to the financial statements.

ROLE OF FINANCIAL STATEMENTS

We walk into a room where a friend is watching a sporting event. Whether it is baseball, football, hockey, or basketball, our first question usually is, What is the score? Financial statements provide important measures of the firm's score. Although the firm is not meeting a competitor in a sporting event at a stadium, the firm is, on a continuous basis, meeting its competition head-on in the marketing arena in a battle for its customers' dollars and in the investing arena in a battle for the investors' capital.

The score is one measure of a team's performance. The score does not capture all other dimensions of the team's performance, such as the number of first downs and batting percentages. These types of "box score" measures present additional attributes for evaluating a team's performance and individual contributions to the team's success. Although assessing the performance of a firm is more complicated because there is no simple "score," financial statements and their projections provide information for judging a company's performance.

This company assessment is extended to assessing the performance of the management team. Management's compensation is often based on the financial information provided by financial statements. Financial statements also form a foundation upon which valuation of the firm is based. The objective for a management team is to maximize the value of the firm. By maximizing (or enhancing) the value of the firm, the management team increases its score. Valuation is a central theme to this book. Financial statements provide the foundation for evaluating the performance of the firm. Chapter 7, Financial Performance Metrics, builds upon the principles developed in this chapter.

Financial statements are based on accounting rules or conventions which are commonly referred to as U.S. GAAP—U.S. generally accepted accounting principles. The use of U.S. GAAP provides a more consistent and comparable basis for assessing a firm. The comparability extends between firms and over time. Audited financial statements generally ensure that statements were prepared in accordance with U.S. GAAP.

A complete description of a firm's financial activities during a year consists of three basic financial statements.

1. An income statement shows the activities as measured by the revenues (or sales) and expenses of the firm throughout the period.
2. A balance sheet provides a snapshot of what the firm owns and what the firm owes at a specific time.
3. A statement of cash flows lists the sources and uses of cash that resulted throughout the period. The statement of cash flows describes the underlying transactions that caused the cash and cash equivalents (from the balance sheet) to change over time.

The accompanying notes to the financial statements, management's discussion and analysis (MD&A), the CEO's letter to shareholders, and many other inclusions in an annual report provide valuable "box score" information for assessing a firm.

Table 2.1 presents an overview of the timing of the primary financial statements. Balance sheets are struck at a moment in time, while

TABLE 2.1

Timing of Primary Financial Statements

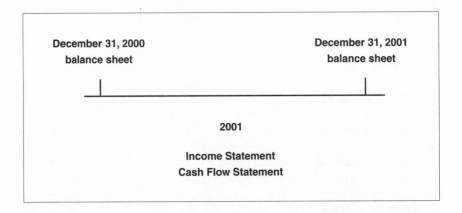

the income statement and cash flow statement measure performance throughout a period of time. In this example, two balance sheets are prepared as of December 31, 2000 and 2001, while the income statement and cash flow measure the activities throughout 2000.

INCOME STATEMENT

The income statement is the most referenced of the three primary financial statements. It records revenues and expenses to derive income over a specified time period—monthly, quarterly, or annually:

$$Revenue - Expenses = Income \tag{2.1}$$

Table 2.2 presents the income statement for Hershey Foods as reported in its 1998 annual report.[1] Consequently, it covers the years 1998, 1997, and 1996. The amounts listed are in thousands of dollars.

---

[1] The senior author was a financial officer of Hershey Foods for over 20 years. Both authors have had considerable consulting interactions with business corporations. Accounting and financial statements are not fully meaningful without experience and knowledge of the business activities of the firms whose financial statements are being analyzed and interpreted. So we shall make considerable use of our background on Hershey Foods and other companies on which we have background knowledge in using actual firms as case examples.

TABLE 2.2

Hershey Food Corporation Income Statement*

	Year Ended December 31, 1998	Year Ended December 31, 1997	Year Ended December 31, 1996
Net sales	$ 4,435,615	$ 4,302,236	$3,989,308
Costs and expenses			
Cost of sales	2,625,057	2,488,896	2,302,089
Selling, marketing, and administrative	1,167,895	1,183,130	1,124,087
Loss on disposal of businesses	—	—	35,352
Total costs and expenses	3,792,952	3,672,026	3,461,528
Income before interest and income taxes	642,663	630,210	527,780
Interest expense, net	85,657	76,255	48,043
Income before income taxes	557,006	553,955	479,737
Provision for income taxes	216,118	217,704	206,551
Net income	$ 340,888	$ 336,251	$ 273,186
Net income per share—basic	$ 2.38	$ 2.25	$ 1.77
Net income per share—diluted	$ 2.34	$ 2.23	$ 1.75
Cash dividends paid per share			
Common stock	$ 0.920	$ 0.840	$ 0.760
Class B common stock	$ 0.835	$ 0.760	$ 0.685

*In thousands of dollars except per share amounts

Hershey Foods Corporation is the number one (largest market share) chocolate and confectionery company in the United States. It is primarily a domestic company with less than 10 percent of its sales coming from outside the United States and even a significantly smaller portion coming from outside North America. Its financial statements are relatively straightforward and will be used throughout this book for illustrative purposes.

The income statement begins with the revenue or net sales of the firm. The term *net sales* indicates that gross sales have been reduced for returned products, discounts taken for prompt payment of invoices, and allowances made for damaged products. In 1998, Hershey Foods had $4.4 billion of net sales. That represents a tremendous amount of peanut butter cups, kisses, Hershey bars, etc., sold in 1998. Although $4.4 billion in net sales is an interesting "score," it lacks context. So immediately a comparison is made to 1997 and 1996. The 1998 net sales were $133 million higher than in 1997, or 3.1 percent higher, and 1997 net sales were $313 million, or 7.8 percent, higher than in 1996.

The income statement is silent about what drove the revenue growth. If further explanation is provided, it must be found elsewhere in the annual report, perhaps in the MD&A. The 1998 net sales growth for Hershey Foods was primarily the result of a highly successful new product, Hershey's Reese Sticks, and modest base business growth. The 1997 surge was the result of a December 30, 1996, acquisition of Leaf North America. The Leaf acquisition included brands such as Jolly Rancher, Milk Duds, and Good & Plenty and contributed the majority of the 1997 revenue increase. Due to the timing of the deal, Leaf's sales were included in 1997 and excluded from 1996, since Hershey owned Leaf for only one day in 1996.

Costs and expenses include at least two lines of distinction: (1) cost of sales and (2) selling, marketing, and administration. The cost of sales captures the manufacturing expenses for the products sold. The cost of sales includes raw material (chocolate, milk, sugar, etc., in Hershey's case), direct labor of the people producing the product, and factory overhead. The factory overhead includes direct and indirect overhead expenses such as electricity, property taxes, insurance, maintenance, salaries, employee benefits, and employment taxes of production supervisors and plant general management, and depreciation expense for the plant and production equipment. Before we discuss the selling, marketing, and administration expense, depreciation expense deserves some special attention.

U.S. GAAP accounting is prepared using accrual-based accounting, which is in sharp contrast to a cash-based accounting. As a side note, this is what drives the distinction between the income statement and the statement of cash flows. Let's say that 3 years ago a piece of manufacturing equipment was purchased for $1000 with an expected life of 10 years. A cash-based system would recognize the $1000 purchase as an equipment expense when that purchase was originally made, and consequently there would be no expense in the current year. An accrual-based accounting system (that is, U.S. GAAP) recognizes that there was cash outflow to buy the equipment 3 years ago, but does not give rise to an immediate expense. Under accrual-based accounting, the expense comes from the consumption of the productive life of the asset. In this case, $100 per year would be recognized as depreciation expense (i.e., purchase price of $1000 apportioned evenly over 10 years of productive life) in the current year and annually over the 10-year life of the equipment.

Although there were no additional equipment purchases in the current year and there never was a check made payable to "depreciation," a $100 depreciation expense would be included in the costs and expenses that are detailed in the income statement. If the depreciating equipment were primarily used for or related to the manufacturing of product, the depreciation would be included in the cost of sales. If the depreciation were associated with corporate headquarters, that expense would be included in selling, marketing, and administrative costs.

Also included in selling, marketing, and administrative costs are those costs associated with (1) selling expenses, such as salespeople's salaries, bonuses, benefits, employment taxes, salespeople's automobiles, office expenses, etc.; (2) marketing expenses, including promotions, advertising, marketing research, salaries, etc.; and (3) administrative expenses, which are characterized by expenses for corporate and divisional staffs, executive compensation, training, consulting fees, research and development, etc. Selling, marketing, and administrative expenses are sometimes referred to as operating expenses or *G&A* (general and administrative) *expenses*.

As illustrated on Table 2.2, there is also an expense that is separately identified on the income statement entitled *loss on disposal of businesses*. In 1996, as part of the Leaf North America acquisition, a separate agreement was constructed that sold the European operations of Hershey Foods to the parent company of Leaf North America, Huhtamaki, from Finland. Most of those operations were acquired just a few years earlier at a cost of $157 million. Leaf agreed to buy them for $122 million, resulting in the loss of $35 million.

This loss is characteristic of *one-time, nonrecurring gains or losses* separately highlighted on the income statement. Other examples of common one-time events that are separately highlighted include

- Restructuring charges—an accumulation of anticipated expenses associated with closing a plant, division, or other business segment
- Discontinued operations—current-period income or loss from a business that has been identified to be discontinued through a shutdown or divestiture
- Accounting change—the cumulative impact for prior years of an implemented change in U.S. GAAP
- Extraordinary gains (losses)

These nonrecurring items may need to be adjusted to obtain a more accurate portrayal of the company's ongoing business. For example, the 1996 loss of $35 million on disposal of businesses depressed income before interest and income taxes by $35 million. Without adjustment, the 1997 growth in income before interest and income taxes is overstated as a 19.4 percent surge, whereas after adjusting for the loss and using a more representative income before interest and income taxes of $563 million (as reported $528 million plus the $35 million loss on disposal of businesses), the adjusted (but more realistic) 1997 growth rate is 11.9 percent.

The next line, income before interest and income taxes, is often simply referred to as earnings before interest and taxes (EBIT). If there are no "other income" or "other expense" items, EBIT is the same as net operating income (NOI). This is the result of subtracting the noted cost of sales and operating expenses from revenue.

Interest expense, net, includes gross interest expense "net" of interest income and of capitalized interest expense. Gross interest expense includes the cost of borrowing funds via long-term debt as part of the permanent capital structure of a firm and short-term debt for working capital needs. Interest income represents the interest *earnings* of cash balances and marketable securities such as bank certificates of deposit, Treasury bills, and commercial paper. Capitalized interest is an accounting convention that reclassifies interest expense on construction in process to the investment in that project. For example, Hershey Foods built a new production facility in 1990 for $120 million. Over its year of construction, the related capital incurred interest expense ($8 million) during that construction period. That $8 million of interest expense was removed from the 1990 interest expense and became part of the plant's investment capital base.

Income before income taxes, or simply pretax income, results from subtracting interest expense from EBIT.

The provision for income taxes is the combined amounts that are owed to the U.S., state, and local governments based on the pretax income. For a discussion of the federal tax environment, see Chapter 5, Business Organization and Taxes.

Net income is the *bottom line* and represents what is left over from sales after all the expenses have been considered. When net income is divided by the number of shares outstanding, net income per share [or earnings per share (EPS)] results. Diluted EPS converts all outstanding options to shares outstanding, thus providing a conservative view on the potential number of shares outstanding and a resulting conservative EPS value.

Also, noted in Table 2.2 are cash dividends paid per share. Dividends are not an expense; dividends are a return of capital to the shareholders (owners) of a corporation. It is the responsibility of the board of directors to determine dividend payments quarterly. In addition, the Hershey Foods August board meeting has usually included a review of Hershey's dividend policy and an increase in the dividend per share.

As an aside, Hershey Foods Corporation has a somewhat unique ownership structure and has a dual class of common stock: the traded common stock (one vote per share but a 10 percent higher dividend) and a supervoting (10 votes per share) Class B common stock that is not publicly traded.

BALANCE SHEET

Balance sheets capture the financial position of a firm at a point in time. Hershey Foods is a calendar fiscal year-end company, which means that its financial year coincides with the calendar. It begins on January 1 and ends on December 31. Table 2.3 presents the Hershey Foods Corporation balance sheet for 1998 and 1997. Additionally, in Table 2.3 at the far right is a column that calculates the change (increase or decrease) from 1997 to 1998 for each line of the balance sheet. This increment or decrement will be used to develop a reconciling cash flow statement in the next section of this chapter.

A balance sheet is founded on the accounting identity equation:

$$\text{Assets} = \text{Liabilities} + \text{Equity} \tag{2.2}$$

Assets and liabilities are further classified as current or long-term according to how quickly they will be converted to cash (assets) or paid off (liabilities). In general, assets with less than a year until they are converted to cash are considered current assets, and liabilities with less than a year until they need to be paid are considered current liabilities. Equation (2.2) can be expanded to reflect this added distinction:

$$\text{Current Assets} + \text{Long-Term Asset}$$
$$= \text{Current Liabilities} + \text{Long-Term Liabilities} + \text{Equity} \tag{2.2a}$$

By accounting conventions, these relationships are based on historical costs. Equity is also referred to as the *book value* of the firm.

The $39 million of cash and marketable securities on Hershey's 1998 balance sheet represents cash on hand (a minimal amount), demand deposits, and checking accounts. These cash funds are required to conduct the *transactions* of the firm. The marketable securities (sometimes referred to as cash equivalents) include temporary investment of "excess" (beyond transactions) cash in financial income-producing investments, which can be converted to cash with relatively small risk of a decline in their stated values. Examples of such investments include certificates of deposit from banks, Treasury bills, and commercial paper.

Hershey's cash balances fluctuate greatly throughout the year and follow a classic fiscal year pattern. The year begins with a modest cash balance. At Hershey it was always important to view the calendar based on "chocolate holidays," the first of which is Valentine's Day. The Hershey Valentine entrants include a giant Kiss and an assortment of snack size candies wrapped in silver and red foil. Hershey does not fully exploit this holiday, and the first quarter ends with modest cash balances intact. The next chocolate holiday is Easter. Once again, Hershey's offerings are limited and include jellybeans, peanut butter eggs,

Cadbury creme eggs, and an assortment of snack-size candy wrapped in pastel foil. Easter is an important season, but there is still opportunity to capitalize on it further. Another modest chocolate holiday is Mother's Day. Hershey's limited boxed chocolate line, Pot of Gold, is a slight player in this occasion. So Hershey ends May with a minor level of positive cash balances.

TABLE 2.3

Hershey Foods Corporation Consolidated Balance Sheets

	December 31, 1998 ($000)	December 31, 1997 ($000)	Change ($000)
Assets			
Current assets			
Cash and cash equivalents	$ 39,024	$ 54,237	$ (15,213)
Accounts receivable—trade	451,324	360,831	90,493
Inventories	493,249	505,525	(12,276)
Deferred income taxes	58,505	84,024	(25,519)
Prepaid expenses and other	91,864	30,197	61,667
Total current assets	1,133,966	1,034,814	99,152
Property, plant, and equipment, net	1,648,058	1,648,237	(179)
Intangibles resulting from business acquisitions	530,464	551,849	(21,385)
Other assets	91,610	56,336	35,274
Total assets	$3,404,098	$3,291,236	$ 112,862
Liabilities and stockholders' equity			
Current liabilities			
Accounts payable	$ 156,937	$ 146,932	$ 10,005
Accrued liabilities	294,415	371,545	(77,130)
Accrued income taxes	17,475	19,692	(2,217)
Short-term debt	345,908	232,451	113,457
Current portion of long-term debt	89	25,095	(25,006)
Total current liabilities	814,824	795,715	19,109
Long-term debt	879,103	1,029,136	(150,033)
Other long-term liabilities	346,769	346,500	269
Deferred income taxes	321,101	267,079	54,022
Total liabilities	2,361,797	2,438,430	(76,633)
Stockholders' equity			
Preferred stock, shares issued: none in 1998 and 1997	—	—	
Common stock, shares issued: 149,502,964 in 1998 and 149,484,964 in 1997	149,503	149,485	

TABLE 2.3

Hershey Foods Corporation Consolidated Balance Sheets (*Continued*)

	December 31, 1998 ($000)	December 31, 1997 ($000)	Change ($000)
Class B common stock, shares issued: 30,447,908 in 1998 and 30,465,908 in 1997	30,447	30,465	
Additional paid-in capital	29,995	33,852	
Unearned ESOP compensation	(25,548)	(28,741)	
Retained earnings	2,189,693	1,977,849	
Treasury—common stock shares, at cost: 36,804,157 in 1998 and 37,018,566 in 1997	(1,267,422)	(1,267,861)	
Accumulated other comprehensive income	(64,367)	(42,243)	
Total stockholders' equity	1,042,301	852,806	189,495
Total liabilities and stockholders' equity	$3,404,098	$3,291,236	$ 112,862

Hershey's largest sales season is in anticipation of back-to-school period and Halloween. In June, Hershey starts expanding its raw material inventories; July and August are heavy production months. Payrolls swell and substantial cash outflows occur. During August, Hershey's modest cash balance turns into a significant shortfall, and a significant level of borrowing against its lines of credit occurs. In late August and September, sales start to soar. October and November are heavy collection months for Hershey. Accounts receivable are collected, and the cash is used to pay off the line-of-credit borrowing. By the end of December, working capital borrowing is fully paid off, and once again a modest level of cash is on hand at year's end.

Accounts receivable—trade or simply accounts receivable—reflects sales made to customers for which Hershey has not yet received payment. Accounts receivable represents the amount that customers owe to Hershey.

Inventories represent the dollar amount of raw material (cocoa beans, sugar, milk, packaging material, etc.), goods in process, and finished candy goods (at the cost of production) that Hershey has on hand. There are alternatives available for valuing the inventory. The two most common are FIFO (first in, first out) and LIFO (last in, first out). Table 2.4 compares the financial impact of FIFO and LIFO inventory methods.

Table 2.4 illustrates two start-up retail companies, a FIFO company and a LIFO company. They both begin operations on January 1 with the purchase of 100 units of inventory at $5 each. Two weeks later, costs increase dramatically. So both companies buy an additional 100 units at the inflated price of $6. Throughout the year, both retailers sell 100 units at $10 each. The resulting income statement impact is seen in Table 2.4. The FIFO company reports that it sold the first 100 units it purchased, resulting in a cost of goods sold of $500, while the LIFO company reports that it sold the last units at a cost of $600. Consequently, the FIFO firm reports higher pretax income, taxes, and net income. On the balance sheet, the FIFO company (which sold the first 100 units that it purchased) is left with 100 units and specifically the last 100 units that it purchased, valued at their cost of $600. The LIFO company reported that it sold the last 100 units it bought at $6 each, so the remaining 100 units of inventory must be the first units purchased (or 100 units at $5 each) for $500.

Again, these are accounting conventions that may or may not be linked to reality. Hershey Foods is a LIFO company for accounting purposes. Accountants at Hershey Foods can look up in the LIFO inventory records that some of the cocoa bean raw material dates back to the 1940s. LIFO is the accounting convention; the reality is that cocoa beans could not survive for 50 years, let alone be used in the production of fine-quality chocolate products. Fortunately, the reality is that

TABLE 2.4

Inventory—FIFO Versus LIFO

Inventory Transactions	FIFO	LIFO
Jan. 1, Buy inventory (100 units @ $5)	$ 500	$ 500
Jan. 15, Buy inventory (100 units @ $6)	$ 600	$ 600
Income Statement		
Sales (100 units @ $10)	$ 1000	$ 1000
Cost of good sold	500	600
Pretax income	$ 500	$ 400
Taxes (40%)	200	160
Net income	$ 300	$ 240
Balance Sheet		
Inventory	$ 600	$ 500

Hershey manages its inventory on a very strict first-in, first-out basis regardless of how the accounting records are kept. The physical inventory is FIFO while the accounting records are kept on a LIFO basis.

The remaining current assets include current deferred tax assets, which will be discussed at the conclusion of this section; prepaid expenses; and numerous miscellaneous other current assets. Notice these prepaid expenses and other exceeded $91 million in 1998. The single largest account within this category is $72 million for capitalized software related to an investment in information technology (IT) and SAP implementation. SAP is a major enterprisewide information system for efficient resource planning that integrates all systems commonly thought of as independent, such as sales, production, logistics, and financials, into one common system.

Property, plant, and equipment, net (or net PP&E) is a long-term asset and summarizes the company's investment in land, building, equipment, and fixtures net of accumulated depreciation. As discussed, depreciation expense represents an estimate of the annual consumption of a fixed asset's value. Accumulated depreciation is the accumulation of all the depreciation expense since the asset was first purchased. Further detail is provided in the accompanying notes:

	1998	1997
Land	$ 30,871	$ 31,340
Building	541,181	540,729
Equipment and fixtures	2,130,735	2,015,161
Total PP&E, gross	2,702,787	2,587,230
Less: Accumulated depreciation	(1,054,729)	(938,993)
PP&E, net	$1,648,058	$1,648,237

PP&E, gross is recorded at the original purchase price. Market value, economic value, replacement value, and current cost are not considered. Only historical cost is recorded in the U.S. GAAP system. This has some noteworthy implications. Land includes $1 million for an 80-acre tract of land on which are located Hershey's major production facilities and division offices. This land was purchased before 1900. There has been land appreciation over the last 100 years, but the land is recorded at its historical cost of $1 million. Land is not a depreciable asset. Another illustration is that, in the process of making milk chocolate, the chocolate paste needs to be *conched* for an extended period. (Conching is equivalent to blending and mixing.) The machines used in this process are called conches. The conches at Hershey are still functional, cost-effective, and production-efficient after 80 years of operation. Although there is significant economic value, these conches are recorded on the books at their original purchase price less their accumulated depreciation. These conches are currently on the books at a zero dollar value. In fact, these conches were fully written off before any of Hershey's current senior management team was born. However, there is tremendous economic value in this equipment, but due to the nature of GAAP accounting for PP&E, only historical cost less accumulated depreciation is recorded.

Intangibles resulting from business acquisitions, which are also referred to as goodwill, represent the extra amount paid for an acquisition beyond the acquired assets. To illustrate, in the 1980s, Hershey Foods bought Dietrich Corporation (Luden's, Fifth Avenue bar, Mello Mints, etc.) for approximately $100 million. A group of accountants determined that Hershey was receiving $60 million of assets (receivables, inventory, and net PP&E) but was also assuming $20 million of liabilities (accounts payable and debt), or net assets of $40 million ($60 million assets less $20 million liabilities). The difference between what Hershey paid ($100 million) and the tangible net assets that it received ($40 million) represents $60 million of goodwill or intangibles resulting from business acquisitions.

The final category of Hershey's assets is a catchall reporting category called *other assets*. These are mainly capitalized software, long-term deferred tax assets, and long-term investments in the debt or equity securities of other firms.

We next turn to the "right hand" side of the balance sheet. Current liabilities usually contain two types of liabilities: (1) payables and accruals and (2) short-term borrowings. Hershey presents three accounts for accounts payable, accrued liabilities, and accrued income taxes. Other common payables include taxes payable and wages payable. Accounts payable and accrued liabilities represent the amounts owed to suppliers for purchases of goods and services. The distinguishing characteristic hinges on whether an invoice was received or not. Accounts payable have been billed by the supplier, whereas for accrued liabilities, charges for services or products have been incurred but have not been billed.

Short-term borrowing represents interest-bearing loans. On the Hershey balance sheet, short-term borrowings are captured as short-term debt and current portion of long-term debt (long-term debt that will mature in less than a year). Sometimes short-term bank borrowing is called "note payable."

Commonly, long-term liabilities include the three liabilities on Hershey's balance sheet. Long-term debt is interest-bearing debt. Other long-term liabilities is another catchall category. However, the largest items in other long-term liabilities are pension liabilities and postretirement benefits other than pension (PBOP). PBOP is similar to a pension liability except it is related to nonpension benefits such as medical insurance for retirees.

Deferred taxes represents the difference between the measure of the total amount of tax obligations incurred by the firm during the accounting period and the amount of taxes actually paid. The sources of these differences are explained in the notes to the financial statements, but in general relate to differences in when expenses are recognized. Chapter 5, Business Organization and Taxes, discusses deferred taxes more fully.

The stockholders' equity section includes four distinct sections:

	Balance Sheet Item	Comment
1.	Preferred stock Common stock Class B common stock Additional paid-in capital	In combination, these accounts represent the proceeds received when stock was originally issued.
2.	Retained earnings	The accumulated net income retained in the corporation since inception.
3.	Treasury stock	A reduction that reflects amounts paid for repurchased shares.
4.	Unearned ESOP compensation Accumulated other income	Miscellaneous impacts that directly are assigned to equity.

The current market value of the equity is not reflected in stockholders' equity. Simply put, stockholders' equity represents the original proceeds from the company first selling shares plus the accumulated earnings that were not paid out in the form of dividends, less the repurchased amount of shares at the existing market prices at the time of repurchase.

The next section introduces the cash flow statement and develops a link between the three financial statements.

ANALYSIS OF CASH FLOWS

The income statement presents revenue, expenses, and income over a period of time. It does not detail cash flow over time due to accrual accounting. The balance sheet represents the financial picture of the firm at a point in time—what it owns and what it owes. The balance sheet includes the cash balances from one period to the next and consequently the change or total amount of cash flow for the period. From the balance sheet in Table 2.3, the Hershey Foods cash balance decreased by $15 million. This represents a negative cash flow for 1998. However, there is no detail as to where the cash came from and where it went.

In November 1987, the Financial Accounting Standards Board (FASB) issued its Statement of Financial Accounting Standards No. 95, Statement of Cash Flows (FASB 95). FASB 95 accepts the use of two methods to measure cash flows: the direct method and the indirect method. The direct method is very similar to cash-based accounting. As an example, the direct method recognizes cash collected from customers and cash paid to suppliers. It also recognizes cash used to buy equipment or pay off loans. The indirect method provides a reconciling link with the balance sheet and income statement. The indirect method derives the cash flow via the existing structure provided by the balance sheet and income statement. The indirect method is discussed in greater detail below.

Table 2.5 classifies the balance sheet changes (from Table 2.3) as sources and uses of cash. In general, a decrease in an asset or an increase in a liability is a source of cash. For example, inventories decreased by $12 million from 1997 to 1998. This provided a source of cash since Hershey sold off $12 million of inventories that it had on hand. At the same time, accounts payable increased by $10 million, which also provided a source of cash to Hershey as it borrowed more from its suppliers.

An increase in an asset or a decrease in a liability is a use of cash. To illustrate, accounts receivable grew by more than $90 million. Hershey financed its customers' purchases by providing trade credit. Instead of immediately demanding cash at the time of purchase, Hershey used its cash to finance its customers' purchases. Hershey also used its cash to pay down more than $150 million of its long-term debt in 1998.

The following summarizes the cash flow implications of changes in the balance sheet:

	Asset Change	Liability Change
Source of cash	Decrease	Increase
Use of cash	Increase	Decrease

FASB 95 requires a segregation of cash flow items on the cash flow statement by

- Cash from operations
- Cash (used for) investments
- Cash from (used for) financing

TABLE 2.5

Balance Sheet Cash Flow Implications
Hershey Foods Corporation, 1998 versus 1997 ($000)

	Balance Sheet Change	Cash Flow Implication	
		Source	Use
Cash and cash equivalents	$ (15,213)	$ 15,213	—
Accounts receivable—trade	90,493	—	$ 90,493
Inventories	(12,276)	12,276	—
Deferred income taxes	(25,519)	25,519	—
Prepaid expenses and other	61,667	—	61,667
Total current assets	99,152		
Property, plant, and equipment, net	(179)	179	—
Intangibles resulting from business acquisitions	(21,385)	21,385	—
Other assets	35,274	—	35,274
Total assets	$ 112,862		
Accounts payable	$ 10,005	10,005	—
Accrued liabilities	(77,130)	—	77,130
Accrued income taxes	(2,217)	—	2,217
Short-term debt	113,457	113,457	—
Current portion of long-term debt	(25,006)	—	25,006
Total current liabilities	19,109		
Long-term debt	(150,033)	—	150,033
Other long-term liabilities	269	269	—
Deferred income taxes	54,022	54,022	—
Total liabilities	(76,633)		
Total stockholders' equity	189,495	189,495	—
Total liabilities and stockholders' equity	$ 112,862		
Total sources and uses of cash		$ 441,820	$ 441,820

Most balance sheet changes are easily classified into one of the three categories noted above. However, to properly segregate changes in (1) plant, property, and equipment, net; (2) other assets; and (3) stockholders' equity, it is necessary to isolate certain key components:

Balance Sheet Item	Annual Change Component	Cash Flow Classification	Source (Use) ($000)
PP&E, net	Capital additions	Investing	$ (161,328)
	Depreciation expense	Operations	152,223
	Assets sold	Investing	9,284
		Balance sheet change	$ 179
Other assets	Capitalized software additions	Investing	$ (42,859)
	Remaining other assets	Operating	7,585
		Balance sheet change	$ (35,274)
Stockholders' equity	Net income	Operations	$ 340,888
	Dividends	Financing	(129,044)
	Share repurchases	Financing	(16,151)
	Miscellaneous other	Financing	(6,198)
		Balance sheet change	$ 189,495

The annual change in net PP&E is equal to capital expenditures less depreciation and assets sold during the period. Other assets includes a major asset of capitalized software related to the SAP software installation. The 1998 addition to capitalized software can be segregated in the investing section, thus leaving a source of more than $7.6 million related to the remaining other assets. Finally, the change to stockholders' equity is equal to net income less dividends less (plus) share repurchase (issuance) and plus or minus the miscellaneous other changes and reclassification within stockholders' equity.

CONSOLIDATED STATEMENTS OF CASH FLOWS

Table 2.6 furnishes Hershey's official consolidated statements of cash flows. The consolidated statements of cash flow provide three comparative years and additional insight into the firm's activities. The first section is cash from operating activities. The first set of items adjusts reported net income for noncash expenses that were deducted to arrive at net income while the second set captures the changes in operating assets and liabilities. Net income is the largest source of cash, but in calculating net income numerous noncash expenses were deducted. These noncash expenses, such as depreciation and amortization of intangibles, did not require a cash payment but were correctly deducted as an expense. Within the cash flow statement, net income is subsequently adjusted to better align with cash flows by "adding back" depreciation and amortization. In a similar fashion, an adjustment must be made for deferred taxes. The change in deferred taxes represents the difference between the tax liability on the income statement and what was actually paid to the taxing authorities. For example, the income statement included a tax liability of $216.118 million. However, in its 1998 tax return, Hershey actually paid taxes of $133.877 million. The difference between the reported liability and the actual payment represents $82.241 million of cash that was not paid but was deferred. So net income needs to be adjusted, and $82.241 million needs to be captured as a "source" of cash. The second set of items in cash from operating activities captures the noninvestment changes in operating assets and liabilities, e.g., accounts receivable and inventories.

The second section of the Consolidated Statement of Cash Flows in Table 2.6 shows cash (used for) investing. Capital additions, also referred to as capital expenditures, are monies that are reinvested in the business to buy new plant, property, and equipment. Due to the major information technology investment that Hershey was making in SAP, an enterprisewide information system for efficient resource planning, Hershey specifically highlighted capitalized software. Also, listed in Table 2.6 were proceeds from the disposal of plant, property, and equipment. Although they did not occur in 1998 for Hershey, the investing section records the cash uses (sources) for acquisitions (or divestitures).

The third section, cash flow from (used by) financing, includes the issuance (or repayment) of debt, dividend payments, equity issuance or repurchase, and some minor other adjustments.

In summary, the cash flow statements show that Hershey made substantial investments in accounts receivable in 1998 and 1997. Hershey was increasing its sales, but not collecting from its customers. This schedule also captures the fluctuations in working capital investment over the 3-year period, the relatively stable level of capital additions (investment), the 1996 acquisition of Leaf North America and 1996 divestiture of Hershey Europe and some Canadian lines of business, and Hershey's steady growth in dividends.

TABLE 2.6

Consolidated Statements of Cash Flows—Hershey Foods Corporation

	Year Ended December 31, 1998 ($000)	Year Ended December 31, 1997 ($000)	Year Ended December 31, 1996 ($000)
Cash flows provided from (used by) operating activities			
Net income	$ 340,888	$ 336,251	$ 273,186
Adjustments to reconcile net income to net cash provided from operations:			
Depreciation and amortization	158,161	152,750	133,476
Deferred income taxes	82,241	16,915	22,863
Loss on disposal of businesses	—	—	35,352
Changes in assets and liabilities, net of effects from business acquisitions and divestitures:			
Accounts receivable—trade	(90,493)	(68,479)	5,159
Inventories	12,276	(33,538)	(41,038)
Accounts payable	10,005	12,967	14,032
Other assets and liabilities	(124,118)	85,074	15,120
Other, net	745	4,018	5,593
Net cash provided from operating activities	389,705	505,958	463,743
Cash flows provided from (used by) investing activities			
Capital additions	(161,328)	(172,939)	(159,433)
Capitalized software additions	(42,859)	(29,100)	—
Business acquisitions	—	—	(437,195)
Proceeds from divestitures	—	—	149,222
Other, net	9,284	21,368	9,333
Net cash (used by) investing activities	(194,903)	(180,671)	(438,073)
Cash flows provided from (used by) financing activities			
Net change in short-term borrowings partially classified as long-term debt	(36,543)	(217,018)	210,929
Long-term borrowings	—	550,000	—
Repayment of long-term debt	(25,187)	(15,588)	(3,103)
Cash dividends paid	(129,044)	(121,546)	(114,763)
Exercise of stock options	19,368	14,397	22,049
Incentive plan transactions	(22,458)	(35,063)	(45,634)
Repurchase of common stock	(16,151)	(507,654)	(66,072)
Net cash (used by) provided from financing activities	(210,015)	(332,472)	3,406

TABLE 2.6

Consolidated Statements of Cash Flows—Hershey Foods
Corporation (*Continued*)

	Year Ended December 31, 1998 ($000)	Year Ended December 31, 1997 ($000)	Year Ended December 31, 1996 ($000)
Increase (decrease) in cash and cash equivalents	(15,213)	(7,185)	29,076
Cash and cash equivalents as of January 1	54,237	61,422	32,346
Cash and cash equivalents as of December 31	$ 39,024	$ 54,237	$ 61,422
Interest paid	$ 89,001	$ 64,937	$ 52,143
Income taxes paid	123,970	181,377	180,347

CASH FLOW PATTERNS

The grouping of cash flows into operating activities, investing activities, and financing activities provides a useful perspective on patterns that firms experience over the life cycle of activities. Representative life cycles of cash flow patterns are demonstrated below:

	Start-up Firm	Growth Firm	Mature Firm	Declining Firm
Operating activities	$ (20)	$ 200	$ 250	$ 150
Investing activities	(400)	(900)	(200)	30
Financing activities	500	800	(60)	(300)
Net increase (decrease) in cash	$ 80	$ 100	$ (10)	$ (120)

During the start-up period for a firm when it is trying to establish both the product and its position in the industry, it may be suffering initial losses from operations. It has heavy investment requirements. Its financing activities are likely to be large enough to cover current needs as well as anticipated future growth. When the product, industry, and firm become more strongly established, a growth period is entered. Profitability increases, and the firm's operating activities begin to throw off substantial positive cash flows. However, with its rapid growth in sales, the firm's investment requirements are still likely to exceed the cash from operating activities. The firm with high profitability is now in a position to have strong access to financial markets. Although investment requirements are very substantial, funds from financing and from operating activities are likely to enable the firm to increase its stock of cash and cash equivalents.

As the firm becomes mature, operating activities throw off more cash at higher levels of sales with reduced profit margins. The need for growth has diminished so that investing activities are reduced. Financing requirements are substantially smaller. The firm is likely to be able to begin paying off some of its debt and pay a higher rate of cash dividends. It can begin to reduce its stock of cash and cash equivalents.

Finally, in the declining phase, sales may decline and profit margins may be severely eroded. Hence the cash flow from operating activities is likely to be reduced. Investing activities are likely to be a small source of positive cash flows because some capacity may be reduced. At this stage, the firm should be paying off some of its obligations. It is likely to engage in substantial repayment of debt, increased dividend payments, and perhaps share repurchases as the firm begins to shrink. The firm is in a position to substantially reduce its stock of cash and equivalents.

From this discussion, note that the need for financing is likely to be greatest when the firm is in a period of growth. Large investment requirements and substantial needs for outside financing are healthy indicators if the profitability of the firm is good. But if the firm needs financing because it is losing money, and its existing accounts receivable and inventories are declining in value, this forecasts disaster. So the information provided by the cash flow patterns is necessary, but not sufficient for evaluating the financial health of a firm. Other performance measures are required, particularly the levels of profitability. More detailed analysis of the performance of the firm is the subject of Chapter 7, Financial Performance Metrics.

FINANCIAL STATEMENTS SUMMARY

In summary, Table 2.1 is repeated as Table 2.7 with highly summarized financial statements attached. The December 1997 balance includes cash of $54 million, stockholders' equity of $853 million, and total assets of $3291 million. During 1998, cash decreased to $39 million as uses of cash exceeded sources by $15 million, which is included in the 1998 changes in cash. The summarized income statement reflects net income of $341 million which flows into the stockholders' equity less dividend payments, share repurchases, and miscellaneous items, to arrive at a 1998 stockholders' equity of $1042 million.

ADDITIONAL REPORTING REQUIREMENTS

In addition to the three primary financial statements discussed above, a company is required to report other information, which is generally

TABLE 2.7

Timing of Primary Financial Statements

			1998				
	12/31/97					**12/31/98**	
	Balance Sheet		*Changes in Equity*			*Balance Sheet*	
Cash	$	54	Equity 12/31/97 $	853	Cash	$	39
Other Assets		3237	'98 net income	341	Other assets		3365
	$	3291		$ 1194		$	3404
Liabilities	$	2438	'98 dividends	$ (129)	Liabilities	$	2362
Equity		853	'98 share repurchase	(16)	Equity		1042
	$	3291	'98 other	(7)		$	3404
			Equity 12/31/98 $	1042			

	1998 Income Statement	
Sales	$	4436
Expenses		4095
Net income	$	341

	1998 Changes in Cash	
Cash 12/31/97	$	54
Sources of cash		427
Uses of cash		(442)
Cash 12/31/98	$	39

detailed in the notes to financial statements. Within the first note, the firm clarifies its accounting policies, which generally includes discussing its inventory, depreciation, and amortization policies; additional expense detail such as advertising and promotion expense and research and development expense; and other accounting issues such as treatment of foreign currency and financial instruments.

Additional notes discuss the firm's acquisitions and divestitures, capital stock position, short-term and long-term debt, lease commitments, income taxes, hedging activities using derivatives, retirement plans, postretirement benefits other than pensions, incentive plans, and stock prices and dividends. These notes discuss the company's activities and/or policies related to each of the topics.

Additional financial statements include a reconciliation of stockholders' equity, a summary of quarterly financial data such as sales and income, line-of-business detail, and international diversification (geographical) data. For businesses with a substantial part (defined as 10 percent) of the business in more than one line of business or with a substantial part (10 percent or more) of the business outside of the United States, additional reporting requirements, for each significant line of business or geographic region, reveal

- Net sales
- Operating income
- Identifiable assets
- Capital expenditures
- Depreciation and amortization expense

Since Hershey Foods is primarily a domestic, single-line-of-business company, Table 2.8 shows the geographic information reported by Heinz, another food company. Even though the data are limited, it is clear that while in total Heinz sales grew by 1 percent from 1996, the U.S. and Asia/Pacific businesses fell almost 5 and 6 percent, respectively. The shortfall was overcome by surges of almost 15 and 39 percent in Europe and Other areas, respectively. In 1998, domestic sales accounted for 53 percent of Heinz' sales and 59 percent of the operating income while utilizing 50 percent of Heinz' assets. Despite the limited data, insights can be gleaned about the Heinz business.

Finally, a summary of key financial data is also provided in an annual report. The summary presents 5 to 11 years' of data for the firm. It may include key financial metrics in addition to the data.

REPORTING REQUIREMENTS

One of the important responsibilities of the chief financial officer (CFO) is to manage all financial reporting requirements, both inside and outside the firm. Table 2.9 lists the numerous reporting requirements to the public, government agencies, and management team. Stockholders receive consolidated financial information from annual reports and quarterly reports as well as SEC filings.

The CFO is responsible for the timely and accurate preparation of the financial statements. The board of directors has access to all reporting but may choose to remain at a consolidated and SEC (Securities and Exchange Commission) level of reporting (lines 1 to 4 in Table 2.9). From time to time, the board may choose to get involved with more day-to-day details of running the company (items 5 to 9).

Consolidated statements, Securities and Exchange Commission filings, and tax filings all require audit by a public accounting firm. The public accounting firm and its subsequent opinion letter attest that the financial reports are fairly prepared in accordance with U.S. GAAP. Shareholders elect a board of directors who, in turn, select (1) an audit committee to oversee the external audit of the firm's accounts and to direct the preparation of an annual report to shareholders and (2) a public accounting firm to perform the audit and to approve (or disapprove) the annual report.

TABLE 2.8

Heinz' Geographical Information

(Dollars in thousands)	Domestic	Foreign	Worldwide	North America	Europe	Asia/ Pacific	Other
1998							
Sales	$4,873,710	$4,335,574	$9,209,284	$5,331,408	$2,453,180	$1,015,885	$ 408,811
Operating income	892,625	627,705	1,520,330	938,289	395,179	132,934	53,928
Operating income excluding restructuring related items*	860,521	647,332	1,507,853	906,114	409,030	138,781	53,928
Identifiable assets	4,075,040	3,948,381	8,023,421	4,522,535	2,332,609	825,029	343,248
Capital expenditures†	187,927	185,827	373,754	212,713	62,211	49,097	49,733
Depreciation and amortization expense	168,076	145,546	313,622	186,602	81,906	30,475	14,639
1997							
Sales	$5,169,779	$4,187,228	$9,357,007	$5,586,730	$2,281,364	$1,129,788	$ 359,125
Operating income	174,280	581,991	756,271	208,585	320,347	166,552	60,787
Operating income excluding restructuring related items††	704,880	613,309	1,318,189	751,685	374,202	130,515	61,787
Identifiable assets	4,474,740	3,963,047	8,437,787	4,941,301	2,241,006	995,762	259,718
Capital expenditures†	192,682	184,775	377,457	213,574	102,677	31,442	29,764
Depreciation and amortization expense	203,587	136,903	340,490	221,249	81,932	29,944	7,365
1996							
Sales	$5,235,847	$3,876,418	$9,112,265	$5,598,286	$2,133,690	$1,085,747	$ 294,542
Operating income	739,807	547,765	1,287,572	801,090	336,481	114,239	35,762
Identifiable assets	4,801,790	3,821,901	6,623,691	5,099,632	2,289,919	978,292	255,848
Capital expenditures†	185,874	148,913	334,787	195,517	65,485	40,294	33,491
Depreciation and amortization expense	206,912	136,897	343,809	224,824	72,530	30,674	15,781

*Excludes domestic and foreign charges for nonrecurring costs related to the implementation of Project Millenia of $64.5 million and $19.6 million, respectively. Also excludes a domestic gain on the sales of the Ore-ida foodservice foods business of $96.6 million.

†Excludes property, plant, and equipment acquired through acquisitions.

††Excludes domestic and foreign charges for restructuring and related costs of $530.6 million and $116.6 million, respectively. Also excludes gains on the sale of an ice cream business in New Zealand and real estate in the United Kingdom of $72.1 million and $13.2 million, respectively.

Congress has accepted the ultimate responsibility for the determination of accounting principles. However, in the Securities Act of 1933, the authority was delegated to the Securities and Exchange Commission. Choosing not to become directly involved in the regulation of accounting principles, the SEC elected to oversee self-regulation by the accounting profession. Public accounting firms are guided by a set of generally accepted accounting principles (GAAP), which are governed by opinions, issued between 1959 and 1973, of the Accounting Principles Board (APB) and by the Financial Accounting Standards Board (FASB) since 1973.

TABLE 2.9

Reporting Requirements

Reporting Requirement	Target Audience						
	Chief Financial Officer	Board of Directors	Public Accounting Firm	Stockholders	Internal Use	Tax Agencies	Securities and Exchange
1. Consolidated Income Statement	Required	Required	Required	Required	Required	—	—
2. Consolidated Balance Sheet	Required	Required	Required	Required	Required	—	—
3. Consolidated Cash Flow Statement	Required	Required	Required	Required	Required	—	—
4. SEC Reports: 10K, 10Q, Other	Required	Required	Required	Required	Required	—	Required
5. Tax Books and Filings	Required	Required	Required	—	—	Required	—
6. Divisional Financial Statements	Required	Required	—	—	Required	—	—
7. Cost Accounting Reports	Required	Required	—	—	Required	—	—
8. Annual Budgets and Financial Plans	Required	Required	—	—	Required	—	—
9. Project Requests and Reviews	Required	Required	—	—	Required	—	—

Internal personnel focus on consolidated reports and financial reports that "drill" more deeply into the organization. The internal reporting requirements are listed as items 5 through 9 in Table 2.9. The term *requirement* is strong in this case since there are no direct legal requirements to implement these tools. However, these tools are generally implemented to strengthen management decision making. For example, a division of a company each may have its own set of financial statements. These statements are not required by law but are prudent management tools. See the discussion of internal reporting below.

The SEC requires that nearly all publicly held corporations submit a standardized annual report, called a 10K, which usually contains more information than the annual report. Firms are required to send the 10K to all stockholders who request it. In addition, there is a quarterly filing called the 10Q. The SEC further requires that whenever a corporation wishes to issue securities to the public, it must file a registration statement that discloses the current financial data as well as such items as the purpose for issuing the securities.

Finally, tax agencies at federal, state, local, and international levels receive their appropriate filings. As briefly discussed above and more fully explained in Chap. 5, tax reporting differs from U.S. GAAP accounting. Tax accounting in general is more cash-oriented than accrual-oriented and makes use of conventions such as accelerated depreciation.

From time to time, additional audiences may require financial statements. These audiences include

- Debtholders, debt rating agencies, and banks
- Suppliers
- Investment analysts
- Employees or potential employees
- Unions

Each of these additional audiences will focus on the publicly reported consolidated financial statements and SEC filings.

INTERNAL FINANCIAL REPORTING

Table 2.9 included four areas of reporting requirements with an internal focus: divisional financial statements, cost accounting reports, annual budgets and financial plans, and project requests and reviews. As previously stated, these activities are not requirements of law, but are financial tools and processes needed to facilitate the efforts of a successful management team.

Division financial statements provide the same financial information as consolidated financial statements and should be prepared in parallel with the organizational structure of the firm. In some companies, these division statements are drilled deeper to product lines, products, sales regions, plants, production lines, and administrative cost centers or areas such as the CFO's office. Each level may have its own full or abbreviated set of financial statements. Often an abbreviated set of financial statements focuses on the income statement or lines on an income statement. For example, reporting of administrative cost centers would involve detailed expense items such as salaries, travel, and training by each administrative area, such as finance, law, and human resources that sum to the related administrative expense on an income statement.

Although external reporting is done annually or quarterly, internal reporting requirements often are monthly or shorter in order to efficiently and effectively facilitate managerial decision making and to allow for timely corrective action. The management team at a leading pharmaceutical company has an internal financial system that provides daily information with a one-day delay on the sales and gross profit (sales less cost of goods sold) of any of its hundreds of products from its many worldwide regions and in total worldwide. Needless to say, external auditors do not audit the more frequent, internal management reporting.

External reporting requirements or external benchmarking and analysis are often oriented as this year versus last year, where two historical periods are compared. A dynamic internal management style compares performance versus expectations, as reflected in annual budgets and plans. A distinction is made between planning (a broader, less detailed, longer-term direction and target-setting process) and annual budgets, which provide day-to-day, detailed operational focus that ties to the plan. Most companies compare this year's performance or financial statements to budgeted financial statements. Budgets embody the financial objectives and aspirations of the firm. Budgets have been already benchmarked to historical performance, and so now current performance need only be compared to the budget.

Financial plans and budgets are control tools used to keep managers in line. At their best, financial plans and budgets are wonderful management tools that:

- Facilitate communications throughout an organization
- Engage all members of the organization, if implemented as a participatory exercise
- Establish a common goal and set of objectives to attain that goal
- Identify performance shortfalls from aspiration levels of performance and facilitate addressing of those shortfalls without the "heat of the battle" immediately pressing

- Prioritize competing strategies
- Determine compensation targets
- Provide a barometer to gauge the progress and effectiveness of implementation

In general, plans remain as internal standards of performance. On occasion, some annual reports discuss general objectives of the firm, such as "double-digit growth" in sales or income or profitability standards as return on assets, return on equity, and margins (see Chap. 7, Financial Performance Metrics).

Finally, project requests and reviews relate to capital investment for new equipment, new plants, new products, and acquisitions or divestitures. Often the underlying process—projecting future cash flows and discounting them at an appropriate risk-adjusted cost of capital—is extended to marketing programs, research and development, investments in information technology, etc. This is the topic of Chap. 9, Capital Investment Decisions.

INTERNATIONAL REPORTING REQUIREMENTS

Cash flow has the virtue of being tangible. It is easy to identify cash when you see it. But extracting cash flows from financial statements for the purposes of financial decision making is quite another matter and is complicated by the fact that financial reporting standards and practices differ from country to country.

In Europe, e.g., a company's tax books and its annual report are the same. Consequently, for tax reasons, earnings are understated relative to what they would be using commonly accepted U.S. accounting standards. For example, in the United States accelerated depreciation is used for tax purposes, but straight-line depreciation is used in the annual report; thus taxable earnings are often less than reported earnings. In Europe, companies use accelerated depreciation for both their annual report and their tax books.

Furthermore, provisions are frequently made to expense against current income, anticipated future costs such as pensions, reorganization, or maintenance. The effect is to understate current earnings. In other words, in a good year companies will "book" additional expenses by increasing their "reserves" for various expenses. In a bad year, the previously booked reserves are reversed, which is reflected as lower expenses and higher income. These reserves and the resulting income management are strongly frowned upon in the United States.

Until very recently European companies could, at their discretion, choose whether to consolidate foreign subsidiaries. If they did not consolidate, their earnings could be substantially understated.

In France, accounting standards allow for the periodic restatement of assets to replacement value. This has no cash impact on the firm except for tax implications. When assets are based on replacement value, earnings are understated relative to U.S. GAAP-derived earnings due to higher depreciation allowances, and stockholders' equity is overstated. The amount by which the assets are written up is usually booked partly to shareholders' equity reserves and partly to deferred taxes.

It is nearly an impossible task to keep track continuously of the changing accounting standards of hundreds of countries. An international accounting standards group is trying to establish international reporting standards across the world. However, accounting numbers in one country are not likely to have the same meaning in different nations. But cash flow has an unambiguous meaning across borders, and in most countries the accounting reports give enough information to extract cash flow information.

SUMMARY

This chapter provided an overview of the three primary financial statements of the firm: income statement, balance sheet, and cash flow statement. Hershey Foods Corporation was used as an illustrative example. Reporting requirements for external and internal audiences as well as the CFO's role in timely preparation that is consistent with U.S. GAAP were discussed. Numerous points were made about the processes and practices of U.S. GAAP including FASB 95 requiring a consolidated statement of cash flows. Analysis of cash flows makes it possible to demonstrate the interrelationship of the three financial statements. Finally, internal and international reporting requirements were discussed.

QUESTIONS AND PROBLEMS

2.1   **Income Statement Preparation.** The following items are listed in alphabetical order. Please prepare an Income Statement from this information and then answer the additional questions:

Item	2000
Administrative Expense	$ 4,000
Administrative Salaries	2,500
Advertising Expense	5,000
Amortization of Goodwill	2,000
Consulting Expenses	500
Direct Labor	14,000
Dividend Payments	1,500
Income Tax Rate	40.0%
Interest Expense	3,000
Investment in New Plant	10,000
Manufacturing Depreciation	7,000
Manufacturing Overhead	6,000
Other Administrative Expense	1,000
Promotional Expenses	5,000
Raw Material Expense	38,000
Receivables	4,500
Research and Development	4,000
Sales	100,000

A.   What is the gross income and gross margin (gross income/sales)?

B.   What is the operating income (earnings before interest and taxes) and operating margin (operating income/sales)?

C.   What items were not included on the income statement? Why were they not included?

2.2   **Balance Sheet Preparation.** The following items are listed in alphabetical order. Please prepare a Balance Sheet from this information and then answer the additional questions:

Item	2000
Accounts Payable	$ 14,000
Accounts Receivable	17,000
Accrued Liabilities	9,000
Accumulated Depreciation	(34,500)
Building	32,000
Cash	2,500
Current Deferred Tax Asset	500
Current Portion of Long-Term Debt	1,500
Deferred Taxes	13,000
Depreciation Expense	7,000
Equipment	21,000
Goodwill	4,300
Inventory	23,500
Land	15,000
Long-Term Debt	5,000
Marketable Securities	14,000
Net Income	7,200
Office Equipment	2,500
Other Current Assets	1,200
Other Long-Term Assets	1,000
Other Long-Term Liabilities	2,000
Pension Liability	23,000
Stockholders' Equity	25,500
Taxes Payable	4,000
Wages Payable	3,000

A.   What dollar amount are the following items:

Item	Amount
1. Current Assets	
2. Gross Plant, Property, and Equipment	
3. Total Assets	
4. Current Liabilities	
5. Total Liabilities	
6. Total Liabilities and Equity	

B.   What items were not included on the balance sheet? Why were they not included?

2.3 **Accounting Relationships.**

A. The beginning balance of Net, Plant, Property, and Equipment was $250 million. During the year, capital expenditures were $75 million and depreciation expense was $45 million. In addition, the company sold $2 million of idle equipment as scrap. What is the ending balance of Net, Plant, Property, and Equipment?

B. Stockholders' equity was $843 million at the beginning of the year. During the year, the company generated $78 million of net income and paid dividends of $33 million. If the ending Stockholders' Equity balance is $778 million, what dollar amount of shares were repurchased throughout the year?

2.4 **Interrelationship of the Financial Statements.** The following is a consolidated balance sheet and income statement for Wal-Mart for the fiscal years ended January 31, 1998 and 1999.

A. Compute the annual dollar change in each balance sheet line item (excluding totals and subtotals). Indicate if that change is a source or use of cash.

($ Millions)	1998	1999	Balance Sheet Changes	
			Source	Use
Cash and Marketable Securities	$ 1,447	$ 1,879	$ —	$ 432
Accounts Receivable	976	1,118		
Inventory	16,497	17,076		
Prepaid Expenses and Other	432	1,059		
Total Current Assets	19,352	21,132	—	—
Gross Plant, Property, and Equipment	30,416	34,464		
Less: Accumulated Depreciation	(6,810)	(8,491)		
Net, Plant, Property, and Equipment	23,606	25,973	—	—
Other Assets and Deferred Charges	2,426	2,891		
Total Assets	$ 45,384	$ 49,996	$ —	$ —
Accounts Payable	$ 9,126	$ 10,257	$ 1,131	$ —
Accrued Liabilities	3,628	4,998		
Accrued Income Taxes	565	501		
Long-Term Debt Due in One Year	1,141	1,006		
Total Current Liabilities	14,460	16,762	—	—
Long-Term Debt	9,674	9,607		
Deferred Income Taxes and Other	2,747	2,515		
Shareholders' Equity	18,503	21,112		
Total Liabilities and Equity	$ 45,384	$ 49,996	$ —	$ —

B.   Combining the information below, construct Wal-Mart's 1999 Cash Flow Statement:

	1999
Net Sales	$ 139,208
Cost of Sales	108,725
Operating Expenses	22,363
Operating Income	8,120
Interest Expense	797
Pretax Income	7,323
Income Taxes	2,740
Net Income	$ 4,583
Other Information:	
Common Stock Dividend	$ 693
Common Stock Repurchase	1,281

SOLUTIONS TO QUESTIONS AND PROBLEMS

Problem 2.1

		2000
Sales		$ 100,000
Cost of Goods Sold		
Raw Material Expense		38,000
Direct Labor		14,000
Manufacturing Overhead		6,000
Manufacturing Depreciation		7,000
Total Cost of Goods Sold		65,000
Gross Income	A.	35,000
Gross Margin	A.	35.0%
Selling, General, and Administrative Expense		
Advertising Expense		5,000
Promotional Expenses		5,000
Research and Development		4,000
Amortization of Goodwill		2,000
Administrative Salaries		2,500
Administrative Expense		4,000
Consulting Expenses		500
Other Administrative Expense		1,000
Total Operating Expenses		24,000
Earnings Before Interest and Taxes*	B.	11,000
Operating Margin	B.	11.0%
Interest Expense		3,000
Pre-Tax Income		8,000
Income Taxes (40%)		3,200
Net Income		$ 4,800
Net Margin		4.8%

* Earnings Before Interest and Taxes is used the same as Operating Income.

C. The following items were not included on the income statement:

1. Dividend Payments are a return of capital, not an expense.

2. Investment in New Plant is a cash flow that will be expensed as depreciation over the life of the new plant.

3. Receivables are a balance sheet account that represents how much money customers owe to you.

Problem 2.2

	2000	
Current Assets		
Cash	$ 2,500	
Marketable Securities	14,000	
Accounts Receivable	17,000	
Inventory	23,500	
Current Deferred Tax Asset	500	
Other Current Assets	1,200	
Total Current Assets	58,700	2.A.1
Property, Plant, and Equipment (PP&E)		
Land	15,000	
Building	32,000	
Equipment	21,000	
Office Equipment	2,500	
Total Gross PP&E	70,500	2.A.2
Accumulated Depreciation	(34,500)	
Total Net PP&E	36,000	
Goodwill	4,300	
Other Long-Term Assets	1,000	
Total Assets	$ 100,000	2.A.3
Current Liabilities		
Accounts Payable	$ 14,000	
Accrued Liabilities	9,000	
Wages Payable	3,000	
Taxes Payable	4,000	
Current Portion of Long-Term Debt	1,500	
Total Current Liabilities	31,500	2.A.4
Long-Term Debt	5,000	
Pension Liability	23,000	
Deferred Taxes	13,000	
Other Long-Term Liabilities	2,000	
Total Liabilities	74,500	2.A.5
Stockholders' Equity	25,500	
Total Liabilities and Equity	$ 100,000	2.A.6

B. Net Income—Net income is the "bottom line" of the income statement and is reflected on the income statement. Indirectly, net income is captured in stockholders' equity.

Depreciation Expense—Depreciation is an annual expense. It is indirectly captured on the balance sheet as an increase in accumulated depreciation.

Problem 2.3

A.
Beginning Balance – Net, PP&E	$ 250
+ Capital Expenditures	75
– Depreciation	(45)
– Equipment Disposal	(2)
Ending Balance – Net, PP&E	$ 278

B.
Beginning Balance – Equity	$ 843
+ Net Income	78
– Dividends	(33)
– Shares Repurchased	??
Ending Balance – Equity	$ 778
Shares Repurchased =	$(110)

Problem 2.4

	1998	1999	Source	Use
Cash and Marketable Securities	$ 1,447	$ 1,879	$ —	$ 432
Accounts Receivable	976	1,118	—	142
Inventory	16,497	17,076	—	579
Prepaid Expenses and Other	432	1,059	—	627
Total Current Assets	19,352	21,132	—	—
Gross, Plant, Property, and Equipment	30,416	34,464	—	4,048
less: Accumulated Depreciation	(6,810)	(8,491)	1,681	—
Net, Plant, Property, and Equipment	23,606	25,973	—	—
Other Assets and Deferred Charges	2,426	2,891	—	465
Total Assets	$45,384	$49,996	—	—
Accounts Payable	$ 9,126	$10,257	1,131	—
Accrued Liabilities	3,628	4,998	1,370	—
Accrued Income Taxes	565	501	—	64
Long-Term Debt Due in One Year	1,141	1,006	—	135
Total Current Liabilities	14,460	16,762	—	—
Long-Term Debt	9,674	9,607	—	67
Deferred Income Taxes and Other	2,747	2,515	—	232
Shareholders' Equity	18,503	21,112	2,609	—
Total Liabilities and Equity	$45,384	$49,996	$ 6,791	$ 6,791

B. Cash Flow Statement

	1999
Operating Cash Flow	
Net Income	$ 4,583
Addback: Depreciation Expense	1,681
	6,264
(Increase) Decrease in Accounts Receivable	(142)
(Increase) Decrease in Inventory	(579)
(Increase) Decrease in Prepaid Expenses and Other	(627)
(Increase) Decrease in Other Assets	(465)
Increase (Decrease) in Accounts Payable	1,131
Increase (Decrease) in Accrued Liabilities	1,370
Increase (Decrease) in Accrued Income Taxes	(64)
Increase (Decrease) in Deferred Taxes and Other	(232)
Cash Flow from Operations	6,656
Investing Cash Flow	
Capital Expenditures	(4,048)
Cash Flow (Used for) Investments	(4,048)
Financing Cash Flow	
Repayment of Current Portion of LTD, Net	(135)
Repayment of Long-Term Debt	(67)
Common Stock Dividends	(693)
Repurchases of Common Stock	(1,281)
Cash Flow (Used for) Financing	(2,176)
Change in Cash—Cash Flow	$ 432

CHAPTER 3

The Time Value of Money

Knowledge of the time value of money is essential to an understanding of most topics in finance. For example, financial structure decisions, project selection, lease-versus-borrow decisions, bond refunding, security valuation, and the whole question of the cost of capital are subjects that cannot be understood without a knowledge of compound interest. Almost all problems involving compound interest can be handled with only a few basic concepts.

THE NATURE OF FINANCIAL DECISIONS

This chapter on the time value of money is key to the main theme of this book. Growth is a major source of value, and the analysis of expected future cash flows is the basis of the calculation of value. This theme is implemented throughout the chapters that follow. In this chapter we present the foundations for the analysis of growth and value.

Most decisions we face in our everyday lives, as well as the decisions that confront business firms, involve a comparison of the present with the future. This involves comparing cash flows at different times—present outlays versus future benefits, or present consumption versus future payments or forgone future benefits. For example, consider an investment of $1000 today that pays $1100 at the end of 1 year. This returns 10 percent on the investment. If the cost of funds is 12 percent, it is not a good investment because we are not earning the cost of funds. If the funds cost 8 percent, we have made a net gain.

Most financial decisions require comparisons of these kinds. Because funds have earning power, $1000 today is not the same as $1000 received 1 year later. If we have $1000 today, we can invest it to have more than $1000 in the future. Financial decisions, therefore, involve the time value of money—decisions across time. Values are determined by the timing of the future cash flows to be received. Funds received next year are worth more than the same amount of funds received in the fifth or tenth year. What is involved is discounted cash flow analysis, representing the fundamental technique for measuring the time value of money. Most financial decisions at both the personal and business levels must take into account the time value of money. The materials in this chapter are, therefore, key to the important topics of managerial finance.

FUTURE VALUE

A person invests $1000 in a security that pays 10 percent compounded annually. How much will this person have at the end of 1 year? To treat the matter systematically, let us define the following terms:

P_0 = principal, or beginning amount, at time 0 (that is, $1000)

r = rate of return or interest rate (that is, 10%)[1]

$P_0 r$ = total dollar amount of interest earned at r

$FV_{r,n}$ = future value at end of n periods at r

When n equals 1, then $FV_{r,n}$ can be calculated as follows:

$$FV_{r,1} = P_0 + P_0 r = P_0(1 + r) \tag{3.1}$$

Equation (3.1) shows that the ending amount $FV_{r,1}$ is equal to the beginning amount P_0 times the factor $1 + r$. In the example, where P_0 is $1000, r is 10 percent, and n is 1 year, $FV_{r,n}$ is determined as follows:

$$FV_{10\%,\ 1\ yr} = \$1000(1.0 + 0.10) = \$1000(1.10) = \$1100$$

Multiple Periods

If the person leaves $1000 on deposit for 5 years, to what amount will it have grown at the end of that period if interest is earned on interest? Equation (3.1) can be used to construct Table 3.1, which shows the answer. Note that $FV_{r,2}$, the balance at the end of the second year, is found as follows:

$$FV_{r,2} = FV_{r,1}(1 + r) = P_0(1 + r)(1 + r) \quad = P_0(1 + r)^2$$

$$= \$1000(1.10)^2 = \$1210.00$$

---

1 In this chapter we use r as the rate of return, or interest rate. In later chapters involving topics such as the cost of capital and valuation, the literature uses k instead of r. In one sense, k is a particular kind of rate of return or discount factor. In another sense, r and k could be used interchangeably.

Similarly, $FV_{r,3}$, the balance after 3 years, is found as

$$FV_{r,3} = FV_{r,2}(1 + r) = P_0(1 + r)^3$$
$$= \$1000(1.1)^3 = \$1331.00$$

In general, $FV_{r,n}$, the compound amount at the end of any future year n, is found as

$$FV_{r,n} = P_0(1 + r)^n \tag{3.2}$$

Equation (3.2) is the fundamental equation of compound interest. Equation (3.1) is simply a special case of Eq. (3.2), where $n = 1$.

The above is straightforward, but some important subtleties need to be drawn out. First, consider simple interest. Under a simple interest contract, the investor would have received interest of \$100 for each of the years. While contracts are sometimes written to provide for simple interest, the powerful logic behind the idea of compound interest is demonstrated by Table 3.1. If the money is invested for 5 years and the interest earned each year is left with the financial institution, interest is earned on the interest. Thus, as shown by column 2 in Table 3.1, the amount of interest earned under compound interest rises each year. Therefore, the value of the amount at the start of the year on which interest is earned during the year includes the interest earned in previous time periods.

Second, the rate of interest applied to the interest earned is *assumed* to be the 10 percent provided for in the 5-year contract. However, it is possible that interest rates would be higher or lower during the 5-year period. If so, the contract could provide for adjusting the interest rate upward or downward over the life of the agreement. But conventional practice in compound interest calculations is to assume

TABLE 3.1

Compound Interest Calculations

Year	(1) Amount at Start of Year PV	(2) Interest Earned (1) × 0.10	(3) Amount at End of Year (1) × (1 + 0.10) $FV_{r,n}$
1	\$1000.00	\$100.00	\$1100.00
2	1100.00	110.00	1210.00
3	1210.00	121.00	1331.00
4	1331.00	133.10	1464.10
5	1464.10	146.41	1610.51

reinvestment at the specified interest rate. Thus, the fundamental equation of compound interest set forth in Eq. (3.2) has important assumptions that should be kept in mind when compound interest rate relationships are utilized in the many individual topics of financial management.

Table 3.1 illustrates how compound interest rate relationships can be developed on a year-by-year basis. We could also use Eq. (3.2) to calculate the future value of $1000 at the end of 5 years. Any calculator with a y^x function would enable us to quickly calculate the results shown in Table 3.1. It is recommended that at these early stages the relationships between equations, tables, regular calculators, and financial calculators will all be explored.

To round out this discussion therefore, we illustrate how the same result of $1610.51 as the future value of $1000 at 10 percent interest can also be obtained from a table. Tables have been constructed for values of $(1 + r)^n$ for wide ranges of r and n. (See Table A.1 in App. A at the end of the book.)

Letting the *future value interest factor* (FVIF) equal $(1 + r)^n$, we can write Eq. (3.2) as $\text{FV}_{r,n} = P_0 \text{FVIF}(r, n)$. It is necessary only to go to an appropriate interest table to find the proper interest factor. For example, the correct interest factor for the illustration given in Table 3.1 can be found in Table A.1. Look down the period column to 5, then across this row to the appropriate number in the 10 percent column, to find the interest factor, 1.6105. Then with this interest factor, the future value of $1000 after 5 years is

$$\text{FV}_{10\%,\, 5\,\text{yr}} = P_0\, \text{F VIF}(10\%,\, 5\,\text{yr}) = \$1000(1.6105) = \$1610.50$$

This is the same figure that was obtained by the other methods.

The equation for the future value interest factor is

$$\text{FVIF}_{r,n} = (1 + r)^n \tag{3.3}$$

This equation can be used to calculate how the interest factor is related to the interest rate and time, as shown numerically in Table 3.2 and graphically in Fig. 3.1.

Table 3.2 and Fig. 3.1 demonstrate the power of compound interest. At a 10 percent interest rate our investment doubles in slightly more than 7 years. At 15 percent, our investment doubles in less than 5 years, and our investment has more than quadrupled in less than 10 years. The nature of the compound interest relationships is the basis for the *rule of 72*. If we divide 72 by the interest rate, we obtain the number of years required for an investment to double. At 6 percent, an investment doubles in 12 years; at 9 percent, in 8 years; at 24 percent, in 3 years. Or if we have the number of years required for an investment to double, we can use the rule of 72 to calculate the compound interest

TABLE 3.2

Interest Factors as a Function of Interest Rates

	$FVIF_{r,n} = (1 + r)^n$			
Period n	0%	5%	10%	15%
1	1.0000	1.0500	1.1000	1.1500
2	1.0000	1.1025	1.2100	1.3225
3	1.0000	1.1576	1.3310	1.5209
4	1.0000	1.2155	1.4641	1.7490
5	1.0000	1.2763	1.6105	2.0114
6	1.0000	1.3401	1.7716	2.3131
7	1.0000	1.4071	1.9487	2.6600
8	1.0000	1.4775	2.1436	3.0590
9	1.0000	1.5513	2.3579	3.5179
10	1.0000	1.6289	2.5937	4.0456

rate. If an investment doubles in 6 years, the interest rate is 12 percent; in 12 years, 6 percent; in 3 years, 24 percent. So if we are told that a stock price will double in 12 years, that represents only a 6 percent return—relatively modest. If a stock price doubles in 3 years, that represents a 24 percent rate of return, which is very good.

PRESENT VALUE

We have observed the power of compound interest to calculate future values. The next concept is the present-value concept, which has numerous applications in finance. The present-value concept leads directly to the *basic principle of investment decisions*, which is this: An investment is acceptable only if it earns at least its opportunity cost. The opportunity cost is what the funds could earn on an investment of equal risk. The *basic principle of investment decisions* may then be stated as follows: An investment is acceptable only if it earns at least the risk-adjusted market interest rate or opportunity cost of funds.

An example will illustrate the relationship between future value, present value, and the basic principle of investment decisions under certainty. We have the opportunity to invest $1000 today for an asset which can be sold 1 year later for $1210; the applicable market rate of interest is 10 percent. We can analyze the decision, using the concepts of future value, present value, and rate of return.

Under future-value analysis, we could invest the $1000 at the market interest rate of 10 percent. At the end of the year, we would have

$$\$1000(1 + 0.10) = \$1100$$

But the asset investment would have a value of $1210, which is higher than the market investment. Alternatively, we can use the concept of present value to compare the two investments.

Finding present values (*discounting*, as it is commonly called) is simply the reverse of compounding, and Eq. (3.2) can readily be transformed into a present value formula by dividing both sides by the discount factor $(1 + r)^n$ and expressing P_0 as $PV_{r, n}$.

$$FV_{r,n} = P_0(1 + r)^n \qquad (3.2)$$

$$\text{Present value} = \frac{FV_{r,n}}{(1 + r)^n} = FV_{r,n} \left[\frac{1}{(1 + r)^n} \right]$$

$$PV_{r,n} = FV_{r,n} [(1 + r)^{-n}] = FV_{r,n} \, PVIF(r, n) \qquad (3.4)$$

The subscript zero in the term P_0 indicates the present. Hence, present-value quantities can be identified by either P_0 or $PV_{r,n}$ or more generally as PV (Present Value).

FIGURE 3.1

Interest Factors as a Function of Interest Rates

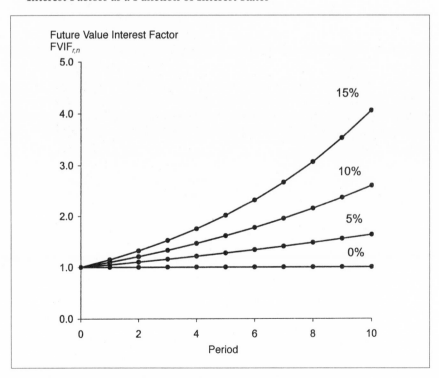

For our simple examples the present values of the two investments are

Market investment $P_0 = \$1100/1.10 = \$1000 = \$1100(0.9091)$

Asset investment $P_0 = \$1210/1.10 = \$1100 = \$1210(0.9091)$

We can calculate the present value by dividing by 1 plus the interest rate expressed as a decimal or by multiplying the future value by $1/(1 + r) = (1 + r)^{-1}$. Finally, we note that the market investment has a rate of return of 10 percent, while the asset investment has a return of 21 percent. To summarize the three comparisons, we have

	Asset Investment	Market Investment
Future value	$1210	$1100
Present value at market rate	$1100	$1000
Rate of return	21%	10%

By all three methods or criteria, the asset investment is superior to an investment at the market rate. In these comparisons we have explained the concept of present value and illustrated its use. More generally, to obtain the present value we divide by $(1 + r)^n$ or multiply by $(1 + r)^{-n}$.

Tables have been constructed for the present-value interest rate factors—$(1 + r)^{-n}$—for various rates r and time intervals n. (See Table A.2.) For example, to determine the present value of $1610.51 to be received 5 years hence when the discount factor is 10 percent, look down the 10 percent column in Table A.2 to the fifth row. The figure shown there, 0.6209, is the present-value interest factor (PVIF) used to determine the present value of $1610.51 payable in 5 years, discounted at 10 percent.

$$PV_{r,n} = P_0 = FV_{10\%,5\,\text{yr}}[\text{PVIF}(10\%, 5\,\text{yr})]$$

$$= \$1610.51(0.6209)$$

$$= \$1000$$

The present value tells us what a future sum or sums would be worth to us if we had those funds today. It is obtained by discounting the future sum or sums back to the starting point, which is the present. Present-value analysis clearly involves discounting future cash flows back to the present. It should be understood, however, that the standard practice in finance is to call all compound interest calculations involving present values *discounted cash flow (DCF) analysis*.

ANNUITIES

Thus far we have discussed the concepts of future value and present value for a single outflow or inflow. We next consider multiple outflows and/or inflows. These are called annuities.

Future Value of an Annuity

An annuity is defined as a series of payments or receipts for a specified number of periods. The payment or receipt may occur at the end of the year or at the beginning of the year. If it occurs at the end of the year, it is called an *ordinary annuity* (or annuity paid in arrears); if it occurs at the beginning of the year, it is called an *annuity due* (or an annuity paid in advance). Mortgage payments are typically made at the end of the period; lease payments are usually made at the beginning of the period. For most problems payments are received at the end of the period, so our emphasis will be on ordinary annuities.

The sum of a geometric series can be expressed as

$$S_n = a\left(\frac{r^n - 1}{r - 1}\right) \tag{3.5}$$

For calculating the future value of an annuity at an interest rate of r and the number of periods reflected in t, denoted by $FVA_{r,t}$, the rate of geometric growth is $1 + r$. Hence we can write

$$FVA_{r,t} = a\left[\frac{(1 + r)^n - 1}{1 + r - 1}\right]$$

Solving for $FVA_{r,t}$ results in Eq. (3.6), which is the formula for calculating the future value of an annuity.

$$FVA_{r,t} = a\left[\frac{(1 + r)^n - 1}{r}\right] \tag{3.6}$$

The interest factor in Eq. (3.6) can also be written with an abbreviation in letters, as shown in Eq. (3.6a).

$$FVA_{r,t} = a\, FVIFA(r,\ t) \tag{3.6a}$$

FVIFA has been given values for various combinations of r and t. To find these, see Table A.3. To find the answer to the 3-year, $1000 annuity problem, simply refer to Table A.3. Look down the 10 percent column to the row for the third year, and multiply the factor 3.3100 by $1000, as shown below:

$$FVA_{r,t} = a\, FVIFA(r,\ t)$$
$$FVA_{10\%,3\ yr} = \$1000(3.3100) = \$3310$$

Notice that the FVIFA for the sum of an annuity is always larger than the number of years that the annuity runs. The reader should verify that the same result can be obtained with a hand calculator, using the formula in Eq. (3.6).

Present Value of an Annuity

Many decisions in finance use the concept of the present value of an annuity. Its basic formulation is used in analyzing investment decisions, in valuation calculations, and in many other applications. We start with a simple investment decision. Abacus Company is considering the purchase of a power saw; the saw will cost $2000 and will generate additional cash flows of $1000 per year for 3 years. The cash flows are considered available at the end of each year (ordinary annuity); the applicable discount rate is 10 percent. Will Abacus gain from the investment?

The present value of an annuity ($PVA_{r,t}$) is expressed in Eq. (3.7).

$$PVA_{r,t} = a\left[\frac{1-(1+r)^{-n}}{r}\right] \tag{3.7}$$

Equation (3.7) can also be written as shown below:

$$PVA_{r,t} = a\,PVIFA_{r,t} \tag{3.7a}$$

We can derive Eq. (3.7) from the future-value formula:

$$PVA_{r,t} = FVA_{r,t}(1+r)^{-n}$$

$$= a\left[\frac{(1+r)^{n}-1}{r}\right](1+r)^{-n} = a\left[\frac{1-(1+r)^{-n}}{r}\right]$$

Using PVIFA, the present value of an annuity interest factor, we can write $PVA_{r,t} = a\,PVIFA_{r,t}$. For our simple numerical example, we have

$$\$1000\left[\frac{1-(1.10)^{-3}}{0.10}\right] = \$1000\left(\frac{1-0.7513}{0.10}\right) = \$2486.85$$

Notice that the PVIFA for the present value of an annuity is always less than the number of years the annuity runs, whereas the FVIFA for the sum of an annuity is larger than the number of years for which it runs.

The analysis is a comparison between the present value of the future cash inflows and the initial investment cash outflow. The present value of the future cash inflows is $2486.85. The net present value NPV of the investment is the present value of benefits less the present value of costs. In our example, the NPV is $2486.85 − $2000 = $486.85. The investment adds value to the firm, so it should be made. (We use the NPV concept, which is the basis for value creation, throughout the book.)

Unequal Payments

Thus far we have used constant annual inflows to develop the basic relationships. The concepts can easily be applied to uneven payments by using the simple present-value formula. The assumed cash inflows and their present value are shown in Table 3.3.

PERPETUITIES

Some securities carry no maturity date. They are a perpetuity—an annuity that continues forever. The future value of a perpetuity is infinite since the number of periodic payments is infinite. The present value of an annuity can be calculated by starting with Eq. (3.8).

$$PVA_{r,\,t} = a\left[\frac{1-(1+r)^{-n}}{r}\right] \qquad (3.8)$$

Notice that the term $(1 + r)^{-n} = 1/(1 + r)^n$ is always less than 1 for positive interest rates. For example, suppose $r = 10$ percent; then

$$(1+r)^{-1}=0.909, (1+r)^{-2}=0.826, (1+r)^{-3}=0.751, \ldots, (1+r)^{-100}=0.000073$$

As the number of years becomes very large (i.e., infinite), the term $(1 + r)^{-n}$ goes to zero. Thus, if the annuity of constant payments is perpetual, we have as our final result

TABLE 3.3

PVA for Unequal Inflows

Period	Cash Inflows	× PVIF$_{10\%,n}$	=	PV of Each Cash Inflow
1	100	0.9091		$ 90.91
2	200	0.8264		165.29
3	300	0.7513		225.39
4	500	0.6830		341.51
5	400	0.6209		248.37
6	600	0.5645		338.68
7	200	0.5132		102.63
	Present value of unequal inflows =			$ 1512.78

$$\text{PVA}_{r,\,\infty} = \frac{a}{r} \tag{3.9}$$

So the present value of a perpetuity is the periodic flow a, divided by the discount factor. Equation (3.9) is a simple expression rich in implications.

Impact of Changing the Discount Rate

Assume that initially $a = \$120$ and $r = 10$ percent; the PV is

$$\text{PV} = \frac{\$120}{0.10} = \$1200$$

If r rises to 12 percent, PV falls to $1000. If r falls to 8 percent, PV rises to $1500. Thus PV is very sensitive to the size of the discount factor. This is also generally true for investments, even if they do not have infinite lives; however, the impact is largest for a perpetuity.

Interrelationships among the Terms

The formula for a perpetuity also facilitates an understanding of another set of relationships. For all the interest formulas we have three basic terms, as shown by Eq. (3.10).

$$\text{Value} = (\text{Periodic Flow}) \times (\text{Interest Factor}) \tag{3.10}$$

For our basic example above, we have

$$\text{Value} = \$120\left(\frac{1}{0.10}\right) = \$120(10)$$

If we know any two of the three terms, we can calculate the third. If we have a value of $1000 and a flow of $120, the discount factor can be solved for and is found to be 12 percent. If we have a value of $1500 and a discount factor of 10 percent, the flow must be $150.

GENERALIZATION OF INTERRELATIONSHIPS

We present some practical illustrations of how we may solve for a third term when we have two of the three factors: present or future value, the periodic flow, and the interest factor.

Determining Interest Rates

In many instances, the present values and cash flows associated with a payment stream are known, but the interest rate is not known. Suppose a bank offers to lend you $1000 today if you sign a note agreeing to pay the bank $1762.30 at the end of 5 years. What rate of interest would you be paying on the loans? To answer the question, we use Eq. (3.2):

$$FV_{r,n} = P_0(1 + r)^n = P_0 FVIF(r, n) \qquad (3.2)$$

We simply solve for the FVIF and then look up this value in Table A.1 along the row for the fifth year:

$$FVIF(r, n) = \frac{FV_{r,\,5\,yr}}{P_0} = \frac{\$1762.30}{\$1000} = 1.7623$$

Looking across the row for the fifth year, we find the value 1.7623 in the 12 percent column; therefore, the interest rate on the loan is 12 percent.

Precisely the same approach is taken to determine the interest rate implicit in an annuity. For example, suppose a bank will lend you $2401.80 if you sign a note in which you agree to pay the bank $1000 at the end of each of the next 3 years. What interest rate is the bank charging you? To answer the question, we solve Eq. (3.7a) for PVIFA and then look up the PVIFA in Table A.4:

$$PVA_{r,t} = a\ PVIFA_{r,t} \qquad (3.7a)$$

$$PVIFA_{r,t} = \frac{PV_{r,\,3\,yr}}{a} = \frac{\$2401.80}{\$1000} = 2.4018$$

Looking across the third-year row, we find the factor 2.4018 under the 12 percent column; therefore, the bank is lending you money at a 12 percent interest rate.

A third illustration of finding interest rates involves determining the growth rates. One method is the endpoints method. Data for ABC's revenue are presented in Table 3.4. We can calculate (geometric average) growth rates using the future-value formula, Eq. (3.2):

$$FV_{r,n} = P_0(1 + r)^n$$

For the revenue stream, the future amount after 5 years of growth to 1996 is $64.7 billion, and the present amount in 1991 is $50.7 million. Substituting these into the formula, we have

$$\$64.7 = \$50.7(1 + r)^5$$

TABLE 3.4

ABC Financial Data

	2001	2000	1996	1991
Revenue ($ billions)	75.9	62.7	64.7	50.7

$$\left(\frac{\$64.7}{\$50.7}\right)^{1/5} - 1 = r$$

$$r = 5.00\%$$

Similarly, for 1996–2000, we have:

$$FV_{r,n} = PV_0 (1 + r)^n$$

$$62.7 = 64.7(1 + r)^4$$

$$\left(\frac{62.7}{64.7}\right)^{1/4} - 1 = r = -0.78\%$$

For 2000–2001, ABC's revenues grew at a compound annual rate of 21.05 percent. For the entire 10-year period 1991–2001, ABC's revenues grew at a compound annual rate of 4.12 percent.

More generally,

$$g = \left(\frac{X_n}{X_0}\right)^{1/n} - 1 \qquad\qquad (3.11)$$

where g = compound (geometric average) growth rate over the period

X_n = endpoint value

X_0 = beginning value

n = number of periods of growth

This example illustrates the strength and weakness of the end-points method. A plus is that it is easy to calculate. A negative is that it may not reflect the data patterns for the periods between the end-points. For the 10 years between 1991 and 2001, ABC's revenues grew at a compound annual rate of 4.12 percent. But in the intervening subperiods, higher and lower (even negative) growth rates were experienced.

NONINTEGER VALUES OF INTEREST RATES

In the interest tables at the end of the book, we have given interest factor values for integer values such as 8 or 9 percent. Sometimes practical problems involve fractional interest rates, such as $8\frac{1}{4}$ percent. Or the interest rate calculation problem you encounter may involve time periods outside the range of the years provided in the tables. (Compounding for periods other than the annual basis given in the tables will be discussed in the following section.) For fractional interest rates, the use of the formulas and a hand calculator enables us to determine the interest factors required. Recall that in the interest rate formulas presented, there was a component (FVIF, PVIF, FVIFA, or PVIFA) for the interest factor. Assuming that our problem involved alternatively using each of the four types of interest factors for an interest rate of $8\frac{1}{4}$ percent and a 10-year period, the formulas and the resulting values are as shown below:

$$FVIF \quad = \quad (1 + r)^n = 1.0825^{10} = 2.2094$$

$$PVIF \quad = \quad 1/(1 + r)^n = 1/1.0825^{10} = 0.4526$$

$$FVIFA \quad = \quad [(1 + r)^n - 1]/r = [1.0825^{10} - 1]/0.0825 = 14.6597$$

$$PVIFA \quad = \quad [1 - (1 + r)^{-n}]/r = [1 - 1.0825^{-10}]/0.0825 = 6.6351$$

Notice that in performing the calculations, we take $(1.0825)^{10}$ and then simply use this result in a slightly different way for each of the four interest factors that we calculate. Many handheld calculators are pre-programmed to carry out these kinds of calculations. However, all these internal programs are based on the logic involved in using each of the four basic compound interest formulas.

Sometimes the problem involves obtaining interest rates when only the interest factors are provided. For example, suppose we make an investment of $663,510, which will yield $100,000 per year for 10 years. We want to know the rate of return on that investment. We use Eq. (3.7a) to find the PVIFA:

$$PVIFA = \$663,510/\$100,000 = 6.6351$$

From our calculations above, we recognize that this result is the PVIFA in which the interest rate is $8\frac{1}{4}$ percent. If we are using a prepro-grammed hand calculator, we can solve for the required interest rate. With a less sophisticated hand calculator, we would have to obtain the result by trial and error. But with hand calculators of any degree of sophistication, if we keep in mind the expressions for the four basic compound interest relations, we can obtain what we need to solve any real-world problem that might come up. This is even true when com-pounding is on a basis other than annual, as we shall demonstrate in the following section.

SEMIANNUAL AND OTHER COMPOUNDING PERIODS

In all the examples used thus far, it has been assumed that returns were received annually. For example, in the section dealing with future values, it was assumed that the funds earned 10 percent a year. However, suppose the earnings rate had been 10 percent compounded semiannually (i.e., every 6 months). What would this have meant? Consider the following example.

You invest $1000 in a security to receive a return of 10 percent compounded semiannually. How much will you have at the end of 1 year? Since semiannual compounding means that interest is actually paid each 6 months, this fact is taken into account in the tabular calculations in Table 3.5. Here the annual interest rate is divided by 2, but twice as many compounding periods are used because interest is paid twice a year. Comparing the amount on hand at the end of the second 6-month period, $1102.50, with what would have been on hand under annual compounding, $1100.00, shows that semiannual compounding is better for the investor. This result occurs because the saver earns interest on interest more frequently. Thus semiannual compounding results in higher effective annual rates. If we required that the annual rates stay at 12 percent, then the semiannual rate would be not 12/2 = 6 percent but rather $(1.12)^{1/2} - 1 = 0.0583 = 5.83$ percent. By market convention, however, the yield to maturity based on compounding at intervals of 6 months is doubled to obtain the annual yield, which understates the effective annual yield.

We can extend this simple example for more frequent compounding within the year. We shall calculate the future sum for 1 year for multiple compounding within the year for an interest rate of 12 percent and an initial principal of $1, as shown in Table 3.6. We see that daily compounding increases the effective annual interest rate by 0.75 percent.

TABLE 3.5

Compound Interest Calculations with Semiannual Compounding

Period	Period Beginning Amount	×	1 + r	=	Ending Amount $(FV_{r,n})$
1	$ 1000.00		1.05		$ 1050.00
2	1050.00		1.05		1102.50

TABLE 3.6

Effective Annual Yields with Multiple Compounding within the Year

Annual	$FV_{r,1} = P_0(1+r)$	=	1.1200	$(q=1)$
Semiannual	$= P_0\left(1 + \dfrac{r}{2}\right)^2$	=	1.1236	$(q=2)$
Quarterly	$= P_0\left(1 + \dfrac{r}{4}\right)^4$	=	1.1255	$(q=4)$
Monthly	$= P_0\left(1 + \dfrac{r}{12}\right)^{12}$	=	1.1268	$(q=12)$
Daily	$= P_0\left(1 + \dfrac{r}{365}\right)^{365}$	=	1.1275	$(q=365)$

Equation (3.12) is a generalization of the procedure for within-the-year compounding, where q is frequency and n is years:

$$FV_{r,n} = P_0\left(1 + \frac{r}{q}\right)^{nq} \tag{3.12}$$

The four interest tables presented can be used when compounding occurs more than once a year. Simply divide the nominal (stated) interest rate by the number of times compounding occurs, and multiply the years by the number of compounding periods per year. For example, to find the amount to which $1000 will grow after 5 years if semiannual compounding is applied to a stated 10 percent interest rate, divide 10 percent by 2 and multiply the 5 years by 2. Then look in Table A.1 at the end of the book under the 5 percent column and in the row for the tenth period, where you will find an interest factor of 1.6289. Multiplying this by the initial $1000 gives a value of $1628.90, the amount to which $1000 will grow in 5 years at 10 percent compounded semiannually. This compares with $1610.50 for annual compounding.

The same procedure is applied in all cases covered—compounding, discounting, single payments, and annuities. To illustrate semiannual compounding in calculating the present value of an annuity, e.g., consider the case described in the section on the present value of an annuity—$1000 a year for 3 years, discounted at 10 percent. With annual discounting or compounding, the interest factor is 2.4869, and the present value of the annuity is $2486.90. For semiannual compounding, look under the 5 percent column and in the year 6 row of Table A.4 to find an interest factor of 5.0757. Then multiply by one-half of $1000, or the $500 received each 6 months, to get the present value of the annuity, or $2537.85. The payments come a little more rapidly (the first

$500 is paid after only 6 months), so the annuity is a little more valuable if payments are received semiannually rather than annually.

CONTINUOUS COMPOUNDING AND DISCOUNTING

By letting the frequency of compounding q approach infinity, Eq. (3.12) can be modified to the special case of *continuous compounding*. Continuous compounding is extremely useful in theoretical finance as well as in practical applications. Also as shown in later chapters, computations are often simplified when continuously compounded interest rates are used.

When we compound continuously, the result is the equation for continuous compounding

$$FV_{r,t} = P_0 \, e^{rt} \tag{3.13}$$

where e is the constant 2.718. Letting $P_0 = 1$, we can rewrite Eq. (3.13) as

$$FV_{r,t} = e^{rt} \tag{3.13a}$$

Expressing Eq. (3.13a) in logarithmic form and noting that ln denotes the log to the base e, we obtain

$$\ln FV_{r,t} = rt \ln e \tag{3.13b}$$

Since e is defined as the base of the system of natural logarithms, ln e must equal 1.0. Therefore,

$$\ln FV_{r,t} = rt \tag{3.13c}$$

For example, if $t = 5$ years and $r = 10$ percent, the product is 0.50. To use Eq. (3.13a) requires a hand calculator with an e^x key. If your hand calculator has an e^x function, use Eq. (3.13a); enter the 0.5 and push the e^x key to obtain 1.648721. If your hand calculator has a ln x key (but not an e^x key) use Eq. (3.13c); enter the 0.5 and push INV and then the ln x key to obtain the same result. Most calculators have some provision for performing logarithmic functions. For annual compounding, the calculation is $(1.1)^5 = 1.610510$.

Continuous Discounting

Equation (3.13) can be solved for P_0 ($= PV_{r,t}$) and used to determine present values under continuous compounding.

$$P_0 = PV_{r,t} = \frac{FV_{r,t}}{e^{r,t}} = FV_{r,t}e^{-rt} \tag{3.14}$$

Thus, if \$1649 is due in 5 years and if the appropriate *continuous* discount rate r is 10 percent, the present value of this future payment is

$$PV = \frac{\$1649}{1.649} = \$1000$$

The present value of an infinite stream of payments growing at a constant rate g with continuous discounting at rate r can be calculated by using Eq. (3.15).

$$PV_{r,\infty} = \frac{a_0}{r-g} \tag{3.15}$$

Equation (3.15) is the formula for the present value of a continuous stream of payments growing to infinity at the constant rate g and discounted at rate r. For example, when $a_0 = \$12$, $r = 12$ percent, and $g = 4$ percent, the (present) value of the stream of inflows is $12/0.08 = \$150$.

THE ANNUAL PERCENTAGE RATE (APR)

Different types of financial contracts use different compounding periods. Most bonds pay interest semiannually. Some savings accounts pay interest quarterly, but the new money market accounts at most financial institutions pay interest daily. Department stores, oil companies, and credit cards also specify a daily rate of interest. In addition, to obtain a home mortgage loan, the lender charges points up front. To compare the costs of different credit sources, it is necessary to calculate the effective rate of interest, or the annual percentage rate (APR), as it is generally called. The APR is always compounded once per year.

To calculate APR, we should recognize that we are simply making another application of Eq. (3.12), where $n = 1$. Equation (3.12) then becomes Eq. (3.16).

$$PV_{r,1} = P_0\left(1 + \frac{r}{q}\right)^q \tag{3.16}$$

The annual effective rate of interest (APR) can be determined as follows:

$$\frac{PV_{r,1}}{P_0} = \left(1 + \frac{r}{q}\right)^q = 1 + APR$$

Solving for the APR, we have

$$APR = \left(1 + \frac{r}{q}\right)^q - 1 \tag{3.16a}$$

Since we have already calculated $1 + APR$ in Table 3.6, the APR in each of the examples is obtained by subtracting 1. For example, the

APR rises from 12.36 percent for semiannual compounding to 12.68 percent for monthly compounding.

We can generalize further. At an interest rate of 12 percent, we want to know the future sum of $100 with quarterly compounding for 5 years. First we use Eq. (3.12):

$$\text{FV}_{r,n} = P_0\left(1 + \frac{r}{q}\right)^{nq} = \$100\left(1 + \frac{0.12}{4}\right)^{5(4)} = \$100(1.03)^{20} = \$180.611$$

Alternatively, we can use the APR in Table 3.6 for quarterly compounding. This is 12.55 percent, which we can use in Eq. (3.2):

$$\text{FV}_{r,n} = P_0(1 + APR)^n = \$100(1.1255)^5 = \$180.604$$

Since the results are the same (except for rounding), we can use either method in making calculations. In many transactions, government regulations require that the lender provide the borrower with a written statement of the APR in the transaction. We have described how it can be calculated.

THE RELATIONSHIP BETWEEN DISCRETE AND CONTINUOUS INTEREST RATES

Discrete growth or compounding can always be transformed to an equivalent continuous version. Let d represent a discrete rate of compounding, while c is a continuous compounding rate. In general,

$$\ln(1 + d) = c \tag{3.17}$$

The continuous rate will, in general, be lower than the discrete rate. For example, if the discrete rate of interest is 12 percent, the continuous rate would be ln 1.12 = 11.33 percent. This is quite logical, since the interest is working harder, e.g., when it is compounding every second than when it is compounding only once a year.

Conversely, if a given interest rate is being compounded continuously, the equivalent discrete rate is larger. Thus, if we are using a nominal 12 percent rate but applying it continuously, the equivalent discrete rate will be higher. The appropriate formula to apply requires solving Eq. (3.18) for d.

$$d = e^c - 1 \tag{3.18a}$$

Compounding a 12 percent nominal rate continuously, we see the equivalent discrete rate is 12.7497 percent. Note that Eq. (3.18a) is the continuous compounding equivalent of Eq. (3.16), which was the expression for calculating the annual percentage rate under discrete compounding. Thus, we see that the equivalent discrete rate when a nominal interest rate is compounded continuously represents the annual percentage rate.

SUMMARY

A knowledge of compound interest and present-value techniques is essential to an understanding of important aspects of finance covered in subsequent chapters: capital budgeting, financial structure, security valuation, and other topics.

The four basic equations with the notation that will be used throughout the book are

$$\text{FV}_{r,n} = P_0\,\text{FVIF}(r,n) \equiv P(1+r)^n \tag{3.2}$$

$$\text{PV}_{r,n} = \text{FV}_{r,n}\,\text{PVIF}(r,n) \equiv \text{FV}_{r,n}\,(1+r)^{-n} \tag{3.4}$$

$$\text{FVA}_{r,t} = a\,\text{FVIFA}(r,t) \equiv a[(1+r)^n - 1]/r \tag{3.6}$$

$$\text{PVA}_{r,t} = a\,\text{PVIFA}(r,t) \equiv a[1-(1+r)^{-n}]/r \tag{3.7}$$

With continuous compounding, the first two formulas become

$$\text{FV}_{r,t} = P_0\,e^{rt} \tag{3.13}$$

$$\text{PV}_{r,t} = \text{FV}_{r,t}\,e^{-rt} \tag{3.14}$$

These interest formulas can be used for either an even or uneven series of receipts or payments. The basic formulas can be used to find (1) the annual payments necessary to accumulate a future sum, (2) the annual receipts from a specified annuity, (3) the periodic payments necessary to amortize a loan, and (4) the interest rate implicit in a loan contract. They are the basis for all valuation formulas. The formulas can also be used with more frequent periods than annual compounding, including semiannual, monthly, daily, and continuous compounding.

The general formula for within-the-year compounding is

$$\text{FV}_{r,n} = P_0\left(1 + \frac{r}{q}\right)^{n,\,q} \qquad q \text{ frequency, } n \text{ years} \tag{3.12}$$

This expression is used in determining the APR (annual percentage rate) implicit in a contract where the *effective interest rate* is not the same as the stated rate because of the frequency of compounding. The formula for the annual percentage rate is

$$\text{APR} = \left(1 + \frac{r}{q}\right)^q - 1 \tag{3.16a}$$

Finally, the relationship between discrete and continuously compounded discount rate is

$$d = e^c - 1 \tag{3.18}$$

where *d* is also the (higher) APR for a continuously compounded discount rate *c*.

QUESTIONS AND PROBLEMS

3.1   The current production target for the 5-year plan of Logo Company is to increase output by 8 percent per year. If the 2000 production is 3.81 million tons, what is the target production for 2005?

3.2   At a growth rate of 9 percent, how long does it take a sum to double?

3.3   If, at age 25, you open an IRA account paying 10 percent annual interest and you put $2000 in at the end of each year, what will be your balance at age 65?

3.4   You are offered two alternatives: a $2000 annuity for 7 years or a lump sum today. If current interest rates are 9 percent, how large will the lump sum have to be to make you indifferent between the alternatives?

3.5   You have just purchased a newly issued $1000 five-year Malley Company bond at par. The bond (bond A) pays $60 in interest semiannually ($120 per year). You are also negotiating the purchase of a $1000 six-year Malley Company bond (bond B) that returns $30 in semiannual interest payments and has 6 years remaining before it matures.

    A.   What is the going rate of return on bonds of risk and maturity of Malley Company's bond A?

    B.   What should you be willing to pay for bond B?

3.6   On December 31, George Smith buys a building for $175,000, paying 20 percent down and agreeing to pay the balance in 20 equal annual installments that are to include principal plus 15 percent compound interest on the declining balance. How much are the equal installments?

3.7   You wish to borrow $50,000 for a home mortgage. The quoted interest rate is 11 percent compounded monthly for a 25-year mortgage.

    A.   What annual percentage rate is equal to 11 percent compounded monthly?

    B.   What will your monthly mortgage payments be (assuming that they are paid at the end of each month)?

3.8   If you have an account that compounds interest continuously and has an effective annual interest yield of 6.18 percent, what is the stated annual interest rate?

3.9 What rate of interest compounded monthly is equivalent to 18 percent compounded continuously?

SOLUTIONS TO QUESTIONS AND PROBLEMS

3.1 $3.81 \times$ FVIF(8%, 5 years) = production during year 2005
$3.81(1.4693) = 5.60$ million tons

3.2 Eight years. Referring to Table A.1 and reading down the 9 percent column, FVIF = 1.9926 (approximately 2) in the eighth year, so at the beginning of the ninth year, the amount will have grown to twice its size.

3.3 Forty total payments are made. Their value is found as the compound value of an annuity. From Table A.3, FVIFA(10%, 40 years) = 442.59.

Compound value = 442.59($2000) = $885,180

Note that the compound value is more than 10 times the total of $80,000 of actual payments.

3.4 From Table A.4, PVIFA(9%, 7 years) = 5.033
Present value = 5.033($2000) = $10,066
At a 9 percent interest rate, you will be indifferent between receiving a lump sum of $10,066 today versus a $2000 annuity for 7 years.

3.5 A. You are receiving $120 interest annually, or $60 semiannually, on a $1000 investment. Thus, the going rate of return is 12 percent compounded semiannually, an effective rate of 12.36 percent.

B. The other bond should provide a similar yield; the price that forces this bond to yield 12 percent, with semiannual compounding, is found as follows:

$$
\begin{aligned}
\text{Price} = \text{PV} &= \sum_{t=1}^{12} \frac{\$30}{(1.06)^t} + \frac{\$1000}{(1.06)^{12}} \\
&= \$30(8.3838) + \$1000(0.4970) \\
&= \$251.51 + \$497 \\
&= \$748.51
\end{aligned}
$$

3.6
Price of building	$175,000
Down payment	35,000
Amount due	$140,000

The present value of a 20-year annuity at 15 percent equals $140,000. The present value of a $1 annuity for 20 years at 15 percent equals $6.2593.

$$\frac{\$140,000}{6.2593} = \$22,366.72 = \text{amount of each installment}$$

Note: Total payments will be $22,366.72 × 20 = $447,334.40, or more than 3 times $140,000.

3.7   A. $$\text{APR} = \left(1 + \frac{r}{q}\right)^{q} - 1$$

$$= \left(1 + \frac{0.11}{12}\right)^{12} - 1 = 11.57\%$$

B.

$$\text{PV} = a\left[\frac{1 - (1 + r)^{-n}}{r}\right]$$

$$\$50,000 = a\left[\frac{1 - (1 + 0.11/12)^{-(12)(25)}}{0.11/12}\right]$$

$$\$50,000 = a(102.03)$$

$$a = \frac{\$50,000}{102.03} = \$490 \text{ monthly payment}$$

3.8 $(1 + d)^{n}$ $= e^{cn}$
      $1 + d$ $= e^{c}$
      1.0618 $= e^{c}$
      $\ln 1.0618$ $= c$
      0.059966 $= c$

c equal approximately 0.06, or 6 percent.

3.9 $\left(1 + \dfrac{d}{m}\right)^{mn} = e^{cn}$ Take the nth root.

$\left(1 + \dfrac{d}{12}\right)^{12} = e^{0.18}$

$\left(1 + \dfrac{d}{12}\right) = \left(e^{0.18}\right)^{1/12}$

$\left(1 + \dfrac{d}{12}\right) = (1.197217)^{1/12}$

$1 + \dfrac{d}{12} = 1.015113$

$\dfrac{d}{12} = 0.015113$

$d = 0.181357 \qquad = 18.14 \text{ percent}$

CHAPTER 4

Financial Markets and Market Efficiency

THE FINANCIAL SYSTEM

The financial manager functions in a complex financial environment because the savings and investment functions in a modern economy are performed by different economic units. Savings surplus units (a "unit" could be a business firm or an individual), whose savings exceed their investment in real assets, own financial assets. Savings deficit units, whose current savings are less than their investment in real assets, incur financial liabilities.

The transfer of funds from a savings surplus unit or the acquisition of funds by a savings deficit unit creates a financial asset or a financial liability. For example, funds deposited in a savings account in a bank represent a financial asset on the account holder's personal balance sheet, but a liability account to the financial institution. Conversely, a loan from a financial institution represents a financial asset on its balance sheet, but a financial liability to the borrower. A wide variety of financial claims, including promissory notes, bonds, and common stocks, are issued by savings-deficit units.

Financial Markets

Financial transactions involve financial assets and financial liabilities. The creation and transfer of such assets and liabilities constitute *financial markets.* The nature of financial markets can be explained by an analogy. The automobile market, e.g., is defined by all transactions in automobiles, whether they occur at auto dealers' showrooms, at wholesale auctions of used cars, or at individuals' homes, because the transactions make up the total demand and supply for autos.

Similarly, financial markets are comprised of all trades that result in the creation of financial assets and financial liabilities. Trades are made through organized institutions, such as the New York Stock Exchange or the regional stock exchanges, or through the thousands of brokers and dealers, who buy and sell securities off the exchange, comprising the *over-the-counter market*. Individual transactions with department stores, savings banks, or other financial institutions also create financial assets and financial liabilities. In recent years computers and the Internet have facilitated systems such as online trading.

Different segments of the financial markets are characterized by different maturities. When the financial claims and obligations bought and sold have maturities of less than one year, the transactions constitute *money markets*. If the maturities are more than one year, the markets are referred to as *capital markets*. Although real capital in an economy is represented by physical assets, e.g., plants, machinery, and equipment, long-term financial instruments are regarded as ultimately representing claims on the real resources in an economy; for that reason, the markets in which these instruments are traded are referred to as capital markets.

Financial Intermediaries

Financial intermediation brings together, through transactions in the financial markets, the savings-surplus units and the savings-deficit units so that savings can be redistributed into their most productive uses. The specialized business firms whose activities include the creation of financial assets and liabilities are called *financial intermediaries*. Without these intermediaries and the processes of financial intermediation, the allocation of savings into real investment would be limited by whatever the distribution of savings happened to be. With financial intermediation, savings are transferred to economic units that have opportunities for profitable investment. In the process, real resources are allocated more effectively, and real output for the economy as a whole is increased.

The major types of financial intermediaries are briefly described in Table 4.1. Commercial banks are defined by their ability to accept demand deposits subject to transfer by depositors' checks. Such checks represent a widely accepted medium of exchange, accounting for more than 90 percent of the transactions that take place. Savings and loan (S&L) associations traditionally received funds from passbook savings and invested them primarily in real estate mortgages that represented long-term borrowing, mostly by individuals.[1] Finance companies are business firms whose main activity is to make loans to other

---

1 New laws by the early 1980s broadened the lending powers of S&L operations so that they increasingly became department stores of finance. Lack of experience with their new areas of operations, excesses and outright fraud, and the perverse incentives provided by deposit insurance (small investments by owners taking on huge debts, resulting in big profits if successful and losses covered by the government if not) resulted in the multibillion-dollar bailouts of the 1990s.

TABLE 4.1

Market Share Changes for Financial Intermediaries (Excluding Government-Sponsored Enterprises and Miscellaneous)

	Percentage of Total Intermediary Assets					
Intermediary	1950	1960	1970	1980	1995	1999
Commercial banks	52	38	37	37	26	21
Life insurance companies	22	20	15	12	13	12
Private pension funds	2	6	9	12	17	19
Savings institutions	14	19	20	19	6	4
State and local pension funds	2	3	5	5	9	12
Mutual funds	1	3	4	2	13	18
Finance companies	3	5	5	5	4	4
Other insurance companies	4	5	4	4	5	3
Money market funds	nr	nr	nr	2	5	6
Credit unions	nr	1	1	2	2	2
Total*	100	100	100	100	100	100*

Source: Compiled from Fed, *Flow of Funds Accounts*
nr—not reported
*May not add to 100 due to rounding.

business firms and to individuals. Life insurance companies sell protection against the loss of income from premature death or disability, and the insurance policies they sell typically have a savings element in them. Pension funds collect contributions from employees and/or employers to make periodic payments upon employees' retirement. Investment funds, also called mutual funds, sell shares to investors and use the proceeds to purchase existing equity and debt securities.

Investment bankers are financial firms that buy new issues of securities from business firms at a guaranteed, agreed-upon price and seek immediately to resell the securities to other investors. Related financial firms that function simply as agents linking buyers and sellers are called investment brokers. Investment dealers are those who purchase for their own account from sellers and ultimately resell to their buyers. While investment bankers operate in the new-issues market, brokers and dealers engage in transactions of securities that have already been issued. These activities are combined in the larger firms. Other sources of funds are other business firms, households, and governments. At any time, some of these will be net borrowers and others net lenders.

The relative size of these institutions is suggested by the data in Table 4.1, which presents the trends in market shares since 1950. Some dramatic changes have taken place. The market share of total assets held by financial intermediaries accounted for by commercial banks dropped from 52 percent in 1950 to 21 percent in 1999. This represents a loss of more than 50 percent of their original market share. The share of life insurance companies dropped from 22 to 12 percent over the same period. This was a decline of about 50 percent. Savings institutions as a group declined by more than 71 percent.

The big winner was private pension funds whose market share grew from 2 to 19 percent. State and local pension funds achieved a six-fold gain in market share. Mutual funds made large gains, and money market funds emerged with a market share of 6 percent. These patterns portray major shifts in the role of financial intermediaries. They reflect the increased use of money market funds at brokerage houses and the substantial growth in both private and public pension funds.

Table 4.2 presents the total assets of major financial intermediaries in the United States in 1995 and 1999. It adds the category of govern-

TABLE 4.2

Asset Growth by Intermediary, 1995–1999

| Intermediary | Assets, Year End ($ Billions) | | | | Growth, Percent |
| | 1995 | | 1999 | | |
	Amount	Percent	Amount	Percent	
Commercial banks	$ 4,097	20	$ 5,526	16	35
Life insurance companies	2,064	10	3,105	9	50
Private pension funds	2,755	14	4,998	15	81
Savings institutions	1,013	5	1,151	3	14
State and local pension funds	1,465	7	3,047	9	108
Mutual funds	1,987	10	4,659	14	134
Finance companies	672	3	956	3	42
Other insurance companies	740	4	891	3	20
Money market funds	745	4	1,585	5	113
Credit unions	311	2	415	1	34
GSEs and related mortgage pools*	3,176	16	5,635	17	77
Miscellaneous†	1,008	5	2,034	6	102
Total††	$20,031	100	$34,001	101	70

*Government-sponsored enterprises + federally related mortgage pools + issuers of asset-backed securities.
†Mortgage companies + real estate investment trusts + security brokers and dealers + funding corporations.
††May not add to 100 due to rounding.
Source: Compiled from Fed, *Flow of Funds Accounts.*

ment-sponsored enterprises and related mortgage pools. The final line is "miscellaneous" consisting of real estate investment trusts (REITs), security brokers, and dealers and funding corporations. Total assets for this group of intermediaries grew from $20 trillion in 1995 to $34 trillion in 1999—a growth rate of 70 percent in 4 years. The total assets of these intermediaries in 1995 were 2.71 times the $7.4 trillion gross domestic product (GDP) for the year; in 1999 the ratio was 3.68 times the $9.248 trillion GDP. The GDP during the 4 years grew by 25 percent; so the growth of assets held by financial intermediaries grew at a rate 2.8 times the growth rate of GDP.

The fastest-growing financial intermediary during this period was mutual funds, with a growth rate of 134 percent, followed by money market funds whose growth was 113 percent. The growth in these two sectors was powered by the strong rise in stock prices during the period. Pension funds of all types experienced high growth, reflecting the rise in their asset values. Real estate and mortgage activities also grew at high rates, reflecting booming real estate markets. Most of the financial intermediaries listed in Table 4.2 are sources of financing to business firms either directly or indirectly. Hence the environment was favorable for funding business growth in general but particularly in the new economy sectors of the Internet, high technology, and biotechnology.

FINANCIAL MODERNIZATION ACT
(GRAMM-LEACH-BLILEY ACT OF 1999)

On November 12, 1999, the Gramm-Leach-Bliley (GLB) Act (also known as the Financial Modernization Act) became law. Its fundamental effect was the repeal of the Glass-Steagall Act of 1933 that established the separation between commercial banking and securities underwriting.

Financial institutions will now have a two-tier system for expanding activities. One entity will be the financial holding company. It can have commercial subsidiaries along with other subsidiaries that are engaged in activities considered "financial in nature," "incidental" to financial activities, or "complementary" to financial activities. Examples of activities include insurance underwriting, real estate development, merchant banking, and securities underwriting. These activities can be performed by affiliates of a bank within a financial holding company. The second entity involves subsidiaries of commercial banks (i.e., financial subsidiaries). These subsidiaries will be able to engage in some expanded activities, such as insurance agency and brokerage activities (but not insurance underwriting), and securities underwriting. The subsidiaries will not be allowed to expand into real estate development, merchant banking, or activities complementary to financial activities.

The act makes provisions intended to limit the risks of new activities. A financial holding company must have well-capitalized and well-managed bank subsidiaries with Community Reinvestment Act (CRA) ratings of satisfactory or higher. These requirements apply similarly for a bank to qualify for having financial subsidiaries. In addition, if a bank is one of the largest 50 insured banks, it must have unsecured long-term debt rated in one of the three highest credit categories.

Other provisions in the act limit credit extensions and require arm's-length activity between a bank and its subsidiaries and between a bank and other financial holding company subsidiaries. The GLB Act does not allow mixing of banking and commerce, and it closed the unitary thrift holding company loophole that allowed commercial firms to enter the banking industry by buying a thrift institution. However, nonbank companies may be involved in the financial services business by acquiring bank holding companies provided that their nonfinancial holdings account for 15 percent or less of the consolidated revenues.

The GLB Act implements *functional regulation*. Each of the institution's functions will be supervised by the appropriate regulator. For example, insurance agency activities will be subject to state insurance regulations, and securities affiliates will be under the Securities and Exchange Commission (SEC) and the National Association of Securities Dealers (NASD) regulations. The Federal Reserve will have oversight for the entire organization.

ROLE OF GOVERNMENT

Government activities have many influences on the financial markets. Government policies have major influences on the state of the economy, on the money supply, and on the amounts and types of financial instruments outstanding.

Federal Reserve System

Fundamental to an understanding of the behavior of the money and capital markets is an analysis of the role of the Federal Reserve System. The Fed, as it is called, has a set of instruments with which to influence the operations of commercial banks, whose loan and investment activities, in turn, have an important influence on the cost and availability of money. The most powerful of the Fed's instruments, and hence the one used most sparingly, is the right to change reserve requirements (the percentage of deposits that must be kept on reserve with the Fed). Most often, the Fed will exercise its option to alter the pattern of open-market operations (the Fed's buying and selling of securities), increasing and decreasing the amount of funds in the public's hands.

Changes may also be made in the interest rate that the Fed charges its borrowers, mainly the commercial banks. This interest charge is called its discount rate for the following reason. A commercial bank makes loans to its customers, resulting in the creation of debt instruments, such as promissory notes. The bank may, in turn, sell these promissory notes to the Fed. When a commercial bank sells debt instruments to the Fed, they are discounted from face value. To illustrate, suppose a bank sells a promissory note in the amount of $1166, which the borrower has promised to pay the bank at the end of 1 year. If the Fed's discount rate at that time is 6 percent, it will pay the discounted value of the promissory note to the bank. This is $1166 divided by 1.06, which is $1100.

Changes in the discount rate change the interest rates paid by banks and, consequently, the rates they charge their customers. In addition, changes in the Fed's discount rate may have *announcement effects*. These changes represent an implicit announcement by Federal Reserve authorities that a change in economic conditions has occurred and that the new conditions call for a tightening or easing of monetary conditions. History shows that increases in the Federal Reserve Bank discount rate have usually been followed by rising interest rate levels, and decreases by lowered levels. When the Federal Reserve System purchases or sells securities in the open market, makes changes in the discount rate, or varies reserve requirements, the supply and price of funds are influenced and the interest rates or returns on most securities change as a result.

Fiscal Policy

The fiscal policy of the federal government may also impact interest rate levels. A cash budget deficit represents a stimulating influence by the federal government, and a cash surplus exerts a restraining influence. However, this generalization must be modified to reflect the way a deficit is financed and the way a surplus is used. To have the most stimulating effect, a deficit should be financed by a sale of securities through the banking system, particularly the central bank, thus providing a maximum amount of bank reserves and permitting a multiple expansion in the money supply. To have the most restrictive effect, the surplus should be used to retire bonds held by the banking system, particularly the central bank, thereby reducing bank reserves and causing a multiple contraction in the supply of money.

The impact of Treasury financing programs varies. Ordinarily, when the Treasury needs to draw funds from the money market, it competes with other potential users of funds, possibly resulting in a rise in interest rate levels. However, the desire to hold down interest rates also influences Treasury and Federal Reserve policy. To ensure the success of a large new offering, Federal Reserve authorities may temporarily ease money conditions, which may soften interest rates. If the

Treasury encounters resistance in selling securities in the nonbanking sector, it may sell them in large volume to the commercial banking system, a move that expands its reserves and thereby increases the monetary base. This change, in turn, may lower the level of interest rates. The opposite effects may also occur. If the money supply expands faster than new goods and new investments, there may be too much money chasing too few goods, with inflation as the result. Lenders may then require an inflation component in the nominal interest rates charged, resulting in a rise in interest rates. This more sophisticated reaction to monetary policy has been called a *rational expectations* model in that it takes into account the longer-term effects of changes in government policy.

TYPES OF FINANCIAL INSTRUMENTS

The basic classification of financial instruments involves three major categories: currency, debt, and equity claims. Currency represents obligations issued by the U.S. Treasury as coins and paper currency. The operations of the commercial banking system result in creating demand deposits (the familiar checking accounts) by which about 90 percent of commercial transactions are conducted. The use of checks on demand deposits, therefore, represents the main form of "money." Debt or credit instruments represent promises to pay to the creditor specified amounts plus interest at a future date or dates. Stock generally means common stock representing the equity or ownership claims on an organization.

The above classification covers the three major types of financial instruments. However, variations on these basic types have produced many different kinds of financial instruments, proliferating into a complex variety of forms particularly in recent years with the development of financial engineering. The great variety of financial instruments now observed has resulted because there are several different types of building blocks, each of which can have different characteristics that can be combined in many different ways. We shall briefly describe some basic building blocks here, some of which will be developed in greater detail in subsequent chapters. The basic building blocks can be outlined as shown in Table 4.3.

We shall briefly explain the categories in Table 4.3 in order to provide a vocabulary and overview for materials covered throughout the book.

Debt Forms

Debt instruments can be freely traded in the credit markets or held by the lender. The distinction is not absolute because receivables held by

TABLE 4.3

Forms of Financial Contracts

Debt Forms	Pricing Contracts
Zero coupon	Forward contracts
Level coupon	Futures contracts
Floating-rate coupon	Swaps
Options	**Ownership Position**
Calls	Long
Puts	Short

lenders can also be sold. Zero coupon forms of debt have long been used in selling U.S. savings bonds—buy a U.S. savings bond for $15 and receive the face amount of $25 at X years in the future. Some debt has a fixed-level coupon like fixed-rate home mortgages. A floating-rate coupon is illustrated by adjustable-rate mortgages (ARMs). The familiar home mortgage also illustrates the concept of amortizing because the periodic (usually monthly) payment made by the borrower includes not only the interest owed but also some portion of principal borrowed.

Pricing Contracts

A forward contract requires the purchase or sale of a particular asset at a specified future date at a price set at the time the contract is made. For example, you promise to buy an automobile from someone in 2 months when you will have gotten together the necessary funds. This protects against a rise in price. Forward contracts may also be entered into to seek to gain from price changes. For example, a forward contract may be made to buy 1000 bushels of wheat for $3 per bushel at the end of 180 days. If the price of wheat were $4.25 at the end of 180 days, the contract owner would have gained $1.25; if the price were $1.75, the contract owner would have lost $1.25.

A futures contract is equivalent in concept to a forward contract. The purchase of a futures contract obligates the purchaser to buy a specified amount at a designated exercise price on the contract maturity date. A futures contract has the same kind of two-sided risk illustrated by the wheat example for the forward contract. By institutional practice, futures contracts seek to reduce default risk by the traders through two requirements. The gain or loss on a futures contract is calculated daily (it is "marked to market" at the end of each day), and cash is settled daily. In addition, participants in futures markets are required to post a bond as a form of guarantee. Empirical studies indicate no statistically significant differences in the price behavior of forward contracts as compared with futures contracts.

A swap contract obligates two parties to exchange specified cash flows at designated intervals. An example would be to exchange the cash flows from a 5-year fixed-rate bond for those of a 5-year floating-rate bond. Many circumstances might stimulate swaps. For example, a business firm may enter into a contract in a country that does not permit floating-rate contracts. Or a firm's assessment of the future results in the decision to prefer a floating-rate debt obligation rather that a fixed-rate obligation. The other end of the swap contract may represent a financial institution that is entering into many such transactions so that its position in fixed-rate versus floating-rate obligations might be closely balanced, so that risk is thereby reduced.

Options

An option gives the owner the right (but not a requirement or obligation) to buy (a call) or sell (a put) an asset by the end of a specified period. For example, a 90-day call on the common stock of Alcoa Corporation with an exercise price of $65 would enable the owner to buy Alcoa common stock at $65 anytime during that 90-day period. For example, if during the 90-day period the call were exercised at a price of $75, the owner of the call would have a $10 gain per share, less what the owner paid for the calls. If a put contract is bought, it gives the owner the right to sell the stock to the seller of the put at a specified price during a specified period. The buyer of the put expects a price decline, in which case the stock can be sold to the seller of the put at the higher price specified in the put contract.

Options as well as forward or futures contracts are called *derivative* securities. They are created by those who trade in them. They usually do not represent claims on business assets, as do debt and equity securities.

Ownership Position

Finally, we consider ownership positions. A long position means that you will gain if the price goes up; typically this means that you are in an ownership position. Owning a call represents a long position; the difference is that the call only gives the owner of the call contract the ability to take an ownership position. To be short means that you will gain if the price goes down. Thus selling short means that you sell stock you do not own. There are institutional arrangements that make this possible. If you sell a stock for $100 and then later the stock goes down to $60, you "cover your position" by buying the stock at $60 and have gained $40 per share. Or you might own 100 shares of stock (a long position) at a price of $100, and you wish to protect yourself from future price decline. You may buy a put, which obligates the seller of the put to pay you $100 per share for your 100 shares. If the price goes down to $60, you will then put the stock to the seller of the put at $100 a share, avoiding a loss of $40 per share less the price you paid for the 100 put contracts plus commissions. In concept, it is also possible to be long or short in call options or long or short in put options.

From this brief overview it is clear that the 10 forms of contracts covered in Table 4.3 could have different payment patterns, different settlement conventions, and different maturities as well as be put together in different combinations. Hence, the number of different contracts that can be formed is limited only by the imagination of the participants to the contracts. The innovations in types of contracts in recent years have resulted in literally hundreds of new forms of financial instruments or securities. It is likely that financial engineering will continue to produce new forms of financial instruments in future years as well.

FINANCIAL MARKET INSTITUTIONS

Within the framework of the broad functions of financial intermediation and the monetary and fiscal policies briefly summarized in the preceding sections is another important set of financial market institutions in the operation of the financial system. One basis for classifying securities markets is the distinction between primary markets, in which stocks and bonds are initially sold, and secondary markets, in which they are subsequently traded. Initial sales of securities are made by investment banking firms that purchase the securities from the issuing firm and sell them through an underwriting syndicate or group. Subsequent transactions take place in organized securities or less formal markets.

The Exchanges

The New York Stock Exchange (NYSE) was founded in 1817. In 1999 the shares traded were $204 billion. The dollar value of stocks listed on the NYSE more than doubled from $6.0 trillion in 1995 to $12.3 trillion in 1999. The NYSE also trades bonds. The par value of bond volume declined from $7.0 trillion in 1995 to $3.2 trillion in 1999. The value of a seat on the NYSE grew from a low of $250,000 in 1990 to a high of $2.65 million in 1999.

The American Stock Exchange (AMEX) serves the organizations that do not meet the listing and size requirements of the NYSE. For years, AMEX was known as the "New York curb exchange" because its trading was conducted on the street outside the offices of the brokers;

the exchange moved indoors in 1921. The dollar volume of shares traded on AMEX has been less than 3 percent of the dollar volume of shares traded on the NYSE.

Traditional commodity markets such as the Chicago Board of Trade (CBOT) and the Chicago Mercantile Exchange (CME) have expanded their operation to include the derivative securities such as futures contracts and options. The stock exchanges have also been adding trading in these derivative securities.

Over-the-Counter (OTC) Security Markets

Over-the-counter security markets is the term used for all the buying and selling activity in securities that does not take place on a stock exchange. In the United States, the OTC market handles transactions in (1) almost all bonds of U.S. corporations; (2) almost all bonds of federal, state, and local governments; (3) open-end investment company shares of mutual funds; (4) new issues of securities; and (5) most secondary distributions of large blocks of stock, regardless of whether they are listed on an exchange.

The exchanges operate as auction markets; the trading process is achieved through agents making transactions at one geographically centralized exchange location. On an exchange, firms known as *specialists* are responsible for matching buy and sell orders and for maintaining an orderly market in a particular security. In contrast, the OTC market is a dealer market; i.e., business is conducted across the country by broker/dealers known as *market makers*, who stand ready to buy and sell securities in a manner similar to wholesale suppliers of goods or merchandise. The exchanges are used to match buy and sell orders that come in more or less simultaneously. But if a stock is traded less frequently (perhaps because it is a new or a small firm), matching buy and sell orders might require an extended period of time. To avoid this problem, some broker/dealer firms maintain an inventory of stocks. They buy when individual investors want to sell and sell when investors want to buy. At one time, these securities were kept in a safe; when they were bought and sold, they were literally passed over the counter.

The National Association of Securities Dealers Automated Quotations (NASDAQ) was founded in 1971. It was the first to use high-technology systems to trade securities. In terms of the number of shares traded, NASDAQ accounts for a greater volume than the NYSE. The dollar volume of shares traded still trails that of the NYSE. In 1982, the National Market System (NMS) was introduced. The National Market System gives price quotations and volume figures for NASDAQ securities throughout the trading day. The third market refers to these transactions from dealer accounts in the OTC market. Unlisted stocks will be handled only in the OTC market, but listed stocks may also be involved in these transactions. They can also include trades of large blocks of listed stocks off the floor of the exchange, with a brokerage house usually acting as intermediary between two institutional investors.

The Fourth Market

The *fourth market* refers to direct transfers of blocks of stock among institutional investors without an intermediary broker. Such transactions have led to the development of Instinet, a computerized quotation system with display terminals to provide communications among major institutional investors. Other automated transaction systems are the Crossing Network and POSIT. Increasingly, computers are used to evaluate companies by investors and traders who then use the fourth market for their transactions.

International Dimensions

The international debt market consists of three major components: foreign bonds, Eurobonds, and Euro commercial paper. Foreign bonds are issued in a foreign country and denominated in that country's currency. Eurobonds are long-term instruments issued and traded outside the country of the currency in which they are denominated. Euro commercial paper is the short-term debt version of Eurobonds.

Globalization has resulted in the rapid growth of derivative international financial products such as Eurodollar futures and options as well as futures and options on foreign currencies and domestic securities that trade globally (e.g., U.S. Treasury securities). Futures and options exchanges have been established worldwide. The strongest competitors to the U.S. exchanges are the London International Financial Futures Exchange (LIFFE) and the Singapore International Monetary Exchange (SIMEX).

To List or Not to List

In order to list their stock, firms must meet exchange requirements relating to such factors as size of company, number of years in business, earning record, the number of shares outstanding, and market value. In the United States, requirements become more stringent as viewed on a spectrum ranging from the regional exchanges toward the NYSE.

The firm itself makes the decision whether to seek to list its securities on an exchange. Typically, the stock of a new and small company is traded over the counter; there is simply not enough activity to justify the use of an auction market for such stocks. As the company grows and establishes an earnings record, expands its number of shares outstanding, and increases its list of stockholders, it may decide to apply for listing on one of the regional exchanges. For example, a west coast company may list on the Pacific Stock Exchange. As the company grows still more, and its stock becomes distributed throughout the country, it may seek a listing on the American Stock Exchange, the smaller of the two national exchanges. Finally if it becomes one of the nation's leading firms, it may, if it qualifies, switch to the Big Board—the New York Stock Exchange.

Some multinationals issue equity in several stock markets. The benefits of international stock listing include greater share liquidity, firm publicity, and prestige. On the other hand, the costs of listing on additional exchanges may not be worth the greater liquidity. In addition, reporting requirements in other countries may increase the costs of overseas listing.

Some believe that listing is beneficial to both the company and its stockholders. Listed companies receive a certain amount of free advertising and publicity, and the status of being listed enhances their prestige and reputation. The exchanges maintain that listing is advantageous in terms of lowering the required rate of return on a firm's common stock. Investors, of course, respond favorably to increased information, liquidity, and prestige. By providing investors with these benefits by listing their company's stocks, financial managers may lower their firms' cost of capital. There may also be costs of obtaining wider ownership of a firm's stocks. These include the risk of attracting possibly unwanted takeover attempts and the cost of disclosing financial data due to Securities and Exchange Commission requirements. With increased computerization and electronic communication, the information gap between listed and unlisted stocks appears to be narrowing.

Benefits Provided by Securities Markets

Securities markets are said to provide at least four economic functions.

1. Security exchanges facilitate the investment process by providing a marketplace to conduct efficient and relatively inexpensive transactions. Investors are thus assured that they will have a place to sell their securities, if they decide to do so. Increased liquidity is provided by the securities markets investors who are willing to accept a lower rate of return on securities than they would otherwise require.

2. They are capable of handling continuous transactions, testing the values of securities. The purchases and sales of securities record judgments on the values and prospects of companies. Those whose prospects are judged favorably by the investment

community have higher values, which facilitates new financing and growth.

3. Security prices are relatively more stable because of the operation of the security markets. Securities markets improve liquidity by providing continuous markets that make for more frequent but smaller price changes. In the absence of active markets, price changes are less frequent but more violent.

4. The securities markets aid in the digestion of new security issues and facilitate their successful flotation.

ROLE OF THE FINANCIAL MANAGER

In Fig. 4.1, the financial manager is shown linking the financing of an organization to its financing sources via the financial markets.

In the aggregate, business firms are savings-deficit units that obtain funds to make investments to produce more goods and services. As part of the process by which funds are allocated to their most productive uses, financial managers have two important areas of responsibility:

FIGURE 4.1

Financial Markets, the Financial Manager, and the Firm

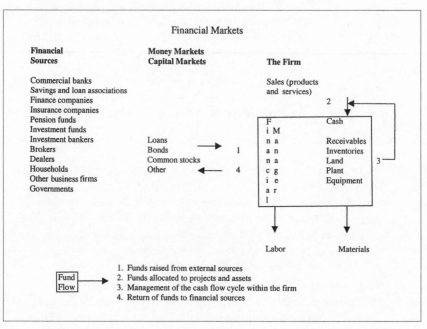

1. To obtain external funds through the financial markets.
    * What financing forms and sources are available?
    * How can the funds be acquired efficiently?
    * What will be the timing and form of returns and repayments to financing sources?
2. To see that the funds obtained are used effectively.
    * To what projects and products should funds be allocated?
    * What assets and resources must be acquired in order to produce the product or service?
    * How should the use of funds be monitored so that they are most effectively distributed among the various operating activities?

It is the financial manager's responsibility to implement these choices in the various financial markets to meet the firm's financing requirements.

MARKET EFFICIENCY

To allocate capital effectively, the financial markets should price securities solely by economic considerations based on publicly available information. In such a market, the prices for a company's securities reflect investors' estimates of the level and riskiness of future cash flows. Since higher stock prices reflect investors' positive assessments of the future, companies with higher expected cash flows will find it easier to raise additional capital. On the other hand, companies with lower expected cash flows will find less favorable terms when they try to raise additional capital. Securities that are priced efficiently guide the financial market in allocating funds to their most productive use.

Efficiency in the stock market implies that all relevant, available information regarding a given stock is instantaneously reflected in its price. Stated another way, an efficient market is one where a security's current price gives the best estimate of its true worth. In an efficient market there are neither free lunches nor expensive dinners.

Informational Efficiency of the Stock Market

One set of tests of market efficiency examines the informational efficiency of security prices. Existing models of efficient stock markets imply that all relevant information regarding a given stock is reflected in its current market price. This notion of market efficiency can be divided into three categories based on the type of information used in making market decisions:

1. *Weak-form* market efficiency hypothesizes that today's security prices fully reflect all information contained in historical security prices. This implies that no investor can earn excess returns by developing trading rules based on historical price or return information.

2. *Semistrong-form* market efficiency says that security prices fully reflect all publicly available information. Thus, no investor could earn excess returns using publicly available sources such as corporate annual reports, NYSE price information, or published investment advisory reports.

3. *Strong-form* market efficiency hypothesizes that security prices fully reflect all information whether it is publicly available or not.

Much empirical evidence supports the first two forms of market efficiency. A direct test of strong-form efficiency is whether insiders with access to information that is not publicly available earn abnormal returns. Studies have found that stock returns following the periods of insider trading have risen significantly. These returns are statistically significant, proving that insiders earn abnormal returns so that the strong-form hypothesis of market efficiency does not hold.

Market Efficiency and Investment Decisions

We have emphasized that the market is an important guide with which to evaluate corporate decisions. At the same time we emphasize that the stock market should not be the only guide used in making corporate decisions. Financial managers may be in a superior position to judge their own firms, or even other firms in the industry. They may recognize that the market does not fully value their firm's future opportunities or, conversely, has an overly optimistic assessment of their firm's prospects. In such conditions, managers should also study economic forces in their firm's markets. Information from market research, laboratory reports, and opinions about sales potential should also be considered when making investment decisions.

Implications for Managerial Decision Making

The existence of efficient markets has important implications for financial managers. Market efficiency means that a firm's share price is the best available estimate of its future cash flows. Despite the sometimes speculative nature of security markets, share prices give the best benchmark for corporate financial choices. Thus decisions should be oriented toward maximizing the market value of the firm. If security prices reflect all publicly available information, then managers can watch their company stock price to find out what the market thinks of recently announced decisions.

SUMMARY

The financial sector of the economy, an important part of the financial manager's environment, is comprised of financial markets, financial institutions, and financial instruments. Financial markets involve the creation and transfer of financial assets and liabilities. The financial manager uses these markets to obtain needed funds for the operation and growth of the business and to employ funds temporarily not needed by the business. Funds are provided by savings-surplus units to be used by savings-deficit units. This transfer of funds creates a financial asset for the surplus unit and a financial liability for the deficit unit. Transfers can be made directly between a surplus and a deficit unit or can involve a financial intermediary, such as a bank. Intermediaries take on financial liabilities in order to create financial assets, typically profiting from their expertise in packaging these assets and liabilities. The operations of intermediaries, and financial markets in general, bring about a more efficient allocation of real resources.

The money markets involve financial assets and liabilities with maturities of less than one year, and the capital markets involve transfers for longer periods. Since most businesses are savings-deficit units, the financial manager is concerned with the choice of financial markets, intermediaries, and instruments best suited to the financing needs of the firm and with the decision of how best to employ excess funds for short periods.

Two major forms of financing are used by business firms: equity financing through common stock and various forms of debt financing. Numerous alternative types of debt instruments exist; they differ in maturity, in terms, and in the degree of risk at which the borrower (the issuer of the debt) will become unable to meet the obligation. Other forms of financial contracts include forward and futures contracts, swaps, options, and combinations thereof.

The initial sale of stocks and bonds is known as the primary market. Subsequent trading takes place in the secondary market, the organized exchanges. The over-the-counter market, the third market, is a dealer market, where broker/dealers throughout the country act as market makers. Sometimes large blocks of stock are traded directly among institutional investors, constituting the fourth market.

Most of the research on capital markets supports the conclusion that they are weak-form and semistrong-form efficient, but are probably not strong-form efficient. A semistrong-form efficient market is one where prices instantaneously and fully reflect all publicly available information. In order for a message to contain relevant information, there must be a security price change when the news is released. This test allows us to separate meaningful information (e.g., quarterly earnings reports) from immaterial information such as corporate name changes. The evidence on block trading shows that block sales contain negative information but, even more important, that prices fully adjust to their new permanent level within 15 minutes after the block transaction becomes publicly available information. Finally, we saw that if information is costly, then there is every reason to believe that costly securities analysis pays off well enough to at least recover its expense.

QUESTIONS AND PROBLEMS

4.1   What are the financial intermediaries, and what economic functions do they perform?

4.2   How could each tool of the Federal Reserve be used to slow down expansion?

4.3   Evaluate each of the arrangements in favor of today's organized securities exchanges relative to OTC markets.

4.4   Why might an investor want to sell short?

4.5   You are told that the market for options is a fair game but that four out of five options expire worthless. How can these two statements be true?

SOLUTIONS TO QUESTIONS AND PROBLEMS

4.1   Financial intermediaries are business units which receive funds in one form and repackage them for the use of savings-deficit units. Through financial intermediation, savings are transferred to economic units which have the opportunity for more profitable investment of them. Real resources are allocated more effectively, and the real output of the economy is thereby increased.

4.2   Raising the reserve requirement would restrict the amount of money banks have available to lend. Raising the discount rate would signal that the Federal Reserve intended to slow down the rate of expansion in the money supply. Open-market sales of securities would reduce the supply of reserves in the commercial banking system.

4.3   Given improved communication, the assurance of a place in which to sell securities is relatively minor, compared to historically. If all the information on buy and sell orders is available via the OTC system, the constant testing of the price of a security will depend on the amount of the stock outstanding and the frequency with which it is traded. There is less dependence on the existence of an organized exchange. It is still true that the exchange has little to do with the flotation of new issues, provided the OTC retail market is active. As OTC communication networks continue to improve, the value of an organized exchange would be further reduced.

4.4   If he thought that the stock were going to go down in price he could make a profit by borrowing the stock (from his broker), selling it, and buying it back later at the lower price to cover the borrowing.

4.5   A game is considered "fair" if the actual probability of winning is equal to the chance of winning based on the underlying probabilities. When your option expires worthless four times out of five, you lose small amounts of money (the option cost), but when the option finishes in the money, you win large amounts. A small probability of large gains offsets a large probability of small losses, so that option investments actually have a positive expected return.

CHAPTER 5

Business Organization and Taxes

Tax laws are constantly revised to achieve both revenue-raising and public policy goals. The Tax Reform Act of 1986 was the most far-reaching in recent years with its much-publicized goals of simplification and fairness. Yet some basic patterns of relations important for financial decisions remain basically unchanged. These basic relations are the emphasis of this brief summary of the key aspects of the tax laws and regulations. It is not intended to substitute for the need to use tax accountants and tax lawyers on real-life matters of complexity.

CORPORATE INCOME TAX

The rate structure of the corporate income tax in 2000 is shown in Table 5.1. For the first $50,000 of corporate taxable income, the tax rate is 15 percent. The next $25,000 of corporate taxable income is taxed at 25 percent, as shown in column 4 of Table 5.1. Thus, the marginal tax rate for a corporate taxable income of $75,000 shown in column 2 is the 25 percent shown in column 4. However, since the tax rate applicable to the first $50,000 of income is 15 percent, and 25 percent is the rate for the next $25,000, the average tax rate for a total corporate taxable income of $75,000 is 18.33 percent. Similarly, for the rest of the table for the taxable income amounts shown in column 2, the applicable marginal rates are shown in column 4. The corresponding average tax rates are shown in column 7. Note that the jump in the marginal tax rate for the $235,000 increment over $100,000 shown in line 4 is 39 percent, which makes the average rate 34 percent. As shown in line 5 for the next increment to $10 million, the marginal and average rates are equal at 34 percent. The marginal rate for the incremental $5 million shown in column 6 is 35 percent. In line 7 for the next increment of $3,333,333, the marginal rate shown in column 4 is 38 percent, which makes the average tax rate 35 percent. Thus, for corporate taxable incomes of $18,333,333 and above, both the marginal and average tax rates remain constant at 35 percent.

From the above we see that differentially lower rates of taxes are applied to the first $75,000 of corporate taxable income. However, the marginal rates for corporate taxable income above $75,000 become 34 percent. For the corporations with very high levels of income, the marginal tax rate of 35 percent is not greatly different from the $25,000 increment over $75,000.

Prior to the Tax Reform Act of 1986 (TRA 86), the maximum corporate rate was 46 percent. Because of the sharp increase in tax rates on corporate taxable income over $100,000, many moderate-sized companies were organized in the form of two or more separate corporations to keep the taxable income of each at a level where lower corporate tax rates were applicable.

Before the Tax Reform Act of 1969 substantially eliminated the advantages of multiple corporations, some retail chains and small loan companies consisted of literally thousands of separate corporations.

Tax Credits

Tax credits are deductions from the tax bill itself, rather than deductions from taxable income, and thus are potentially very valuable. The investment tax credit program was typical. It was first included in the federal income tax laws in 1962 as an incentive for investment. Under the program, business firms could deduct from their income tax liability a specified percentage of the dollar amount of new investment in each of certain categories of capital assets. Tax credits, like tax rates and depreciation methods, are subject to congressional changes reflecting public policy considerations. During the economic boom in

TABLE 5.1

Income Tax Rates—Corporations, 2000
Taxable Income

Line	Over— (1)	But Not Over— (2)	Tax Is: (3)	+	Marginal Tax Rates, Percent (4)	Of the Amount Over— (5)	Taxes Paid on Column 2 Income (6)	Average Tax Rates, Percent (7)
1	$ —	$ 50,000			15	$ —	$ 7,500	15.00
2	50,000	75,000	$ 7,500	+	25	50,000	13,750	18.33
3	75,000	100,000	13,750	+	34	75,000	22,250	22.25
4	100,000	335,000	22,250	+	39	100,000	113,900	34.00
5	335,000	10,000,000	113,900	+	34	335,000	3,400,000	34.00
6	10,000,000	15,000,000	3,400,000	+	35	10,000,000	5,150,000	34.33
7	15,000,000	18,333,333	5,150,000	+	38	15,000,000	6,416,667	35.00
8	18,333,333	—			35	—		35.00

the early part of 1966, for example, the investment tax credit was suspended in an effort to reduce investment; it was reinstated later that year, suspended again in 1969, reinstated in 1971, and modified by almost every tax bill since. The Tax Reform Act of 1986 largely eliminated the investment tax credit on capital assets. The tax credits that remain include those for investment in targeted jobs (employers may deduct a percentage of first-year wages paid to "disadvantaged" individuals), incremental research and development, alternative sources of business energy (including solar, geothermal, and ocean thermal), and low-income housing.

Corporate Capital Gains and Losses

Corporate taxable income consists of two kinds: profits from the sale of capital assets (capital gains and losses) and all other income (*ordinary income*). *Capital assets* (e.g., buildings or security investments) are defined as assets not bought or sold in the ordinary course of a firm's business. Gains and losses on the sale of capital assets are defined as capital gains and losses. Tax laws distinguish between *long-term, medium-term, and short-term* capital gains, based on the length of time the asset is held (12 months or less, 12 to 18 months, or more than 18 months, respectively, under various tax laws).

For corporations, most of the tax difference between capital gains and ordinary income have been eliminated. Corporate capital gains are taxed at the same rates as ordinary income. Capital losses of corporations are deductible only from capital gains. The net long-term gain or loss and net short-term gain or loss are balanced off to obtain the net capital gain or loss for the year. However, a corporation cannot take a deduction in the current year for a net capital loss. But a 3-year carryback and a 5-year carryforward not including the loss year are available. Capital loss carryovers are used in the order they are incurred. All carrybacks and carryovers are treated as short-term capital losses. The capital loss carrybacks are deductible only up to the point of not creating a net operating loss or increase. In addition, capital loss carryovers may be denied if a substantial change of ownership takes place.

Deductibility of Interest and Dividends

Interest payments made by a corporation are a deductible expense to the firm, but dividends paid on its common stock are not. This differential treatment of dividends and interest payments has an important effect on the methods by which firms raise capital.

Suppose a corporation has earned $1100 million before interest, taxes, and dividends. It has paid $100 million in interest expense and $200 million in dividends. Since the interest expense is deductible and the dividend expense is not, the corporation's taxable income is $1000 million. If a 35 percent corporate tax rate were paid, the taxes paid would be $350 million. The $200 million dividends would be paid from the after-tax income of $650 million. If the recipient of the dividends is subject to personal income taxes, double taxation results from the tax paid by the corporation and the personal taxes paid on the dividends received.

Dividend Income

If the dividends were received by another corporation, triple taxation would be involved. For this reason, dividends received by one corporation from another are partially exempted from taxation according to the schedule in Table 5.2. Thus, 70–80 percent of dividend income received by one corporation from another is exempted from further corporate taxation. Eighty percent ownership of another corporation permits consolidated reporting so that the dividend income is eliminated.

Net Operating Losses Carryover

For most businesses, net operating losses (NOLs) can now be carried forward for 20 years. The allowable carryback period for net operating losses is 2 years, thereby giving firms a 22-year period in which to absorb losses against future profits or to recoup taxes paid on past profits. The purpose of permitting this loss averaging is to avoid penalizing firms whose incomes fluctuate widely.

The Tax Reform Acts of 1976 and 1986 limit the use of a company's net operating losses in periods following a change in ownership. The carryover is disallowed if the following conditions exist: (1) 50 percent or more of the corporation's stock changes hands during a 2-year period as a result of purchase or redemption of stock, and (2) the corporation changes its trade or business. (There are other important

TABLE 5.2

Deductions for Corporate Dividend Income

Percentage of Ownership by Corporate Shareholder	Deduction Percentage
Less than 20	70
20 or more (but less than 80)	80
80 or more (consolidated return)	100

restrictions on the acquisition of a loss company, but they are too complex to be covered in this brief summary.)

Net operating loss carryovers also figure prominently in the calculation of the alternative minimum tax, which was strengthened by the Tax Reform Act of 1986 to ensure that all profitable corporations pay some taxes.

Unreasonable Accumulations

A penalty tax may be imposed on improperly accumulated income. The Internal Revenue Code states that earnings accumulated by a corporation are subject to penalty rates *if the purpose of the accumulation is to enable the stockholders to avoid the personal tax.* Earnings retention can be justified if the firm is paying off debt, financing growth, or increasing marketable securities to provide the corporation with a cushion against possible cash drains caused by losses. How much a firm should properly accumulate for uncertain contingencies is a matter of judgment.

DEPRECIATION

Depreciation refers to allocating the cost of an asset over its life. Suppose a business firm buys a piece of equipment that costs $200,000 and is expected to last 5 years. The equipment will increase gross profits (earnings before interest, taxes, depreciation and amortization, or EBITDA) to $500,000 per year. Without depreciation, the entire cost of the equipment would be a business expense against the first year's income alone; this is equivalent to depreciating the asset over 1 year. The pattern of accounting net income would be as indicated below (we assume interest costs are zero to focus on depreciation):

CASE 1

Immediate Write-off

	Year 1	Years 2–5
EBITDA	$ 500,000	$ 500,000
Depreciation	200,000	—
EBIT	300,000	500,000
Taxes (34%)	102,000	170,000
Net income	$ 198,000	$ 330,000

The cardinal assumption of depreciation is that because the equipment contributes revenues over the entire 5-year period, its cost should be allocated over the same period. If we accept this assumption, then the immediate write-off illustrated understates net income for year 1 and overstates net income for years 2 through 5.

Now assume that the firm uses straight-line depreciation, so that one-fifth of the cost of the equipment is allocated against each year's revenues. Accounting net income is now the same for each of the 5 years as illustrated:

CASE 2
___

Straight-Line Depreciation—Accounting Net Income

	Years 1–5
EBITDA	$ 500,000
Depreciation	40,000
EBIT	460,000
Taxes (34%)	156,400
Net income	$ 303,600

Depreciation and Cash Flows

We have illustrated the effect of depreciation on accounting earnings. However, depreciation is a special kind of tax-deductible expense in that it is *not* a cash outlay. Whether we consider depreciation or not, the only cash outflow in our example occurs in year 1 when the equipment is initially purchased. For case 1, therefore, cash flows and accounting net income are the same, but for case 2, the noncash nature of depreciation expense causes cash flows to be different from accounting income. Now we calculate the cash flows for case 2.

CASE 2
___

Straight-Line Depreciation—Cash Flows

	Year 1	Years 2–5
EBITDA	$ 500,000	$ 500,000
Depreciation	40,000	40,000
EBIT	460,000	460,000
Taxes (34%)	156,400	156,400
Net income	303,600	303,600
Add back depreciation	+ 40,000	+ 40,000
Less cost of equipment	– 200,000	—
Cash flow	$ 143,600	$ 343,600

Because depreciation is not a cash charge, it is added back to net income to determine cash flows. Cash flows must also be adjusted in year 1 to reflect the cash outlay that took place when the equipment was purchased. The effect of depreciation is to reduce the cash outflow on income taxes. Recall that in case 1, the cash outflow for taxes in years 2 to 5 (the years for which we have no depreciation expense) is $170,000, while in case 2, cash outflows for taxes are the same every year, at $156,400.

Without for the moment considering the time value of money, the sum of net income (equal to cash flows) for case 1 is $1,518,000. This is the same as the sum of accounting net income for case 2; and it is the same as the sum of cash flows for case 2. Also, in each case, the total dollar amount of cash outlay for income taxes is identical to $782,000. So what is the point of depreciation? The only effect is on the *timing of cash flows.*

Using a 10 percent discount rate, we calculate the present value of cash flows for case 1 and case 2:

		Case 1		Case 2	
Year	PV Factor	Cash Flow	Present Value	Cash Flow	Present Value
1	0.9091	$ 198,000	$ 180,002	$ 143,600	$ 130,547
2	0.8264	330,000	272,712	343,600	283,951
3	0.7513	330,000	247,929	343,600	258,147
4	0.6830	330,000	225,390	343,600	234,679
5	0.6209	330,000	204,897	343,600	213,341
		$1,518,000	$1,130,930	$1,518,000	$1,120,655

The present value of cash flows is $10,265 greater for case 1 (immediate write-off) than for case 2. (If we calculated the present value of cash outlays for taxes, that would explain the difference.)

Thus, if businesses valued cash flow over accounting income, firms would prefer to write off assets as they were purchased, rather than depreciate them over their useful lives. This is not permitted, however, by either accounting conventions or tax laws. Given that assets must be depreciated, firms will generally want to depreciate them as quickly as possible.

Accelerated Depreciation

There are two ways for a firm to write off assets more quickly. One is to shorten the period over which the asset is depreciated. The other is to use an accelerated depreciation method (such as sum-of-years'-digits or double-declining-balance method). U.S. tax laws permit firms to do both, most recently via a procedure known as the modified accelerated cost recovery system (or MACRS, pronounced "makers"). The initial accelerated cost recovery system (ACRS or "acres") was incorporated into the Tax Reform Act of 1986; the modified system applies to assets placed in service after 1986.

Under MACRS, there is no need to estimate the expected useful economic life of an asset. Instead, assets are categorized into several classes, each with its own *class life* and *recovery period* over which the asset is to be depreciated. These statutory lives are generally shorter than the economic lives of the assets; furthermore, MACRS allows an accelerated depreciation method, specifically, 200 percent (or double-declining balance) depreciation for most classes of assets. (Fifteen-year and twenty-year assets are depreciated using the 150 percent declining-balance method, and real property must be depreciated over 27.5 or 39 years using the straight-line method.) The effect of MACRS is to accelerate depreciation, increasing the depreciation tax shelter and thus increasing cash flows.

Sale of Depreciable Assets

If a depreciable asset is sold, then the sale price (actual salvage value) minus the then-existing book value, which reflects the depreciation taken up to the sale, is added to operating income and taxed at the firm's marginal rate.

Benefit for Small Companies

Under Section 179 of the Tax Code, companies are allowed to expense up to $18,000 worth of equipment per year. This allowance is scheduled to increase slightly each year after 1998. For small businesses, this is equivalent to depreciating some equipment over a single year.

Tax Purposes versus Reporting Purposes

Firms are required to depreciate assets. For the purposes of income tax reporting, they must use either the MACRS method or the straight-line method; for reasons we have illustrated, virtually all firms will choose the method which provides the faster write-off. Accelerated depreciation reduces the cash outlay for taxes early in the asset's life, giving the firm the use of that cash for other purposes.

The use of accelerated depreciation increases cash flows (over straight-line depreciation), while reducing accounting net income. Firms are allowed by law to keep two sets of books—one for taxes and one for reporting to investors. If stockholders of business firms value cash flows over net income, they will support the use of accelerated depreciation methods. Considerable evidence shows that stockholders *do* value cash flows, and that they are not misled by accounting techniques that affect only reported net income rather than underlying cash flows. Nevertheless, most firms use accelerated depreciation for tax purposes, but straight-line depreciation (with its higher reported net income) for stockholder reporting purposes. The use of straight-line depreciation minimizes the negative effect on accounting net income and is said to "normalize" or stabilize reported income, especially when asset purchases are "lumpy."

PERSONAL INCOME TAX

Of some 16 million business firms filing tax returns in the United States, about 13 million are organized as sole proprietorships or partnerships. The income of these firms is taxed as personal income to the owners or the partners. The net income of a proprietorship or partnership provides a basis for determining the individual's income tax liability. Thus, as a business tax, the individual income tax can be as important as the corporate income tax.

The personal income tax is conceptually straightforward, although many taxpayers find it confusing. Virtually all the income a person or family receives goes into determining the tax liability.

Total income from all sources is called gross income. All taxpayers are permitted to make deductions from their gross income before computing any tax. These deductions are of two types: deductions and personal exemptions.

Deductions

Taxpayers may choose to itemize deductions, such as state and local taxes, mortgage interest, and charitable contributions, or they may claim the standard deduction, whichever is higher. Under the Tax Reform Act of 1986, the standard deduction was changed from a constant amount to a deduction indexed to inflation.

Personal Exemptions

A personal exemption is allowed for the taxpayer and for each of the taxpayer's dependents. The apparent intent of the personal exemption is to exempt the first part of income from taxation, enabling individuals to obtain the basic necessities of life, such as food, clothing, and shelter. Consistent with this intent, the personal exemption is phased out for very high-income taxpayers. As with the standard deduction, the personal exemption (and the threshold income level at which the phase-out mechanism to eliminate it kicks in) are now indexed to inflation.

Itemized Deductions

Itemized deductions include such items as state and local income and property taxes (but not sales tax); mortgage interest on first and qualifying second homes (all other personal interest expense deductions have been phased out under TRA 86); job-related moving expenses; casualty losses; and charitable contributions. Some itemized deductions are deductible only to the extent that they exceed some percentage of adjusted gross income (AGI); these include employee business expenses, investment expenses, tax counsel and preparation fees, continuing education, job-hunting expenses, subscriptions to professional journals, and travel, meals, and entertainment expenses (limited to 80 percent of the amount incurred). Medical expenses are deductible to the extent that they exceed some percentage of AGI.

Tax Rates for the Personal Income Tax

To illustrate the nature of the personal tax structure, the schedules for married persons filing jointly for 2000 are shown in Table 5.3. The tax rates in Table 5.3 start at 15 percent. The rates rise to 36 percent for taxable income of $161,450. Above $288,350, the rate rises to a maximum of 39.6 percent. For federal income taxes at high levels of income, the personal tax rates are 39.6 percent, somewhat higher than the corporate income tax rates at 35 percent. When state income taxes are taken into account, personal income tax rates may rise as high as 50 percent and corporate income tax rates to about 40 percent. It is mainly at income levels of up to about $1 million that it may be useful to evaluate the tax advantages of operating as a corporation versus an individual proprietorship or partnership. When a business has income of several million dollars or more, it is likely that the superior fund-raising

TABLE 5.3

Married Filing Jointly or Qualifying Widow(er)—Schedule Y-1, 2000

| Taxable Income | | | | % of | Of the Amount |
Over	But Not Over	Pay	+	Excess	Over
$ —	$ 43,850	$ —		15	$ —
43,850	105,950	6,577.50		28	43,850
105,950	161,450	23,965.50		31	105,950
161,450	288,350	41,170.50		36	161,450
288,350	—	86,854.50		39.6	288,350

capabilities of a corporation and the limited liability of its shareholders make the corporate form preferred.

Capital Gains and Losses

The Taxpayer Relief Act of 1997 changed both the holding periods for defining categories of gains and losses and the applicable tax rates. These are summarized in Table 5.4.

Tax Deferrals

Many tax deferral plans are available. They include 401(k) plans, traditional IRAs, and the new Roth IRA created by the Taxpayer Relief Act of 1997. Our summary treatment will not cover the details of these plans. They are discussed in *The Wall Street Journal, Lifetime Guide to Money,* 1997, and various summaries provided by brokerage houses.

CHOICES AMONG ALTERNATIVE FORMS OF BUSINESS ORGANIZATION

Taxes are an important influence in choosing among alternative forms of business organization. In the following sections, the nature of the various alternatives and their advantages and disadvantages are described. Then the tax aspects are considered.

From a technical and legal standpoint, there are three major forms of business organization: the sole proprietorship, the partnership, and the corporation.* In terms of numbers, 72 percent of business firms are operated as sole proprietorships, 8 percent are partnerships, and 20 percent are corporations. By dollar value of sales, however, about 89 percent of business is conducted by corporations, about 5 percent by sole proprietorships, and about 6 percent by partnerships. The remain-

TABLE 5.4

Tax Rates on Individual Capital Gains

Classification	Holding Period	Top Rates, Percent
Short-term	Up to 12 months	Ordinary income, to 39.6
Middle-term	12–18 months	28
Long-term	More than 18 months	20

---

*Other less common forms of organization include business trusts, joint stock companies, and cooperatives.

der of this section describes and compares the characteristics of these alternative forms of business organization.

Sole Proprietorship

A sole proprietorship is a business owned by one individual. Going into business as a sole proprietor is very simple; a person merely begins business operations. However, cities or counties may require even the smallest establishments to be licensed or registered. State licenses may also be required.

The proprietorship has key advantages for small operations. It is easily and inexpensively formed, requires no formal charter for operations, and is subject to few government regulations. Further, it pays no corporate income taxes, although all earnings of the firm are subject to personal income taxes, regardless of whether the owner withdraws the funds for personal use.

The sole proprietorship also has important limitations. Most significant is its inability to obtain large sums of capital. Further, the proprietor has unlimited personal liability for business debts; creditors can look to both business assets and personal assets to satisfy their claims. Finally, the proprietorship is limited to the life of the individual who creates it. For all these reasons, the sole proprietorship is limited primarily to small business operations. However, businesses frequently are started as proprietorships and then converted to corporations when their growth causes the disadvantages of the proprietorship form to outweigh its advantages.

Partnership

A partnership is the association of two or more persons to conduct a business enterprise. Partnerships can operate under different degrees of formality, ranging from an informal oral understanding to a written partnership agreement to a formal agreement filed with the state government. Like the sole proprietorship, the partnership has the advantages of ease and economy of formation as well as freedom from special government regulations. Partnership profits are taxed as personal income in proportion to the partners' claims, whether or not the profits are distributed to them.

One of the advantages of the partnership over the sole proprietorship is that it makes possible a pooling of various types of resources. Some partners contribute particular skills or contacts, while others contribute funds. However, there are practical limits to the number of co-owners who can join in an enterprise without destructive conflict, so most partnership agreements provide that the individual partners cannot sell their share of the business unless all the partners agree to accept the new partner (or partners).

If a new partner comes into the business, the old partnership ceases to exist and a new one is created. The withdrawal or death of any of the partners also dissolves the partnership. To prevent disputes under such circumstances, the articles of the partnership agreement should include terms and conditions under which assets are to be distributed upon dissolution. Of course, dissolution of the partnership does not necessarily mean the end of the business; the remaining partners may simply buy out the one who left the firm. To avoid financial pressures caused by the death of one of the partners, it is common practice for each partner to carry life insurance naming the remaining partners as beneficiaries. The proceeds of such policies can be used to buy out the investment of the deceased partner.

A number of drawbacks stemming from the characteristics of the partnership limit its use. They include impermanence, difficulty of transferring ownership, and unlimited liability (except for limited partners). Partners risk their personal assets as well as their investments in the business. Further, under partnership law, the partners are jointly and separately liable for business debts. This means that if any partner is unable to meet the claims resulting from the liquidation of the partnership, the remaining partners must take over the unsatisfied claims, drawing on their personal assets if necessary.

Limited Partnership (LP)

A limited partnership consists of at least one general partner and multiple limited partners. Each limited partner's risk of loss is limited to her or his investment in the entity. Only the general partners are liable to creditors. Limited partnerships are common in real estate and oil exploration investments.

Limited-Liability Partnership (LLP)

Owners of an LLP are also general partners. But an LLP partner cannot be held liable for a malpractice committed by other partners. Partners in a registered LLP are still treated as general partners for commercial debt—they are jointly and severally liable. The LLP is often used by large accounting firms and by large law firms. LLPs are taxed as partnerships under the federal tax code. An LLP must have formal documents of organization and register with the state. Because the LLP is a general partnership in most respects it is not required to pay state franchise taxes on its operations.

Corporation

A corporation is a legal entity created by a government unit—mostly states in the United States. It is a separate entity, distinct from its owners and managers. This separateness gives the corporation four major advantages: (1) It has an unlimited life—changes of owners and managers do not affect its continuity. (2) It permits limited liability—stockholders are not personally liable for the debts of the firm. (3) The residual risk of the owners is divided into many units so that the risk exposure in any one firm can be small and diversification by investors across many firms is facilitated. (4) It permits easy transferability of ownership interest in the firm—the divided ownership interests can be transferred far more easily than partnership interests.

While a proprietorship or a partnership can commence operations without much paperwork, the chartering of a corporation involves more legal formalities. First, a certificate of incorporation is drawn up; in most states, it includes the following information: (1) name of proposed corporation, (2) purposes, (3) amount of capital stock, (4) number of directors, (5) names and addresses of directors, and (6) duration (if limited). The certificate is notarized and sent to the secretary of the state in which the business seeks incorporation. If approved, the corporation officially comes into being.

The actual operations of the firm are governed by two documents: the charter and the bylaws. The corporate charter technically consists of a certificate of incorporation and, by reference, the general corporation laws of the state. Thus, the corporation is bound by the general corporation laws of the state as well as by the unique provisions of its certificate of incorporation. The bylaws are a set of rules drawn up by the founders of the corporation to aid in governing the internal management of the company. Included are such points as (1) how directors are to be elected (all elected each year or, say, one-third each year, and whether cumulative voting will be used), (2) whether the preemptive first right of purchase is granted to existing stockholders in the event new securities are sold, and (3) provisions for management committees, such as an executive committee or a finance committee, and their duties. Also included is the procedure for changing the bylaws themselves, if necessary.

S Corporations

Subchapter S of the Internal Revenue Code provides that some small, incorporated businesses may still elect to be taxed as proprietorships or partnerships if some technical requirements are met, e.g., a maximum of 75 shareholders. Thus, the firm may enjoy the protection of the limited liability provided by incorporation but still retain some tax advantages.

These benefits are particularly useful to a small new firm that may incur losses while it seeks to become established in its beginning years. Its operating losses may be used on a pro rata basis by its stockholders as deductions against their ordinary income. In the past, this stimulated persons in high marginal personal income tax brackets to invest in small, new, risky enterprises. Similarly, new firms making large capital investments were likely to generate more investment tax credits than they could use, even with carryforwards; these credits could also be passed through the high-income stockholders. While the Tax Reform Act of 1986 has eliminated the investment tax credit, S corporations are expected to remain popular, not on account of their losses, but for their profits. Even with the surtaxes on higher levels of income, the maximum personal income tax rate is not 39.6 percent; the maximum corporate rate is 35 percent. If other aspects of incorporation are attractive, especially the limited-liability feature, then perhaps organizing as an S corporation is the preferred alternative.

Limited-Liability Corporation (LLC)

The limited-liability corporation (LLC) has increased in use since 1988 when the IRS ruled that a qualifying LLC would be treated as a partnership for tax purposes. An advantage of an LLC is that none of the owners are personally liable for its debts. This is an advantage over a limited partnership in which general partners have personal liability for partnership recourse debts. Also, limited partners cannot participate in its management, but all owners of an LLC have the legal right to do so.

With respect to an S corporation, the LLC also has advantages. An LLC can have an unlimited number of partners. An LLC may make special allocations, but S corporations are unable to do so. While S corporation shareholders are limited, any taxpayers including corporations, other partnerships, trusts, and nonresident aliens can be owners of an LLC.

TAX ASPECTS OF THE FORMS OF ORGANIZATION

To a small, growing firm, there may be advantages in the corporate form of organization. There is "double taxation" of dividends, but salaries paid to principals in the corporation are a tax-deductible expense and so are not subject to double taxation. However, by splitting organizational earnings between the corporation and the individual, both may be put into a lower tax bracket. Also of importance is the fact that all the earnings of partnerships and proprietorships are taxable at the personal income tax rate, whether the earnings are reinvested in the business or withdrawn from it.

SUMMARY

This chapter provides some basic background on the tax environment within which business firms operate. For corporations, the tax rate is 15 percent on income up to $50,000, 25 percent on the next increment of $25,000, and 34 percent on all income over $75,000. A 5-percent surtax on taxable income between $100,000 and $335,000 effectively applies a 34 percent rate to all increments of income for high-income corporations. Any operating loss incurred by the corporation can be carried back 3 years and forward 15 years against income in those years.

Of the dividends received by a corporation owning stock in another firm, 70 to 80 percent may be excluded from the receiving firm's taxable income depending on how much stock is owned. Dividends paid are not a tax-deductible expense. Regardless of its profitability, a corporation does not have to pay dividends if it needs funds for expansion or other legitimate business purposes. If, however, earnings are retained merely to enable stockholders to avoid paying personal income taxes on dividends received, the firm is subject to an improper accumulations tax. Interest received is taxable as ordinary income; interest paid is a tax-deductible expense.

Depreciation is a special kind of tax-deductible business expense in that it does not represent a cash outflow on taxes. However, firms may use alternative methods to maximize reported net income for purposes of reporting to shareholders.

Unincorporated business income is taxed at the personal tax rates of the owners. The 2000 rates begin at 15 percent up to $43,850 and reach a maximum of 39.6 percent for taxable income over $288,350.

Sole proprietorships and partnerships are easily formed. All earnings (losses) are taxed as regular income of the owner or partner. Owners and partners are also personally liable for the debts of the business. The corporation has the advantage of limiting the liability of the participants, but it is generally more expensive to organize. Once organized, a corporation provides an easy means to transfer ownership to others. Corporate earnings paid as dividends are subject to double taxation. The other tax differences between corporations and proprietorships or partnerships depend on the facts of individual cases.

QUESTIONS AND PROBLEMS

5.1 Which is the more relevant tax rate—the marginal or the average—in determining the form of organization for a new firm? Discuss aspects of the tax laws that make the form of organization less important.

5.2 For tax purposes, how does the treatment of interest expense compare with the treatment of common stock dividends from each of the following standpoints: a firm paying the interest or dividend, an individual recipient, and a corporate recipient?

5.3 Why is personal income tax information important to the study of business finance?

5.4   What are the advantages and disadvantages of the use of a sole proprietorship versus a partnership for conducting the operations of a small business firm?

5.5   Under what circumstances does it become advantageous for the small business to incorporate?

5.6   A corporation had net taxable income of $60,000 in 1991.

    A.   How much income tax must the corporation pay?

    B.   What is the marginal tax rate?

    C.   What is the average tax rate?

5.7   Martin Corporation had net operating income of $40,000. It also had $20,000 of interest expense and $35,000 of interest income during 2000.

    A.   How much income tax must the corporation pay?

    B.   What is the marginal tax rate?

    C.   What is the average tax rate?

5.8   The Green Corporation had net income from operations of $130,000 in 2000, including $30,000 in dividend income on small holdings of stocks of various major publicly held corporations.

    A.   How much tax must the corporation pay?

    B.   What is the average tax rate?

    C.   What is the marginal tax rate?

SOLUTIONS TO QUESTIONS AND PROBLEMS

5.1   In general, the average tax rate is relevant in deciding on a form of organization. On new or incremental projects, the marginal tax rate is relevant.

    The main feature of the tax law which makes the form of organization less important is the subchapter S corporation provision. This provision makes it possible for a firm to be organized as a corporation with its limited liability feature, and yet allows the gains or losses of the firm to be treated more flexibly. For example, the stockholders of the subchapter corporation may elect to treat the firm's losses as if the firm were a partnership; the losses pass through to the individual partners' personal incomes reducing their personal tax liability.

5.2   A.   Interest expense is treated as a business expense. For tax purposes, interest expense is deducted before arriving at taxable income. Dividends paid are not tax-deductible.

B.   Interest and dividend income are taxed as ordinary income for the individual taxpayer.

C.   Interest received by a corporation is taxed as ordinary income. Dividends are treated in one of the two ways. First, 70 to 80 percent of the dividends received by a corporation may be excluded, the remaining being taxed as ordinary income. However, if the receiving corporation owns 80 percent or more of the payer corporation and files a consolidated return, the dividends are completely tax-exempt.

5.3   Because the great majority of firms are organized as individual proprietorships or as partnerships. For these firms, the personal income tax is equivalent to a business tax. Also, the dividend policies of corporations should take into account the personal tax status of their shareholders; this obviously requires a knowledge of the personal tax structure.

5.4   Advantages of sole proprietorship: Easily and inexpensively formed. No formal charter required. Subject to few government regulations. Pays no corporate income taxes.

Limitations of sole proprietorship: Inability to raise large sums of capital. Unlimited liability for business debts. Life of the proprietorship is limited to the life of the individual who runs it.

Proprietorship in relationship to partnership: Partnership can pool funds and abilities of a number of persons. It may make provisions for continuity if one or more partners leaves firm or dies. Disadvantage of partnership versus sole proprietorship is conflicts that may arise among partners.

5.5   There may be tax advantages. It becomes advantageous for the small business to incorporate if limited liability or continuity is very important. However, lenders may require personal guarantees from the main owners of small business.

5.6   A.   Income tax on $60,000

$50,000	@15%	=	$ 7,500
10,000	@25%	=	2,500
$60,000			$10,000

B.   The marginal tax rate is the rate charged on the next dollar of net income. For this firm, the marginal tax rate is 25 percent.

C.   The average tax rate is total taxes as a percentage of net taxable income. For this firm, the average tax rate is

$$\frac{\$10,000}{\$60,000} = 0.1667 = 16.67\%$$

5.7   A.   Since interest income and interest expense are taxed in the same way as operating income and operating expense, net taxable income can be determined directly:

Net operating income	$40,000
Plus: Interest revenue	35,000
Less: Interest expense	20,000
Net taxable income	$55,000

Tax:

$50,000	@ 15%	=	$7,500
5,000	@ 25%	=	1,250
$55,000			$8,750

B.   The marginal tax rate is the rate on the next dollar of taxable income. In this case, the marginal rate is 25 percent.

C.   The average tax rate is total taxes as a percentage of net taxable income. In this case,

$$\frac{\$8,750}{\$55,000} = 0.1591 = 15.91\%$$

5.8   A.   Green Corporation income tax:

Net income	$130,000
Less 70% of dividends	
($30,000 × 0.70)	21,000
Net taxable income	$109,000

Tax:

$50,000	@ 15%	=	$7,500
25,000	@ 25%	=	6,250
34,000	@ 34%	=	11,560
+ 5% surtax on 9,000		=	450
			$25,760

B.   Average tax rate on net taxable income is

$$\frac{\$25,760}{\$130,000} = 0.1982 = 19.82\%$$

C.   The marginal tax rate is the tax rate on the next dollar of taxable income. The marginal tax rate is 39 percent.

CHAPTER 6

Interest Rates in the International Economy

HOW THE MARKET DETERMINES
INTEREST RATES AND RATES OF RETURN

Interest rates and rate-of-return data provide information from which financial managers can determine the opportunity costs of investments. The return on investment must exceed the market rate on projects of equivalent risk. In this section, our objective is to explain the underlying factors that determine interest rates (e.g., the rate on U.S. government bonds) and rates of return (e.g., the rate of return on common stocks).

Different assets and securities may have different rates of return. For example, Ibbotson and Sinquefield [Annual Yearbooks] compile data on various types of securities over the time period since 1926. Their data plus government data sources suggest the patterns shown in Table 6.1.

Why have rates of return varied over a long period? As we shall see, the pretax nominal rate of return on any asset can be explained by four components: the expected real rate of return, expected inflation over the life of the asset, liquidity of the asset, and riskiness of the asset. For example, most of the difference between the rate of return on common stocks, 10 to 13 percent, and that on long-term government

TABLE 6.1

Historical Rate-of-Return Patterns, Percent

Common stocks	10–13
Stocks of smaller companies	14–16
Long-term corporate bonds	6.5–8.00
Long-term U.S. government bonds	5–7.5
Short-term U.S. Treasury bills	3.5–5.0
Inflation	2–3

Source: Ibbotson Associates. Stocks Bonds Bills and Inflation (SBBI), Annual Yearbooks; plus government data sources.

bonds, 5 to 7.5 percent, can be explained by the extra risk of common stock. Equation (6.1) shows that interest rates are a function of four components:

Nominal rate of return = $f[E(\text{real rate}), E(\text{inflation}),$
$E(\text{liquidity premium}), E(\text{risk premium})].$ (6.1)

Note that each term on the right-hand side is preceded by an expectations operator E. For example, $E(\text{inflation})$ is the market's estimate of expected future inflation. Investors try to estimate what inflation will be, and consequently the market rates of return on securities with different lives will reflect the market's expectation of inflation over the life of the asset.

The real rate of interest, in a world without inflation or uncertainty, is the rate that equates the demand for funds with supply. Funds are demanded in order to invest them in profitable projects. The demand schedule is downward-sloping because we assume that as more money is invested, investors begin to run out of profitable projects and as a result, the expected rate of return on marginal investment declines. The supply schedule is upward-sloping because higher and higher rates of return are needed to induce suppliers to lend greater amounts of money. Projects that earn more than the real rate will be undertaken, and the funds will be acquired to finance them.

IMPORTANCE OF INTERNATIONAL FINANCE

International finance in recent years has taken on great significance. Widely fluctuating exchange rates have affected not only profits and losses from changes in foreign currency values but also the ability to sell abroad and to meet import competition. For example, suppose that a Japanese auto producer needs to receive 1.2 million yen per car to cover costs plus a required return on equity. At an exchange rate of 200 yen to the dollar, a rate which existed in the late 1970s, the Japanese producer would have to receive $6000 for an automobile sold in the United States. When the exchange rate is 265 yen to the dollar, as existed in early 1985, dividing 1.2 million yen by 265 tells us that the dollar amount required now is $4528. Thus, the Japanese producer is in a position to either reduce its dollar price by approximately 25 percent and still receive the same number of yen or take higher profit margins on sales in the United States. In 2000, the yen fluctuated in the region somewhat over 110 to the dollar. The U.S. wholesale price to yield 1.2 million yen to the Japanese auto company would be $10,909. Thus the competitive position of the Japanese producer in selling in the U.S. market is reduced by the stronger yen. Of course, the success of Japanese auto companies in the United States has not been completely due to changes in foreign exchange rates alone. Auto producers in Japan have achieved improved production processes that have resulted in greater productivity and high-quality cars. But exchange rate movements have also been a factor, as the above example illustrates.

From the standpoint of U.S. companies selling products abroad, the rising value of the dollar in relation to foreign currencies has the opposite consequence. It is more difficult for U.S. firms to sell abroad, and it is much more attractive for foreign firms to sell in the United States. For example, suppose that a U.S. producer is selling a product in the United Kingdom, and to meet competition, the product has to be sold for 500 pounds. When the pound had a value of $2.25, as it did in the late 1970s, the dollar amount received by the U.S. seller would be $1125. By March 1985, the value of the pound had fallen to $1.07. If the U.S. producer continued to sell the product for 500 pounds, it would now receive $535. If the original $1125 represented a dollar price necessary to earn its cost of capital, the U.S. firm would find it difficult to survive with a price that had declined more than 50 percent. Or alternatively, to continue to realize a dollar price of $1125 at the exchange rate of $1.07 to the pound would require a new selling price of 1051 pounds, a price increase of more than 100 percent expressed in pounds. On June 1, 2000, the British pound traded at $1.5173. At this level, the price of 500 pounds would represent $758.65. A price of $1125 would require 741 pounds, representing a price increase of 48 percent in pounds over the original 500 pounds.

These are not just hypothetical examples. They reflect the actual patterns of foreign exchange movements during recent years. There have been upward and downward fluctuations in the value of the dollar in relation to the currencies of developed countries such as Japan and West Germany. For less developed countries, the movements have represented a one-way street as shown in Table 6.2. From 1954 through 1975, the value of the Mexican peso was stable at 12.5 pesos to the U.S. dollar. Subsequent devaluations caused a continued erosion, so that 2846 pesos was required for $1 by June 1990—the peso had declined from U.S. $0.08 in value to a small fraction of one cent.

Thus, changes in foreign currency values in relation to the dollar have been both substantial and uncertain. Most business firms, as well as individuals, have experienced some of the effects of these changes in currency values that have taken place and are likely to continue—with magnitudes and directions of movements subject to considerable uncertainty. These changes have particularly severe effects on a manufacturing firm. Its inputs may include imported materials, and its products may be exported or become part of an exported product. Some large companies earn more than one-half of their profits abroad. Even for smaller companies, it is not uncommon to find that, if international sales can be developed to about one-fourth of total sales, earnings from

TABLE 6.2

Number of Foreign Currency Units per U.S. Dollar

	1965	1975	1980	6/21/90	12/26/97	6/30/00
Japan X	360.90	305.15	215.45	153.9	130.39	106.02
E	0.00277	0.00328	0.00464	0.006498	0.007669	0.009432
Index	100	118	168	235	277	341
Germany X	4.00	2.62	1.76	1.6778	1.7734	2.0485
E	0.2500	0.3817	0.5682	0.5960	0.5639	0.4882
Index	100	153	227	238	226	195
Mexico X	12.50	12.50	22.83	2,846.00	8.125*	9.825*
E	0.08	0.08	0.0438	0.0003514	0.1235	0.1018
Index	100	100	55	0.44		

X = number of FCs (foreign currency units) per dollar.
E = dollar value of one FC (foreign currency unit).
Index is of dollar value, with 1965 = 100.
*After a new currency was created.
Source: International Monetary Fund, *International Financial Statistics*, monthly issues; and "Foreign Exchange,"
The Wall Street Journal, June 21, 1984, p. 52; March 28,1985, p. 49; June 22, 1990, p. C10; July 5, 2000, p. C18.

foreign sales or operations are likely to be as high as 40 to 50 percent of total earnings. International operations often enable the smaller firm to achieve better utilization of its investment in fixed plant and equipment.

IMPACT OF EXCHANGE RATE FLUCTUATIONS

A difference between international business finance and domestic business finance is that international transactions and investments are conducted in more than one currency. For example, when a U.S. firm sells goods to a French firm, the U.S. firm usually wants to be paid in dollars and the French firm usually expects to pay in francs. Because of the existence of a foreign exchange market in which individual dealers and many banks trade, the buyer can pay in one currency and the seller can receive payment in another.

Since different currencies are involved, a rate of exchange must be established between them. The conversion relationship of the currencies is expressed in terms of their price relationship. If foreign exchange rates did not fluctuate, it would make no difference whether firms dealt in dollars or any other currency. However, since exchange rates do fluctuate, firms are subject to exchange rate fluctuation risks if they have a net asset or net liability position in a foreign currency. When net claims exceed liabilities in a foreign currency, the firm is said to be in a *long* position, because it will benefit if the value of the foreign currency rises. When net liabilities exceed claims in regard to foreign currencies, the firm is said be in a *short* position, because it will gain if the foreign currency declines in value.

Expressing Foreign Exchange Rates

The foreign exchange rate represents the conversion relationship between currencies and depends on demand and supply relationships between the two currencies. The foreign exchange rate is the price of one currency in terms of another. Exchange rates may be expressed in dollars per foreign currency unit or units of foreign currency per dollar. An exchange rate of $0.050 to FC1 shows the value of one foreign currency unit in terms of the dollar. We shall use E_0 to indicate the spot rate, E_f to indicate the forward rate* at present, and E_1 to indicate the actual future spot rate corresponding to E_f. An exchange rate of FC2 to $1 shows the value of the dollar in terms of the number of foreign currency units it will purchase. We use the symbol X with corresponding subscripts to refer to the exchange rate expressed as the number of foreign currency units per dollar.

Measuring the Percentage of Devaluation or Revaluation

Assume that there has been a devaluation of the French franc from 3 per U.S. dollar to 4 per U.S. dollar. This can be expressed as the percentage change in the number of French francs required to purchase 1 U.S. dollar $(= D_{fd})$.

For example, where $X_0 = 3$ and $X_1 = 4$,

$$\% \text{ change} = (X_1 - X_0)/X_0 = (4-3)/3 = \tfrac{1}{3} \text{ or } 33\tfrac{1}{3}\% = D_{fd}$$

There has been an increase of $33\tfrac{1}{3}$ percent in the number of French francs required to equal one U.S. dollar, which is a $33\tfrac{1}{3}$ percent appreciation in the franc value of the dollar.

Thus, the change of value in terms of FC per dollar is

$$D_{fd} = \frac{X_1 - X_0}{X_0} = \frac{1/E_1 - 1/E_0}{1/E_0} = \frac{E_0}{E_1} - 1 = \frac{E_0 - E_1}{E_1} \qquad (6.2a)$$

The change in value in terms of dollars per FC is

$$D_{df} = \frac{E_1 - E_0}{E_0} = \frac{1/X_1 - 1/X_0}{1/X_0} = \frac{X_0}{X_1} - 1 = \frac{X_0 - X_1}{X_1} \qquad (6.2b)$$

---

*Recall that a forward contract is a purchase or sale at a price specified now (the *forward rate*), with the transaction to take place at some future date.

Using Eq. (6.2b), the devaluation of the French franc using its U.S. dollar value is

$$\frac{X_0 - X_1}{X_1} = \frac{3 - 4}{4} = -\frac{1}{4} = -25\%$$

Because of the risks of exchange rate fluctuations, transactions have developed in a forward, or futures, foreign exchange market. This market enables a firm to hedge in an attempt to reduce risk. Individuals also may speculate by means of transactions in the forward market. Forward contracts are normally for a 30-, 60-, or 90-day period, although special contracts for longer periods can be arranged by negotiation.

The cost of this protection is the premium or discount of the forward contract over the current spot rate, which varies from 0 to 2 or 3 percent per year for currencies that are considered reasonably stable. For currencies undergoing devaluation in excess of 4 to 5 percent per year, the required discounts may be as high as 15 to 20 percent per year. When it is probable that future devaluations may exceed 20 percent per year, forward contracts are usually unavailable.

The magnitude of the premium or discount required depends on the forward expectations of the financial communities of the two countries involved and on the supply and demand conditions in the foreign exchange market. Since members of the financial communities are usually well informed about the expected forward exchange values of their respective currencies, the premiums or discounts quoted are very closely related to the probable occurrence of the changes in the exchange rates.

BASIC PARITY CONDITIONS

Three basic relationships are discussed:

1. The Fisher effect (FE)
2. The interest rate parity theorem (IRPT)
3. The purchasing power parity theorem (PPPT)

Fisher Effect

The Fisher effect states the relationship between interest rates and the anticipated rate of inflation. While it can also be regarded as purely a relationship for a domestic economy, it is utilized as well in developing some of the international relationships. The Fisher effect states that nominal interest rates rise to reflect the anticipated rate of inflation. The Fisher effect can be stated in a number of variations of Eq. (6.3).

$$\frac{P_0}{P_1} = \frac{1+r}{1+R_n}$$

$$1 + r = (1 + R_n)\frac{P_0}{P_1}$$

(6.3)

$$r = \left[(1 + R_n)\frac{P_0}{P_1}\right] - 1$$

(6.3a)

$$R_n = \left[(1 + r)\frac{P_1}{P_0}\right] - 1$$

(6.3b)

where P_0 = initial price level

P_1 = subsequent price level

P_1/P_0 = rate of inflation

P_0/P_1 = relative purchasing power of currency unit

r = real rate of interest

R_n = nominal rate of interest

While the Fisher effect can be stated in a number of forms, its basic idea can be conveyed by a simple numerical example. Over a given period, if the price index is expected to rise by 10 percent and the real rate of interest is 7 percent, then the current nominal rate of interest is

$$R_n = (1.07)(1.10) - 1 = 17.7\%$$

Similarly, if the nominal rate of interest is 12 percent and the price index is expected to rise by 10 percent over a given period, the current real rate of interest is

$$r = 1.12(100/110) - 1 = 1.018 - 1 = 0.018 = 1.8\%$$

Interest Rate Parity Theorem (IRPT)

The interest rate parity theorem is an extension of the Fisher effect to international markets. It holds that the ratio of the forward and spot exchange rates will equal the ratio of foreign and domestic gross interest rates. The formal statement of the interest rate parity theorem can be expressed as in Equation (6.4).

$$\frac{X_f}{X_0} = \frac{1 + R_{f0}}{1 + R_{d0}} = \frac{E_0}{E_f}$$

(6.4)

where X_f = current forward exchange rate expressed as FC units per $1

E_f = current forward exchange rate expressed as dollars per FC 1

X_0 = current spot exchange rate expressed as FC units per $1

E_0 = current spot exchange rate expressed as dollars per FC 1

R_{f0} = current nominal foreign interest rate

R_{d0} = current nominal domestic interest rate

Thus, if the foreign interest rate is 15 percent while the domestic interest rate is 10 percent and the spot exchange rate is $X_0 = 10$, the predicted current forward exchange rate will be

Annual Basis

$$X_f = \frac{1 + R_{f0}}{1 + R_{d0}}(X_0)$$

$$= \frac{1.15}{1.10}(10) = 10.45$$

Quarterly Basis

$$X_f = \frac{1 + R_{f0}/4}{1 + R_{d0}/4}(X_0)$$

$$= \frac{1.0375}{1.025}(10) = 10.12$$

Thus, the indicated foreign forward rate is 10.45 units of foreign currency per $1, and the foreign forward rate is at a discount of 4.5 percent on an annual basis. If the time period of a transaction is 90 days, we have to rework the problem, first changing the interest rates to a quarterly basis. The discount on the 90-day forward rate would now be 1.22 percent on the quarterly basis, since the 90-day forward rate would be 10.122.

The approximation for the IRPT is

$$R_{fo} - R_{do} \cong \frac{X_f - X_0}{X_0}$$

The data for the annual example are used to illustrate the approximation:

$$0.15 - 0.10 \cong \frac{10.45 - 10}{10}$$

$$0.05 \cong 0.45$$

The IRPT can also be used to illustrate another general proposition for international finance. In the absence of market imperfections, risk-adjusted expected real returns on financial assets will be the same in foreign markets as in domestic markets. Equilibrium among the current exchange rate, the forward exchange rate, the domestic interest rate, and the foreign interest is achieved through the IRPT.

Purchasing Power Parity Theorem (PPPT)

The purchasing power parity doctrine states that currencies will be valued for what they will buy. If a U.S. dollar buys the same basket of goods and services as 5 units of a foreign currency, we have an exchange rate of 5 foreign currency units to the dollar or 20 cents per foreign currency unit. An attempt to compare price indexes to computed purchasing power parity assumes that it is possible to compile comparable baskets of goods in different countries. As a practical matter, the parity rate is, in general, estimated from changes in the purchasing power of two currencies with reference to some past base period when the exchange rate was theoretically in equilibrium. In formal terms, the PPPT may be stated as in Eq. (6.5).

$$CX = \frac{X_1}{X_0} = \frac{P_{f1}/P_{f0}}{P_{d1}/P_{d0}} = RPC \tag{6.5}$$

where $\dfrac{X_1}{X_0} = \dfrac{E_0}{E_1}$

X_0 = FC units per dollar now
X_1 = FC units per dollar one period later

E_0 = $\dfrac{1}{X_0}$ =dollars per FC unit now

E_1 = $\dfrac{1}{X_1}$ =dollars per FC unit one period later

CX = $\dfrac{X_1}{X_0}$ =change in exchange rate

P_{f0} = initial price level in the foreign country.
P_{f1} = foreign country price level one period later.
P_{d0} = initial domestic price level.
P_{d1} = domestic price level one period later.

$RPC = \dfrac{P_{f1}/P_{f0}}{P_{d1}/P_{d0}}$ = relative price change

= ratio of inflation rates.

A few numerical examples will illustrate some of the implications of the purchasing power parity doctrine. Let us assume that for a given period, foreign price levels have risen by 32 percent while domestic price levels have risen by 20 percent. If the initial exchange rate is FC 10 to $1, the subsequent new exchange rate will be

$$\frac{1.32}{1.20} = \frac{X_1}{10}$$
$$1.2X_1 = 13.2$$
$$X_1 = 11$$

It will now take 10 percent more foreign currency units to equal $1, because the relative inflation rate has been higher in the foreign country. Alternatively, with an exchange rate of FC 10 to $1, let us assume that foreign prices have risen by 17 percent while domestic prices have risen by 30 percent. The new expected exchange rate will be

$$\frac{1.17}{1.30} = \frac{X_1}{10}$$
$$1.3X_1 = 11.7$$
$$X_1 = 9$$

In this instance, the number of foreign currency units needed to buy $1 will drop by 10 percent. Thus, the value of the foreign currency has increased by 10 percent due to the differential rates of inflation in domestic versus foreign prices.

Empirical studies indicate that while the purchasing power parity relationship does not hold perfectly, it tends to hold in the long run. More fundamentally, the doctrine predicts that an equilibrium rate between two currencies will reflect market forces and that random deviations from the central tendency will tend to be self-correcting. This suggests the existence of some strong equilibrating forces. Furthermore, the PPPT argues that the relations between exchange rates will not be haphazard but will reflect underlying economic conditions and changes in these conditions. The relationships are not precise because of a number of factors. These include (1) differences in incomes or other endowments between the two countries, (2) differences in government monetary and fiscal policies, (3) large capital movements motivated by changes in relative political risks or differences in prospective economic opportunities, (4) transportation costs, (5) lags in market responses, (6) differences between the two countries in the price ratios of internationally traded goods to domestically traded goods, (7) the impact of risk premium influences, and (8) differences in rates of productivity growth.

Risk Position of the Firm in Foreign Currency Units

The risk position of a firm in relation to possible fluctuations in foreign exchange rates can be clarified by referring to expected receipts or obligations in foreign currency units. If a firm is expecting receipts in foreign currency units (if it is long in the foreign currency units), its risk is that the value of the foreign currency units will fall (devaluing the foreign currency in relation to the dollar). If a firm has obligations in foreign currency units (if it is short in the foreign currency units), its risk is that the value of the foreign currency will rise and it will have to buy the currency to repay the obligations at a higher price.

SUMMARY

In this chapter we analyze how interest rates are determined, taking into account international influences. The globalization of international financial markets makes it impossible to understand interest rate determination without taking international exchange rate influences into account. We begin with the observed nominal pretax rates of return. Four influences are operating:

Nominal rate of return = $f[$ E(real rate), E(inflation), E(liquidity premium), E(risk premium)$]$

The risk premium includes the risk of exchange rate fluctuations. Assets can be grouped according to how they fit these characteristics. For example, one can collect all Aaa-rated corporate bonds with 10 years to maturity. Within this group, all four factors are held constant. Consequently, all securities within the group are close economic substitutes and will have the same nominal rate of return.

Some fundamental exchange rate relationships provide a basis for understanding interest rates in an international setting. Because a different set of relationships is involved, the following key symbols have been used: D = devaluation, E = dollars per foreign currency (FC) unit, X = FC units per dollar, P = price level, R = the nominal interest rate, and r = real rate of interest. And D_{fd} is the change in the number of FC units per dollar:

$$D_{fd} = \frac{X_1 - X_0}{X_0} = \frac{E_0 - E_1}{E_1} \tag{6.2a}$$

Alternatively, D_{df} is the change in the dollar value of a foreign currency unit.

$$D_{df} = \frac{E_1 - E_0}{E_0} = \frac{X_0 - X_1}{X_1} \tag{6.2b}$$

In addition to presenting the requirements for consistent foreign exchange rates, three fundamental exchange rate relationships were explained.

1. Fisher effect (FE)

$$R_n = \left[(1 + r)\frac{P_1}{P_0} \right] - 1 \tag{6.3b}$$

2. Interest rate parity theorem (IRPT)

$$\frac{X_f}{X_0} = \frac{1 + R_{f0}}{1 + R_{d0}} = \frac{E_0}{E_f} \tag{6.4}$$

3. Purchasing power parity theorem (PPPT)

$$CX = \frac{X_1}{X_0} = \frac{P_{f1}/P_{f0}}{P_{d1}/P_{d0}} = RPC \tag{6.5}$$

For an understanding of interest rate relationships, these three fundamental parity conditions need to be taken into account. PPPT relates relative inflation rates to exchange rate movements. The Fisher effect relates nominal interest rates and real interest rates through the influence of inflation. Differences in interest rates between different countries are linked to movements between current spot exchange rates and future exchange rates.

International business transactions are conducted in more than one currency. If a firm is expecting receipts in foreign currency units, its risk is that the value of the foreign currency units will fall. If it has obligations to be paid in foreign currency units, its risk is that the value of the foreign currency will rise. To reduce foreign exchange risk, firms can engage in transactions in the forward foreign exchange market. They can also borrow at current spot exchange rates the amount of foreign currency needed for future transactions. These two forms of hedging are essentially insurance and, therefore, involve costs. Firms also take protective actions against long or short positions in foreign currencies resulting from the balance sheet positions of their foreign subsidiaries. Protective actions include hedging and relating the investments in operations abroad to the firm's worldwide foreign exchange risk profiles over time.

QUESTIONS AND PROBLEMS

6.1   Given below are the yields to maturity on a 5-year bond:

Years to Maturity	Yield to Maturity
1	8.0
2	9.0
3	10.0
4	10.5
5	10.8

    A.   What is the implied forward rate of interest for the third year?

    B.   What (geometric) average annual rate of interest would you receive if you bought a bond at the beginning of the third year and sold it at the beginning of the fifth year?

6.2   You have priced two pure discount bonds, each with 5 years to maturity and with a face value of $1000. They pay no coupons. The first bond sells for $780.58, and the second sells for $667.43.

    A.   What are their yields to maturity?

    B.   Why does the second bond sell for less than the first?

C.   If their default risk is uncorrelated with the rest of the economy, then their expected cash flows can be discounted at the riskless rate, which is 5 percent. If they have the same expected yield, what is the probability of default for the second bond? (Assume that if the bond defaults, you receive nothing, but if it does not default, you receive the full face value.)

6.3   In March 1991, the U.S. dollar was worth 137 yen. In October 2000, the rate was 108 yen.

A.   What is X_0 (1991)? What is X_1 (2000)?

B.   What is E_0 (1991)? What is E_1 (2000)?

C.   What was the percentage devaluation or revaluation of the yen in terms of the U.S. dollar?

D.   What was the percentage devaluation or revaluation of the dollar in terms of the yen?

6.4   If the exchange rate between francs and dollars is Fr 7.546 = $1.00, and between pounds and dollars is £1 = $1.4623, what is the exchange rate between francs and pounds?

6.5   *The Wall Street Journal*, on October 12, 2000, listed the following information on the exchange rates between the dollar and the German mark:

X_0 = 2.2500 DM/$
E_0 = $0.4444/DM
X_F (90 days) = 2.2399 DM/$
E_F (90 days) = $0.4464/DM

The U.S. prime rate on that day was 9.5 percent. What is the implied German interest rate?

6.6   The treasurer of a company in Mexico borrowed $10,000 in dollars at a 12 percent rate when the exchange rate was 9 pesos to the dollar. His company paid the loan plus interest 1 year later, when the exchange rate was 9.5 pesos to the dollar.

A.   What rate of interest was paid, based on the pesos received and paid by the treasurer?

B.   Show how your result illustrates the interest rate parity theorem.

SOLUTIONS TO QUESTIONS AND PROBLEMS

6.1   A.   Implied forward rate, year 3:

$$1 +_2 f_3 = \frac{(1 +_0 R_3)^3}{(1 +_0 R_2)^2} = \frac{(1.10)^3}{(1.09)^2} = 1.120276$$

$$_2 f_3 = 0.1203 = 12.03\%$$

B.

$$(1 +_2 f_3)(1 +_3 f_4) = \frac{(1 +_0 R_4)^4}{(1 +_0 R_2)^2} = \frac{(1.105)^4}{(1.09)^2} = \frac{1.4909}{1.1881} = 1.25486$$

25.49 percent is the 2-year rate of interest. The average 1-year rate is

$$(1.25486)^{0.5} - 1 = 0.1202 \equiv 12.02\%$$

This is equal to the geometric mean of the two forward rates.

$$1 +_3 f_4 = \frac{(1 +_0 R_4)^4}{(1 +_0 R_3)^3} = \frac{(1.105)^4}{(1.10)^3} = \frac{1.4909}{1.3310} = 1.1201352$$

$$(1 +_2 f_3)(1 +_3 f_4) = (1.120276)(1.1201352) = (1.25486)^{1/2} = 1.1202$$

Note:

Maturity in Years	YTM	% Increase	Implied Forward Rates	
1	8.0	—	8.0000	for year 1
2	9.0	12.5	10.0093	for year 2
3	10.0	11.1	12.0276	for year 3
4	10.5	5.0	12.01352	for year 4
5	10.8	2.9	12.00817	for year 5

$$\frac{(1.09)^2}{(1.08)^1} = \frac{1.1881}{1.08} = 1.100093$$

$$\frac{(1.108)^5}{(1.105)^4} = \frac{1.669932}{1.490902} = 1.1200817$$

6.2   **A.**   **Bond A**   **Bond B**

$$\$780.58 = \frac{1000}{(1+r)^5} \qquad\qquad \$667.43 = \frac{1000}{(1+r)^5}$$

$$\$780.58(1+r)^5 = 1000 \qquad \$667.43(1+r)^5 = 1000$$

$$(1+r)^5 = 1.281099 \qquad\qquad (1+r)^5 = 1.498284$$

$$1+r = 1.05079 \qquad\qquad\quad 1+r = 1.08422$$

$$r = 5.079\% \qquad\qquad\qquad\quad r = 8.422\%$$

B.   The second bond sells for less than the first because it has a higher yield to maturity. This indicates that the second bond is considered to be a riskier investment than the first bond. Thus, to compensate investors for taking on additional risk, additional return must be realized.

C.   If we discount the expected cash flows of the second bond at the riskless rate R_F, then the correct formula is

$$PV = \frac{(1-p)(\text{face value})}{(1+R_F)^n} + \frac{p(\$0)}{(1+R_F)^n} = \frac{p(\$0)+(1-p)(\text{face value})}{(1+R_F)^n}$$

where p is defined as the probability of default. Substituting in the correct numbers, we have

$$\$667.43 = \frac{(1-p)1000}{(1.05)^5}$$

$$\frac{667.43(1.05)^5}{1000} - 1 = -p$$

$$1 - \frac{667.43(1.276282)}{1000} = p$$

$$1 - 0.851829 = p$$

$$p = 0.14817$$

Thus the probability of default of the second bond is approximately 15 percent.

6.3   **A.**   1991: $X_0 = 137$ yen per dollar $\left.\phantom{\begin{matrix}a\\b\end{matrix}}\right\}$ Dollar has devalued
              2000: $X_1 = 108$ yen per dollar $}$ in relation to yen

B.   1991: $E_0 = 1/137 = \$0.007299$
                    yen per dollar $\left.\phantom{\begin{matrix}a\\b\\c\\d\end{matrix}}\right\}$ Yen has revalued
              2000: $E_1 = 1/108 = \$0.009259$ in relation to dollar
                    yen per dollar

C.   Yen has been revalued in terms of the dollar:

$$\% \text{ change} = (E_1 - E_0)/E_0$$
$$= (0.009259 - 0.007299) / 0.007299$$
$$= 0.26853$$
$$= 26.85\% \text{ increase in value of yen in relation to dollar between 1991 and October 2000}$$

D.   Dollar has been devalued in terms of the yen:

$$\% \text{ change} = (X_1 - X_0)/X_0 = D_{yd}$$
$$= 108 - 137/137$$
$$= -0.211679$$
$$= -21.168\% \text{ or a decrease in value of dollar in relation to the yen of 21\% between 1991 and October 2000}$$

6.4 $1 = fr 7.546

£1 = \$1.4623

fr 1 = £ ?

By the principles of consistent cross rates, the product of the right-hand sides of the three relations must equal 1.

$$(7.546)(1.4623)(X) = 1$$
$$11.0345X = 1$$
$$X = £0.090625/ \text{ fr } 1$$

The Wall Street Journal carries a table of "Key Currency Cross Rates" in its Financial Section.

6.5   The German interest rate is lower than the U.S. rate. By the interest rate parity theorem (IRPT):

$$\frac{X_f}{X_0} = \frac{1 + R_{f0}/4}{1 + R_{d0}/4}$$

$$\frac{2.2399}{2.2500} = \frac{1 + R_{f0}/4}{1 + 0.095/4}$$

$$0.995511 = \frac{1 + R_{f0}/4}{1 + 0.2375}$$

$$1.019154 = 1 + \frac{R_{f0}}{4}$$

$$\frac{R_{f0}}{4} = 0.019154$$

$$R_{f0} = 0.076618 \approx 7.66\%$$

6.6   A.   Loan $10,000

Interest   1,500

Amount paid $11,200 × 9.5 =106,400 pesos

Loan amount $10,000 × 9.0 = 90,000 pesos

Interest   16,400 pesos

$$\text{Interest rate} = \frac{16,400}{90,000} = 18.22\%$$

B.   IRPT

$$\frac{1 + R_{f0}}{1 + R_{d0}} = \frac{X_f}{X_0}$$

$$\frac{9.5}{9.0}(1.12) = 1 + R_{f0}$$

$$1.0556(1.12) = 1 + R_{f0}$$

$$1.182272 = 1 + R_{f0}$$

$$R_{f0} = 18.22\%$$

If the interest rate in Mexico were below 18.22 percent, e.g., 15 percent, it would have been cheaper to borrow in pesos than to borrow in dollars at 12 percent, which was an effective rate of 18.22 percent in pesos.

PART TWO

FINANCIAL PLANNING AND CONTROL

CHAPTER 7

Financial Performance Metrics

Effective planning and control are central to enhancing enterprise value. Financial plans may take many forms, but any good plan must be related to the firm's existing strengths and weaknesses. The strengths must be understood if they are to be used to proper advantage, and the weaknesses must be recognized if corrective action is to be taken. For example, are inventories adequate to support the projected level of sales? Does the firm have too heavy an investment in accounts receivable, and does this condition reflect a lax collection policy? For efficient operations, does the firm have too much or too little invested in plant and equipment? The financial manager can plan future financial requirements in accordance with forecasting and budgeting procedures, but the plan must begin with the type of financial analysis developed in this chapter.

Financial performance metrics provide a relative basis for comparing a company with itself over time or a company versus competitors within its industry. Metrics provide a comparative basis for evaluating suppliers and customers and can be used for historical analysis as well as projected performance. Financial performance metrics also know no international boundaries and are useful in assessing company performance throughout the world. It has often been said that accounting and financial statements are the languages of business. Extending this further, financial analysis using financial performance metrics provides the "literature" of business.

Traditional financial ratio analysis focused on the numbers. The value of this approach is that quantitative relations can be used to diagnose strengths and weaknesses in a firm's performance. But the world is becoming more dynamic and subject to rapid changes. It is not enough to analyze operating performance. Financial analysis must also include consideration of strategic and economic developments for the firm's long-run success. Financial management as well as general senior management is demanding evaluative standards by which the firm's performance can be rapidly measured and an appropriate course charted. Operational managers also are seeking performance metrics that can aid them in running the business on a day-to-day or week-to-week basis. These metrics should immediately provide actionable feedback to improve the immediate operations of the firm. Management's intense interest in financial performance metrics has dramatically risen as more and more annual and long-term incentive compensation is tied to attaining acceptable levels of performance as measured by financial performance metrics.

The firm's external stakeholders, which traditionally included stockholders and creditors, are also broadening to include employees, consumers, customers, social and environmental considerations, suppliers, the government, and regulatory interests. Each of these constituencies has a particular interest in the firm's performance and judges the success or failure of that firm by using a variety of performance metrics.

Different sources and different analysts use different lists or combinations of financial ratios for analysis. There is no one list of metrics that can be universally applied to all situations. The lists of metrics provided in this chapter are intended to be suggestive only. For some situations, even more lists of more elaborate financial ratios might be useful, and for other decisions, only a few ratios would be sufficient. There is no one set of metrics that must be used all the time, only those ratios for the decision at hand.

A number, such as 3, is neither good nor bad. It needs to be placed in a context. It needs to be compared to a similarly measured value for another time period or against another organization. From decade to decade and within an industry, minimal acceptable levels of strength change, and in the case of some ratios, there are no established minimal acceptable levels.

There are potentially thousands of ratios and metrics to discuss. Many of these ratios have several permutations or slight variation differences. Take one number and divide it by another number, and you have created a ratio. Whether the resulting ratio makes any sense and you can use that number for business decision making is another question. The numbers are not an end in themselves. They are aids to stimulate questions, further investigation, and generate additional analysis with the ultimate goal of better economic analysis for improved managerial decisions.

Financial analysis is a combination of science and art. This chapter seeks to cover the science part; the art comes with practice and experience—from many hours of number crunching and use of numbers to make decisions on the firing line. Good finance managers are made, not born.

This chapter (1) develops an analytical foundation by reviewing traditional financial analysis and financial performance metrics, (2) illustrates competitive financial analysis and its managerial implications, and (3) introduces some of the "new" financial performance metrics. Rest assured that this chapter does not review thousands or even hundreds of ratios, but this chapter focuses on the major categories of ratios and the fundamental ratios within each category.

COMPARATIVE BASIS STANDARDS

Hershey Foods Corporation will again be the central company in this analysis. Hershey's financial statements are discussed in Chap. 2, Financial Statements and Cash Flows. Financial ratio performance standards come from a number of sources:

- Company historical performance
- Performance established as a target or objective within a plan
- Single or multiple competitors
- Industry averages and standards
- Best-demonstrated practices companies

Historical performance establishes a baseline of performance upon which an organization seeks to build and improve. If a specific metric receives particular focus, that objective may be elevated to a strategic objective. Another source of performance standards comes from competitive benchmarking with other companies in the firm's industry group. Finally, certain key companies have been identified as having the best-demonstrated practices. They usually have the optimal financial performance metrics and represent a superior way of conducting a certain aspect of business.

The analysis in this chapter first focuses on Hershey's performance versus itself in basic financial statement analysis. The financial performance metrics are introduced by comparing Hershey Foods Corporation to H.J. Heinz Company for the years 1996 through 1998. Finally, the whole food processing industry, as identified by Hershey Foods, is used to present and enhance the DuPont ratio analysis process.

Industry data can be used to obtain standards for evaluating the ratios that are calculated for an individual company. Listed below are many specialized producers of industry data, both private and government sources:

- Dun & Bradstreet: D&B provides ratios calculated for a large number of industries. The data give industry norms (common-size financial statements) and 14 ratios, with the median, lower, and upper quartiles, for more than 800 types of business activity based on their financial statements.

- Robert Morris Associates: Another group of useful financial ratios can be found in the annual *Statement Studies*, compiled and published by Robert Morris Associates, the national association of bank loan officers. Average common-size balance sheet and income statement data and 17 ratios are calculated for 341 industries. Five-year data are presented for four size categories and the total industry.

- Quarterly financial report for manufacturing corporations: The Bureau of the Census in the U.S. Department of Commerce publishes quarterly financial data on manufacturing companies. The data include an analysis by industry groups and by asset size, as well as financial statements in a common-size format.

- Trade associations and professional societies: Trade associations and professional societies will often compile data related to a specific industry or a particular function, e.g., treasury management functions.

- Financial services: Specialist firms that compile and publish financial data, such as Value Line, Standard & Poor's, and Moody's, develop industry composites. Brokerage firms such as Merrill Lynch, Paine Webber, and Morgan Stanley Dean Witter periodically publish industry studies.

- Financial press: Financial periodicals such as *Business Week, Forbes,* and *Fortune* publish quarterly or annual studies that center on financial performance metrics with companies grouped by industry.

However, one problem that may arise is that many diverse firms may be included in the industry category. The general industry data may be fine for a quick comparison, but most companies, investment analysts, and professionals construct their own industry groups. With the considerable diversification by firms, selected firms may be more comparable than industry groupings. This was the case at Hershey Foods. Hershey wanted to compare itself to major, branded food companies. Companies were selected that in general were larger than Hershey or companies that compete more directly in a broader snack food industry.

Table 7.1 captures the comparative industry group used by Hershey Foods. Some companies are not included in this industry group. M&M Mars is not included in this industry group since Mars is a private organization and not required to publicly disclose its financial information. Nestle is also not included since it is a Swiss company and is subject to different accounting practices and different reporting requirements. Kraft Foods (formerly Kraft-General Foods), the largest domestic food company, is not included because it is a division of Philip Morris and not subject to full disclosure as if it were a separate

TABLE 7.1

1998 Net Sales ($ million)

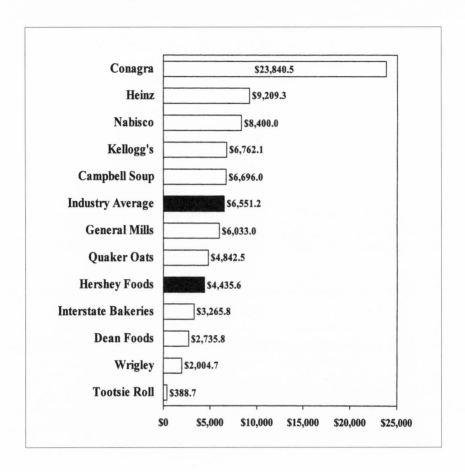

company. Although Tootsie Roll is less than one-tenth Hershey's size, Tootsie Roll is included in Hershey's industry because it is the only other publicly traded confectionery company in the United States.

Table 7.1 also demonstrates a graphical technique (bar chart) to illustrate the companies in this industry group. Table 7.2 presents the 1998 annual growth in net sales and our first comparative metric, annual growth. Hershey finished the year with slightly higher growth than the industry average. Dean Foods was the sole food processing company in this industry group to experience double-digit growth, which it achieved primarily through acquisitions. The industry group will be revisited within the DuPont analysis section.

TABLE 7.2

1998 Annual Growth in Net Sales

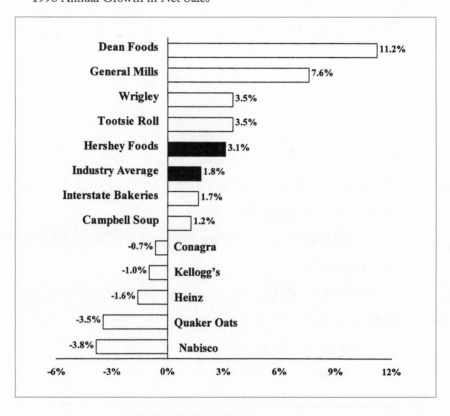

Basic Financial Statement Analysis

Basic financial statement analysis begins by examining income statements and balance sheets on a relative basis, including

- Representing line items on an income statement as a percent of sales and line items on a balance sheet as a percent of total assets (common-size statement)
- Analyzing the annual growth rate of each line item
- Indexing each line item as a percentage of the first year, 1996 (common base year)

This kind of analysis provides the most fundamental level of analysis. After we discuss the specific calculations, we review Hershey. Tables 7.3 and 7.4 analyze Hershey's income statement and balance sheet, respectively. Panels A on each table provide the actual information.

TABLE 7.3

Income Statement Analysis
Hershey Foods Corporation 1996, 1997, and 1998 ($000)

	A. Income Statement			B. Percent of Net Sales			C. Annual Growth (Percent)			D. Index Value		
	1996	1997	1998	1996	1997	1998	1997	1998	CAGR*	1996	1997	1998
Net sales	$3,989,308	$4,302,236	$4,435,615	100.0	100.0	100.0	7.8	3.1	5.4	100.0	107.8	111.2
Costs and expenses												
Cost of sales	2,302,089	2,488,896	2,625,057	57.7	57.9	59.2	8.1	5.5	6.8	100.0	108.1	114.0
Selling, marketing, & administrative	1,124,087	1,183,130	1,167,895	28.2	27.5	26.3	5.3	-1.3	1.9	100.0	105.3	103.9
Loss on disposal of business	35,352	—	—	0.9	—	—	-100.0	—	—	100.0	—	—
Total costs and expenses	3,461,528	3,672,026	3,792,952	86.8	85.4	85.5	6.1	3.3	4.7	100.0	106.1	109.6
Income before interest and income taxes	527,780	630,210	642,663	13.2	14.6	14.5	19.4	2.0	10.3	100.0	119.4	121.8
Interest expense, net	48,043	76,255	85,657	1.2	1.8	1.9	58.7	12.3	33.5	100.0	158.7	178.3
Income before income taxes	479,737	553,955	557,006	12.0	12.9	12.6	15.5	0.6	7.8	100.0	115.5	116.1
Provision for income taxes	206,551	217,704	216,118	5.2	5.1	4.9	5.4	-0.7	2.3	100.0	105.4	104.6
Net income	$ 273,186	$ 336,251	$ 340,888	6.8	7.8	7.7	23.1	1.4	11.7	100.0	123.1	124.8

*CAGR is compound annual growth rate from 1996 to 1998.

In Table 7.3, the percent of net sales (panel B) is calculated as each line item on the income statement divided by net sales:

1998 Cost of sales as a percent of net sales

$$= \frac{\text{cost of sales}}{\text{net sales}} = \frac{\$2,625,057}{\$4,435,615} = 59.2\%$$

Annual growth (panel C) is calculated as

1998 Annual growth in net sales

$$= \frac{1998 \text{ net sales}}{1997 \text{ net sales}} - 1 = \frac{\$4,435,615}{\$4,302,236} - 1 = 3.1\%$$

The compound annual growth rate (CAGR) from 1996 to 1998 (also in panel C) is calculated as

$$1998 \text{ Net sales CAGR} = \left(\frac{1998 \text{ net sales}}{1996 \text{ net sales}}\right)^{0.5} - 1$$

$$= \left(\frac{\$4,435,615}{\$3,989,308}\right)^{0.5} - 1 = 5.4\%$$

This is exactly the same as the compound annual growth rates determined in Chap. 3, The Time Value of Money.

Finally, the index value (panel D) is calculated as

$$1998 \text{ Index value of net sales} = \frac{1998 \text{ net sales}}{1996 \text{ net sales}} \times 100$$

$$= \left(\frac{\$4,435,615}{\$3,989,308} \times 100 = 111.2\right)$$

The index value shows the accumulated growth from the base year. This is also referred to as the common base-year analysis.

From Table 7.3, 1997 was a year of growth for Hershey well beyond the growth experienced in 1998 (panel C), in part related to the year-end 1996 acquisition of Leaf North America. However, in both years, cost of sales rose faster than net sales, and consequently cost of sales as a percentage of net sales rose from 57.7 percent in 1996 to 59.2 percent in 1998 (panel B). Offsetting this rise in cost of sales, selling, marketing, and administrative expenses fell to 26.3 percent of net sales by 1998. This is also seen as the index value of the selling, marketing, and administrative expense lagged the index value of net sales for 1998 (103.9 versus 111.2, respectively, in panel D). Income before interest and taxes surged in 1997 by 19.4 percent on net sales growth of 7.8 percent (panel C). Interest expense also surged in 1997 as Hershey took on long-term debt to pay for its year-end 1996 acquisition of Leaf North America and stock repurchases. Over this 3-year time frame, income tax rates fell steadily. Net income dramatically increased in 1997 by 23.1 percent (panel C) and grew to 7.8 percent of net sales (panel B). In 1998, net income grew only 1.4 percent (panel C).Table 7.4 provides the same type of analysis for the balance sheet as found in Table 7.3 for the income statement. In Table 7.4, panel B, the percent of total assets is

TABLE 7.4

Balance Sheet Analysis
Hershey Foods Corporation 1997 and 1998 ($000)

	A. Balance Sheet			B. Percent of Total Assets			C. Annual Growth			D. Index Value		
	1996	1997	1998	1996	1997	1998	1997	1998	CAGR*	1996	1997	1998
Cash and cash equivalents	$ 61,422	$ 54,237	$ 39,024	1.9	1.6	1.1	-11.7	-28.0	-20.3	100.0	88.3	63.5
Accounts receivable — trade	294,606	360,831	451,324	9.3	11.0	13.3	22.5	25.1	23.8	100.0	122.5	153.2
Inventories	474,978	505,525	493,249	14.9	15.4	14.5	6.4	-2.4	1.9	100.0	106.4	103.8
Deferred income taxes	94,464	84,024	58,505	3.0	2.6	1.7	-11.1	-30.4	-21.3	100.0	88.9	61.9
Prepaid expenses and other	60,759	30,197	91,864	1.9	0.9	2.7	-50.3	204.2	23.0	100.0	49.7	151.2
Total current assets	986,229	1,034,814	1,133,966	31.0	31.4	33.3	4.9	9.6	7.2	100.0	104.9	115.0
Property, plant, and equipment, net	1,601,895	1,648,237	1,648,058	50.3	50.1	48.4	2.9	0.0	1.4	100.0	102.9	102.9
Intangibles resulting from business acquisitions	565,962	551,849	530,464	17.8	16.8	15.6	-2.5	-3.9	-3.2	100.0	97.5	93.7
Other assets	30,710	56,336	91,610	1.0	1.7	2.7	83.4	62.6	72.7	100.0	183.4	298.3
Total assets	$3,184,796	$3,291,236	$3,404,098	100.0	100.0	100.0	3.3	3.4	3.4	100.0	103.3	106.9
Accounts payable	$ 134,213	$ 146,932	$ 156,937	4.2	4.5	4.6	9.5	6.8	8.1	100.0	109.5	116.9
Accrued liabilities	357,828	371,545	294,415	11.2	11.3	8.6	3.8	-20.8	-9.3	100.0	103.8	82.3
Accrued income taxes	10,254	19,692	17,475	0.3	0.6	0.5	92.0	-11.3	30.5	100.0	192.0	170.4
Short-term debt	299,469	232,451	345,908	9.4	7.1	10.2	-22.4	48.8	7.5	100.0	77.6	115.5
Current portion of long-term debt	15,510	25,095	89	0.5	0.8	0.0	61.8	-99.6	-92.4	100.0	161.8	0.6
Total current liabilities	817,274	795,715	814,824	25.7	24.2	23.9	-2.6	2.4	-0.2	100.0	97.4	99.7
Long-term debt	655,289	1,029,136	879,103	20.6	31.3	25.8	57.1	-14.6	15.8	100.0	157.1	134.2
Other long-term liabilities	327,209	346,500	346,769	10.3	10.5	10.2	5.9	0.1	2.9	100.0	105.9	106.0
Deferred income taxes	224,003	267,079	321,101	7.0	8.1	9.4	19.2	20.2	19.7	100.0	119.2	143.3
Total liabilities	2,023,775	2,438,430	2,361,797	63.5	74.1	69.4	20.5	-3.1	8.0	100.0	120.5	116.7
Total stockholders' equity	1,161,021	852,806	1,042,301	36.5	25.9	30.6	-26.5	22.2	-5.3	100.0	73.5	89.8
Total liabilities and stockholders' equity	$3,184,796	$3,291,236	$3,404,098	100.0	100.0	100.0	3.3	3.4	3.4	100.0	103.3	106.9

*CAGR is compound annual growth rate from 1996 to 1998.

calculated as each line item on the balance sheet divided by total assets

1998 Cash as a percent of total assets

$$= \frac{\text{cash}}{\text{total assets}} = \frac{\$39,024}{\$3,404,098} = 1.1\%$$

Annual growth (panel C) is calculated as

$$1998 \text{ Annual growth in cash} = \frac{1998 \text{ cash}}{1997 \text{ cash}} - 1 = \frac{\$39,024}{\$54,237} - 1 = -28.0\%$$

The compound annual growth rate from 1996 to 1998 (also in panel C) is calculated as

$$1998 \text{ Cash CAGR} = \left(\frac{1998 \text{ cash}}{1996 \text{ cash}}\right)^{0.5} - 1$$

$$= \left(\frac{\$39,024}{\$61,422}\right)^{0.5} - 1 = -20.3\%$$

This is exactly the same as the compound annual growth rates determined in Chap. 3, The Time Value of Money.

Finally, the index value (panel D) is calculated as

$$1998 \text{ Index value of cash} = \frac{1998 \text{ cash}}{1996 \text{ cash}} \times 100$$

$$= \frac{\$39,024}{\$61,422} \times 100 = 63.5$$

The index value shows the accumulated growth (or decline in this case) from the base year. This is also referred to as the common base-year analysis.

Cash and cash equivalents as presented above and in Table 7.4 have been declining over the past 2 years. Their importance on the balance sheet has declined to only 1.1 percent of total assets (panel B), or a 20.3 percent CAGR decline since 1996 (panel C) to an index value of only 63.5 of its 1996 level (panel D). Over the past 2 years (1996 to 1998), Hershey's accounts receivables grew by 22.5 percent in 1997 and 25.1 percent in 1998 (panel C), to reach a 1998 index value of 153.2 (panel D) and 13.3 percent of total assets (panel B). This 4.0 percent surge in accounts receivable as a percent of total assets (from 9.3 percent in 1996 to 13.3 percent in 1998, panel B) reflects the largest increase in any asset. Almost $157 million was invested in accounts receivable to help Hershey's customers buy products from Hershey. Inventories and property, plant, and equipment, net showed modest increases over the 3-year period with slight declines in 1998.

In the liabilities and stockholders' equity section, the biggest tradeoff occurred in 1997 when Hershey repurchased more than $500 million of its equity primarily through the issuance of debt. Thus total stockholders' equity dropped from 36.5 percent of 1996 total assets to only 25.9 percent of total assets in 1997 (or a 10.6 percent drop in value, panel B). Long-term debt, on the other hand, swelled by 10.7 points as a percent of total assets from 1996 to 1997. In 1998, Hershey generated more than $340 million in net income. Most of that amount was retained and boosted stockholders' equity by almost $190 million.

Financial Ratio Analysis

The basic financial statement analysis presented above, common-size statement analysis, growth analysis, and common base-year or indexed statements, is the most fundamental of all analysis. Although the components of the basic financial statement analysis are appropriate for comparisons between companies, the analysis was illustrated above as a way of examining a company versus itself over time.

Table 7.5 provides 1998 summary statistics to compare Hershey Foods with Heinz. Many food industry experts have admired the steady

TABLE 7.5

1998 Summary Statistics ($ Millions, except per share)

	1998	
	Hershey	**Heinz**
Sales	$4435.6	$9209.3
Cost of goods sold	2625.1	5711.2
Operating income	642.7	1520.3
Interest expense	85.7	226.0
Pretax income	557.0	1255.0
Net income	340.9	801.6
Cash and cash equivalents	39.0	99.4
Accounts receivable	451.3	1071.8
Inventory	493.2	1328.8
Current assets	1134.0	2686.5
Net plant, property, and equipment	1648.1	2394.7
Total assets	3404.1	8023.4
Current liabilities	814.8	2164.3
Short-term debt	345.9	301.0
Current portion of LTD	0.1	38.6
Long-term debt (LTD)	879.1	2768.3
Stockholders' equity	1042.3	2216.5
Stock price per share	62.188	53.313
Shares outstanding	143.1	366.0
Dividends per share	0.92	1.23

and continuous performance of Heinz. It is an international, well-diversified food processing company. If we compare the "raw data" for Hershey Foods and Heinz, the best that we can say is that Heinz has more than double the sales, income, cash and other assets, liabilities, and stockholders' equity of Hershey Foods. This provides a rather uninspiring and uninformative analysis of the two companies. Hershey will be compared to Heinz throughout this next section for the years 1996, 1997, and 1998.

Table 7.6 overviews comparative financial ratio analysis and lists five broad groups of ratios:

- *Liquidity*: How liquid is the company? These metrics measure the firm's ability to meet its maturing short-term obligations.
- *Activity*: How effectively is the company managing its assets? These metrics measure how effectively the company is using its resources.
- *Leverage*: How is the company financed? These metrics measure the extent to which the firm's assets have been financed by debt.
- *Profitability*: How profitable is the company? These metrics measure management's overall effectiveness in generating profits in relation to its sales or investment.
- *Market*: How does the company's performance "translate" in the stock market? These metrics measure the firm's relationship to the broader stock market.

In addition, the basic financial statement analysis discussed above included two additional categories of financial ratios:

- *Growth*: How has the company been growing? These metrics include annual growth rates and compound annual growth rates over extended periods (see Chap. 3, The Time Value of Money) of key balance sheet and income statement items and measure the firm's ability to maintain its economic position in the growth of the economy and industry.
- *Cost management*: What are the underlying cost trends relative to other measures? These metrics include measuring expenses as a percent of each sales dollar, as in the common size income statement in Table 7.3.

Within each of these categories are numerous individual performance metrics. The most common metrics are discussed below.

Liquidity Ratios

Liquidity ratios measure the firm's ability to pay off its maturing short-term obligations. The broadest view of liquidity is captured in the current ratio.

TABLE 7.6

Performance Metrics

	Hershey			Heinz		
	1996	**1997**	**1998**	**1996**	**1997**	**1998**
Liquidity						
Current ratio	1.21	1.30	1.39	1.12	1.05	1.24
Net working capital	$168.9	$239.1	$319.2	$331.6	$132.7	$522.2
Quick ratio	0.63	0.67	0.79	0.57	0.55	0.63
Cash ratio	0.08	0.07	0.05	0.04	0.07	0.05
Activity						
Total asset turnover	1.25	1.31	1.30	1.06	1.11	1.15
Fixed asset turnover	2.49	2.61	2.69	3.48	3.77	3.85
Capital turnover	1.87	2.01	1.96	1.50	1.59	1.73
Accounts receivable turnover	13.54	11.92	9.83	7.54	8.36	8.59
Accounts receivable days outstanding	27.0	30.6	37.1	48.4	43.6	42.5
Inventory turnover	4.85	4.92	5.32	3.87	4.12	4.30
Inventory days outstanding	75.3	74.1	68.6	94.4	88.5	84.9
Leverage						
Debt to equity	1.74	2.86	2.27	2.19	2.46	2.62
Financial leverage	2.74	3.86	3.27	3.19	3.46	3.62
Capitalization ratio	45.5%	60.1%	54.0%	55.4%	58.6%	58.4%
Interest coverage	11.73	8.26	7.50	5.40	5.79	6.55
Profitability, percent*						
Net margin	7.7	7.8	7.7	7.2	7.6	8.7
Pretax margin	12.9	12.9	12.6	11.2	12.0	13.6
Operating margin	14.1	14.6	14.5	14.1	15.0	16.5
Gross margin	42.3	42.1	40.8	36.6	36.9	38.0
Return on assets	9.7	10.2	10.0	7.6	8.4	10.0
Return on net assets	11.5	12.2	11.6	9.4	10.6	12.9
Return on capital	15.8	17.9	17.3	13.7	15.0	18.2
Return on equity	26.6	39.5	32.7	24.4	29.1	36.2
Market						
Price/earnings	21.7	26.3	26.1	18.9	21.5	24.3
Market to book	5.76	10.38	8.54	4.62	6.25	8.80
Shareholder returns	36.4%	42.9%	1.9%	44.8%	25.2%	30.8%
Dividend yield	1.7%	1.4%	1.5%	3.0%	2.7%	2.3%

*Hershey 1996 values use a normalized net income.

The *current ratio* is calculated as current assets divided by current liabilities. Current assets include cash and marketable securities, accounts receivable, inventory, and any other line items that comprise current assets. Current assets are categories that will be converted to cash in the coming year. Current liabilities include accounts payable, accrued liabilities, other payables and accruals, short-term debt, and current portion of long-term debt. Current liabilities represent items that must be paid in the coming year. So the current ratio is calculated by taking current liabilities or obligations that need to paid off in the coming year and dividing that into current assets or items that you will convert to cash in the coming year. Said differently, the current ratio shows that for every dollar you owe in the coming year, you have X dollars to pay it off. For Hershey for 1998

$$\text{Hershey's 1998 current ratio} = \frac{\text{current assets}}{\text{current liabilities}} = \frac{\$1134.0}{\$814.8} = 1.39$$

For every $1 that Hershey Foods owes over the coming year, it has $1.39 with which to pay it off.

As late as the mid-1980s, a strong current ratio had a value greater than 2. However, in the past 15 years, companies have altered their current asset structure with such processes as *just-in-time* inventory management, more aggressive management of accounts receivable, and a limiting of cash and cash equivalents. In addition, with the increased efficiencies of interest rate swaps, a number of companies have been taking advantage of lower short-term interest rates as they have made a strategy of "rolling over" short-term borrowing as a part of their permanent capital structure. Consequently, companies have systematically shed current assets while purposefully increasing their current liabilities, thus lowering the current ratio standard.

Ratios, including the current ratio, tend to have performance standards related to the industry. Restaurants or fast foods have a current ratio standard that is less than 1! Its current liabilities exceed its current assets. Think about McDonald's and the components of its current assets and current liabilities. On the current assets side, McDonald's does have cash, but only minimal accounts receivable. When was the last time that you went to McDonald's and slapped down your "Mickey D charge card" and charged your purchase? McDonald's has very limited franchise fee receivables. As far as inventory, again think about McDonald's business. It has no finished goods inventory or goods in process. They only have raw material inventory with limited shelf life. On the liability side, McDonald's has all the normal liabilities such as accounts payable, wages payable, taxes payable, accrued liabilities, short-term debt, and current portion of long-term debt. So McDonald's has all the normal liabilities but a thinner level of current assets. Consequently, a current ratio approaching 1.00 would be deemed a strong ratio for the restaurant and fast food businesses.

Nonetheless, the higher the current ratio, the stronger the firm's performance. Again, anything taken to an extreme could actually show signs of an underlying weakness. For example, a current ratio of 8.00 could show

- Hoarding of cash
- Noncollection of receivables
- Inventory buildup
- Inefficient use of "free" financing from suppliers
- Limited short-term borrowings

Industry, competitor, and self-comparisons are instrumental in determining performance strengths and weaknesses.

Table 7.6 compares Hershey Foods Corporation with the H.J. Heinz Company for the period 1996 through 1998. With regard to the current ratio, Hershey Foods has steadily improved this measure. In 1998, for every $1 that it owed (current liabilities) in the coming year, Hershey had $1.39 with which to pay it off (current assets). Hershey's current ratio is stronger than Heinz's current ratio and has followed a steady path of improvement.

A related metric, although not a comparative metric since it is expressed in absolute not relative terms, is net working capital. Net working capital is simply current assets (CA) less current liabilities (CL), and it represents the amount left over after a firm pays off all its immediate liabilities. For Hershey Foods in 1998, working capital was $319.2 million:

$$\text{Hershey's 1998 net working capital}$$
$$= \text{CA} - \text{CL} = \$1134.0 - \$814.8 = \$319.2$$

Although Hershey has been increasing its net working capital over this period, it is of only limited value to compare the net working capital of Hershey to the net working capital of Heinz. Heinz is a significantly larger company, and so a comparison to the Heinz 1998 net working capital of $522.2 million is almost meaningless. It is interesting to note that a negative net working capital (current assets less than current liabilities) is equivalent to a current ratio of less than 1.00.

The *quick ratio*, or the acid test ratio, is similar to the current ratio except inventories are eliminated from the current assets. Why do companies go bankrupt? There are numerous answers to that question, but in the end it boils down to the fact that no one wants the company's product. There are some companies that make a highly desirable product and are successful in spite of inadequate managerial processes and leadership. There are other organizations with great management talent, but a product that no one wants. These latter companies are doomed to failure.

The quick ratio eliminates inventory from current assets. That is, what if you could not realize any value for your finished goods, or your goods in process or even your raw material? The quick ratio for Hershey in 1998 was

$$\text{Hershey's 1998 quick ratio} = \frac{\text{current assets} - \text{inventory}}{\text{current liabilities}}$$

$$= \frac{\$1134.0 - \$493.2}{\$814.8} = 0.79$$

For every $1 that Hershey owes over the coming year, it has $0.79 to pay it off in current assets excluding inventories. Hershey has been steadily increasing its quick ratio over the past few years. Heinz took a slight dip and then rebounded in 1998 but not to the level of Hershey Foods. The quick ratio shows that Hershey is in a relatively better position than Heinz.

Another way of stating the quick ratio is to examine the remaining current assets that are used in the numerator. For every $1 that Hershey owes over the coming year, it has $0.79 of cash and cash equivalents, accounts receivable, deferred tax assets, and prepaid expenses and other current assets to pay it off. But what if the accounts receivable are noncollectible or partially noncollectible, what if deferred tax assets are not realized, and what if prepaid expenses and other assets could not be readily (or fully) converted to cash? Permutations of an "adjusted" quick ratio abound for any specific situation.

The *cash ratio* is the most restrictive liquidity ratio and assumes that only cash and cash equivalents are available to pay off current liabilities. The cash ratio is calculated as

$$\text{Hershey's 1998 cash ratio} = \frac{\text{cash and cash equivalents}}{\text{current liabilities}}$$

$$= \frac{\$39.0}{\$814.8} = 0.05$$

For every $1 Hershey owes, within the next year, at the end of 1998, Hershey has $0.05 to pay it off. This metric has been steadily declining for Hershey over this 3-year time span, while Heinz has bounced around, ending in 1998 at exactly the same level as Hershey Foods. As mentioned, this is the most restrictive of all the liquidity ratios.

Activity Ratio

The activity ratios measure how effectively the company is using its resources. Throughout this section, income statement and balance sheet line items are used for comparison. In all cases, year-end balance sheet values are used. This provides the most conservative metric. These metrics could also be calculated using the beginning balance or an average of the beginning and ending balances. More elaborate averaging techniques could also be used, such as averaging the last four or five quarters of balance sheets. Unless there are some pressing business rationales or massive sudden changes in business, the use of year-end, average, or beginning-of-the-year balance sheet values will have minimal impact on telling the story that underlies the analysis. Yes, there will be different exact, specific numbers, but the underlying trends will be consistent. For simplistic illustration, year-end balance sheet values are used is this section and throughout this chapter.

The total asset turnover ratio gives the broadest and more strategically focused measure. Additional activity measures target specific areas of management for closer, day-to-day scrutiny.

Total asset turnover is defined as sales divided by total assets:

$$\text{Hershey's 1998 total asset turnover} = \frac{\text{sales}}{\text{total assets}}$$

$$= \frac{\$4435.6}{\$3404.1} = 1.30$$

For every \$1 of assets, Hershey generates \$1.30 in sales. Over the past 3 years, Hershey showed general improvement and utilized its assets more effectively. The improving trend is also the result of sales growing faster than total assets. Compared to Heinz, which also has shown steady improvement, Hershey generates \$0.15 more in sales for every \$1 of assets than did Heinz in 1998.

The difference may be the result of Hershey's superior sales force; or it may be the result of more efficient production facilities; or it may be the result of factors such as asset mix, product mix, or other factors not related to management efficiency. The total asset turnover alerts management to overall efficiency differences. The other activity ratios make the analysis more operational by identifying key areas for management's attention. Before we address these operational ratios, consider another more strategic turnover metric, capital turnover.

Capital turnover is of interest because total capital represents the portion of total assets that is financed by sources carrying explicit capital costs, i.e., interest-bearing debt and stockholders' equity. It is calculated as

$$\text{Hershey's 1998 capital turnover} = \frac{\text{sales}}{\text{total capital}} = \frac{\$4435.6}{\$2267.4} = 1.96$$

The total capital is calculated as follows:

	1998
Short-term debt	\$ 345.9
Current portion of long-term debt	0.1
Long-term debt	879.1
Stockholders' equity	1042.3
Total capital	\$2267.4

Once again, Hershey is demonstrating superior performance in this metric compared to Heinz. However, Heinz is on a steadily improving trend while Hershey slipped a bit in 1998. Similar to the total asset turnover, more analysis is necessary before any conclusions can be drawn.

Fixed asset turnover, or the rate of fixed asset utilization, is critical because investments in plant and equipment are both large and of long duration. A mistake in fixed asset investments may be reversed, but the consequences are likely to be long-lasting. To focus on plant and equipment investment, the fixed asset turnover centers on net plant, property, and equipment and is determined as follows:

Hershey's 1998 fixed asset turnover

$$= \frac{\text{sales}}{\text{net property, plant, and equipment}} = \frac{\$4435.6}{\$1648.1} = 2.69$$

Hershey's performance shows continuous improvement over this 3-year span. However, when compared to Heinz, Hershey is significantly overmatched. Heinz generates $1.16 more in sales for every $1 invested in fixed assets. Although this metric points to superior managerial performance at Heinz, this difference could be due to a number of reasons, such as plant production configuration and the age of the plants. The plant production configuration, i.e., how many different products are produced at the same manufacturing facility, affects the plant utilization rate. It is much more efficient to produce one product at a specific facility than to produce a variety of diverse products. The age of the plants and equipment is also important. Older facilities presumably are operationally less efficient, but are represented on the books in depreciated dollar amounts based on their original purchase price. Newer facilities tend to be more efficient, cost more, and are initially underutilized. All these aspects affect this metric.

Unfortunately, Hershey would not be able to analyze Heinz's plants more specifically due to the lack of available *public* plant-specific data. However, the managerial objectives remain clear for Hershey: Generate more sales or reduce the investment in net plant, property, and equipment. Continuous improvement objectives can be implemented at the manufacturing facility level within Hershey.

Additional activity ratios examine accounts receivable and inventory.

Accounts receivable turnover is calculated similar to the other turnovers:

Hershey's 1998 accounts receivable turnover

$$= \frac{\text{credit sales}}{\text{accounts receivable}} = \frac{\$4435.6}{\$451.3} = 9.83$$

It is assumed that all Hershey's sales are made on credit. This measure suggests that 9.83 times a year, Hershey collects all its accounts receivables from its customers. Even though Hershey's performance is better than Heinz's performance, there is concern for the underlying trend. In 1996, Hershey collected its receivables 13.5 times a year and has been on a steady decline since that period. Heinz, on the other hand, shows improving trends throughout this 3-year period.

Very closely related to the accounts receivable turnover ratio is another activity ratio called the average collection period. The *average collection period* measures the length of time that it takes to collect from a customer. It is calculated by dividing 365 days in a year by the accounts receivable turnover:

Hershey's 1998 average collection period

$$= \frac{365}{\text{accounts receivable turnover}} = \frac{365}{9.83} = 37.1 \text{ days}$$

In 1998, Hershey took 37.1 days to collect from its customers. This is more than 5 days better than Heinz (42.5) in 1998. But once again, it is the trend that is of concern for Hershey. In the past 2 years, Hershey's customers were taking more than 10 days longer to pay their bills. Over the same period, Heinz reduced the time its customers took to pay by almost 6 days (from 48.4 to 42.5 days).

Usual credit terms are 2/10 net 30, which means that if you pay in the first 10 days, you get a 2 percent discount. If you do not pay in the first 10 days, the entire amount (no discounts) is payable in 30 days. Under these circumstances, an average collection period of 30 days or less is a standard of excellence. For the first time in more than 10 years, Hershey's performance slid above this 30-day mark.

The final activity ratio examined in this section is the inventory turnover ratio. Inventory turnover is calculated using the cost of goods sold instead of sales, to eliminate the "profit" component and more accurately reflect this metric since inventory is carried at cost, not the anticipated selling price:

$$\text{Hershey's 1998 inventory turnover} = \frac{\text{cost of goods sold}}{\text{inventory}}$$

$$= \frac{\$2625.1}{\$493.2} = 5.32$$

In 1998, Hershey sold off its entire inventory 5.32 times in the year. That is, it cleaned out its warehouses, sold everything off the shelves 5.32 times in 1998. This ratio has shown steady improvement at Hershey as it became an important operational objective over this time period. Again, Hershey's performance is better than Heinz's performance, although Heinz is also showing improving trends.

A variation of the inventory turnover is to measure the number of days of inventory on hand. This is accomplished by dividing 365 days in the year by the number of turnovers per year:

$$\text{Hershey's 1998 inventory days outstanding} = \frac{365}{\text{inventory turnover}}$$

$$= \frac{365}{5.32} = 68.6 \text{ days}$$

Every 68.6 days Hershey sells off its entire inventory, which is more than 16 days better than Heinz's performance. Once again the product line influences this ratio. Hershey's products, in general, have a shorter shelf life than Heinz's products. It is paramount that Hershey not ship "dated" old product to its customers, and consequently Hershey carries lower levels of inventory.

This metric can be applied at a lower level within a firm. This metric can be applied by decomposing inventory into its main components: raw material, goods in process, and finished goods. Standards of performance can be established for these individual inventory components.

In the early 1990s, the management at Dell Corporation elevated inventory days outstanding from simply an operating metric to a strategic performance metric. Dell changed its "business model" to build-on-order. Build-on-order means that each computer is custom-built for each sales order, resulting in no finished goods inventory. Dell enhanced supplier relationships and a just-in-time inventory system. The result: Hundreds of millions of dollars were eliminated in inventory investment! Inventory days outstanding dropped to 7 days in an industry where the average inventory days outstanding is greater than 40 days.

Activity ratios provide an overview of how effectively a company is using its assets. The activity ratios listed above provide a review of the major metrics in this category. Once again, this is not an exhaustive list. Turnovers can be calculated by taking any balance sheet item and dividing it into sales or cost of goods sold. This past discussion provided an analytical framework that can be used to build other turnovers, as specific business needs dictate.

Leverage Metrics

Leverage metrics have a number of implications. First, creditors look at equity, or owner-supplied funds, as a cushion or base for the use of debt. If owners provide only a small proportion of total financing, the risks of the enterprise are borne mainly by the creditors. Second, by raising funds through debt, the owners gain the benefits of achieving control of the firm with limited commitment. Third, the use of debt with a fixed interest rate magnifies both the gains and losses to the owners. Fourth, the use of debt with a fixed interest cost with a specified maturity increases the risks that the firm may not be able to meet its obligations. Decisions about the use of leverage must balance hoped-for higher returns against the increased risk of the consequences firms face when they are unable to meet interest payments or maturing obligations.

Leverage metrics measure the extent to which a firm is financed by debt. One group of leverage metrics uses the balance sheet identity relationship:

$$\text{Assets} = \text{liabilities} + \text{stockholders' equity}$$

This group of leverage metrics uses total liabilities (including accounts payable, accrued liabilities, deferred taxes, other long-term liabilities, and interest-bearing debt) synonymously with debt. Another group of leverage ratios centers on balance sheet relationships, but defines debt as interest-bearing debt only. The third group of leverage metrics concentrates on income statement relationships and the ability of the firm to pay.

In the term *debt to equity*, *debt* refers to total liabilities. It is calculated as

$$\text{Hershey's 1998 debt-to-equity ratio} = \frac{\text{debt (or liabilities)}}{\text{stockholders' equity}}$$

$$= \frac{\$2361.8}{\$1042.3} = 2.27$$

For every $1 of stockholders' equity, Hershey supports $2.27 worth of liabilities. A higher debt-to-equity ratio indicates that the firm is using more total liabilities to finance its assets. At Heinz in 1998, every $1 of equity supported $2.62 worth of liabilities or $0.35 more of liabilities than at Hershey Foods. For Heinz, this ratio reveals a steadily increasing dependency on the use of debt; for Hershey Foods, the general trend is rising with some fluctuation.

Financial leverage is closely aligned to the debt-to-equity ratio. Financial leverage measures the extent to which the shareholders' equity investment is magnified by the use of total debt (or liabilities) in financing its total assets. Financial leverage illustrates the number of dollars of assets for every $1 of stockholders' equity:

$$\text{Hershey's 1998 financial leverage} = \frac{\text{assets}}{\text{stockholders' equity}}$$

$$= \frac{\$3404.1}{\$1042.3} = 3.27$$

At Hershey Foods, every $1 of stockholders' equity supported $3.27 of assets. Financial leverage can also be determined by adding 1 to the debt-to-equity ratio:

Hershey's 1998 financial leverage $= 1 + \dfrac{\text{debt (or liabilities)}}{\text{stockholders' equity}}$

$$= 1 + \frac{\$2361.8}{\$1042.3} = 3.27$$

As an algebraic note, remember the old high school algebra "trick" that 1 can equal any number divided by itself (identity property). In the equation above, let 1 be equity/equity. That allows the combination of terms (equity + debt), which per the accounting identity equals total assets:

$$1 + \frac{\text{debt}}{\text{equity}} = \frac{\text{equity}}{\text{equity}} + \frac{\text{debt}}{\text{equity}} = \frac{\text{equity} + \text{debt}}{\text{equity}} = \frac{\text{assets}}{\text{equity}}$$

The accounting identity equation also captures this relationship:

$$\text{Assets} = \text{Liabilities} + \text{Stockholders' equity}$$
$$\$3.27 \ = \$2.27 + \$1.00$$

Additional leverage metrics can be constructed from this relationship.

These metrics look at what percentage of the assets is financed with liabilities and what percentage is financed with stockholders' equity:

$$\frac{\text{Liabilities}}{\text{Assets}} = \frac{\$2361.8}{\$3404.1} = 69.4\%$$

$$\frac{\text{Stockholders' equity}}{\text{Assets}} = \frac{\$1042.3}{\$3404.1} = 30.6\%$$

These ratios must total 100 percent. The underlying relationships portrayed by these four ratios, trends, and competitive comparisons do not change. What is different is the focus of presentation and associated discussions. How is the management team more comfortable in discussing leverage, in relationship to percent of assets or percent of equity? That should determine how the analysis is presented.

Balance sheet line items such as accounts payable, accrued liabilities, and long-term liabilities including deferred taxes stem from the operations of the business. Those liabilities are sometimes referred to as spontaneous operating liabilities. The second group of leverage ratios centers on financial liabilities, interest-bearing debt, and total capital. Total capital consists of interest-bearing debt and stockholders' equity.

The *capitalization ratio* calculates the percentage that interest-bearing debt represents of the total capital pool:

Hershey's 1998 capitalization ratio

$$= \frac{\text{interest-bearing debt}}{\text{interest-bearing debt} + \text{equity}} = \frac{\$1225.1}{\$2267.4} = 54.0\%$$

Fifty-four percent of Hershey's financing comes from interest-bearing debt.

Variations of this ratio differ in what is considered in the numerator. Are short-term debt, notes payable, and current portion of long-term debt part of the permanent financial capital structure of the firm, or are short-term debt, notes payable, and current portion of long-term debt just another form of operating liabilities? The answer lies in the motives of the corporation. Many companies have incorporated a long-term financing strategy of rolling over short-term borrowings. With the financial flexibility provided by swaps and other instruments and the relatively calm debt markets of the past few years, many firms save millions of dollars annually by taking advantage of lower short-term interest rates, and they finance a portion of their permanent assets with short-term borrowings. In these cases it is clear that short-term borrowings are part of the permanent financial structure and should be included as interest-bearing debt in the capitalization ratio.

Other companies within other industries could argue that all short-term financing supports temporary working capital needs. They may chose to exclude short-term borrowings for purposes of the capitalization ratio and narrow the metric to

Hershey's 1998 long-term capitalization ratio

$$= \frac{\text{long-term debt}}{\text{long-term debt} + \text{equity}} = \frac{\$879.1}{\$1921.4} = 45.8\%$$

This more narrowly focused metric centers on long-term debt as a percent of a similarly narrowed definition of capital. In this example, 45.8 percent of Hershey's capital pool (excluding short-term borrowings) comes from long-term debt. Both variations of the capitalization ratio are appropriate depending on the circumstances. It appears that the food industry incorporates short-term borrowings into its permanent capital structures. Consequently, the former version of the capitalization ratio (including short-term borrowings) would be more appropriate for the food industry.

Interest coverage is the final leverage ratio. Interest coverage utilizes the income statement and examines how many times the interest could be paid off with operating income:

Hershey's 1998 interest coverage

$$= \frac{\text{EBIT}}{\text{interest expense}} = \frac{\$642.7}{\$85.7} = 7.50$$

EBIT represents earnings before interest and taxes and is often called *operating income*. Simply put, for every $1 that Hershey owes for interest expense, Hershey earns $7.50 in operating income that could be used to pay the interest. From a banker's perspective, the higher this ratio, the stronger the company. Everything else remaining constant, as leverage and interest expense increase, this ratio declines. Interest coverage reflects a consistent pattern of increasing leverage for Hershey, as did the other leverage metrics in this section.

To demonstrate more fully the informational content of the leverage ratios, look at leverage patterns for Heinz in Table 7.6. The leverage metrics are seemingly in conflict. The debt-to-equity and the financial leverage ratios indicate a company that is systematically increasing its leverage. The capitalization ratio portrays a company with relatively unchanging leverage, while the interest coverage metric shows an upward trend that is consistent with a company decreasing its leverage. So is Heinz becoming more or less leveraged?

As with most things, it depends. Heinz is not (in relative terms) increasing its interest-bearing debt, which gives rise to an almost constant capitalization ratio. In fact, Heinz is reducing its debt while also repurchasing its stock. Both transactions are of relatively the same magnitude, and so the capitalization ratio remains almost constant. The improving interest coverage ratio can be explained by Heinz's improvement in operating income coupled with a slightly lower interest cost. Heinz is, however, increasing its operating leverage. Non-interest-bearing current liabilities are increasing as are long-term operating liabilities. So Heinz is a company that is increasing its operating liabilities while reducing its interest-bearing debt in the same proportion as it is repurchasing its stock and increasing its profitability.

Profitability Ratios

Profitability ratios measure management's overall effectiveness at generating profits. One common set of profitability ratios examines some measure of income as a percent of sales, while another group of metrics focuses on income in relation to some measure of investment as captured by the balance sheet.

As the profitability metrics are considered, the proper focus is on income from continuing operations or normalized profit (see Chap. 2, Financial Statements and Cash Flows). Hershey's 1996 normalized net is $308.6 million and is used throughout the discussion below.

Net margin is one of the most frequently cited metrics. Senior management often sets targets and objectives that involve the net margin. Often a senior manager's bonus is tied directly or indirectly to the net margin. Simply, the net margin reflects the number of pennies of income for every dollar of sales:

$$\text{Hershey's 1998 net margin} = \frac{\text{net income}}{\text{sales}} = \frac{\$340.9}{\$4435.6} = 7.7\%$$

For every $1 of sales, Hershey Foods generated $0.077 of net income, i.e., income after paying all its operating expenses, interest, and taxes. This is consistent with the net margin in 1996, but down 0.1 from 1997. Over this same period, Heinz showed tremendous improvement, rising from $0.072 for every $1 in sales in 1996, to $0.076 in 1997, and surging to $0.087 for every $1 of sales in 1998. Now, $0.015 per dollar of sales does not sound like much, but when multiplied by Heinz 1998 sales of $9209.3 million, that $0.015 improvement accounts for $138.1 million additional net income!

There are two ways to improve your net margin. One way is to reduce expenses; the other way is to increase prices. Generally the higher net margin the better, but again anything taken to an extreme becomes a weakness. Kellogg's was the perennial leader of the food industry with net margins approaching 10 percent in the late 1980s. Also, in the late 1980s and early 1990s, Kellogg's was the number one cereal company in the United States with the largest market share. In the early 1990s, Kellogg's went through a series of price increases that boosted its margin to more than 11.0 percent. Of course as consumers, we were all less than thrilled to pay $4 and $5 for a box of cereal.

Companies that produce generic and store-brand cereals seized the opportunity. Competition heated up. We, as consumers, even learned that we could eat cereal that did not come in a box, but rather came in a cello-phane bag. Prices fell and heavy expenses were incurred for store cou-pons, promotions, and advertising. Kellogg's sales declined, its number one market share eroded, and its net margins shrank to only 8.1 percent. Kellogg's strict adherence to raising prices for a higher net margin eventu-ally cost the company. All ratios must be carefully balanced.

The *pretax margin* reveals how profitable the firm is before con-sidering the effects of income taxes. It is calculated as

$$\text{Hershey's 1998 pretax margin} = \frac{\text{pretax income}}{\text{sales}}$$

$$= \frac{\$557.0}{\$4435.6} = 12.6\%$$

In 1998, Hershey Foods had a pretax margin of 12.6 percent which was down 0.3 percent from 1997. That 0.3 percent reflects a $13.3 million drop in pretax profitability for a 1998 sales level of $4435.6 million. When compared to Hershey's net margin (7.7 percent), the pretax mar-gin shows that $0.049 (12.6 percent – 7.7 percent) of every dollar of Her-shey's sales went to pay income taxes.

In 1996, Heinz significantly trailed Hershey's pretax profitability by 1.7 percent (11.2 versus 12.9 percent). By 1998, Heinz was 1.0 percent higher (better) than Hershey in this metric. More will be said about the pretax margin later when we talk about the DuPont analysis.

Operating margin is calculated as

Hershey's 1998 operating margin

$$= \frac{\text{operating income}}{\text{sales}} = \frac{\$642.7}{\$4435.6} = 14.5\%$$

For every $1 of sales, Hershey Foods generated $0.145 of operating income or earnings before interest and tax. This represents the profitability of the corporation before considering financing costs (interest) and income taxes. For Hershey, this metric follows a similar pattern to the previous profitability metrics: 1998 encountered a slight annual downturn in performance. Heinz continued its onward and upward profitability trend.

The difference between EBIT and pretax income is interest expense. In Table 7.5, Hershey's 1998 operating income ($642.7 million) less interest expense ($85.7 million) equals pretax income of $557.0 million. Similarly, the difference between the operating margin and pretax margin represents interest expense as a percent of sales, or in this case $0.019 of every sales dollar goes to pay interest expense.

Gross margin develops a profitability relationship between gross income and sales, where

Gross income = sales – cost of goods sold

Gross income represents the inherent profitability for making a product. Cost of goods sold encompasses total cost of production: raw material, direct labor, plant overhead, etc. After it absorbs the costs of making the product, how profitable is the company?

$$\text{Hershey's 1998 gross margin} = \frac{\text{sales – cost of goods sold}}{\text{sales}}$$

$$= \frac{\$4435.6 - \$2625.1}{\$4435.6} = 40.8\%$$

In Hershey's case for 1998, it made more than $0.40 for every dollar of sales for its products.

When compared to Heinz, Hershey's product mix, selling prices, costs of ingredients, productivity of labor, etc., produce greater profitability for its chocolate and confectionery than Heinz does for its wide variety of diverse product lines. Hershey's superior gross margin was evident in all three years. However, in 1998, due to rising cocoa and milk prices, which could not be passed on to consumers, Hershey's gross margin slid while Heinz's gross margin improved.

So far the profitability metrics examined numerous measures of profitability compared to sales. This next series of profitability metrics looks at understanding the amount of profitability for every dollar of investment. In these cases, profitability and investment definitions vary with the particular focus of the analysis.

Assets represent the total investment made by the corporation on behalf of its stockholders. As discussed in Chap. 2, accounting values do not represent current values, fair market values, or even replacement value of assets. In fact, a fair portion of the balance sheet captures only historical costs of the assets. Still other "asset" values go unacknowledged, such as the value of intellectual property, strong brands, technology, and highly knowledgeable employees. Despite these frailties, a balance sheet does reasonably capture and represent assets on a consistently measured basis among organizations.

Return on assets measures the return (income) for every dollar of assets:

$$\text{Hershey's 1998 return on assets} = \frac{\text{net income}}{\text{total assets}}$$

$$= \frac{\$340.9}{\$3404.1} = 10.0\%$$

In 1998, Hershey generated slightly more than $0.10 on every dollar of assets, which was minimally higher than 1996, but lower than 1997. Heinz also generated $0.10 on every dollar of assets, which reflects a continually improving trend.

Many companies establish internal profitability metrics. Hershey called its metric RONA (or return on net assets). Many companies have a similarly defined metric that goes by many different names:

- RONA, or return on net assets
- RONI, or return on net investment
- ROIC, or return on invested capital
- ROCI, or return on capital invested
- ROGEC, or return on gross employed capital

While these measures may have slight variations in the definition of the denominator, we will use a fairly common variety of net asset definition:

Net assets = total assets – non-interest-bearing current liabilities

In Hershey's 1998 case, non-interest-bearing current liabilities total $468.8 million: $156.9 million accounts payable, $294.4 million accrued liabilities, and $17.5 million accrued income taxes. Net assets were

Net assets = $3404.1 – $468.8 = $2935.3

Said differently, net assets represent the capital (equity, long-term debt, short-term debt, and current portion of long-term debt) and long-term operating liabilities such as deferred taxes and other long-term liabilities. The return on net assets represents the return on total assets less spontaneous current operating liabilities:

$$\text{Hershey's 1998 return on net assets} = \frac{\text{net income}}{\text{net assets}}$$

$$= \frac{\$340.9}{\$2935.3} = 11.6\%$$

Hershey's RONA fluctuated over the time period from 11.5 to 12.2 percent, ending 1998 at 11.6 percent. Once again, Hershey's 1998 performance trails Heinz's, which has shown consistent improvement since 1996.

Return on capital narrows the investment base further. Capital is defined as equity and interest-bearing debt, or more specifically, equity, short-term debt, notes (or loans) payable, current portion of long-term debt, and long-term debt. Compared to the net assets definition above, capital excludes deferred tax liabilities and other long-term liabilities.

In this case, the numerator is not net income. Net income excludes interest expense, an explicit cost of the debt component of capital. To neutralize the impact of leverage and to provide a more consistent view of return on capital, the return on capital is calculated with after-tax operating income, which is calculated by first estimating the average income tax rate:

$$\text{Hershey's 1998 tax rate} = \frac{\text{income tax expense}}{\text{pretax income}} = \frac{\$216.1}{\$557.0} = 38.8\%$$

Hershey's $216.1 million of tax expenses equates to an average income tax rate of 38.8 percent. Next, using the 38.8 percent tax rate, income taxes are estimated for operating income (EBIT). The estimated taxes are $249.4 million (operating income of $642.7 million times 38.8 percent) and result in after-tax operating income of $393.3 million. This is equal to net income ($340.9) plus (1 − tax rate) times interest expense 0.612(85.7) or 52.4.

The return on capital is 17.3 percent:

$$\text{Hershey's 1998 return on capital} = \frac{\text{after-tax operating income}}{\text{capital}}$$

$$= \frac{\$393.3}{\$2267.4} = 17.3\%$$

For every $1 of capital (interest-bearing debt and equity), Hershey generated $0.173 in 1998, which showed a downturn from 1997 and trailed Heinz's performance for the year.

Return on equity is the final profitability metric and is the most narrow definition of a capital base used in the return metrics. Return on equity for Hershey in 1998 was 32.7 percent:

$$\text{Hershey's 1998 return on equity} = \frac{\text{net income}}{\text{equity}}$$

$$= \frac{\$340.9}{\$1042.3} = 32.7\%$$

For every $1 of total stockholders' equity (original investment and retained earnings offset by share repurchases), Hershey Foods generated $0.327 of income after paying all production costs, operating expenses, interest expense, and income taxes. Once again, a similar performance path is noted: 1998 is down from 1997 but better than 1996. Also, Hershey's performance exceeded Heinz's performance in 1996 and 1997, but now trails the Heinz 1998 performance.

Market-Related Metrics

The market-related metrics incorporate current stock prices into the performance metrics.

Price/earnings ratios compare the market price per share to earnings per share. This widely used measure is simply called the *P/E* ratio and is often reported within a stock listing in a daily business newspaper such as *The Wall Street Journal*. This metric is calculated as

$$\text{Hershey's 1998 price/earnings ratio} = \frac{\text{market price per share}}{\text{earnings per share}}$$

$$= \frac{\$62.19}{\$2.38} = 26.1$$

Broadly interpreted, the *P/E* ratio indicates that for every $1 of Hershey's earnings the stock market (or actually an investor) is willing to pay $26.10.

The higher the growth rate of the firm, the higher the price/earnings ratio. The past few years have seen a tremendous increase in *P/E* ratios as stock prices (for a variety of reasons) have grown faster than earnings. The 1998 *P/E* ratio for Heinz was 24.3, which is slightly below Hershey's *P/E* ratio.

The *market-to-book* ratio measures the value that financial markets attach to the management and organization of the firm as a going concern. The ratio can be calculated based on the current market price:

$$\text{Hershey's 1998 market-to-book ratio} = \frac{\text{market price per share}}{\text{book value per share}}$$

$$= \frac{\$62.19}{\$7.28} = 8.54$$

Book value per share is calculated by taking stockholders' equity ($1042.3 million) divided by the number of shares outstanding (143.1

million shares), or $7.28. The other way to calculate the market-to-book ratio is to calculate a total market value for the firm. This market capitalization (or total market value of the firm) is calculated by multiplying the number of shares outstanding (143.1 million shares) by the market price per share. In Hershey's case at the end of 1998, the market capitalization was $8900 million, and the resulting market-to-book ratio is

$$\text{Hershey's 1998 market-to-book ratio} = \frac{\text{market capitalization}}{\text{stockholders' equity}}$$

$$= \frac{\$8900}{\$1042} = 8.54$$

In any case, the ratio calculates to the same value, 8.54. The distinction is the ease of use and a specific focus. Hershey's market value of equity is $8.9 billion. The historical "book value" of stockholders' equity is a less meaningful value, as we discussed in Chap. 2, Financial Statements and Cash Flows. Stockholders' equity represents the original proceeds that equity investors invested in Hershey in the 1927 Hershey initial public offering, along with the proceeds of subsequent stock issuance and earnings retained (not paid out as dividends) in the corporation offset by shares repurchased.

The market-to-book ratio suggests that for every $1 of Hershey's net book value (or stockholders' equity) the market is willing to pay $8.54. Since the balance sheet does not capture the value of brands, intellectual property, proprietary processes, knowledge workers, etc., some argue that the market-to-book ratio reflects the relative value of these intangibles. This point is dramatically seen in extremely high market-to-book ratios for the "new economy" companies.

Hershey sells at a substantial premium to its book value, in part, due to its brands and cash flow generation ability. Also, Hershey sells at a substantial premium due to recent stock buybacks. Since 1994, Hershey has repurchased more than $1.3 billion of its stock in the stock market. This reduces the book value of the equity and generally tends to boost stock prices. Therefore, the market-to-book multiple is increased. In fact, if that $1.3 billion is added back to the book value of equity with no downward adjustment to stock prices, the market-to-book ratio falls from 8.54 to 3.85, which is still above the traditional level for Hershey Foods.

Heinz, which has also engaged in share repurchasing, has a comparable 1998 market-to-book ratio of 8.80. This is slightly higher and on the surface suggests that the market values Heinz's intangibles more than Hershey's intangibles. However, since stockholders' equity is subject to significant impacts based upon the amount of share repurchases, it is difficult to strongly suggest that the market values Heinz's intangibles more.

Shareholder returns have become the touchstone of much financial analysis. The theme of enhancing shareholder value is the subject of many books and articles and is highlighted in the annual reports of many individual companies. The shareholder return measures what shareholders actually earn over a period of time. This is a widely used measure in making comparisons between the market returns among a wide range of financial instruments.

Shareholder return is defined as the sum of capital appreciation and dividend yield over a period of time. The period of time can be a month, quarter, year, or a number of years. The shareholder return for Hershey for 1998 was

Hershey's 1998 shareholder return

$$= \frac{\text{stock price}_{12/31/98} - \text{stock price}_{1/1/98} + \text{dividends}_{1998}}{\text{stock price}_{1/1/98}}$$

$$= \frac{\$62.19 - \$61.94 + \$0.92}{\$61.94} = \frac{\$0.25 + \$0.92}{\$61.94} = 1.9\%$$

In 1998, the stock of Hershey Foods provided a return of only 1.9 percent to its stockholders. In other words, if you bought the stock on January 1, 1998, you would have paid $61.94 for that share. At year end (whether you sell your share or not) the value of that share rose $0.25 to $62.14. The 1998 capital appreciation was 0.4 percent. In addition, you received a dividend of $0.92 throughout 1998, which represents a dividend yield of 1.5 percent.

Many companies throughout the food processing industry in both 1998 and 1999 felt this anemic shareholder return. However, Heinz provided a solid 30.8 percent shareholder return in 1998. Over a longer period, from 1994 to 1997, Hershey's stock price appreciated 36.8 percent per year ($24.19 on December 31, 1994, and $61.94 on December 31, 1997) along with an average dividend yield of 2.3 percent for a total annual shareholder return from 1994 to 1997 of 39.1 percent!

Dividend yield represents the dividend received over a period of time compared to the initial price of the stock. In the example above,

$$\text{Hershey's 1998 dividend yield} = \frac{\text{dividends}_{1998}}{\text{stock price}_{1/1/98}}$$

$$= \frac{\$0.92}{\$61.94} = 1.5\%$$

Dividend yield measures the *current return* of owning a share of stock.

The market ratios blend current stock market conditions into the comparative analysis of companies.

Table 7.7 summarizes the metrics discussed above, their calculation, and the general direction that indicates a stronger performance.

TABLE 7.7

Summary of Financial Performance Metrics

Financial Performance Metric	Calculation	Strength
Liquidity		
Current ratio	Current assets / Current liabilities	Higher
Net working capital	Current assets − Current liabilities	Higher
Quick ratio	(Current assets − inventories) / Current liabilities	Higher
Cash ratio	Cash / Current liabilities	Higher
Activity		
Total asset turnover	Sales / Total assets	Higher
Fixed asset turnover	Sales / Fixed assets	Higher
Capital turnover	Sales / (Interest-bearing debt + Equity)	Higher
Accounts receivable turnover	Sales / Accounts receivable	Higher
Accounts receivable days outstanding	365 days / Accounts receivable turnover	Lower
Inventory turnover	Cost of goods sold / Inventory	Higher
Inventory days outstanding	365 days / Inventory turnover	Lower
Leverage		
Debt to equity	Liabilities / Equity	Lower
Financial leverage	Assets / Equity	Lower
Capitalization ratio	Interest-bearing debt / (Interest-bearing debt + Equity)	Lower
Interest coverage	Earnings before interest and tax / Interest expense	Higher
Profitability		
Net margin	Net income / Sales	Higher
Pretax margin	Pretax income / Sales	Higher
Operating margin	Operating income / Sales	Higher
Gross margin	(Sales − Cost of goods sold) / Sales	Higher
Return on assets	Net income / Assets	Higher
Return on net assets	Net income / (Assets − Non-interest-bearing current liabilities)	Higher
Return on capital	EBIT (1 − Tax rate) / (Interest-bearing debt + Equity)	Higher
Return on equity	Net income / Equity	Higher
Market		
Price/earnings ratio	Stock price per share / Earnings per share	Higher
Market-to-book ratio	Market value / Book value	Higher
Shareholder returns	(Capital appreciation + Dividends) / Beginning stock price	Higher
Dividend yield	Dividend per share / Beginning price	Higher

Other Ratios

Two other types of ratios were mentioned above: growth metrics and cost management metrics.

Annual growth rates and compound annual growth rates over an extended period were illustrated in the basic financial statement analysis section. Growth can be calculated on any income statement (Table 7.3) or balance sheet (Table 7.4) line items. Five-year and 10-year growth rates provide a long-term barometer of the firm's health and its abilities to conduct business.

Cost management ratios take many forms. In the basic financial statement analysis, we looked at costs as a percent of sales. Cost management stresses that lower costs (as a percent of sales) are a sign of strength. Again, balance is key. Hershey Foods could improve its cost of goods sold as a percent of sales by reducing the quality of its products. While such a strategy could reduce costs in the short run, in the long run, reduced quality would negatively impact one of Hershey's core competitive strengths, a quality product.

Examining specific, individual expenses as a percent of sales creates additional cost management measures. That is, some expenses such as research and development, advertising, and depreciation are reported in the footnotes or supplemental schedules of annual reports. Each of these expenses can be calculated as a percent of sales (e.g., R&D expense/sales) for a historical period and compared to other firms in the industry. Using nonreported, internal numbers, all functional areas can be viewed as a percent of sales and tracked over years of experience with appropriate targets and boundaries set.

Finally, other relative cost management ratios can be calculated based on other statistics. One of the most common of these ratios is sales per employee. Some consider the year-to-year change in this ratio as a measure of productivity.

DUPONT RATIO ANALYSIS

With so many numbers and so many ratios, where do we begin our diagnosis of a company's fiscal health? The DuPont ratio analysis is a systematic approach to financial analysis that was originally developed by analysts at DuPont. It does not add to our "bag" of analytical metrics, but it does help us organize the metrics to tell a clear and concise story.

A System of Metrics

DuPont analysis uses metrics that were introduced earlier in the chapter.

The first part of the analysis examines the return on assets as a function of profitability and turnover. Profitability is measured using net margin, while turnover is measured using total asset turnover:

$$\text{Net margin} \times \text{asset turnover} = \text{return on assets}$$

$$\frac{\text{Net income}}{\text{Sales}} \times \frac{\text{sales}}{\text{total assets}} = \frac{\text{net income}}{\text{total assets}}$$

The algebra is trivial! Sales cancel, and we are left with net income divided by total assets, or the return on assets.

Next, we can take the return on assets and multiply it by financial leverage:

$$\text{Return on assets} \times \text{financial leverage} = \text{return on equity}$$

$$\frac{\text{Net income}}{\text{Total assets}} \times \frac{\text{total assets}}{\text{equity}} = \frac{\text{net income}}{\text{equity}}$$

Once again, the algebra is trivial! Total assets cancel, and we are left with net income divided by equity, or the return on equity.

Yes, we could have directly calculated the return on assets or return on equity. However, by isolating the individual operating components, we can address strengths and weaknesses in the firm.

For example, Table 7.8 compares the performance of Hershey and Heinz in 1992 and 1998. In 1992, both Hershey and Heinz generated $0.075 of net income for every $1 of sales as determined by the net margin of 7.5 percent. Hershey used its assets more effectively than Heinz did in 1992. Hershey generated $1.21 of sales for every $1 of assets while Heinz only generated $1.03 of sales for every $1 of assets. This resulted in return on assets for Hershey and Heinz of 9.1 and 7.8 percent, respectively.

For every $1 of assets, Hershey generated $1.21 in sales. Those sales were profitable at the rate of $0.075 for every sales dollar, or $0.091 for $1.21 in sales. In total, that $1 of assets generated $1.21 in sales, which generated $0.091 of income. In 1992, the margin was neutral in performance to Heinz, while the total asset turnover was superior for Hershey Foods. Therefore, Hershey's return on assets was stronger than Heinz's return on assets.

Commodity, or low value-added, businesses typically have low margins and more rapid turnover. Years earlier, Iowa Beef, which as the named implies is a meat processor, typified a commodity business. A meat processor has very limited assets. The plant is essentially a steel-shell building with refrigeration units. Inventory is walked off of a railroad car, processed with a great deal of manual labor, and wheeled onto a railroad car at the opposite end of the building. Inventory is not left "hanging around," no pun intended. The meat processing business is a

TABLE 7.8

Hershey and Heinz DuPont Analysis

		Hershey		Heinz	
		1992	1998	1992	1998
Net margin	Net income / Sales	7.5%	7.7%	7.5%	8.7%
×	×				
Total asset turnover	Sales / Total assets	1.21	1.30	1.03	1.15
=	=				
Return on assets	Net income / Total assets	9.1%	10.0%	7.8%	10.0%
×	×				
Financial leverage	Total assets / Equity	1.82	3.27	2.92	3.62
=	=				
Return on equity	Net income / Equity	16.6%	32.7%	22.8%	36.2%

low-margin, low-profitability business. However, the turnover is much more rapid. In 1980, Iowa Beef's net margin was 1.15 percent. It made just a little more than a penny on every dollar's sale, but the company turned its assets 11.13 times per year. This resulted in a very impressive 12.8 percent return on assets.

Adding financial leverage to the DuPont analysis highlights Hershey's largest weakness in 1992: limited leverage. In 1992, Hershey Foods was a very traditional and conservative company. Debt was considered a "four-letter word" and was not an option without an operating decision driving the increase in leverage. In 1992, every $1 of equity supported $1.82 worth of assets. At the same time at Heinz, every $1 of equity generated $2.92 worth of assets. Remember, Hershey's return on assets was far superior to that of Heinz. However, when the full array of financial performance tools was used, Hershey chose not to emphasize leverage and lost to Heinz on the return to equity. Operations were fine; financing was not!

Before we look at the impact of the six intervening years, a reflection on the meaning of the full DuPont analysis is in order. In 1992, every $1 of Hershey's equity supported $1.82 worth of assets. Those assets generated sales at the rate of $1.21 of sales for every $1 of assets. Therefore that $1 of equity (which supported $1.82 of assets) generated $2.20 worth of sales. Those sales generated profits at the rate of $0.075 for every $1 of sales. Finally, that $1 of equity (which supported $1.82 of assets and generated $2.20 in sales) resulted in $0.166 worth of income. Compared to Heinz, every $1 of equity supported $2.92 worth of assets. Those assets generated sales at the rate of $1.03 of sales for every $1 of assets. Therefore that $1 of equity (which supported $2.92 of assets) generated $3.01 worth of sales. Those sales generated profits at the rate of $0.075 for every $1 of sales. Finally, that $1 of equity (which supported $2.92 of assets and generated $3.01 in sales) resulted in $0.228 worth of income.

Hershey was not even close to Heinz in the return-to-equity metric in 1992. By using the DuPont analysis, management at Hershey could zero in on the root cause of this shortfall and could decide to address the issue of leverage. Also, by 1998 Heinz could address its return-on-asset shortfall.

The results: By 1998, Heinz closed the return-on-asset gap as both companies improved their profitability and turnover, but Heinz increased its profitability by one full percentage point above Hershey. Both companies also increased their leverage, but Hershey increased its leverage more and narrowed the return-on-equity difference.

Final Analysis: Operational Implementation

The DuPont analysis is an effective tool for observing and analyzing your company's strengths and weaknesses as well as the actions of competitors. However, metrics that are left in the board room are of minimal benefit in today's fast-paced business environment. The DuPont analysis can be driven from the board room to the shop floor. Everyone can contribute to the success of the organization.

The messages can be clearly stated for all managers and employees:

- Generate sales and sales growth through production of consistent, quality products; effective marketing campaigns; a dedicated, well-trained sales force; and successful new-product introductions.
- Minimize production costs by effectively purchasing raw material, minimizing downtime, minimizing waste and rework, and reducing overhead expenses.
- Minimize selling, general, and administrative expenses by effectively purchasing all supplies, investing in effective marketing campaigns, and holding the line on all spending.
- Limit the investment in working capital by collecting receivables more quickly, managing inventories, developing effective supplier and customer relations to optimize the supply chain throughput, and extending payables where possible.
- Minimize the investment in fixed capital by productively employing idled equipment, and investing in projects with returns that exceed the cost of capital.

- Review the capital structure of the firm, and take corrective action to optimize the amount of leverage employed. This primarily affects the corporate treasurer's office.

Operational and financial metrics can be employed in individual firm and business unit annual performance objectives.

Economic Value Added

Economic value added, or EVA, is a "new" financial performance metric that has been recently popularized by the consulting firm of Stern Stewart and Company. The metric actually originated in 1890 by Alfred Marshall and was used in the 1960s, when it was called *residual income.*

Conceptually, EVA puts on a dollar basis the difference between a company's return on net assets (or return on invested capital) and the company's cost of capital (see Chap. 10). EVA can also be thought of as after-tax operating income (also called net operating profit after taxes) less a capital charge:

$$EVA = NOPAT - (IC * COC)$$

where: EVA   = economic value added

NOPAT = net operating profit after tax

IC   = invested capital

COC   = cost of capital

As advocated by Stern Stewart, NOPAT and invested capital require U.S. GAAP and non-U.S. GAAP adjustments to convert *accounting profit* to *economic profit.* There are potentially 164 adjustments to convert net income to NOPAT and total assets to invested capital. Truly, the "devil is in the detail" of measuring NOPAT and invested capital.

EVA is a new financial performance metric that some firms feel gives them superior insights into managing their business. However, research studies do not find superior company performance as a result of adopting EVA. Each company must decide whether information provided is worth the added complexities and costs of maintaining "another set of non-U.S. GAAP books."

SUMMARY

Financial performance analysis starts with the fundamental financial statements of the firm: income statements, balance sheets, and cash flow statements. Ratios are classified into seven categories:

- Liquidity
- Activity
- Leverage
- Profitability
- Market
- Growth
- Cost management

To be useful, metrics must be related to some standards. One approach is to use the firm's own historical patterns, which involves comparing its metrics for a number of years to determine if it is improving or deteriorating. A second approach is to make comparisons with other firms in the same industry or with best-demonstrated practices firms. Sometimes industry composite data supplied from outside sources will be useful. Sometimes it is necessary to select more directly comparable firms as a basis for relating the ratios of a given firm to those of comparable companies.

The basic financial statement analysis and DuPont ratio analysis were introduced as a systematic approach to structuring a financial analysis. Additional investigation would be required to enrich the analysis.

QUESTIONS AND PROBLEMS

7.1   **Performance metric application.** Summarized below is 1998
       financial information for seven actual companies in seven dif-
       ferent industries. Please identify the companies and match
       the names to the column numbers below:

				Unidentified Companies			
	1	**2**	**3**	**4**	**5**	**6**	**7**
Percent of sales							
Cost of goods sold	16.1	78.1	0.0	77.9	68.1	76.4	50.9
Operating expenses	41.9	16.1	81.5	11.4	23.7	9.0	42.2
Percent of assets							
Cash and cash equivalents	62.3	3.8	3.0	43.2	12.1	1.3	17.9
Accounts receivable	6.5	2.2	0.7	34.8	18.5	3.4	10.2
Inventory	0.0	34.2	0.6	5.5	18.4	1.3	45.5
Current assets	71.1	42.3	5.0	91.7	64.1	6.8	77.2
Net plant, property, and equipment	6.7	47.4	89.2	8.0	18.9	71.3	18.0
Current liabilities	25.6	33.5	15.7	63.2	40.0	12.9	27.7
Interest-bearing debt	0.0	21.2	43.4	0.4	9.8	28.8	27.5
Equity	74.4	42.2	43.2	30.3	50.2	57.9	48.8
DuPont analysis							
Net margin	29.4%	3.2%	12.6%	7.7%	6.3%	7.7%	7.7%
Total asset turnover	0.683	2.784	0.464	2.888	1.398	1.267	1.106
Return on assets	20.1%	8.9%	5.8%	22.1%	8.7%	9.8%	8.5%
Financial leverage	1.345	2.368	2.316	3.301	1.990	1.726	2.048
Return on equity	27.0%	21.0%	13.5%	73.0%	17.4%	16.9%	17.4%
Other metrics							
Current ratio	2.77	1.26	0.32	1.45	1.60	0.53	2.78
Accounts receivable days outstanding	34.92	2.93	5.12	44.00	48.33	9.67	33.72
Inventory days outstanding	n/a	57.33	n/a	8.85	70.38	4.95	295.07

Company	Number
Applebee's	
Wal-Mart	
Dell	
Microsoft	
Royal Caribbean	
Tiffany's	
Hewlett-Packard	

7.2   **International analysis.** The following information is from Table 2.18, Heinz's geographical information. To analyze the business, complete the table below and answer the associated questions.

	Domestic	Foreign	Total	North America	Europe	Asia	Other
1998							
Sales	$4874	$4335	$9209	$5331	$2453	$1016	$409
Operating income*	861	647	1508	906	409	139	54
Identifiable assets	4075	3948	8023	4522	2333	825	343
1997							
Sales	5170	4187	9357	5587	2281	1130	359
Operating income*	705	613	1318	752	374	130	62
Identifiable assets	4475	3963	8438	4941	2241	996	260
1996							
Sales	5236	3876	9112	5598	2134	1086	294
Operating income*	740	548	1288	801	337	114	36
Identifiable assets	4802	3822	8624	5100	2290	978	256

Annual growth rates

Sales

   1996–1997

   1997–1998

   CAGR (96–98)

Operating income*

   1996–1997

   1997–1998

   CAGR (96–98)

Identifiable assets

   1996–1997

   1997–1998

   CAGR (96–98)

DuPont analysis

1998

   Margin

   Turnover

   ROIA†

1997

   Margin

   Turnover

   ROIA†

1996

   Margin

   Turnover

   ROIA†

*Operating income excludes restructuring related items and is before income tax.
†ROIA stands for Return on Identifiable Assets.

A. Which is the fastest growing region with respect to sales? Operating income? Identifiable assets?

B. Which region showed the greatest improvement in asset utilization (turnover)?

C. Which region is the most profitable?

7.3 **DuPont analysis application.** Using the DuPont analysis, discuss the comparative business approach of Tootsie Roll and ConAgra.

1998	Tootsie Roll	ConAgra
Net margin	17.4%	2.6%
Total asset turnover	0.797	2.037
Return on assets	13.8%	5.4%
Financial leverage	1.229	4.211
Return on equity	17.0%	22.6%

SOLUTIONS TO QUESTIONS AND PROBLEMS

7.1

	Microsoft	Wal-Mart	Royal Caribbean	Dell	Hewlett-Packard	Applebee's	Tiffany's
Capital-intensive (NPPE* percent)		X	X			X	
Low inventory DOS†			X			X	
Low accounts receivable DOS		X				X	
Heavy debt loads			X				
Low capital intensity	X			X	X		X
Low-inventory DOS	X			X			
Extended inventory DOS							X
Low cost of goods	X						
Higher debt loads							X

*NPPE: net property, plant, and equipment.
†DOS: days of sales.

7.2

	Domestic	Foreign	Total	North America	Europe	Asia	Other
1998							
Sales	$4874	$4335	$9209	$5331	$2453	$1016	$409
Operating income*	861	647	1508	906	409	139	54
Identifiable assets	4075	3948	8023	4522	2333	825	343
1997							
Sales	5170	4187	9357	5587	2281	1130	359
Operating income*	705	613	1318	752	374	130	62
Identifiable assets	4475	3963	8438	4941	2241	996	260
1996							
Sales	5236	3876	9112	5598	2134	1086	294
Operating income*	740	548	1288	801	337	114	36
Identifiable assets	4802	3822	8624	5100	2290	978	256
Annual growth rates							
Sales							
1996–1997	−1.3%	8.0%	2.7%	−0.2%	6.9%	4.1%	22.1%
1997–1998	−5.7%	3.5%	−1.6%	−4.6%	7.5%	−10.1%	13.9%
CAGR (96–98)	−3.5%	5.8%	0.5%	−2.4%	7.2%	−3.3%	17.9%
Operating income*							
1996–1997	−4.7%	11.9%	2.3%	−6.1%	11.0%	14.0%	72.2%
1997–1998	22.1%	5.5%	14.4%	20.5%	9.4%	6.9%	−12.9%
CAGR (96–98)	7.9%	8.7%	8.2%	6.4%	10.2%	10.4%	22.5%
Identifiable assets							
1996–1997	−6.8%	3.7%	−2.2%	−3.1%	−2.1%	1.8%	1.6%
1997–1998	−8.9%	−0.4%	−4.9%	−8.5%	4.1%	−17.2%	31.9%
CAGR (96–98)	−7.9%	1.6%	−3.5%	−5.8%	0.9%	−8.2%	15.8%
DuPont analysis							
1998							
Margin	17.7%	14.9%	16.4%	17.0%	16.7%	13.7%	13.2%
Turnover	1.20	1.10	1.15	1.18	1.05	1.23	1.19
ROIA†	21.1%	16.4%	18.8%	20.0%	17.5%	16.8%	15.7%
1997							
Margin	13.6%	14.6%	14.1%	13.5%	16.4%	11.5%	17.3%
Turnover	1.16	1.06	1.11	1.13	1.02	1.13	1.38
ROIA†	15.8%	15.5%	15.6%	15.2%	16.7%	13.1%	23.8%
1996							
Margin	14.1%	14.1%	14.1%	14.3%	15.8%	10.5%	12.2%
Turnover	1.09	1.01	1.06	1.10	0.93	1.11	1.15
ROIA†	15.4%	14.3%	14.9%	15.7%	14.7%	11.7%	14.1%

*Operating income excludes restructuring related items and is before income tax.
†ROIA stands for return on identifiable assets.

7.2   (Continued)

	1996	1997	1998	**CAGR** 1996–98
Fastest growth in:				
Sales	n/a	Other	Other	Other
Operating income	n/a	Other	Domestic	Other
Identifiable assets	n/a	Foreign	Other	Other
Most improvement in:				
Asset utilization	n/a	Other	Asia	Europe/Asia
Most profitable:				
Operating margin	Europe	Other	Domestic	n/a
ROIA*	North America	Other	Domestic	n/a

*ROIA stands for Return on Identifiable Assets.
n/a = not available.

7.3   Although ConAgra has a low pretax margin and Tootsie Roll has a high pretax margin, ConAgra's return on equity exceeds Tootsie Roll's return on equity. This occurs despite a higher tax rate faced by ConAgra. ConAgra more effectively uses its assets to generate sales, as seen by the more favorable turnover; for every $1 of assets ConAgra generates over $2.00 of sales, while Tootsie Roll generates less than $0.80 of sales. Additionally, the management team at ConAgra uses leverage to its benefit, while Tootsie Roll remains the most conservative of the industry. That is, every $1 of equity supports $4.21 of assets at ConAgra, but only $1.23 of assets at Tootsie Roll. ConAgra's assets generate sales at the rate of $2.04 per dollar of asset, or that $1 of equity (which supports $4.21 in assets) generates $8.59 in sales. Each dollar of sales generates $0.026 of income, so that $1 of equity (which generates $8.59 in sales) yields $0.226 of net income.

CHAPTER 8

Financial Working Capital Management

Once the firm's broad financial plans have been established, the next step is to set up detailed plans of operations—budgets. A complete budget system encompasses all aspects of the firm's operations over the planning horizon; modifications in plans as required by variations in factors outside the firm's control, especially the level of economic activity, are accounted for by use of flexible budgets.

The budget system provides an integrated picture of the firm's operations as a whole. Therefore, the budget system enables the manager of each division to see the relation of his or her part of the enterprise to the totality of the firm. For example, a production decision to alter the level of work-in-process inventories, or a marketing decision to change the terms under which a particular product is sold, can be traced through the entire budget system to show its effects on the firm's overall profitability.

THE BUDGET SYSTEM

Budgets are developed for every significant activity of the firm. Within each budget program are individual budgets such as a materials budget, a personnel requirements budget, and a facilities or long-run capital expenditures budget. Projections of revenue and cost elements result in the budgeted or pro forma income statement. The projected balance sheet builds on the forecasts of the requirements for the various types of assets to support the anticipated sales. Of particular interest is the cash budget.

Cash Budgeting

The cash budget indicates the combined effects of the budgeted operations on the firm's cash flow. If an increase in the volume of operations results in a negative cash flow, the cash budget will show the amount of additional financing required and its timing. The cash budget indicates the amount of funds needed month by month, or even week by week or day by day (for a firm with widely fluctuating receipts and disbursements), and is one of the financial manager's most important tools. An illustrative case example is therefore provided for a textile company.

The textile company is analyzing the seasonal nature of its cash flows to formulate a proposal for a credit line from its commercial banks. The pattern of its sales is as follows: January through July, November, and December at $100,000; August at $200,000, September at $300,000, and October at $400,000.

Cash received on sales amounts to 10 percent in the current month of sales, 70 percent in the month following the sales. Obligations for labor, both direct and indirect, incurred each month are $10,000 per month plus 20 percent of sales in the current month plus 10 percent of sales in the following month. Raw materials purchases are $30,000 plus 20 percent of next month's sales. Salaries for general administrative expenses are $6000 per month. Selling expenses are 10 percent of current monthly sales. Depreciation charges are $5000 per month. Estimated quarterly income tax payments of $11,000 are paid in January, April, July, and October and are one-fourth of the estimated annual current profits. Cash on hand on January 1 is $50,000. A minimum cash balance of $20,000 needs to be maintained for transaction purposes.

The nature of the textile company's business is highly seasonal. The pattern of cash flows is set out in the cash budget developed in Table 8.1. In the top portion a worksheet is used to determine the collections on sales and the payments for labor and raw materials. The data from the work sheet are used in the cash budget, which begins with the receipts from collections. Next, each payment category is listed for each month. The difference between cash receipts and cash payments is the net increase or decrease in cash during the month. For January, the net decrease in cash is $17,000. The initial cash of $50,000 is reduced by $17,000 to an end-of-month amount of $33,000. Since the desired level of cash is $20,000, the firm has excess cash of $13,000 as of the end of January. This same type of analysis is carried out for each month. The bottom line, excess cash or borrowing needed, represents the cumulative borrowing requirements for the firm at the end of each month.

Because collections are made during the two months following sales, the rise in sales volume from August through October causes the cash position to become negative, causing a maximum borrowing need of $167,000 by the end of September. As the accounts receivable are collected, the firm moves into a positive cash position by November, ending the year with excess cash of $154,000. Thus, although the firm has a negative cash change during each of the first nine months of the year, it ends the year with a positive cash position. It begins the year with an initial amount of cash in excess of the desired level because of the negative cash change for each month. On the basis of the pattern revealed

TABLE 8.1
Cash Budget, 2000 ($000)

Worksheet	Jan.	Feb.	Mar.	Apr.	May	June	July	Aug.	Sept.	Oct.	Nov.	Dec.
Sales	100	100	100	100	100	100	100	200	300	400	100	100
Collections:												
1st month	10	10	10	10	10	10	10	20	30	40	10	10
2d month	70	70	70	70	70	70	70	70	140	210	280	70
3d month	20	20	20	20	20	20	20	20	20	40	60	80
Total	100	100	100	100	100	100	100	110	190	290	350	160
Labor	40	40	40	40	40	40	50	80	110	100	40	40
Payments	40	40	40	40	40	40	50	80	110	100	40	40
Raw materials	50	50	50	50	50	50	70	90	110	50	50	50
Payments	50	50	50	50	50	50	50	70	90	110	50	50
Cash Budget												
Receipts:												
Collections	100	100	100	100	100	100	100	110	190	290	350	160
Payments:												
Labor	40	40	40	40	40	40	50	80	110	100	40	40
Raw materials	50	50	50	50	50	50	50	70	90	110	50	50
G&A salaries	6	6	6	6	6	6	6	6	6	6	6	6
Selling expenses	10	10	10	10	10	10	10	20	30	40	10	10
Income taxes	11			11			11			11		
Total payments	117	106	106	117	106	106	127	176	236	267	106	106
Net cash gain (loss)	(17)	(6)	(6)	(17)	(6)	(6)	(27)	(66)	(46)	23	244	54
Initial cash	50	33	27	21	4	(2)	(8)	(35)	(101)	147	(124)	120
EOM cash	33	27	21	4	(2)	(8)	(35)	(101)	(147)	(124)	120	174
Desired cash	20	20	20	20	20	20	20	20	20	20	20	20
Excess cash: (borrowing needed)	13	7	1	(16)	(22)	(28)	(55)	(121)	(167)	(144)	100	154

by the cash budget, it will be necessary for the firm to make arrangements for financing at least $167,000 by September. But it will be able to repay the loan by the end of November. During the months the firm has cash in excess of its requirements, the textile company uses the funds in short-term investments that will provide interest or other forms of return. Note that depreciation is a noncash expenditure.

The Nature of the Budgeting Process

Historically, budgeting was treated as a device to limit expenditures. The more modern approach is to view the budgeting process as a tool for obtaining the most productive and profitable use of the company's resources. Budgets are reviewed to compare plans and results—a process called *controlling to plan*. It is a continuous monitoring procedure, reviewing and evaluating performance with reference to previously established standards.

Budgets imposed in an arbitrary fashion may represent impossible targets at the one extreme, or standards that are too lax at the other. If standards are unrealistically high, frustrations and resentment will develop. If standards are unduly lax, costs will be out of control, profits will suffer, and morale will become flabby. However, a set of budgets based on a clear understanding and careful analysis of the firm's operations can play an important positive role.

Budgets, therefore, can provide valuable guides to both high-level executives and middle-management personnel. Well-formulated and effectively developed budgets make subordinates aware of the fact that top management has a realistic understanding of the nature of operations in the business firm. Thus, the budget also becomes an important communication link between top managers and the divisional personnel whom they guide.

Profit Planning—Breakeven Analysis

In a sense, all topics of financial management are concerned with profit planning. All decisions are oriented to improving sales, improving efficiency, controlling costs, and making the most effective utilization of investments. Hence, all these decisions contribute to profit improvement and are a part of profit planning. Breakeven analysis has a particular function to perform: It is a type of profit planning approach for studying the relationships among sales, fixed costs, and variable costs.

In general, by incurring fixed costs, the firm can reduce costs of operations if a sufficient volume of business is generated. For example, many operations in manufacturing, such as cutting pieces of metal or punching out holes from pieces of metal, can be performed less expensively with machinery if a sufficient volume of business is involved.

Therefore, if only two pieces of metal are to be cut, or only three holes punched out of a piece of metal per day, it would be cheaper to have a worker do it as a part of her or his other duties. On the other hand, if millions of pieces of metal or millions of holes must be punched out per day, the job will be done less expensively by automating it.

Therefore, the essence of breakeven analysis is to provide a guide for making decisions among alternative ways of doing things. Four types of decisions may be involved: (1) When a firm is planning a general expansion in the level of operations, it has to make a choice between the extent to which additional fixed plants will be purchased and whether additional facilities will be rented or leased. (2) A similar type of decision is involved in connection with new products. The basic question here is how large the sales volume on a new product must be if the firm is to break even. (3) In analyzing whether to modernize or automate its operations, the firm has to choose between the use of fixed costs versus variable costs. (4) The most general and central aspect is involved in competitive strategies. At a sufficient volume of operation and with a sufficient investment, the firm may be able to reduce its costs so that it may reduce its prices. Thus, breakeven analysis is a tool to be used in the firm's effort to achieve cost leadership in its industry. This is in part a matter of cost efficiency and in part a matter of utilizing fixed costs and equipment that will reduce the per unit cost at projected levels of operations.

The central ideas involved in breakeven analysis are illustrated by Table 8.2. Here the situation for three firms is set forth. In each case they have the same selling price of $6 per unit. Firm A has the smallest dollar amount of fixed costs, but the highest variable cost per unit. Firm C has the highest amount of fixed costs but the lowest amount of variable costs per unit. As would be expected, firm C achieves its breakeven point at the largest sales volume, 50,000 units, or a total of $300,000. Firm A, in contrast, achieves a breakeven at 30,000 units with sales of $180,000. At a low volume of 10,000 units, firm C achieves the greatest loss of the three.

The nature of breakeven analysis may be illustrated by a series of charts reflecting the data for each of the three firms, as shown in Fig. 8.1. The nature of the breakeven charts can be explained by using the data for firm B. Its fixed costs are $120,000. Volume produced is measured on the horizontal axis. Income is measured on the vertical axis. The revenue line is constructed by graphing the units sold on the horizontal axis against sales dollars on the vertical axis. For the corresponding volume of units sold, total costs are graphed from the corresponding column of figures from Table 8.2. The slope of the total income line is $6 per unit; the slope of the total cost line is the variable cost per unit, which is $3. Thus, in the illustration for firm B, the slope of the selling price line is twice as steep as the slope of the total cost line; but the total cost line starts from a higher position on the vertical axis. Thus some required volume has to be achieved before the greater slope of the total revenue line overcomes the higher starting point of the total cost line. The point at which the two lines intersect is the breakeven point. By contrasting the three different combinations of fixed costs and variable costs, we have illustrated different degrees of operating leverage.

TABLE 8.2

Profit Planning

Firm A	Firm B	Firm C
Selling price = $6	Selling price = $6	Selling price = $6
Fixed costs = $60,000	Fixed costs = $120,000	Fixed costs = $200,000
Variable costs = $4	Variable costs = $3	Variable costs = $2

Units Sold (Q)	Sales	Costs	Profit
Firm A			
10,000	$ 60,000	$100,000	–$ 40,000
20,000	120,000	140,000	–20,000
30,000	180,000	180,000	0
40,000	240,000	220,000	20,000
50,000	300,000	260,000	40,000
60,000	360,000	300,000	60,000
90,000	540,000	420,000	120,000
Firm B			
10,000	$ 60,000	$150,000	–$ 90,000
20,000	120,000	180,000	–60,000
30,000	180,000	210,000	–30,000
40,000	240,000	240,000	0
50,000	300,000	270,000	30,000
60,000	360,000	300,000	60,000
90,000	540,000	390,000	150,000
Firm C			
10,000	$ 60,000	$220,000	–$160,000
20,000	120,000	240,000	–120,000
30,000	180,000	260,000	–80,000
40,000	240,000	280,000	–40,000
50,000	300,000	300,000	0
60,000	360,000	320,000	40,000
90,000	540,000	380,000	160,000

FIGURE 8.1

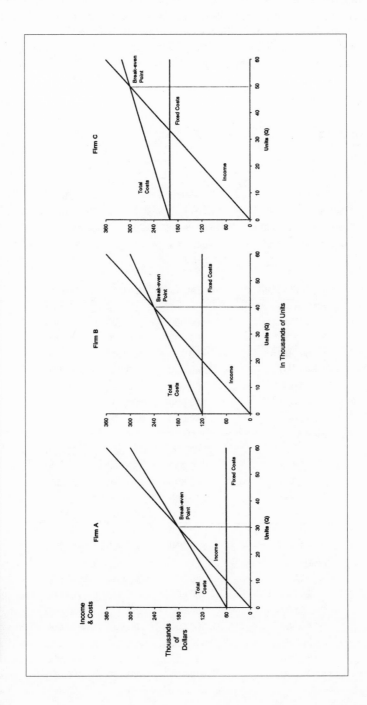

The degree of operating leverage, starting from some specified level of units sold, is defined as the percentage change in operating income resulting from the percentage change in units sold.

Degree of operating leverage

$$= \frac{\text{percent change in operating income (OI)}}{\text{percent change in units sold } Q} \qquad (8.1)$$

Thus for firm B in Fig. 8.1, the degree of operating leverage (OL) at 50,000 units of sales is

$$
\begin{aligned}
\text{Degree of OL}_B &= \frac{\Delta(OI)/OI}{\Delta Q/Q} \\
&= \frac{(\$60,000 - \$30,000)/\$30,000}{(60,000 - 50,000)/50,000} \\
&= \frac{\$30,000/\$30,000}{10,000/50,000} \\
&= \frac{100\%}{20\%} \\
&= 5.0
\end{aligned}
$$

A simplified formula for calculating the degree of operating leverage can also be set forth.

$$\text{Degree of operating leverage of point } Q = \frac{S - VC}{S - VC - FC} \qquad (8.2)$$

Thus the degree of operating leverage is sales S minus variable costs VC divided by sales minus variable costs minus fixed costs FC. Using the formula in Eq. (8.2), the degree of operating leverage at 50,000 units is

$$OL = \frac{\$300,000 - \$150,000}{\$30,000} = \frac{\$150,000}{\$30,000} = 5$$

The two methods, of course, give the same answer: The operating leverage is 5. The significance of the result 5 is that having moved past its breakeven point at 50,000 units sold, any percentage change in units sold will magnify the percentage in profits by a multiple of 5. That is, as you can see in Table 8.2, an increase in the number of units sold from 50,000 to 60,000, or 20 percent, results in an increase in B's profit from $30,000 to $60,000, or 100 percent. A 20 percent increase in the number of units sold results in a 100 percent increase in profits (i.e., 20 percent times the 5, the degree of operating leverage).

Cash Breakeven Analysis

Of particular interest is to translate ordinary breakeven analysis to cash breakeven analysis. Some of the firm's revenues may be in receivables, so that not all sales will represent cash inflows. Some of the firm's fixed costs may be noncash outflows, such as depreciation. The concept of a cash breakeven chart will be illustrated by assuming that $50,000 of fixed costs for firm C is depreciation charges. If $50,000 of the $200,000 fixed costs of firm C is depreciation, the cash fixed costs are only $150,000. The cash breakeven point would therefore be lower than the 50,000 units of profit breakeven point. The cash breakeven point drops to $37,500.

Breakeven analysis using straight-line relationships is useful as a first approximation to understand the general nature of the problem. More sophisticated analysis will require modifications in the relationships set forth. However, even in more complex situations, the basic concepts and principles involved are often indicated by linear breakeven analysis.

INVESTMENT IN CURRENT ASSETS

Gross working capital has traditionally been defined as the firm's total current assets. The term has a double meaning: (1) an investment requirement and (2) liquid assets. Current assets represent the amount of *near cash* or liquid investment a firm must have in order to support its sales volume. Cash, marketable securities, accounts receivable, and inventories constitute assets that are relatively more liquid than fixed assets to meet the claims of short-term creditors. The current asset-debt relationship is conveyed by the concept of net working capital, defined as current assets minus current liabilities. Thus, the management of working capital requires an understanding of the principles both of determining the correct amount and mix of current assets and raising funds to finance these assets.

Investments in current assets are important for at least three reasons. (1) Current assets generally represent more than one-half of the total assets of a business firm. Since current assets is the largest category of investment by the firm, changes in working capital policies may cause substantial variations in financing required. If a firm's average collection period is 30 days and its credit sales are $2000 per day, its investment in accounts receivables will be $60,000. If its average collection period increases to 50 days, its investment in receivables will rise to $100,000. But with an average collection period of 10 days, its investment in receivables would be $20,000. Thus a reduction in investment from $100,000 to $20,000 is equivalent to avoiding $80,000 in financing that otherwise would be required. (2) There is a direct relationship between the growth of sales and the need to finance additional assets of the firm. For example, if the standard for an industry is an average collection period of 30 days and credit sales are $2000 per day, the initial situation above, the investment in accounts receivable will be $60,000. If sales rise to $3000 per day, the investment in accounts receivable will increase to $90,000. The growth of sales also produces requirements for additional inventories and for cash balances. (3) Investments in current assets are especially important for small firms. A small firm can reduce its investment in fixed assets by buying used equipment and by renting or leasing plant and equipment, but it is not possible to reduce the investment in current assets to the same degree.

Cash Management

Cash management is the first task of controlling the investment in current assets. *Cash* refers to the firm's holdings of currency and demand deposits (checking accounts) at commercial banks. Since demand deposits are used in about 90 percent of the volume of business transactions, it is likely to be the major type of cash item.

Sound working capital management requires investment in cash for a number of reasons. Holding cash for transactions enables the firm to conduct its ordinary business of purchasing, selling, and so on. Another reason for holding cash has been referred to as the precautionary motive, similar to the idea of "safety stocks" discussed in inventory management below. Also, it is essential that the firm have sufficient funds to take cash discounts. Since the current and quick ratios are key items in credit analysis, the firm must meet the financial standards or norms of the line of business in which it is engaged in order to maintain its credit standing. A strong credit standing enables the firm to purchase goods from trade suppliers on favorable terms and to maintain its line of credit with banks and other sources of financing. The firm should have sufficient liquidity to meet emergencies such as strikes, fires, or the marketing campaigns of its competitors. This in turn affects the borrowing flexibility of the firm, determining the firm's ability to borrow additional cash as required. The speculative motive (the third reason) for holding cash involves being ready for favorable business opportunities that may come along from time to time.

Building upon her or his knowledge of cash flows (developed in the preceding chapters), the financial manager may be able to improve the inflow-outflow pattern of cash. He or she can do so by better synchronization of flows and by reduction of float. Float refers to funds in transit. For example, checks received from customers in distant cities are subject to two types of delays: the time required for the check to travel in the mail and the time required for clearing through the banking system.

To reduce these two types of float, a *lock box plan* can be used. If a firm makes sales in large amounts at far distances, it can establish a lockbox in a post office located in the customer's area. It can arrange to have customers send payments to the postal box in their city and then have a bank pick up the checks and deposit them in a special checking account. The bank then has the checks cleared in the local area and remits by wire to the firm's bank deposit.

Mathematical models have been developed to help determine the optimal cash balances. These models are variations on basic inventory models, whose nature will be conveyed by the discussion of inventory models in the last section of this chapter.

Marketable Securities

Firms report varying amounts of marketable securities among their current assets. One motive for holding marketable securities or *near monies* is to use them as a buffer or safety stock against cash shortages. Alternatively, a firm may have cash which is temporarily invested in marketable securities for a number of reasons, such as seasonal or cyclical business fluctuations. Also because of uncertainties as to future needs, a firm may have cash funds to invest in temporary investments for a few weeks to several years, or indefinitely. At the end of 1999, Ford Motor Company held $18.9 billion in marketable securities, sometimes also called *short-term investments*.

Management of Investment Receivables

In recent years firms' investments in accounts receivables have been growing. This has been true particularly of larger firms that have access to capital markets and utilize their greater fundraising ability to extend credit to their customers.

The major determinants of the level of receivables are (1) volume of credit sales, (2) seasonality of sales, (3) rules for credit limits, (4) terms of sales and credit policies of individual firms, and (5) collection policies. The ratio of receivables to sales generally ranges from 8 to 12 percent; or on average, approximately one month's sales are in receivables. However, wide variations are experienced among firms, reflecting the differential impact of the factors listed above.

The basis of a firm's credit policy is its industry characteristic credit terms; generally, a firm must meet the terms provided by other firms in the industry. However, a central task in formulating credit policy is an evaluation of the creditworthiness of the potential customer.

To evaluate the credit risk, the credit manager considers the five C's of credit: character, capacity, capital, collateral, and conditions. (1) *Character* refers to the probability that customers will try to honor their obligations. This factor is of considerable importance because every credit transaction implies a promise to pay. Experienced credit professionals frequently emphasize that the moral factor is the most important issue in a credit evaluation. (2) *Capacity* refers to the ability of the customer to pay. This is judged by reviewing his or her past record of payments, observing the customer's plant or store, evaluating her or his business methods. (3) *Capital* is measured by the general financial position of the firm as indicated by financial ratio analysis, with special emphasis on the tangible net worth (stockholders' equity less intangibles such as goodwill) of the enterprise. (4) *Collateral* is represented by assets that the customer may offer as a pledge for security of the credit extended. (5) Finally, *conditions* refer to the impact of general economic trends on the firm, or to special developments in certain areas of the economy that may affect the customer's ability to meet her or his obligations.

The five C's of credit represent the factors by which the creditworthiness of a customer is judged. Information on these items is obtained from the firm's previous experience with the customer, supplemented by a well-developed system of information-gathering groups. Two major sources of external information are available for this purpose. The first is the work of the local credit associations. By periodic meetings of local groups and by direct communication, information on experience with debtors is exchanged. More formally, credit interchange, a system developed by the National Association of Credit Management for assembling and distributing information of debtors' past performance, is also provided. The interchange reports show the paying record of the debtor, industries from which he or she is buying, and the trading areas in which purchases are being made. The second source is the work of the credit-reporting agencies, the best known of which is Dun & Bradstreet. Agencies that specialize in coverage of a limited number of industries also provide credit information.

The terms of credit set forth the conditions under which a discount may be granted and the date that payment is due. Terms of 2/10, net 30, mean that a 2 percent discount from the sales price is granted if payment is made within 10 days; if the discount is not taken, the entire amount is due 30 days from the invoice date. Terms of net 60 indicate that no discount is offered. A toy manufacturer may utilize season dating such as 2/10, net 30, November 1 dating. These terms indicate that the effective invoice date is November 1, so the discount may be taken until November 10, or the full amount paid on November 30. Season dating may induce some customers to buy early, reducing storage costs for the toy manufacturer and giving earlier indications as to total sales for the season.

Collection policy describes the processes by which the firm seeks to obtain payment of its accounts receivable. Collection policies should seek a balance between pressure to avoid excessive investment in receivables and maintaining customers' goodwill. Collection policies should seek to expand sales to the point at which the present value of returns from incremental sales equals the present value of incremental costs. The collection processes are also an opportunity to provide customer counseling to help increase the ability to pay his or her bills.

Managing Inventory Investments

The major determinants of investments in inventory are level of sales, length and technical nature of production processes, durability versus perishability or style factor in the end product, ordering costs, and storage costs. Although wide variations occur, inventory-to-sales ratios are generally concentrated in the 12 to 20 percent range. Within limits set by the economics of a firm's industry, there exists a potential for improvement in inventory control by use of computers and operations research.

Managing assets of all kinds is basically an inventory-type problem—the same method of analysis applies to cash, receivables, and fixed assets as applies to inventories themselves. First, a basic stock must be on hand to balance inflows and outflows of the items, with the size of the stock depending upon the patterns of flows, whether regular or irregular. Second, because the unexpected may always occur, it is necessary to have safety stocks on hand. These safety stocks represent the little extra necessary to avoid the cost of not having enough to meet current needs. Third, additional amounts may be required to meet future growth needs. These are anticipation stocks. Related to anticipation stocks is the recognition that there are optimum purchase sizes, defined as economic order quantities (EOQs). In borrowing money, in buying raw materials for production, or in purchasing plant and equipment, it is usually cheaper to buy more than just enough to meet immediate needs.

Holding costs (carrying costs) represent storage costs, insurance, depreciation, and the cost of funds tied up in the inventory. The cost of ordering inventories consists of the cost of placing orders, shipping and handling, and so on. They are the fixed costs of purchasing and recording an order. The total cost of inventories is obtained by combining these rising and declining elements of cost. The total cost of holding inventories is minimized by choosing an optimal ordering quantity. The economic order quantity represents the minimum point on the total cost curve associated with various sizes of ordering quantities.

The basic inventory model recognizes that certain costs (carrying costs) rise as average inventory holdings increase, but that other costs (ordering costs and stockout costs) fall as average inventory holdings rise. The economic ordering quantity model is designed to locate an

TABLE 8.3

Inventory Problem Scenario

1. Estimated annual sales = 490,000 units (S)
2. Safety stock = 5000 units
3. Ordering costs = $400 per order ($F$)
4. Holding costs (per unit) (C) = $2.00 per unit per year

optimal order size that will minimize total inventory costs. The data required in formal procedures determining the optimal order quantity and the associated considerations are set forth in Table 8.3.

From the data in Table 8.3, an analysis of cost patterns for a range of order sizes is set forth in Table 8.4. The logic of Table 8.4 is conveyed by explaining the numbers in the column which begins with an order size of 14,000 units. The estimated annual sales of 490,000 units is divided by the order size of 14,000 to obtain the number of orders, 35. Average inventory is the safety stock of 5000 units plus one-half the order size of 14,000, or 7000, to total 12,000 units. Holding cost of $2 per unit multiplied by the average inventory of 12,000 gives the total holding cost of $24,000. The ordering costs of $400 per order multiplied by the number of orders, 35, equal the total ordering costs, or $14,000. The total costs represent the sum of ordering costs of $14,000 plus holding costs of $24,000, for a total of $38,000.

TABLE 8.4

Numerical Solution for EOQ

1. Order size Q	1,000	5,000	10,000	14,000	49,000	245,000
2. Number of orders $N = S/Q$	490	98	49	35	10	2
3. Ordering costs ($400 × N)	$196,000	$39,200	$19,600	$14,000	$ 4,000	$ 800
4. Average inventory* A	5,500	7,500	10,000	12,000	29,500	127,500
5. Holding costs ($2 × A)	$ 11,000	$15,000	$20,000	$24,000	$59,000	$255,000
Total costs (3 + 5)	$207,000	$54,200	$39,600	$38,000	$63,000	$255,800

*Average inventory = A = Safety stock plus (order size)/2.

As shown in Table 8.4 and Fig. 8.1: As the order size is increased, average inventory rises and holding costs increase; as the order size increases, ordering costs decline. The lowest total cost is achieved at an order size of 14,000 units. The EOQ formula can also be used to obtain the same result for the optimal order quantity.

We can then verify that EOQ represents that order quantity that achieves the minimum total inventory costs. The EOQ formula is

$$EOQ = \sqrt{\frac{2FS}{C}}$$

where EOQ = economic ordering quantity, or optimum quantity to order each time an order is placed
     F = fixed costs of placing and receiving an order (ordering costs)
     S = annual sales in units
     C = carrying cost per unit of inventory (holding costs)

Using the EOQ formula, the solution to the problem posed is as follows:

$$\text{Optimal order quantity} = \sqrt{\frac{(2)(400)(490,000)}{2.00}} = 14,000 \text{ units}$$

The result is the same as illustrated in Fig. 8.2 and is the order quantity with the minimum cost.

FIGURE 8.2

Inventory Costs in Relation to Order Size

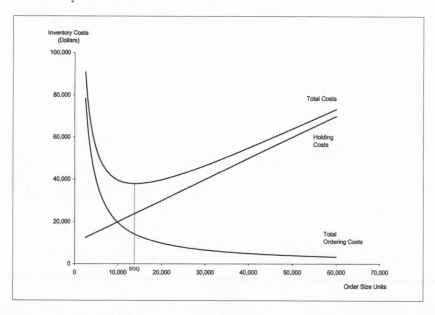

The entire approach to inventory management has been profoundly changed by new Internet transaction procedures.

SHORT-TERM FINANCING

Short-term credit is defined as debt originally scheduled for payment within 1 year. Ranked by their relative importance in supplying credit to business, the main sources of short-term financing are (1) trade credit, (2) commercial banks, and (3) commercial paper.

Trade Credit

In the ordinary course of events, a firm buys its supplies and materials on credit from other firms, recording the debt as an account payable. Accounts payable, or trade credit as it is commonly called, is the largest single category of short-term credit, representing about 40 percent of the current liabilities of nonfinancial corporations. The percentage is somewhat larger for smaller firms, since they may not qualify for financing from other sources.

Whether trade credit costs more or less than other forms of financing is a moot question. If the buyer does not have forms of financing alternative to trade credit, the costs to the buyer may be commensurate with the risks to the seller. However, in some instances, trade credit is used simply because the user may not realize how expensive it is. In such circumstances, careful financial analysis may lead to the substitution of alternative forms of financing for trade credit.

Commercial Banks

Commercial bank lending appears on the balance sheet as notes payable and is second in importance to trade credit as a source of short-term financing. Banks occupy a pivotal position in the short-term and intermediate-term money markets. Measurement of the effective (true) rate of interest depends upon the method of charging interest by the lender, as shown by Table 8.5. If the interest is paid at the maturity of the loan, the stated rate of interest is the effective rate of interest, or 8 percent. If the bank deducts the interest in advance (discounts the loan), the effective rate of interest is increased to 8.7 percent.

A compensating balance of 20 percent raises the effective interest rate to 10 percent. If the loan is repaid in 12 monthly installments, the effective rate of interest is doubled. The borrower has the full amount of money only during the first month, and by the last month he or she has already repaid eleven-twelfths of the loan and so has the use of only one-half of the face amount of the loan. Under the discounting

TABLE 8.5

Cost of Bank Credit

1. Simple interest method

$$\text{Cost} = \frac{\$8000}{\$100,000} = 8.0\%$$

2. Effect of discount

$$\text{Cost} = \frac{\$8000}{\$100,000 - \$8000} = 8.7\%$$

3. Effect of compensating balance

$$\text{Cost} = \frac{\$8000}{\$100,000 - \$20,000} = 10\%$$

4. Interest rate on average amount of amortized loan

$$\text{Cost} = \frac{\$8000}{\$50,000} \cong 16\%$$

5. Interest rate on discounted amortized loan

$$\text{Cost} = \frac{\$8000}{\$92,000/2} \cong 17.39\%$$

method, the effective cost of the installment loan would be 17.39 percent.

Banks now have close relationships with their borrowers. Since there is considerable personal contact over the years, the borrower's business problems are frequently discussed; thus the bank often provides informal management counseling services. With heightened competition between commercial banks and other financial institutions, the aggressiveness of banks has increased. Modern commercial banks now offer a wide range of financial business services. In addition, most large banks have business development departments that provide counseling to firms and serve as intermediaries on a wide variety of their requirements.

Commercial Paper

Commercial paper consists of promissory notes of large firms and is sold primarily to other business firms, insurance companies, pension funds, and banks. Maturities of commercial paper vary from 2 to 6 months, with an average of about 5 months. The rates on prime commercial paper vary, but they are generally below those on prime business loans.

Several advantages may be achieved by use of the commercial paper market. (1) It permits the broadest and most advantageous distribution of paper. (2) It provides more funds at lower rates than do other methods. (3) The borrower avoids the inconveniences and expense of financing arrangements with a number of institutions, each possibly requiring a compensating balance. (4) Publicity and prestige accrue to borrowers as their product and paper become more widely known. (5) Finally, the commercial paper dealer frequently offers valuable advice to clients.

A basic limitation of the commercial paper market is that the amount of funds available is limited to the excess liquidity that corporations, the main suppliers of funds, may have at any particular time. Another disadvantage is that a debtor who may be experiencing temporary financial difficulties will not be able to obtain credit extensions because commercial paper dealings are impersonal.

Use of Security in Short-Term Financing

Sometimes a potential borrower's credit rating is not sufficiently strong to justify an unsecured loan. If the borrower can pledge some forms of collateral as security to be claimed by the lender in the event of default, the lender may extend credit to an otherwise unacceptable firm. The most common types of collateral used for short-term credit are accounts receivables and inventories.

Accounts receivable financing can be done either by pledging the receivables or by selling them outright—factoring. When the receivables are pledged, the borrower retains the risk that the person or firm who owes the receivable will not pay; but this risk is typically passed on to the lender when factoring is involved. Because the factor takes the risk of default, she or he will typically investigate the purchaser's credit. Therefore, the factor can perform three services—a lending function, a risk-bearing function, and a credit-checking function. When receivables are pledged, the lender typically performs only the first of these three functions. Consequently, factoring is more expensive than pledging accounts receivable.

The nature of factoring can be conveyed by an illustrative example. The selling firm A receives an order of $12,000 payable in 30 days after delivery. The factor checks and approves the order. After the goods are shipped, the factor makes funds available to the seller. The factoring commission for credit checking is 2 percent of the invoice price, or $240. If the interest expense is computed at the prime rate plus a 2 percent premium, e.g., at a 10 percent annual rate on the invoice price, it will be

$$\frac{1}{12} \times 0.10 \times 12,000 = \$100$$

The factor will, in addition, hold back a reserve (in this instance assumed to be 10 percent of the invoice) until the account has been collected to provide for disputes over damaged goods, goods returned by the buyers, and so on. When funds are received from the factor, the accounting entry on the seller's books will be as follows:

Cash	10,460	
Interest expense	100	
Factoring commission	240	
Reserve due from factor on collection of account	1,200	
Accounts receivable		12,000

When the factor collects the face of the invoice at the end of the 30 days, the reserve held back is paid to the seller. The process is a continuous one, so the amount actually remitted by the factor occurs when the reserve exceeds some specified percentage of accounts receivable on which the factor has made advances.

Loans may also be secured by inventories. When inventories are held in public warehouses, a trust receipt is issued and conveyed to a lender in a loan transaction. When the technique, known as a field warehousing arrangement, is used, the inventory pledged for a loan is under the physical control of a warehouse company, which releases the inventory only on order from the lending institution. Payments are then remitted to the lender by the seller of goods when received from the buyers. Canned goods, lumber, steel, coal, and other standardized products are the type of goods usually covered in field warehouse arrangements.

Short-term financing is particularly important for meeting the fluctuating needs of business firms and particularly important for new and smaller firms. The risks and limited financing alternatives available to new and smaller firms make it difficult for them to obtain long-term financing. The main reason for this is that lenders on a long-term basis are committing themselves to the future of the firm, and repayment depends upon the firm's success over an extended period. Hence, since the risks of newer and smaller firms are large, lenders may be unwilling to make long-term commitments. Thus, short-term financing (often secured) is generally the lifeblood of new and smaller firms.

WORKING CAPITAL POLICY

The decision criteria for analysis of investment in current assets have been set forth, and the nature and costs of alternative sources of short-term financing were described. These two streams of analysis are now brought together by a consideration of working capital policy. Working capital policy involves decisions with respect to (1) the mix of current and fixed assets, (2) the mix of short-term debt and long-term debt, and (3) the relation between current assets and current liabilities. The third aspect has already been covered in connection with financial ratio analysis as the current ratio, which is a measure of the firm's liquidity or solvency.

Although both current assets and fixed assets are functions of expected sales, only current assets can readily be adjusted to actual sales in the short run. Hence, the burden of making adjustments to short-run fluctuations in sales must be carried by working capital management. The investment in fixed assets can be reduced by renting or leasing rather than owning fixed assets.

In some respects, life is made easier for the managers of a firm by following a slack policy with regard to investment in current assets. For example, if inventories are ample, the risk of loss of sales due to stockout is lower. If credit terms are more liberal or if collections are lax, a firm may be able to increase sales, but only at the expense of greater investment in current assets and possibly higher bad debt loss ratios.

Alternatively, a firm could follow a very tight or aggressive policy toward investment in current assets. Inventories could be held to a minimum, credit terms could be very tight, and collections could be very vigorously pursued. But this alternative working capital policy is likely to have an adverse effect on sales. A balanced investment policy would be required.

Slack working capital is indicated to have higher fixed costs because of excessive investment in inventory associated with greater warehousing expenses, and so on. Thus, tight working capital policy is associated with lower fixed costs. However, tighter working capital policy will have higher variable costs because there will be more frequent ordering of goods for inventory. Also, on inventory stockouts greater expenses may be incurred to attempt to obtain inventory under emergency conditions. The cost conditions for the optimal policy will be between these two extremes.

The larger the percentage of funds obtained from long-term sources, the more conservative the firm's working capital policy. Short-term debt normally carries a lower interest rate than long-term debt. However, during periods of tight money, short-term interest rates may be higher than long-term interest rates. The greater the short-term debt, the greater the probability that during a period of tight money the firm may not be able to renew its short-term debt. On the other hand, the use of short-term debt provides the firm with added flexibility under those circumstances when the need for funds fluctuates or is seasonal. When the need for funds is seasonal, e.g., short-term loans are liquidated within the year, it would be more expensive to cover such financing by long-term debt.

SUMMARY

The four primary reasons for holding cash are the transactions motive, the precautionary motive, to meet future needs, and to satisfy bank compensating balance requirements. The two major aspects of a cash flow system involve the gathering and disbursement of cash, with the firm's objective to speed collections and legitimately slow disbursements.

Float arises from lags in the payment process (mail, processing, and bank clearing delays). Float is an advantage to the firm as a buyer and a disadvantage to the firm as a seller. An efficient cash-gathering system will focus on reducing negative mail float with decentralized collections and a lockbox system. The use of the lockbox also reduces processing time by starting checks through the bank clearing process before they have been recorded in the firm's accounting system.

Companies' liquidity policies vary with individual circumstances and needs. In selecting the firm's portfolio of marketable securities, the financial manager must consider financial risk, interest rate risk, purchasing power risk, liquidity or marketability, taxability, and relative yields. The securities which have best suited the financial manager's objectives are short-term U.S. government issues, plus those of the very strongest domestic and foreign banks and corporations.

In establishing a credit policy, a firm formulates its credit standards and its credit terms. Credit standards that are too strict will lose sales; credit standards that are too easy will result in excessive bad-debt losses. To determine optimal credit standards, the firm relates the marginal costs of credit to the marginal profits on the increased sales. Individual customers are evaluated on the five C's of credit: character, capacity, capital, collateral, and conditions, all of which indicate the likelihood that the buyer will pay its obligations. Credit analysis and the evaluation of prospective customers typically include analysis of financial ratios, the average age of accounts receivable, and record of past payments. They also incorporate the experience of the credit manager in similar situations.

The terms of credit specify the credit period and the use of cash discounts. Longer credit periods stimulate sales, but the optimal credit period balances the marginal profits on increased sales against the costs of carrying the higher amounts of accounts receivable. Similarly, an optimal cash discount policy balances the benefit of increased sales and the costs of discounts taken.

The basic inventory model recognizes that certain costs (carrying costs) rise as average inventory holdings increase, but that certain other costs (ordering costs and stockout costs) fall. The two sets of costs make up the total costs of ordering and carrying inventories, and the EOQ model is designed to locate an optimal order size that will minimize total inventory costs.

Short-term financial management encompasses working capital management and involves all aspects of the administration of current assets and current liabilities. The first policy question deals with the determination of the level of total current assets to be held. Current assets vary with sales, but the ratio of current assets to sales is a policy matter. A firm that elects to operate aggressively will hold relatively small stocks of current assets, a policy that will reduce the required level of investment and increase the expected rate of return on investment. However, an aggressive policy also increases the likelihood of losing sales because of lack of inventories or because of an excessively tough credit policy.

The second policy question concerns the relationships among types of assets and the way these assets are financed. One policy calls for matching asset and liability maturities by financing current assets with short-term debt and fixed assets with long-term debt or equity. But this policy is unsound, because current assets include "permanent" investments that increase as sales grow. In our judgment, the financing of current assets should recognize that some portion bears a constant relationship to sales, so that this portion represents permanent investment. This would call for financing the permanent portion of current assets with the permanent portion of short-term debt (the spontaneous portion provided by accounts payable and accruals) plus the use of long-term debt and equity financing as required. Temporary or seasonal fluctuations would be financed by short-term debt that is periodically paid off.

QUESTIONS AND PROBLEMS

8.1   Brown Company is short on cash and is attempting to determine whether it would be advantageous to forgo the discount on this month's purchases or to borrow funds to take advantage of the discount. The discount terms are 2/10, net 45.

   A.   What is the maximum annual interest rate that Brown Company should pay on borrowed funds? Why?

   B.   What are some of the intangible disadvantages associated with forgoing the discount?

8.2   Walnut Industries projects that annual cash usage of $3.75 million will occur uniformly throughout the forthcoming year. Walnut plans to meet these demands for cash by periodically selling marketable securities from its portfolio. The firm's marketable securities are invested to earn 5.2 percent, and the cost per transaction of converting funds to cash is $40.

A.   Use the inventory model to determine the optimal transaction size for transfers from marketable securities to cash.

B.   What will be Walnut's average cash balance?

C.   How many transfers per year will be required?

8.3   Futon Company has been reviewing its credit policies. The credit standards it has been applying have resulted in annual credit sales of $5 million. Its average collection period is 30 days, with a bad debt/loss ratio of 1 percent. Futon is considering a reduction in its credit standards. As a result, it expects incremental credit sales of $400,000, on which the average collection period (ACP) would be 60 days and on which the bad debt/loss (BDL) ratio would be 3 percent. The variable cost ratio (VCR) to sales for Futon is 70 percent. The required return on investment in receivables is 15 percent. Evaluate the relaxation in credit standards that Futon is considering. (Use 0.04 percent per 365 days/year.)

8.4   You are given the following information:
Annual demand: 2800 units
Cost per order placed: $5.25
Carrying cost: 20 percent
Price per unit: $30

A.   Fill in the blanks in the table below.

Order size	35	56	70	140	200	2800
Number of orders	____	____	____	____	____	____
Average inventory	____	____	____	____	____	____
Carrying cost	____	____	____	____	____	____
Order cost	____	____	____	____	____	____
Total cost	____	____	____	____	____	____

B.   What is the EOQ?

8.5   Warner Flooring Corporation is attempting to determine the optimal level of current assets for the coming year. Management expects sales to increase to approximately $1.2 million as a result of asset expansion presently being undertaken. Fixed assets total $500,000, and the firm wishes to maintain a 60 percent debt ratio. Warner's interest cost is currently 10 percent on both short-term debt and longer-term debt (which the firm uses in its permanent capital structure). Three alternatives regarding the projected current asset level are available to the firm: (1) an aggressive policy requiring current assets of only 45 percent of projected sales, (2) an average policy of 50 percent of sales in current assets, and (3) a conservative policy requiring current assets of 60 percent of sales. The firm expects to generate earnings before interest and taxes at a rate of 12 percent on total sales.

A. What is the expected return on equity under each current asset level? (Assume a 40 percent tax rate.)

B. In this problem, we have assumed that the earnings rate and the level of expected sales are independent of current asset policy. Is this a valid assumption?

C. How would the overall riskiness of the firm vary under each policy? Discuss specifically the effect of current asset management on demand, expenses, fixed-charge coverage, risk of insolvency, and so on.

SOLUTIONS TO QUESTIONS AND PROBLEMS

8.1   A.   The computed annual interest rate of a 2/10, net 45 discount is 21.28 percent; $[2/98 \times 365/35]$; the APR =

$(1 + 0.2128/10.43)^{10.43} - 1$ = 23.45 percent, so any effective rate on borrowed funds less than 23.45 percent is advantageous to the firm.

B.   The answer to A suggests that if the firm can borrow at a rate less than 23.45 percent, it should do so and take the cash discounts offered. But even if the cost of borrowing were greater, the intangibles of not taking cash discounts should be considered. They are (1) recognition that the firm is a high-risk borrower because lenders would charge high interest rates; (2) possibility that the firm has used up its other possible sources of borrowing and could not raise funds at almost any rate of interest.

8.2   A.

$$c = \sqrt{\frac{2bT}{i}}$$

$b = \$40$

$T = \$3,750,000$

$i = 5.2\%$

$$c = \sqrt{\frac{2(40)(3,750,000)}{0.052}}$$

$= 75,955.45 \approx \$76,000$

B.   Average cash balance = $76,000/2 = $38,000

C.   Transfers per year = $3,750,000/$76,000 = 49.34 ≈ 50, or about every 7 days

8.3   Reduction in credit standards, change on incremental sales only.

$$\Delta NPV = \frac{\Delta Sales(1 - b_1)}{(1 + k_1)^{t_1}} - \Delta Costs$$

Variable cost ratio (VCR) as a percent of sales = 70 percent.

$\Delta Sales$	$400,000/yr	=	$1095.89/day
b_1	3%		
t_1	60 days		
k_1	15%/yr	=	0.04%/day

$\Delta Costs = 0.7(400,000) = 280,000/yr = $767.12/day$

$$\Delta NPV = \frac{1095.89(1 - 0.03)}{(1.0004)^{60}} - 767.12$$

$$= \frac{1063.01}{1.02429} - 767.12$$

$$= 1037.81 - 767.12$$

$$= $270.69/day \text{ or } $98,800/year$$

Since the ΔNPV is positive, credit standards should be reduced.

8.4   A.

Order Size	35	56	70	140	200	2800
Number of orders	80	50	40	20	14	1
Average inventory	18	28	35	70	100	1400
Carrying cost	$108.00	$168.00	$210.00	$420.00	$600.00	$8400.00
Order cost	420.00	262.50	210.00	105.00	73.50	5.25
Total cost	$528.00	$430.5	$420.00	$525.00	$ 673.0	$8405.25

B.

$$EOQ = \sqrt{\frac{2VU}{CP}}$$

$$= \sqrt{\frac{2(5.25)(2800)}{(0.2)(30)}}$$

$$= 70$$

8.5   A.   Return on equity may be computed as follows:

Sales	$1,200,000 Aggressive	$1,200,000 Average	$1,200,000 Conservative
Fixed assets	$ 500,000	$ 500,000	$ 500,000
Current assets	45%	50%	60%
(% of sales × sales)	540,000	600,000	720,000
Total assets	$ 1,040,000	$ 1,100,000	$ 1,220,000
Debt (60% of assets)	$ 624,000	$ 660,000	$ 732,000
Equity	416,000	440,000	488,000
Total claims	$ 1,040,000	$ 1,100,000	$ 1,220,000
EBIT (12% × 1.2 mil.)	$ 144,000	$ 144,000	$ 144,000
Interest (10%)	62,400	66,000	73,200
Earnings before taxes	$ 81,600	$ 78,000	$ 70,800
Taxes (40%)	32,640	31,200	28,320
Earnings	$ 48,960	$ 46,800	$ 42,480
Return on equity	11.8%	10.6%	8.7%

B.   No, this assumption would probably not be valid in a real-world assumption. A firm's current asset policies, particularly with regard to accounts receivable, i.e., discounts, collection period, and collection policy, may have a significant effect on the demand for its output. The exact nature of this function may be difficult to quantify, however. Determining an "optimal" current asset level will require knowledge of the industry, competition faced, strength of general economic conditions, and judgment.

C.   As the answers to part A indicate, the more aggressive policies may lead to higher returns. However, as the current asset level is decreased, presumably some of this reduction comes from accounts receivable. This can be accomplished only through higher discounts, a shorter collection period, and/or tougher collection policies. As outlined above, this would in turn have some effect on sales, possibly lowering profits. Tighter receivable policies might involve some additional costs (collection, etc.) but would also probably reduce bad-debt expenses. Lower current assets would also imply lower liquid assets; thus, the firm's ability to handle contingencies would be impaired. Higher risk of inadequate liquidity would increase the firm's risk of insolvency and thus increase its chance of failing to meet fixed charges. Attempting to attach numerical values to these potential losses and probabilities would be extremely difficult.

PART THREE

INVESTMENT AND FINANCING STRATEGIES

CHAPTER 9

Capital Investment Decisions

The capital investment decision combines many aspects of accounting and finance. Chapter 2 introduced financial statements and cash flows, which provide the basic information necessary for financial evaluation. Chapter 3 provided the fundamental tool, the time value of money, which is necessary to value future cash flows. Chapter 7 discussed financial performance metrics. Building upon these topics, this chapter advances our discussion on evaluating corporate investment decisions by discussing the capital investment program and introducing evaluation techniques and methods for projecting operating cash flows.

A number of business factors combine to make business investment perhaps the most important financial management decision. Further, all departments of a firm—production, marketing, logistics, and so on—are vitally affected by the investment decisions; so all executives, no matter what their primary responsibility, must be aware of how capital investment decisions are made and how to interact effectively in the processes.

OVERVIEW OF INVESTMENT ANALYSIS

The broad application of the techniques presented in this chapter makes these tools germane to a wide variety of corporate investment decisions. A four-phase approach to investment analysis, along with a successful implementation, characterizes a value increasing investment program. Each organization also imposes managerial directives designed to balance evaluation and control with analytical appropriateness.

Applications of Investment Analysis

The investment analysis techniques presented in this chapter are widely applicable. Each investment begins with identifying a need, clarifying the investment proposal, considering alternatives, and developing cash flow projections. Table 9.1 lists many types of investment decisions where the application of these techniques is appropriate.

Capital expenditure analysis represents the traditional capital investment analysis (also referred to by some as *capital budgeting*). Capital expenditures include investments in equipment and plants. These expenditures may reduce production costs, reduce working capital investment, speed production, expand production capacity, or enhance product quality. Incremental cash flows are used to measure investment results.

Investment analysis can also be applied to business investments that are treated as expenses, such as the investment in an advertising campaign or research and development. Thirty-second commercials in the 2000 Super Bowl cost $2 million each. Individual advertisement campaigns can cost tens of millions of dollars with annual advertising and promotion budgets exceeding $100 million for many large companies. Some companies spend in excess of $1 billion for research and development each year. Although these expenditures are treated as expenses (period costs) and not capitalized (included on the balance sheet), these transactions involve sizable expenditures that ultimately must provide economic returns.

New product introductions also require rigorous analysis. New products require investment in equipment and marketing expenses (advertising and promotions). Before embarking on a new product, an investment analysis captures the projected sales, income, and cash flows and determines the economic viability of that product.

TABLE 9.1

Applications of Investment Analysis

- Capital expenditure analysis
  - Investments in equipment
  - Investments in plants
- Major operating decisions
  - Advertising campaigns
  - Research and development
- New product introduction
- Information technology
- Mergers and acquisitions
  - External acquisition targets
  - Divisional valuation
    - Using internal strategic plans
  - Divestiture analysis

In the "new economy," many companies invest heavily in information technology. Whether it is technology aimed at the Internet and a changing business model or the implementation of an upgraded enterprisewide solution such as an enterprise resource planning (ERP) system, companies are embracing technology and significantly investing in it. Investors and senior managers demand a return on this investment. The traditional investment analysis techniques provide a useful evaluation framework.

Finally, these analytical tools form the basis for financial evaluation of acquisition or divestiture candidates. Identification of a candidate occurs. Development of projected future cash flows leads to an application of the valuation tools included in this chapter.

Four Phases of a Successful Capital Program

While nothing can guarantee the success of corporate investments, a four-phase approach increases the likelihood of success. The four phases are

- Planning
- Project or capital evaluation
- Status reporting
- Postcompletion reviews

Of course, successful implementation is paramount to a successful investment.

Capital Expenditure Planning

The planning phase originates with the strategic financial plan. In the strategic financial plan, capital expenditures are estimated in total with limited supporting details or "major" projects may be specifically identified with minor capital expenditures estimated in total. Capacity reviews augmented with facilities reviews and merged with new product ideas identify future capital investment needs. Advanced identification leads to advanced planning and evaluation.

Table 9.2 illustrates a planning capital expenditure summary that details the major projected capital expenditures estimated in the strategic financial plan. Some of these planned expenditures are carryovers from 1997 and 1998. If a 1997 project does not have carryover into the planning period, that project's expenditures are combined and reported on the "miscellaneous" line. So, for example, 1997 saw hundreds of capital projects initiated and completed. The production line 1 renovation began in 1997, carried through 1998, and will be completed in 1999. This project is detailed. However, the other 1997 capital expenditures are accumulated and listed in total. More 1998 projects are detailed because there is more carryover.

TABLE 9.2

Strategic Plan: Capital Expenditure Summary ($ Millions)

	Actual Expenditures		Planned Expenditures					Total	
	1997	1998	1999	2000	2001	2002	2003	Plan Only	Total
Cost Savings									
Production Line 1 Renovation	$ 4.8	$15.1	$ 2.0	$ —	$ —	$ —	$ —	$ 2.0	$ 21.9
Production Line 2 Renovation	—	5.0	17.0	3.0	—	—	—	20.0	25.0
Production Line 3 Renovation	—	—	6.0	19.0	4.0	—	—	29.0	29.0
Production Line 21 Renovation	—	3.8	12.0	—	—	—	—	12.0	15.8
Production Line 22 Renovation	—	2.8	12.0	—	—	—	—	12.0	14.8
Production Line 23 Renovation	—	—	3.0	10.0	—	—	—	13.0	13.0
Production Line 24 Renovation	—	—	3.0	10.0	—	—	—	13.0	13.0
Production Line 25 Renovation	—	—	—	15.0	—	—	—	15.0	15.0
Production Line 31 Replacement	—	—	—	—	25.0	15.0	—	40.0	40.0
Production Line 32 Replacement	—	—	—	—	—	20.0	10.0	30.0	30.0
Truck Fleet Replacement	4.0	4.5	4.5	5.0	5.0	5.5	5.5	25.5	34.0
Miscellaneous Cost Savings	76.4	48.8	19.5	27.0	55.0	59.5	84.5	245.5	370.7
Total Cost Savings	$85.2	$80.0	$79.0	$89.0	$89.0	$100.0	$100.0	$457.0	$622.2
Capacity Expansion									
New Milk Handling Line	$ —	$ 2.3	$15.0	$ —	$ —	$ —	$ —	$ 15.0	$ 17.3
New Scale/ Packaging Line	—	—	18.0	3.0	—	—	—	21.0	21.0
Automated Warehousing Robotics	—	—	—	15.0	2.0	—	—	17.0	17.0
Plant: Orlando Location	—	—	—	—	—	5.0	40.0	45.0	45.0
Miscellaneous Capacity	25.3	24.8	—	—	—	—	—	—	50.1
Total Capacity	$25.3	$27.1	$33.0	$18.0	$ 2.0	$ 5.0	$ 40.0	$ 98.0	$150.4
New Product									
Sweet Treats	$ —	$ —	$20.0	$25.0	$ —	$ —	$ —	$ 45.0	$ 45.0
Love'O'Chocolate	—	—	—	12.0	30.0	5.0	—	47.0	47.0
Joy Bites	—	—	—	—	15.0	45.0	—	60.0	60.0
Miscellaneous New Products	27.3	29.1	—	—	—	3.0	30.0	33.0	89.4
Total New Products	$27.3	$29.1	$20.0	$37.0	$45.0	$ 53.0	$ 30.0	$185.0	$241.4

TABLE 9.2

Strategic Plan: Capital Expenditure Summary ($ Millions) (*Continued*)

	Actual Expenditures		Planned Expenditures					Total	
	1997	1998	1999	2000	2001	2002	2003	Plan Only	Total
Miscellaneous									
Information Technology	$ 8.5	$ 5.1	$ 9.0	$ 8.0	$ 8.0	$ 10.0	$ 9.0	$ 44.0	$ 57.6
Regulatory and Safety	4.0	5.0	5.0	4.0	4.0	5.0	4.0	22.0	31.0
Administrative	3.8	2.2	3.0	3.0	4.0	4.0	4.0	18.0	24.0
Learjet Replacement	12.6	—	—	—	15.0	—	—	15.0	27.6
Research and Development	6.0	9.1	8.0	8.0	10.0	10.0	10.0	46.0	61.1
Miscellaneous	0.2	3.7	3.0	3.0	3.0	3.0	3.0	15.0	18.9
Total Miscellaneous	$35.1	$25.1	$28.0	$26.0	$44.0	$32.0	$30.0	$160.0	$220.2
Total Capital Expenditures	$172.9	$161.3	$160.0	$170.0	$180.0	$190.0	$200.0	$900.0	$1234.2

Notice, in this example, capital expenditures are broken into four categories for planning purposes:

- Cost savings
- Capacity expansion
- New products
- Miscellaneous

At the time when the strategic financial plan is prepared, longer-term capital expenditures have not been detailed. Funds are included in the strategic financial plan without all the necessary details in the outer years. The advanced planning leads to a more detailed annual budget.

Good capital planning and budgeting will improve the timing of asset acquisitions and the quality of assets purchased. Since the production of capital goods involves a relatively long work-in-process period, a year or more of waiting may be involved before the additional capital goods are available. Another reason for the importance of capital budgeting is that asset expansion typically involves substantial expenditures. A firm contemplating a major capital expenditure program may need to plan its financing several years in advance to be sure of having the funds required for the expansion.

Capital Evaluation and Authorization

Plan or budget identification of a capital project usually is not authorization to proceed with the project. Authorization (or acceptance) of a project happens during the evaluation phase, which is also called the project approval phase.

While serving a vitally important financial and economic function, a good investment analysis process possesses similar managerial and organizational qualities as a good strategic planning process. Strong investment evaluation and authorization

- Facilitates communication among the senior executives of an organization
- Sets a business direction
- Prioritizes opportunities and requirements
- Establishes business performance standards and objectives

Significant investment analysis involves many areas within an organization. A new product decision involves research and development, marketing, sales, engineering, production, logistics, finance, human resources, legal, corporate communications, etc. All areas of the organization need to be involved in the decision process, albeit to varying degrees. Even in a simple equipment replacement analysis championed by manufacturing and engineering, marketing and sales must be involved to provide consistent product projections.

To facilitate the investment analysis process, a capital authorization request includes several supporting sections and or schedules:

- Summary cover page
- Decision case cash flow assumptions
- Decision case cash flow amounts
- Decision case net present-value analysis
- Project description
- Sensitivity and/or scenario analysis
- Investment components, potential vendor, and cost basis
- Quarterly expenditure budget

Table 9.3 illustrates a summary cover page. The interesting thing about this page is that it supports the collaborative nature of capital investment analysis, by providing numerous areas to capture all the appropriate signatures: project originator, project sponsor, analyst/engineer who completes the capital authorization request, and of course management. Not all the signatures are necessary for every project. The form includes administrative header and identification information, an abbreviated project description, budget information, project anticipated expenditure summary, numerous financial indicators, and, of course, the signatures.

The project description includes a full and complete write-up of the project, its rationale, justification of the key assumptions, alternatives considered and rejected, "fit" with strategic objectives, details of budget inclusion, and key technical data, if appropriate. Sensitivity and scenario analysis examine the degree to which changes in key assump-

tions affect the net present value. A detailed list of equipment components and potential vendors is provided for technical (operational)
consideration. The cost basis is provided to understand if the expenditure estimate is a vendor quote (little volatility) or an estimate with
maybe significant volatility. Finally for detailed budgeting, including a
detailed financing budget, the final schedule of the capital authorization request documents anticipated expenditures by quarter.

Capital Status Reporting

After project evaluation and management approval, a project manager
is assigned to implement the project on (or below) budget and on (or
before) schedule. Status reporting tracks the project investment. This
process reports the total budgeted amounts, project spending, and
project commitments (signed contracts that have not been billed by
the vendor). By using this report, the project manager can track the
project's initial investment compared to the authorized approval. By
using a summary status report that consolidates a number of project
status reports, senior management can monitor the implementation
progress of all projects.

Postcompletion Reviews

Postcompletion reviews are an often-overlooked phase of capital
investment. Even companies that conduct postcompletion reviews
often consider this to be their weakest phase of the capital expenditure
process. Postcompletion reviews are conducted any time (1 year, 3
years, or whenever) after the project is completed.

   The review compares the project's original approved cash flows
and economic evaluation indicators (discussed later in this chapter)
with the cash flows and indicators based on updated operating performance and information. That is, actual project costs and investment
returns are compared to the projected investment estimates when the
project was approved. In the case of a 3-year review, 3 years of actual
performance are substituted for the first 3 years of projected performance. Finally, the cash flows for the remaining years are reestimated,
given new information and current performance. Based upon this combination of actual investment, current performance, and reforecasted
future performance, the economic evaluation indicators are recalculated and improvement or shortfalls addressed.

   Postcompletion reviews are excellent learning tools for the organization. However, they are time-consuming, provide little immediately
"actionable" guidance, and continue to incorporate projections. Nonetheless, postcompletion reporting remains a valuable learning tool
from which judgments can be made about future capital evaluations,
requests, and authorizations.

TABLE 9.3

Capital Authorization Request Summary

Division / Department	Cost Center	Date Prepared	Prepared By	Project Number
Project Title		Starting Date	Closing Date	Internal Reference

Project Description   [ ] Budgeted ($000s) $ _____   [ ] Not Budgeted

Summary of Project Expenditures
($000s)

New Fixed Assets	$ -
Transferred Fixed Assets	-
Capitalized Expense	-
Prior Approvals	-
Total Capital Requested	$ -
Operating Expenses	-
Working Capital	-
Other	-
Total Other Requested	$ -
Total Project Amount	$ -

Financial Indicators

Net Present Value @ _____ %	
Terminal Rate of Return @ _____ %	
Internal Rate of Return	
Payback Period – Years	
Maximum Cash Exposure	
Project Life – Years	

Project Analysis Signatures

Cost Estimates By	
Technical Development By	
Financial Data By	

Management Signatures

Board of Directors	Chief Executive Officer
Chief Operating Officer	Division President
Chief Financial Officer	Vice President
Vice President	Vice President
Vice President	Vice President
Vice President	Vice President
Request Originator	Sponsor

The next section provides an additional overview of the capital management process.

Additional Managerial Issues

In addition to the four phases of the capital investment process, each corporation must decide on a number of other issues related to capital investment.

Project Categories

Most companies categorize projects by the nature of their expenditures. In this way, management can broadly monitor where its capital is being invested. The categories relate to the underlying rationale of the expenditure. For example, in Table 9.2, we categorized projects by their nature. These categories are similar to the categories used at Hershey Foods and at many companies. While these are common categories, each company defines its own group of categories. In a separate survey, one company used 26 different categories, including five varieties of new products.

Project Dependence

When evaluating two projects that are mutually exclusive, you can choose one or the other project, but you cannot choose both. Mutually exclusive projects are alternative means of accomplishing the same objective. On the other hand, when you are evaluating independent projects, the acceptance of one project does not diminish the need to invest in the other project. For example, the decision to buy a forklift truck is independent of the decision to add a new packaging machine.

Project Cash Flow Interrelationship

Understanding the distinctions between products that are substitutes or complements is important when determining the project's cash flows. Kellogg's introduction of a new, ready-to-eat cereal may cause the sales of existing cereals to decline to some degree. Cash flows from projects with substitution implications must be reduced for the lost revenues, income, and cash flows from the "cannibalized" sales of existing products. Complementary projects enhance the total organization's cash flows beyond the immediate project. Those additional, complementary cash flows must augment the project's cash flow. The project's impact on the organization's total cash flow must be determined and considered when the project is evaluated.

Budget Identification and Spending

While it is helpful to specifically identify projects within the annual budget process, it is not uncommon that while 100 percent of the budgeted capital expenditures are spent, only one-half is spent on identified projects. The other half is spent on unidentified projects that result from changes in priorities, market conditions, etc.

Budget Authorization

For most companies, the annual capital budget amount is separate from expenditure authorization. Just because a project is identified at budget time, that does not authorize the project. Each project must undergo its own evaluation and authorization.

Project Evaluation Threshold

As previously mentioned, the economic evaluation techniques are appropriate for many, if not all, expenditures. However, if a project analysis were required every time that someone needed a pencil, many person-hours of effort would be wasted. On the other hand, manufacturing should not be given carte blanche for investments in new production facilities costing several hundreds of millions of dollars. A careful balance must be struck, such as all projects over $100,000.

Authorization Levels

Each company must decide how deeply into the organization capital authorization should be allowed and at what dollar level. For example, should a senior engineer be allowed to authorize capital expenditures? Table 9.4 illustrates authorization levels. In this example, directors can approve up to $10,000, vice presidents up to $100,000, and so on. The CEO can approve up to $2 million with any project exceeding an estimated $2 million requiring board-level approval. Each corporation must find a structure that provides enough control without hampering operations with needless bureaucracy.

TABLE 9.4

Project Evaluation and Approval

- Each project undergoes its own focused review
  - All projects > $100,000
- Approval authority
  - Director: $10,000
  - Vice president: $100,000
  - Senior vice president: $500,000
  - President: $1 million
  - CEO: $2 million
  - Board: $2+ million

OVERVIEW OF THE INVESTMENT PROCESS

Table 9.5 summarizes the investment process. The process begins by projecting operating cash flows for a potential investment. The projected cash flows are the basis upon which capital investment techniques are applied and the investment efficacy determined. The basics of determining cash flows are introduced later in this chapter. The major capital investment evaluation techniques include

> Payback period (PBP)
> Net present value (NPV)
> Internal rate of return (IRR)
> Terminal rate of return (TRR) or modified internal rate of return (MIRR)

Additional techniques covered in this chapter include

> Discounted payback period (DPBP)
> Profitability index (PI)

These techniques will be fully developed throughout this chapter.

Notice, the economic indicators do not include the financial performance metrics of Chap. 7, Financial Performance Metrics. The financial performance metrics detailed in Chap. 7 are viable metrics used to set objectives and performance standards, benchmark against other organizations, and manage the business, but they are inappropriate measures for investment decision making. Accounting-based perfor-

TABLE 9.5

Overview of Investment Process

- Evaluation of projected future cash flows
- Major techniques
  - Payback period
  - Net present value
  - Internal rate of return
  - Terminal rate of return
- Additional investment techniques
  - Discounted payback period
  - Profitability index
- Subject to hurdle rate
  - Risk-adjusted cost of capital

mance measures (including accounting based rates of return) differ greatly from economic rates of return. While accounting metrics can result from future financial statement projections, the nature of the accounting returns differs from that of the economic returns discussed in this chapter. The major differences are summarized:

Accounting Returns	Economic Returns
Single time periods	Multiple time periods
Discrete time	Continuous time
Accrual income–based	Cash flow–based
Historical book values	Market values

Accounting returns are determined for discrete, single time periods (month, quarter, year, etc.) while economic returns consider a continuous time frame over multiple periods. Accounting returns are based on income (accrual) while economic returns center on cash flows. Accounting returns can vary widely over the life of an asset as the asset depreciates, since accounting returns use historical book values.

The following sections describe the common economic performance metrics used to evaluate investment decisions.

MAJOR INVESTMENT EVALUATION TECHNIQUES

The following sections discuss in detail the calculation of each investment evaluation technique as well as review the strengths and weaknesses of each technique.

The point of capital budgeting—indeed, the point of all financial analysis—is to make decisions that will maximize the value of the firm. The capital budgeting process is designed to answer two questions: (1) Which among mutually exclusive investments should be selected? (2) How many projects, in total, should be accepted?

When one is comparing various capital budgeting criteria, it is useful to establish some guidelines. The optimal decision rule will have four characteristics:

1.   It will appropriately consider all cash flows.
2.   It will discount the cash flows at the appropriate market-determined opportunity cost of capital.
3.   It will select from a group of mutually exclusive projects the one that maximizes shareholders' wealth.
4.   It will allow managers to consider each project independently of all others. This has come to be known as the *value additivity principle.*

The value additivity principle implies that if we know the value of separate projects accepted by management, then simply adding their values V_j will give us the value of the firm. If there are N projects, then the value of the firm will be

$$V = \sum_{j=1}^{N} V_j \qquad j = 1, ..., N \qquad (9.1)$$

For example if the added market values for four projects (j=1, 2, 3, 4 and N=4) are \$370, \$150, \$90, and \$210, V will equal \$820. This is a particularly important point because it means that projects can be considered on their own merit without the necessity of looking at them in an infinite variety of combinations with other projects.

We now consider alternative capital investment analysis techniques. We shall see that only one technique—the net present value method—satisfies all four of the desirable properties for capital budgeting criteria.

Data for the Evaluation

Some illustrative data provide a basis for the evaluation of the alternative criteria. Table 9.6 gives the cash flows for two cleverly labeled projects, projects A and B. They both have the same life, 3 years, and they require the same investment outlay, \$400. Their cash flows are similar but inverted.

Payback Period

Payback period (PBP) represents the number of years required to return the original investment. As illustrated in Table 9.7, project A has a $1\frac{1}{2}$-year payback period while project B has a payback period of $2\frac{1}{3}$ years. Project A costs \$400, but pays back \$300 cash in the first year and \$200 cash in the second year. To calculate the payback period, we must include the total cash flow generated in the first year (\$300). This leaves \$100 outstanding until the project is paid back. Assuming level

TABLE 9.6

Hypothetical Projects

A	Projects	B
$ (400)	Cost (outflow year 0)	$ (400)
300	Cash inflow year 1	100
200	Cash inflow year 2	200
100	Cash inflow year 3	300

TABLE 9.7

Payback Period

	A	Projects	B	
	$ (400)	Cost (outflow year 0)	$ (400)	
	300	Cash inflow year 1	100	
	200	Cash inflow year 2	200	
	100	Cash inflow year 3	300	
		Accumulated Cash Inflow		
	$ 300	Year 1	$ 100	
	500	Year 2	300	
	600	Year 3	600	
	$1\frac{1}{2}$ years	Payback period	$2\frac{1}{3}$ years	

cash flows throughout the year, it takes an additional $\frac{1}{2}$ year (or the remaining outstanding $100 divided by the project's $200 second-year cash flow). In total, the project pays back in $1\frac{1}{2}$ years. Project B generates $100 in the first year and $200 in the second year for a total of $300 over the first 2 years. This leaves $100 until project B is paid back or $\frac{1}{3}$ of the third year ($100/$300), assuming level cash flows throughout the year.

If the projects were independent (not mutually exclusive) projects, management would need to establish some cutoff criterion for the acceptable length of payback. This criterion should correspond to the underlying business. For example, most domestic manufacturing firms use a rule-of-thumb payback period of 3 years or less. In that case, both of these projects would be acceptable.

If management adhered strictly to the payback method with a 3-year acceptance criterion but projects A and B were mutually exclusive, project A would be preferred to project B because it has a shorter payback period.

Two arguments can be given for the use of the payback method. (1) It is easy to use. (2) For a company in a tight cash position, it may be of great interest to know how soon it gets back the dollars it has invested.

However, the payback period has significant drawbacks that may result in the wrong investment decision:

- The payback period does not look beyond the payback period. That is, suppose project B-1 has identical cash flows to project B, with the exception of the final year:

Year	Cash Flow Project B-1
Year 0	$ (400)
Year 1	100
Year 2	200
Year 3	3000

Project B-1 has a payback period of 2.03 years. Project A is still preferred, and the organization misses out on the substantial third year cash flow.

- The payback period does not consider the time value of money. Consequently, an independent project such as project M has an acceptable 2-year payback period, but it never returns a positive contribution on the investment:

Year	Cash Flow Project M
Year 0	$(400)
Year 1	100
Year 2	300
Year 3	—

In other words, yes, the project pays back its investment, but it never pays an adequate (or any—in this case) return on the investment. The discounted payback period eliminates this shortcoming and is discussed later in this chapter.

Nonetheless, while the payback period is not the primary investment evaluation tool, many decision makers may continue to use it as a rule of thumb.

Net Present Value

Net present value (NPV) is the present value of the projected future cash flows, discounted at an appropriate cost of capital or hurdle rate, less the cost of the investment.

Table 9.8a graphically depicts the net present value of project A. The projected cash flows are discounted back to today (year 0) by using the tools developed in Chap. 3, Time Value of Money. For example, the first-year cash flow (CF) of $300 is discounted for 1 year at 10 percent.

$$\text{Present value} = \frac{\text{future value}}{(1+r)^N} = \frac{\$300}{(1+0.10)^1} = \$273 = \text{PV}(CF_1) \quad (9.2)$$

$$= \frac{\$200}{(1+0.10)^2} = \$165 = \text{PV}(CF_2)$$

$$= \frac{\$100}{(1+0.10)^3} = \$75 = \text{PV}(CF_3)$$

TABLE 9.8a

Graph of Net Present Value

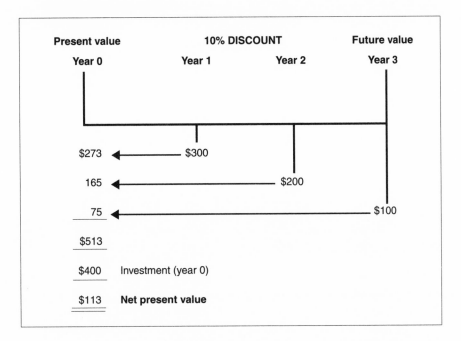

This project is worth $513 (the sum of the present values), but the investment requirement is only $400. Subtracting the investment cost from the present value of the cash flows results in a net present value of $113.

More generally, net present value can be written as

$$\frac{CF_1}{(1+k)^1} + \frac{CF_2}{(1+k)^2} + \cdots + \frac{CF_N}{(1+k)^N} - I_0 = NPV$$

$$\sum_{t=1}^{N} \frac{CF_t}{(1+k)^t} - I_0 = NPV \qquad (9.3)$$

Table 9.8b compares the net present values for both project A and project B. If these projects are independent, accept both projects since both have positive net present values and add value for the organization. If the projects are mutually exclusive, rank the projects based upon the size of the net present value; project A is the investment choice under mutual exclusivity.

The NPV of the project is exactly the same as the increase in shareholders' wealth. This fact makes it the correct decision rule for

TABLE 9.8b

Net Present Value

	Net Present Value, 10 Percent Discount Rate	
A	**Projects**	**B**
$273	Present value of year 1 cash flow	$ 91
165	Present value of year 2 cash flow	165
75	Present value of year 3 cash flow	225
$513	Total present-value cash flow	$481
400	*Less*: Investment (year 0)	400
$113	Net present value (10%)	$ 81
$ 47	**Net present value 20 percent discount rate**	$ (4)

capital budgeting purposes. The NPV rule also meets the other three general principles required for an optimal capital budgeting criterion. It takes all cash flows into account. All cash flows are discounted at the appropriate market-determined opportunity cost of capital in order to determine their present values (see Chap. 10). Also, the NPV rule obeys the value additivity principle. The net present value of a project is exactly the same as the increase in shareholders' wealth. To see why, start by assuming a project has zero net present value. In this case, the project returns enough cash flow to do three things:

1. To pay off all interest payments to creditors who have lent money to finance the project
2. To pay all expected returns (dividends and capital gains) to shareholders who have put up equity for the project
3. To pay off the original principal I_0, which was invested in the project

Thus, a zero NPV project earns a fair return to compensate both debtholders and equity holders, each according to the returns they expect for the risk they take. A positive NPV project earns more than the required rate of return, and equity holders receive all excess cash flows because debtholders have a fixed claim on the firm. Consequently, equity holders' wealth increases by exactly the NPV of the project. It is this direct link between shareholders' wealth and the NPV definition that makes the NPV criterion so important in decision making.

For our analysis of project A, further assume that there are 113 shares outstanding, and the effects of this project could be effectively communicated and implemented. The stock price should reflect an immediate $1 per share increase ($113/113 shares).

Notice in Table 9.8b, at a 20 percent cost of capital, the NPVs of both projects decrease. Project B's NPV turns negative and consequently indicates that project B is not a good investment. Project B should be rejected, and only project A accepted regardless of whether these are mutually exclusive projects or independent projects.

Internal Rate of Return

The internal rate of return (IRR) is the interest rate that equates the present value of projected future cash flows to the investment expenditure. It is the discount rate where the net present value equals $0:

$$\frac{CF_1}{(1+IRR)^1} + \frac{CF_2}{(1+IRR)^2} + \cdots + \frac{CF_N}{(1+IRR)^N} - I_0 = \$0$$

$$\sum_{t=1}^{N} \frac{CF_t}{(1+IRR)^t} - I_0 = \$0 \qquad (9.4)$$

Notice that the IRR formula, Eq. (9.4), is simply the NPV formula, Eq. (9.3), solved for that particular value of k that causes the NPV to equal zero. The same basic equation is used for both methods, but in the NPV method, the discount rate k is specified as the market-determined opportunity cost of capital, while in the IRR method, the NPV is set equal to zero and the value of IRR that forces the NPV to equal zero is found. Table 9.9a graphically demonstrates the IRR for project A and arrives at an IRR of 28.9 percent. Notice, at 28.9 percent NPV = $0.

TABLE 9.9a

Graph of Internal Rate of Return

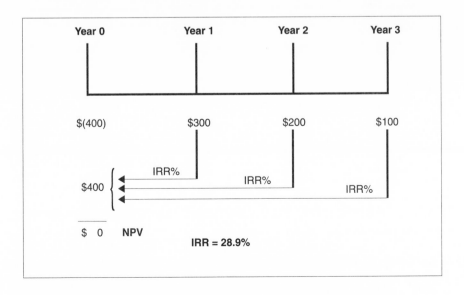

Programs found in financial calculators or personal computers can readily calculate the internal rate of return. With an ordinary calculator, the internal rate of return can also be found by trial and error. First, compute the present value of the cash flows from an investment using an arbitrarily selected interest rate, for example, 10 percent. Then compare the present value so obtained with the investment's cost. If the present value is higher (lower) than the cost figure, try a higher (lower) discount rate and go through the procedure again. Continue until the present value of the flows from the investment is approximately equal to its cost. The discount rate that brings about this equality is defined as the internal rate of return. Table 9.9b shows the trial-and-error IRR computations for project A.

In Table 9.9c, the IRRs for both projects A and B are presented. Project B has an IRR of 19.4 percent. If the projects are independent projects, the IRR should be compared to a risk-adjusted cost of capital, or a hurdle rate. If the IRR exceeds this risk-adjusted cost of capital, the project should be accepted. If the project's IRR is less than the risk-adjusted cost of capital, the project should be rejected. If the projects are mutually exclusive and exceed the hurdle rate, choose the one with the larger IRR. In this example, choose project A!

The internal rate of return implicitly assumes reinvestment of the intermediate cash flows at the IRR. Although Eq. (9.4) does not specifically address reinvestment, fundamentally reinvestment at the IRR is assumed. For projects A and B, what if you cannot reinvest at their internal rates of return? Management would enjoy having 28.9 percent return projects (like project A) just sitting around waiting for funding.

TABLE 9.9b

Calculating IRR, Project A

	Project A Cash Flow	Trial 1 10.0%	Trial 2 20.0%	Trial 3 30.0%	Trial 4 25.0%	Trial 5 28.0%	Trial 6 29.0%	Trial 7 28.9%
			Discounted Cash Flow Value					
Cash inflows								
Year 1	$300	$273	$250	$231	$240	$234	$233	$233
Year 2	200	165	139	118	128	122	120	120
Year 3	100	75	58	46	51	48	47	47
Total present value		$513	$447	$395	$419	$404	$399	$400
Investment		400	400	400	400	400	400	400
Net present value		$113	$ 47	$ (5)	$ 19	$ 4	$ (1)	$ (0)
								IRR is 28.9%!

TABLE 9.9c

Internal Rate of Return

A	Projects	B
28.9%	Internal rate of return	19.4%
	Net Present Value at Internal Rate of Return	
28.9%	IRR—discount rate	19.4%
$233	Present value of year 1 cash flow	$ 84
120	Present value of year 2 cash flow	140
47	Present value of year 3 cash flow	176
$400	Total present-value cash flow	$400
400	*Less:* Investment (year 0)	400
$ 0	Net present value (IRR %)	$ 0

What if other 28.9 percent return opportunities do not exist?What if the best the company can do is to reinvest at 10 percent, its cost of capital? The terminal rate of return (or modified internal rate of return) explicitly addresses the reinvestment assumption.

Terminal Rate of Return

Terminal rate of return (TRR) or modified internal rate of return (MIRR) is the discount rate that equates the cost of the investment with the accumulated future value of the intermediate cash flows that are assumed to be reinvested at an appropriate risk-adjusted cost of capital.

Table 9.10a illustrates calculation of the TRR for project A. The calculation is a two-step process. The first step explicitly reinvests the intermediate cash flows at 10 percent, the cost of capital. For example, the first-year cash flow is invested for 2 years, between the end of the first and third years. The first-year cash flow of $300 accumulates to $363 by the end of year 3 [i.e., $300 $(1 + 0.1)^2$]. The second-year cash flow of $200 grows to $220 with reinvestment for 1 year at 10 percent, and the third-year cash flow of $100 remains $100 since it lacks time to grow. In total, the accumulated future value of the intermediate cash flows that are assumed reinvested at 10 percent, the cost of capital, is $683.

Step 2 compares the investment to the accumulated future value (FV) of the projected and reinvested cash flows. The lower portion of Table 9.10a illustrates this final step.

$$\text{TRR project A} = \left(\frac{\text{accumulated FV}}{\text{investment}} \right)^{1/n} - 1$$

$$= \left(\frac{\$683}{\$400} \right)^{0.333} - 1 = 19.5\% \qquad (9.5)$$

TABLE 9.10a

Graph of Terminal Rate of Return
or Modified Rate of Return

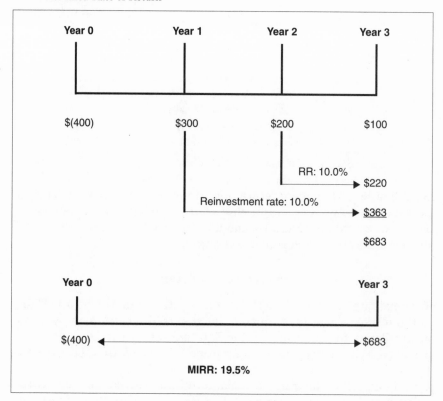

For project A, the terminal rate of return is 19.5 percent and reflects the interest rate that equates the cost of the investment ($400) with the accumulated future value of $683.

Table 9.10b compares the TRR for both projects A and B. Project B has an accumulated future value (assuming 10 percent reinvestment) of $641 in year 3 which equates to a 17.0 percent TRR.

The reinvestment rate assumption is actually an inaccurate use of terminology for what should be called the *opportunity cost assumption*. The real issue is: Given the risk of the project, at what rate can funds be invested (or reinvested) somewhere else for the same level of risk? All investment projects of equal risk will have the same opportunity cost from the point of view of all investors. We have assumed that projects A and B are equally risky and that all investors require at least a 10 percent rate of return in order to invest in the projects. The rate of 10 percent is the appropriate opportunity cost of capital for the assumed level of risk of the project. That is why we discount the cash flows at a 10 percent rate when calculating the NPV. When calculating the TRR, if the reinvestment rate is a risk-adjusted cost of capital (or hurdle rate), the reinvestment rate is neutral to the accept/reject decision. Thus the appropriate reinvestment rate is the opportunity cost of capital.

If the projects are independent projects, the TRR should be compared to the reinvestment rate—the risk-adjusted, opportunity cost of capital. If the TRR exceeds this opportunity cost, the project should be accepted. If the project's TRR is less than the risk-adjusted cost of capital, the project should be rejected. If the projects are mutually exclusive and exceed the reinvestment rate, choose the one with the larger TRR. In this example, again, choose project A!

Before we leave the TRR discussion, let us revisit the implicit reinvestment assumption included in the internal rate of return using the terminal rate of return framework. That is, the IRR assumes reinvestment at the IRR. Table 9.11a illustrates this graphically for project A. In Table 9.11a, the intermediate cash flows are reinvested at 28.9 percent, project A's IRR. The resulting accumulated future value of the intermediate cash flows is $856 compared to an investment of $400 and yields a terminal rate of return of 28.9 percent, which is equal to the IRR! The major shortcoming of the IRR method is that it makes an inappropriate opportunity cost assumption—reinvestment at the IRR. There is a substantial difference between the accumulated future value of $856 (28.9 percent reinvestment, the IRR) and $683 (10.0 percent reinvestment, the cost of capital). Table 9.11b details both projects A and B.

TABLE 9.10b

Terminal Rate of Return

A	Projects	B
$363	Future value of year 1 cash flow	$121
220	Future value of year 2 cash flow	220
100	Future value of year 3 cash flow	300
$683	Total future value	$641
$400	Investment (year 0)	$400
19.5%	Terminal rate of return	17.0%
28.9%	Internal rate of return	19.4%

TABLE 9.11a

Graph of TRR Format Applied to IRR
Project A, IRR Reinvestment Rate

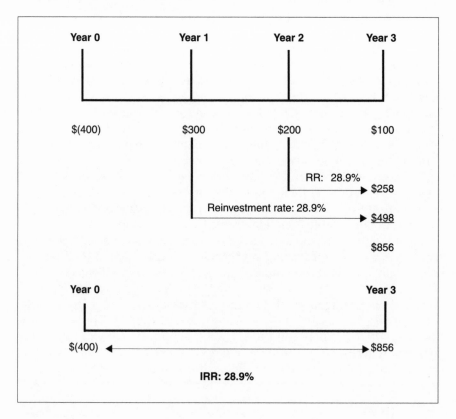

TABLE 9.11b

TRR Format Applied to IRR
Project A, IRR Reinvestment Rate

A	Projects	B
28.9%	Reinvestment rate—IRR	19.4%
$498	Future value of year 1 cash flow	$143
258	Future value of year 2 cash flow	239
100	Future value of year 3 cash flow	300
$856	Total future value	$682
$400	Investment (year 0)	$400
28.9%	Internal rate of return	19.4%

So far, all the investment evaluation techniques lead to choosing project A under terms of mutual exclusivity. Are the techniques always consistent? What if conflicts arise? Which is the best approach? These questions will be addressed in the upcoming section.

INVESTMENT TECHNIQUE— CONFLICT RESOLUTION

It is apparent that the only structural difference between the NPV and IRR methods lies in the discount rates used in the two equations—all the values in the equations are identical except for IRR and k. Further, we can see that if IRR > k, then NPV > $0. Accordingly, it would appear that the two methods give the same accept/reject decisions for specific projects—if a project is acceptable under the NPV criterion, it is also acceptable if the IRR method is used. However, the following example illustrates that this statement is incorrect. Consider the pattern of cash flows in Table 9.12, which contains information about two additional, mutually exclusive projects, cleverly labeled C and D. Both projects cost $700 and have varying (and inverted) cash flows. Although these numbers were contrived to illustrate a point, this conflict is sometimes evident in evaluating investment opportunities that stretch over 10 to 12 years. These numbers were contrived to fit in a 3-year window.

Using net present value, which project would you prefer at a 10 percent cost of capital? The one with the higher net present value, project C ($409 NPV versus project D's NPV of $329), should be

TABLE 9.12

Method Conflicts

C	Projects	D
$ 700	Investment year 0	$ 700
50	Cash inflow year 1	1000
150	Cash inflow year 2	100
1250	Cash inflow year 3	50
$ 409	Net present value at 10%	$ 329
278	Net present value at 15%	278
169	Net present value at 20%	232
29.7%	Internal rate of return	55.0%
28.2%	Terminal rate of return 10%	25.1%
28.6%	Terminal rate of return 15%	28.6%
29.0%	Terminal rate of return 20%	32.0%

accepted. At 15 percent, both projects have the same NPV, so the choice should be made for "strategic" or other reasons. At a 20 percent cost of capital, project D is preferred.

But why should life be so difficult? Project D's IRR is almost double the IRR of project C (55.0 versus 29.7 percent). Choose project D using the IRR! Yes, that is true, if you can reinvest at 55.0 percent. But what if the appropriate opportunity cost of capital for this type of project is substantially lower and consequently you cannot reinvest at 55.0 percent?

Using the terminal rate of return with a 10 percent reinvestment rate, choose project C. With a 15 percent reinvestment rate, strategic rationale and other criteria need to be considered since the TRRs are identical at 28.6 percent. At a reinvestment rate of 20 percent, choose project D.

Notice, with the same investment amount, NPV and TRR give consistent accept/reject decisions and project rankings. Notice, also, TRR provides a more realistic view of the rate of return provided by both projects, but especially project D.

Additional IRR Issues

In addition to the reinvestment rate issue, the IRR is an inferior capital budgeting criterion because (1) it violates the value additivity principle and (2) it can result in multiple IRRs for the same project.

The value additivity principle demands that managers be able to consider one project independently of all others. Table 9.13 presents the cash flows, NPV, and IRR for projects R and S, which are mutually exclusive, and project T, which is independent of them. If the value additivity principle holds, we should be able to choose the better of the two mutually exclusive projects without having to consider the independent project. If we used the IRR rule to choose between projects R and S, we would select project R. But if we considered combinations of projects, then the IRR rule would prefer projects S and T to projects R and T. The IRR rule prefers project R in isolation but project S in combination with the independent project. In this example, the IRR rule does not obey the value additivity principle. The implication for management is that it would have to consider all possible combinations of projects and choose the combination which has the greatest internal rate of return. If, e.g., a firm had only five projects, it would need to consider 32 different combinations.

The NPV rule always obeys the value additivity principle. Given that the opportunity cost of capital is 10 percent, we would choose project R as being the best either by itself or in combination with project T. Note that the combinations of R and T or S and T are simply the sums of the NPVs of the projects considered separately. Conse-

TABLE 9.13

Value Additivity Rule Comparing NPV and IRR

	Projects			Combined Projects	
Years	R	S	T	R and T	S and T
0	$(100)	$(100)	$(100)	$(200)	$(200)
1	0	225	450	450	675
2	550	0	0	550	0
NPV*	$ 354	$ 105	$ 309	$ 663	$ 414
IRR	135%	125%	350%	213%	238%

*NPV assumes a 10% discount rate.

quently, if we adopt the NPV rule, the value of the firm is the sum of the values of the separate projects.

Multiple rates of return are another difficulty with the IRR rule. A classic example of this situation has come to be known as the oil well pump problem. An oil company is trying to decide whether to install a high-speed pump on a well that is already in operation. The estimated incremental cash flows are given below. The pump will cost $1600 to install. During its first year of operation, it will produce $10,000 more oil than the pump that is currently in place. But during the second year, this high-speed pump produces $10,000 less oil because the well has been depleted. The question is whether to accept the rapid pumping technique, which speeds up cash flows in the near term at the expense of cash flows in the long term. The following summarizes the net present value at 10 percent as well as the IRRs:

	Cash Flow	NPV at 10%	Net Present Value / IRR	
			at 25%	at 400%
Year 0	$(1,600)	$(1,600)	$(1,600)	$(1,600)
Year 1	10,000	9,091	8,000	2,000
Year 2	(10,000)	(8,265)	(6,400)	(400)
Total	$ (1,000)	$ (774)	$ 0	$ 0

If the opportunity cost of capital is 10 percent, the NPV rule rejects the project because it has negative NPV at that rate. If we are using the IRR rule, the project has two IRRs, 25 and 400 percent. Since both exceed the opportunity cost of capital, the project would probably be accepted. A separate question is: What IRR would you report to management, 25 or 400 percent?

Mathematically, the multiple IRRs are a result of Descartes' rule of signs, which implies that every time the cash flows change signs, there may be a new (positive, real) root to the problem. For the above example, the signs of cash flows change twice. There are two roots, i.e., two IRRs, and neither has any economic meaning.

ADDITIONAL INVESTMENT EVALUATION TECHNIQUES

Two additional investment evaluation techniques are briefly discussed below: (1) discounted payback period and (2) profitability index.

Discounted Payback Period

Discounted payback period is a variation of the payback period and reflects the number of years required to return the original investment based on estimated future cash flows, which are discounted at an appropriate cost of capital or hurdle rate. One of the shortcomings of the payback period technique, as discussed above, is that it does not consider the time value of money. Using discounted cash flows as illustrated in Table 9.14 eradicates this issue.

TABLE 9.14

Additional Capital Evaluation Technique: Discounted Payback Period

A	Projects	B
$(400)	Investment (year 0)	$(400)
300	Cash inflow year 1	100
200	Cash inflow year 2	200
100	Cash inflow year 3	300
	Cash flows discounted at 10%	
$ 273	Present value of year 1 cash flow	$ 91
165	Present value of year 2 cash flow	165
75	Present value of year 3 cash flow	225
	Accumulated discounted cash inflow	
$273	Year 1	$ 91
438	Year 2	256
513	Year 3	481
1.77 years	**Discounted payback period (10%)**	**2.64 years**
1+(127/165)		2+(144/225)

Returning to projects A and B and discounting their cash flows at the 10 percent cost of capital result in the discounted cash flows in Table 9.14. In the first year, project A experiences $273 of discounted cash inflow and requires an additional $127 to cover the investment of $400. The second year provides a discounted cash flow of $165. Assuming even cash flow throughout the year, project A needs 0.77 ($127/$165) of the second year's cash flow to repay the investment. Project A's discounted payback period is 1.77 years. Notice project B has a discounted payback period of 2.64 years. Project A remains the preferred project if these projects are mutually exclusive.

Although this approach improves upon the payback period by considering the time value of money, strict adherence to this technique does not look beyond the payback period. To extend the illustration from earlier in this chapter, project B-1 has identical cash flows (CF) as project B, with the exception of the final year:

Year	Cash Flow Project B-1	Discounted CF at 10%
Year 0	$ (400)	$ (400)
Year 1	100	91
Year 2	200	165
Year 3	3,000	2,254

Project B-1 has a discounted payback period of 2.06 years. Project A is still preferred, and the organization continues to miss out on the substantial third-year cash flow.

Profitability Index

The profitability index (PI) is a variation of net present value. It is calculated as the present value of estimated future cash flows, discounted at an appropriate cost of capital or hurdle rate, divided by the cost of the investment:

$$\sum_{t=1}^{N} \frac{CF_t}{(1+k)^t} \div I_0 = PI \tag{9.6}$$

Of course, the NPV subtracts the investment amount from the present value of the cash flow. The profitability index suggests that for every dollar invested, you receive a dollar return equal to the PI.

Table 9.15 demonstrates the profitability index for projects A and B. The NPV remains as calculated in Table 9.8b—$113 for project A and $81 for project B. Using the PI, once again, project A is preferred. Every dollar invested in project A provides a return of $1.28 versus a return of $1.20 for project B.

TABLE 9.15

Additional Capital Evaluation Technique: Profitability Index

A	Projects	B
$173	Present value of year 1 cash flow	$ 91
165	Present value of year 2 cash flow	165
75	Present value of year 3 cash flow	225
$513	Total present-value cash flow	$481
400	*Less*: investment (year 0)	400
$113	Net present value (10%)	$ 81
	Profitability index (10%)	
1.28	Present value / investment	1.20
($513/$400)		($481/$400)

A basic difficulty with the profitability index is indicated by an example. Suppose one investment involves an outlay of $1 and returns $2.20 in 1 year, or a present value of $2 (at 10 percent discount rate). Its net present value is $1, and its profitability index is 2.0. Another investment requires an outlay of $1 million and at the end of the year has a return of $1.65 million, or a present value of $1.5 million (at a 10 percent discount rate). Its NPV is $0.5 million, and its PI is 1.5. Under the NPV rule, the larger investment with the larger NPV is clearly superior. Under PI, the firm would select the smaller project (with a PI of 2.0) and enhance its value by only $1 (NPV). If the firm can finance all available investments, the profitability index would not provide a ranking that the firm would want to follow.

Notice, also, in this example with such wide disparity in the size of the two competing projects, the terminal rate of return also breaks down. In this example, the smaller project has a TRR of 120 percent while the larger project has a TRR of "only" 65 percent. Strict adherence to the PI or TRR rules may lead to the wrong decision when comparing two mutually exclusive projects that widely differ in investment size.

Advantages of the NPV Method

We have established that the NPV rule is the correct economic criterion for ranking investment projects. It avoids the deficiencies of the alternative methods. It discounts cash flows at the appropriate opportunity cost of funds. It obeys the value additivity principle. Following the NPV rule maximizes the value of the firm.

Although NPV is the preferred investment valuation technique, one application caveat should be pointed out when comparing projects with different lives. If a company evaluates two alternatives with differing project lives, the projects must be compared on common ground by assuming project replication until common life is obtained.

The following lists the cash flows for two mutually exclusive projects which both cost $100. Project K has a 4-year life and an $11 NPV (at a 10 percent discount rate) while project L has only a 2-year life and a $7 net present value. Applying the NPV rule would lead us to accept project K and reject project L. However, the projects are not comparable because project L covers only a 2-year period while project K covers 4 years. Assuming that project L can be replicated for another 2 years, the last two columns indicate the cash flows and resulting net present value of replicating project L to cover the same 4-year period as project K. Under the project L replication cash flow, the second year cash flow amount of $38 is the second investment of $100 offset by the positive $62 of cash flow from the first investment in project L.

| | Cash Flows | | Net Present Value | | Project L Replication | |
	K	L	K	L	Cash Flow	NPV
Year 0	$(100)	$(100)	$(100)	$(100)	$(100)	$(100)
Year 1	35	62	32	56	62	56
Year 2	35	62	29	51	(38)	(31)
Year 3	35	0	26	0	62	47
Year 4	35	0	24	0	62	42
Total	n/a	n/a	$ 11	$ 7	n/a	$ 14

The replication of project L provides the higher NPV and project L should be accepted. Project K should be rejected.

DETERMINING PROJECT CASH FLOW

Identifying the appropriate cash flows is the application challenge of capital investment analysis. Projected cash flows form the foundation for all the investment analysis techniques and applications. Determining cash flows is one of the most important steps in the capital investment analysis process. In practice, in evaluating investment proposals, discussions about the derivation of assumptions and the resulting cash flows dominate reports and presentations. Reasonable assumptions that are realized when the project is implemented assure the organization that it will enhance shareholders' value to the level of the projected net present value.

We want to isolate incremental after-tax cash flows that occur solely as a result of the project's implementation. For some projects, it is easy to identify the resulting cash flows; for other projects it is much more difficult to isolate the impact on resulting cash flow. For a cost savings project, engineering studies can validate productivity (labor) savings. The life of the project can, again, be determined through engineering studies and experience with similar types of equipment. These cash flows are easy to determine. But what about cash flows from a new product, a new process, or information technology? What about the cash flows that result from years of research and development investment or advertising investment to build brand awareness? These cash flows become a lot more tentative and more difficult to quantify. Nonetheless, a reasonable cash flow or a range of reasonable cash flows must be identified and evaluated.

The remaining portion of this chapter reviews general concepts that support the development of cash flows, defines specific structures to analyze cash flows, and illustrates cash flow models for investment evaluation.

Cash Flow Terminology

This section provides added terminology before we begin the discussion of determining cash flows.

Funds Availability

There are two extremes of funds availability: unlimited funds and capital rationing. Unlimited funds are a financial situation in which a firm is able to accept all independent projects that provide an acceptable rate of return. The authors know of no such organization. Every organization has funding limitations. At the other end of the funds availability continuum lies capital rationing. Capital rationing has two forms: hard capital rationing force on the organization by the financial markets and soft capital rationing, which is management-imposed.

Capital Decisions

As we saw earlier, the first job of capital investment analysis is to identify a project for acceptance or rejection. When two competing, mutually exclusive projects have acceptable returns (or net present values), the decision becomes one of ranking the projects. Capital authorization facilitates, first, the accept/reject decision and, second, project ranking.

Sunk Costs

A *sunk cost* is a cost (or cash outlay) that has already been made. There is nothing to do to change the fact that cash was expended during some previous time period. Sunk costs have no relevance to the immediate decision and should not be considered as part of the investment.

As an example, before the introduction of a new product, a company such as Hershey Foods may decide to do a year-long test market that often costs millions of dollars depending on the size and duration of the test. After a successful test market study, the investment is "scaled up" to accommodate the projected sales level suggested by the test, resulting operating cash flows are estimated, and the project's net present value is calculated. The sunk cost of the test market should not be imposed on the investment analysis. Those costs have already been spent and should not be considered further.

Opportunity Costs

Opportunity costs represent cash flows that could be realized from the best alternative use of a surplus asset that will be engaged in the proposed project. What if a project proposal includes the use of an idle asset that was once used by the business? What value should be attributed to the asset? As in many things, the answer is that it all depends, and we need more additional information.

If the asset has no alternative use and has no current market value or scrap value, that asset should be included at a zero dollar value in the analysis. On the other hand, if you can sell the asset in the open market, that value should be included as part of the project's investment. If you can sell the idle asset as only scrap value, that limited amount should be included in the investment analysis. On the summary page, Table 9.3, this value is included as a transferred fixed asset.

In addition to the difficulty of identifying alternative uses and estimating alternative values, the procedure is often confounded by the asset's book value. The book value of the idle asset has no role in the investment analysis and should not be considered in arriving at the investment amount.

Cost Savings versus Cost Avoidance

Cost savings occur whenever a project's implementation reduces expenses from the current level of expenditures. *Cost avoidance* occurs whenever a project's implementation reduces expenses from a projected level of expenditures. In the case of the analysis of a cost avoidance project, management must first rely on the projected expense pattern without the capital investment. Management must be convinced that without this expenditure, expenses will immediately escalate, and it must be convinced that this capital will save the estimated, projected future expense. Analytically, there is no difference in the designation of the annual cash flow, but there may be a difference in the risk surrounding the nature of the expense.

CAPITAL EVALUATION:
THE BASIC REPLACEMENT DECISION

From this point forward, we shall use the NPV method for all capital evaluation decisions. A cash flow projection includes three interlinked cash flow sections:

- Initial investment: relevant cash outflow (or investment) at the beginning of the investment proposal
- Operating cash flow: relevant, after-tax, incremental cash inflows or outflows from the project throughout its life
- Terminal cash flow: after-tax, nonoperating cash flow occurring in the final year of the project

The following replacement decision is an example of a typical problem. It illustrates the use of cash flows for capital evaluation decisions. It emphasizes that all project cash flows must be represented as changes in the firm's cash flows. And it demonstrates the NPV method of discounted cash flows. Although the project is totally hypothetical, it does maintain our Hershey Foods theme.

Straight-Line Depreciation Example

Hershey Foods Corporation, more specifically the Hershey Chocolate Company, purchased a machine 5 years ago at a cost of $7500. The machine had an expected life of 15 years at the time of purchase and a zero estimated salvage value at the end of 15 years. It is being depreciated on a straight-line basis and has a book value of $5000 at present. The division president reports that, for $12,000 (including installation), a new machine can be bought which, over its 10-year life, will expand sales from $10,000 to $11,000 per year since the product will be aesthetically more appealing and consistent. Further, it will reduce labor and raw materials usage sufficiently to cut operating costs from $7000 to $5000. The new machine has an estimated salvage value of $2000 at the end of 10 years. The old machine's current market value is $1000 and the old machine's market value in 10 years is expected to be zero. Taxes are estimated at a 40 percent rate, and the firm's cost of capital is 10 percent. Should Hershey buy the new machine?

  The decision calls for six steps: (1) Estimate the initial investment attributable to the new investment, (2) determine the incremental operating cash flows, (3) project the terminal cash flows or expected salvage value, (4) add the terminal cash flows to the operating cash flows, (5) find the present value of the total incremental cash flows, and (6) determine whether the NPV is positive. These steps are explained further in the following sections.

Step 1: Estimate Initial Investment

The net initial cash outlay consists of these items: (1) payment to the manufacturer of the new equipment, (2) proceeds from the sale of the old machine, and (3) tax effects (savings). Hershey must make a $12,000 payment to the manufacturer of the machine, and it receives $1000 for selling the old asset. In addition, its next quarterly tax bill will be reduced because of the loss it will incur when it sells the old machine:

	Old Machine
Selling price	$ 1000
Tax book value	5000
Taxable gain (loss)	(4000)
Taxes savings (40%)	1600
After-tax gain (loss)	$(2400)
Selling price	$ 1000
Taxes savings	1600
Cash flow	$ 2600

The tax savings of $1600 on the taxable loss further reduces the initial investment:

	Initial Investment
Purchase price	$12,000
After-tax proceeds from selling the old asset	(2,600)
Initial investment	$ 9,400

The net initial investment is $9600.

If additional working capital is required as a result of a capital investment decision such as sales expansion investments (as opposed to cost-reducing replacement investments), this additional working capital must be taken into account. We assume that Hershey will not need any additional working capital, so this factor is ignored in this example.

Step 2: Determine Annual Incremental Operating Cash Flows

Column 1 below shows this particular product line's estimated income statement and cash flow as they would be without the new machine; column 2 shows the statement as it would look if the new investment were made; and column 3 shows the incremental impacts.

	(1) Current Levels	(2) Projected Levels	(3) Difference Better (Worse)
Sales	$10,000	$11,000	$1,000
Operating costs	7,000	5,000	2,000
Depreciation	500	1,000*	(500)
Operating income	2,500	5,000	2,500
Taxes (40%)	1,000	2,000	(1,000)
After-tax operating income	$ 1,500	$ 3,000	$1,500
After-tax operating income	$ 1,500	$ 3,000	$1,500
Depreciation	500	1,000	500
Cash flow	$ 2,000	$ 4,000	$2,000

*The projected depreciation is calculated as (Cost of Asset – Salvage Value) / Project Life.

Sales improve by $1000 while operating expenses also improve (are reduced). However, depreciation increases by $500 per year, which results in a net $2500 improvement in operating income. After a 40 percent tax impact, the after-tax operating income improves by $1500. When the $500 incremental depreciation is added back, a favorable $2000 after-tax cash impact is realized.

Another way of looking at the annual incremental cash flows is to isolate the after-tax cash flow impact of each item. For example, sales are expected to rise by $1000. This results in $1000 more taxable income upon which $400 (or 40 percent) in taxes must be paid, resulting in after-tax operating income of $600. Operating costs improve (decrease) by $2000 or $1200 after consideration of taxes on the savings. Finally, although depreciation is not a cash flow item, it is a tax-deductible expense. The additional $500 of depreciation provides a tax reduction (or tax shield) of $200. The tax shield provides an additional positive cash flow while the depreciation expense has no direct impact on cash flow. In summary:

Item	Calculation (Tax Rate = 40%)	Cash Flow
Additional sales	$1,000 × (1 – tax rate)	$ 600
Reduced expenses	$2,000 × (1 – tax rate)	1200
Added depreciation	$500 × (tax rate)	200
	Total cash flow impact	$2000

Either approach results in the same incremental cash flow impact, $2000, for each of the 10 years of projections. However, the former approach promotes a consistent framework that we will use for additional analyses.

Step 3: Project the Terminal Cash Flows or Expected Salvage Value

The new machine has an estimated salvage value of $2000. That is, Hershey expects to be able to sell the machine for $2000 after 10 years of use. In year 10, the tax book value is also $2000, or the $12,000 purchase price less 10 years of $1000 depreciation per year. Notice that the salvage value is a return of capital, not taxable income, so it is not subject to income taxes. Of course, when the new machine is actually retired 10 years hence, it might be sold for more or less than the expected $2000. So either taxable income or a deductible loss could arise, but $2000 is the best present estimate of the new machine's salvage value. This results in no taxable gain or loss on the disposal of the new asset, no additional tax payments (or savings), and a cash flow impact of $2000. If additional working capital had been required and included in the initial cash outlay and annual operating cash flow, this amount would be added to the salvage value of the machine because the working capital would be recovered if and when the project was abandoned.

Step 4: Total the Annual Operating Cash Flows and Terminal Cash Flow

Since we are interested in total cash flow, add the terminal cash flow to the annual operating cash flows.

Step 5: Find the Present Value of the Future Cash Flows

We have explained in detail how to measure the annual benefits. The next step is to determine the present value of the benefit stream. This can be accomplished via

$$\sum_{t=1}^{N} \frac{CF_t}{(1+k)^t} - I_0 = NPV \tag{9.7}$$

While this is a general model, the specific case in hand can be solved more straightforwardly using the interest factor for a 9-year, 10 percent annuity, which is found to be 5.7590 from Table A.4. This factor, when multiplied by the first 9 years' $2000 incremental operating cash flow, results in a present value of $11,518. The present value of the final year's cash flow is found by multiplying the present-value interest factor (10 years, 10 percent) of 0.3855 (Table A.2) by the year 10 cash flow of $4000 ($2000 incremental operating cash flow and $2000 terminal cash flow). This results in a present value of the final year's cash flow of $1542. The total gross present value of the 10 years of cash flows is $13,060 ($11,518 + $1542).

Step 6: Determine the Net Present Value

The project's net present value is found as the sum of the present values of the inflows, or benefits, less the outflows, or costs:

$$\text{Net present value} = \begin{matrix} \text{Gross present value} \\ \text{of total cash flow} \end{matrix} - \text{Initial investment}$$

$$= \$13,060 - \$9400$$

$$= \$3660 \tag{9.8}$$

Since the NPV is positive, the project should be accepted.

Capital Evaluation Worksheet

Table 9.16 presents a worksheet for evaluating capital projects. The top section shows net cash flows at the time of investment; since all these flows occur immediately, no discounting is required and the interest factor is 1.0. The lower section of the table shows future cash flows— benefits from increased sales and/or reduced costs, depreciation, and salvage value. These flows occur over time, so it is necessary to convert them to present values. The NPV as determined in this format, $3660, agrees with the figure calculated above.

REPLACEMENT ANALYSIS WITH ACCELERATED DEPRECIATION

Next we consider the effect of MACRS depreciation on the replacement analysis. Accelerated depreciation, on both the old and the new equipment, complicates the computations somewhat, but the logic is the same.

Step 1: Estimate Cash Outlay

The old machine had an initial cost of $7500 and a 15-year life. Using straight-line depreciation, its book value was $5000 after 5 years. Most manufacturing equipment is considered a 7-year class life under MACRS, as listed in Table 9.17. When the 7-year life MACRS depreciation (see Table 9.17 for depreciation rates over the 8-year period due to a half-year convention in the first and last years) is applied to the original $7500, five years of depreciation or $5827 has already been depreciated, leaving a balance of $1673 to be depreciated over the next 3 years. This is less than the book value under straight-line depreciation because MACRS results in higher depreciation earlier in the life of the asset and a shorter life is applied.

The current market value of the old machine is assumed to be $1000, as before. Selling the machine for $1000 will result in a loss of $673—the difference between its book and market value. This loss results in tax savings equal to (loss)(tax rate) = ($673)(0.4) = $269. This

TABLE 9.16

Replacement Decision, Straight–Line Depreciation

	Initial Investment	Year 1	Year 2	Year 3	Year 4	Year 5	Year 6	Year 7	Year 8	Year 9	Year 10
Purchase Price	$(12,000)										
After-Tax Proceeds—Sale of Old Asset	2,600										
Incremental Operating Cash Flow											
Sales		$1,000	$1,000	$1,000	$1,000	$1,000	$1,000	$1,000	$1,000	$1,000	$1,000
Operating Costs		2,000	2,000	2,000	2,000	2,000	2,000	2,000	2,000	2,000	2,000
Depreciation		(500)	(500)	(500)	(500)	(500)	(500)	(500)	(500)	(500)	(500)
Operating Income		2,500	2,500	2,500	2,500	2,500	2,500	2,500	2,500	2,500	2,500
Taxes (40%)		(1,000)	(1,000)	(1,000)	(1,000)	(1,000)	(1,000)	(1,000)	(1,000)	(1,000)	(1,000)
After-Tax Operating Income		$1,500	$1,500	$1,500	$1,500	$1,500	$1,500	$1,500	$1,500	$1,500	$1,500
After-Tax Operating Income		$1,500	$1,500	$1,500	$1,500	$1,500	$1,500	$1,500	$1,500	$1,500	$1,500
Depreciation		500	500	500	500	500	500	500	500	500	500
Incremental Operating Cash Flow		$2,000	$2,000	$2,000	$2,000	$2,000	$2,000	$2,000	$2,000	$2,000	$2,000
Terminal Cash Flow											$2,000
Total Cash Flow	$(9,400)	$2,000	$2,000	$2,000	$2,000	$2,000	$2,000	$2,000	$2,000	$2,000	$4,000
Present Value 10.0%	$(9,400)	$1,818	$1,653	$1,503	$1,366	$1,242	$1,129	$1,026	$933	$848	$1,542
	$13,060	Gross Present Value (PV – Cash Flow Years 1–10)									
Net Present Value	$3,660										

249

does not affect the purchase price of the new equipment, but it does reduce the tax savings on the disposal of the old asset, thus increasing the net initial cash outflow:

			Initial Investment
Purchase price			$12,000
After-tax proceeds from selling the old asset	Selling price	$1,000	(1,269)
	Tax savings	269	
Initial Investment			$10,731

The initial investment increases to $10,731.

Step 2: Determine Annual Incremental Operating Cash Flows

For capital evaluation analysis, the cash flows that are discounted are incremental after-tax operating cash flows. Depreciation is not a direct cash charge, so operating cash flows are not directly affected by the switch to MACRS; however, after-tax cash flows are affected because of the change in the tax shelter resulting from the use of accelerated depreciation. Furthermore, because the depreciation expense is not constant from year to year under accelerated depreciation as it is under straight-line depreciation, annual benefits will vary. The incremental depreciation is calculated in the footnote of Table 9.18, which details all the annual after-tax cash flows.

TABLE 9.17

MACRS Depreciation

Class	Examples
3-Year	Equipment used in research
5-Year	Autos, computers
7-Year	Most industrial equipment and office furniture and fixtures

	Property Class		
Year	3-Year	5-Year	7-Year
1	33.33%	20.00%	14.29%
2	44.44%	32.00%	24.49%
3	14.82%	19.20%	17.49%
4	7.41%	11.52%	12.49%
5		11.52%	8.93%
6		5.76%	8.93%
7			8.93%
8			4.45%

TABLE 9.18

Replacement Decision, MACRS Depreciation

	Initial Investment	Year 1	Year 2	Year 3	Year 4	Year 5	Year 6	Year 7	Year 8	Year 9	Year 10
Purchase Price	$(12,000)										
After-Tax Proceeds—Sale of Old Asset	1,269										
Incremental Operating Cash Flow											
Sales		$1,000	$1,000	$1,000	$1,000	$1,000	$1,000	$1,000	$1,000	$1,000	$1,000
Operating Costs		2,000	2,000	2,000	2,000	2,000	2,000	2,000	2,000	2,000	2,000
Depreciation*		(1,045)	(2,269)	(1,765)	(1,499)	(1,072)	(1,072)	(1,072)	(534)	—	—
Operating Income		1,955	731	1,235	1,501	1,928	1,928	1,928	2,466	3,000	3,000
Taxes (40%)		782	292	494	600	771	771	771	986	1,200	1,200
After-Tax Operating Income		$1,173	$ 439	$ 741	$ 901	$1,157	$1,157	$1,157	$1,480	$1,800	$1,800
After-Tax Operating Income		$1,173	$ 439	$ 741	$ 901	$1,157	$1,157	$1,157	$1,480	$1,800	$1,800
Depreciation		1,045	2,269	1,765	1,499	1,072	1,072	1,072	534	—	—
Incremental Operating Cash Flow		$2,218	$2,708	$2,506	$2,400	$2,229	$2,229	$2,229	$2,014	$1,800	$1,800
Terminal Cash Flow											
Residual Value—No Gain (Loss)											$1,200
Total Cash Flow	$(10,731)	$2,218	$2,708	$2,506	$2,400	$2,229	$2,229	$2,229	$2,014	$1,800	$3,000
Present Value 10.0%	$(10,731)	$2,016	$2,238	$1,883	$1,639	$1,384	$1,258	$1,144	$ 939	$ 763	$1,157
		$14,421	Gross Present Value (PV – Cash Flow Years 1–10)								
Net Present Value	$3,690										
* Incremental Depreciation		14.29%	24.49%	17.49%	12.49%	8.93%	8.93%	8.93%	4.45%	0.00%	0.00%
New Equipment—8-Year MACRS		$1,715	$2,939	$2,099	$1,499	$1,072	$1,072	$1,072	$534	—	—
Old Equipment—8-Year MACRS (Last 3 Years)		670	670	334	—	—	—	—	—	—	—
Incremental Depreciation		$1,045	$2,269	$1,765	$1,499	$1,072	$1,072	$1,072	$534	—	—

Step 3: Project the Terminal Cash Flows or Expected Salvage Value

The new machine has an estimated salvage value of $2000. That is, Hershey expects to be able to sell the machine for $2000 after 10 years of use. The MACRS depreciation technique fully depreciates an asset over the project category's life. Consequently, a salvage value of $2000 results in a taxable gain of $2000 and an after-tax salvage value cash flow of $1200:

	New Machine
Selling price	$2000
Tax book value	0
Taxable gain (loss)	2000
Taxes (40%)	(800)
After-tax gain (loss)	$1200
Selling price	$2000
Taxes	(800)
Cash flow	$1200

Again, if additional working capital had been required and included in the initial cash outlay and annual operating cash flow, this amount would be added to the salvage value of the machine because the working capital would be recovered if and when the project was abandoned.

Step 4: Total the Annual Operating Cash Flows and Terminal Cash Flow

See Table 9.18.

Step 5: Find the Present Value of the Future Cash Flows

See Table 9.18.

Step 6: Determine the Net Present Value

The project's net present value is found as the sum of the present values of the inflows, or benefits, less the outflows, or costs:

$$\text{NPV} = \begin{array}{c} \text{Gross present value} \\ \text{of total cash flow} \end{array} - \text{Initial investment}$$

$$= \$14{,}421 - \$10{,}731$$

$$= \$3690$$

As before, the net present value is positive, indicating that the replacement project should be accepted. The following example examines cash flow development for a new-product project.

THE NEW PRODUCT DECISION

New product growth is an objective embraced by almost all organizations. New products are the lifeblood of an organization and ensure that the firm will renew itself and meet the changing needs, desires, and tastes of its customers and consumers. Hershey Foods for years has ridden the wave of successful new products. Some corporations throw hundreds of new products annually into the marketplace and hope that a few products stick. Hershey's philosophy is more focused and methodical. As a result, Hershey introduces a few new products each year and has enjoyed the success of launching some major new brands throughout the 1990s.

The following describes the process of evaluating a new product. This project and its underlying assumptions are completely hypothetical, but illustrative of the necessary evaluation to validate the economic viability of an investment in a new product.

This new product capitalizes upon Hershey's knowledge of the confectionery market and its strengths in producing, selling, and distributing the product. The new product builds on valuable relationships with customers (such as Wal-Mart, K-Mart, and Food Lion) and the consumer's favorable impressions of Hershey's quality and value. The hypothetical new product is a new candy bar with swirled white chocolate and milk chocolate and macadamia nuts inclusions.

The launch of a new product takes cooperative teamwork that seamlessly unites all functions within the organization. In this example, the new product idea jointly "bubbled up" from sales, marketing, and research and development. A multifunctional new-product task team is quickly assembled to analyze the product's viability.

- Marketing develops an initial sales projection along with an annual growth profile, through test panels and test marketing. Originally, gross product sales were estimated at $65 million for the initial year. However, it was estimated that this new product would "cannibalize" or displace approximately $5 million of sales of other Hershey products. These cannibalized sales are relevant and an incremental impact of accepting this project. Consequently, the first year's sales were estimated at $60 million. In addition, after a second-year reduction in sales, sales of this product would increase at 5 percent until the 10th year, when the product would be discontinued. The second-year sales reduction occurs for a number of reasons: Consumer initial trials are heaviest in the first year, the retail inventory pipeline is filled in the first year, and marketing promotional and advertising expenses are significantly reduced in the second year.
- Marketing and sales also estimate that they will need $23 million for advertising, consumer coupons, and trade promotions to

support the initial new product launch. This is in addition to an ongoing expenditure level of 15 percent of sales, which also includes hiring a brand manager and an assistant.

- Engineering and manufacturing estimate the configuration and number of lines necessary to fulfill the marketing projections. In this example, engineering estimates that the corporation needs to buy two production lines for $50 million. It also estimates that in 10 years, the assets will have a residual value of $5 million before tax considerations.

- Manufacturing, with the help of research and development and cost accounting, estimates it will cost 62 percent (for every sales dollar) to produce this product. This pays for the raw material (cocoa, sugar, milk, nuts, etc.), the direct labor, and overhead.

- Accounting and finance estimate the tax rate and calculate the tax depreciation (MACRS) on the asset. Accounting and finance, with the input of the complete team, estimate that ongoing working capital investment at 8 percent of sales. That is, the initial investment (year 0) includes working capital investment to support the first year's sales of 8 percent. Annually, additional investment (or divestment as in the first year) also is required to support the projected sales for the next year. The investment made in inventory (to ensure that inventory is on hand to complete sales transactions) and receivables (to finance customers' purchases) is offset by spontaneous, operating financing provided by suppliers through accounts payable. Notice, all the working capital is recovered in the final year.

- Finance also determines an appropriate cost of capital for this project.

The top portion of Table 9.19 documents the key assumptions from above. The lower portion dollarizes the assumptions and evaluates them, using the same six-step process as introduced in the evaluation of a replacement asset.

In this analysis, you can see that sales approach $80 million by the final year. Also, the after-tax operating income displays a loss for the first 2 years due to the additional product launch expenses. After the third year, the product contributes positive after-tax operating income through the remainder of its life. This project produces positive cash flows throughout all years of operation. The terminal cash flows include a $3 million after-tax residual value along with working capital recovery of more than $6 million. In total, the project generates cash flows with a gross present value of $58.8 million compared to an initial investment of $54.8 million, which results in a positive $4.0 million net present value.

The project should be accepted and the value of Hershey's stock should rise by $4.0 million.

Notice, if the previously described test market sunk cost of $5 million is included in this analysis, the project is unacceptable with a negative net present value (NPV=–$1). The $5 million test market costs should not be considered in this analysis. Those costs have long been spent. Accepting or rejecting this project does not change the sunk costs for the test market. By rejecting this project, the organization forgoes $4 million in value and does not recover any of its sunk costs.

But what if our collective judgment about the assumptions is incorrect? We treated these assumptions as certain. What if these cash flows are not certain? The next sections discuss different techniques to understand the uncertainty underlying assumptions and their valuation impacts.

Assumption Uncertainty

To better understand the impact of uncertainty on a capital evaluation, we will use the new product example from above and review sensitivity analysis and scenario analysis. Uncertainty underlies any projection. Each organization needs to find the approach that best assists it in understanding and dealing with uncertainty in capital investment analysis.

Sensitivity Analysis

Sensitivity analysis is done by varying each assumption individually and observing the resulting change in the net present value. Table 9.20 tests the impact on the net present value for a reasonable, conservative change in each assumption. For example, if the purchase price of the new assets escalates to $55 million from the original estimate of $50 million, the net present value drops to $0.5 million, or a decrease of more than $3.5 million. Table 9.20 documents the NPV reduction that results from each of the changes noted on the table.

Notice some changes in assumptions have little impact while other changes in assumptions have overwhelming consequences. The working capital support (percent of incremental sales), tax rate, and residual value have minimal impact. Other assumptions, such as purchase price, initial sales levels, growth rates, expenses as a percent of sales, and cost of capital, have a major impact.

Scenario Analysis

Scenario analysis examines different business models or different circumstances by combining adjustments in a number of assumptions simultaneously. Table 9.21 illustrates three different scenarios, busi-

TABLE 9.19
New-Product Decision ($000)

	Initial Investment	Year 1	Year 2	Year 3	Year 4	Year 5	Year 6	Year 7	Year 8	Year 9	Year 10
				KEY ASSUMPTIONS							
Purchase Price of New Equipment	$(50,000)										
Working Capital (% of Incremental Sales)	8.0%										
Initial Sales		$60,000									
Sales Growth			–10.0%	5.0%	5.0%	5.0%	5.0%	5.0%	5.0%	5.0%	5.0%
Cost of Sales (Excluding Depreciation—% of Sales)		62.0%	62.0%	62.0%	62.0%	62.0%	62.0%	62.0%	62.0%	62.0%	62.0%
Operating Costs (% of Sales)		15.0%	15.0%	15.0%	15.0%	15.0%	15.0%	15.0%	15.0%	15.0%	15.0%
Additional Product Launch Expense		$18,000	$5,000	—	—	—	—	—	—	—	—
Tax Rate		40.0%	40.0%	40.0%	40.0%	40.0%	40.0%	40.0%	40.0%	40.0%	40.0%
Residual Value											$5,000
Cost of Capital 10.0%											

CAPITAL EVALUATION

	Year 0	1	2	3	4	5	6	7	8	9	10
Purchase Price	$(50,000)										
Initial Working Capital	(4,800)										
Incremental Operating Cash Flow											
Sales		$60,000	$54,000	$56,700	$59,535	$62,512	$65,637	$68,919	$72,365	$75,983	$79,783
Cost of Sales		(37,200)	(33,480)	(35,154)	(36,912)	(38,757)	(40,695)	(42,730)	(44,866)	(47,110)	(49,465)
Depreciation*		(7,145)	(12,245)	(8,745)	(6,245)	(4,465)	(4,465)	(4,465)	(2,225)	—	—
Gross Income		15,655	8,275	12,801	16,378	19,289	20,477	21,724	25,274	28,874	30,317
Operating Expenses		(9,000)	(8,100)	(8,505)	(8,930)	(9,377)	(9,846)	(10,338)	(10,855)	(11,398)	(11,967)
Additional Product Launch Expense		(18,000)	(5,000)	—	—	—	—	—	—	—	—
Operating Income		(11,345)	(4,825)	4,296	7,448	9,913	10,632	11,386	14,419	17,476	18,350
Taxes (40%)		4,538	1,930	(1,718)	(2,979)	(3,965)	(4,253)	(4,555)	(5,768)	(6,990)	(7,340)
After-Tax Operating Income		$ (6,807)	$(2,895)	$2,578	$4,469	$5,948	$6,379	$6,832	$8,651	$10,486	$11,010
After-Tax Operating Income		$ (6,807)	$(2,895)	$2,578	$4,469	$5,948	$6,379	$6,832	$8,651	$10,486	$11,010
Depreciation		7,145	12,245	8,745	6,245	4,465	4,465	4,465	2,225	—	—
Additional Working Capital		480	(216)	(227)	(238)	(250)	(263)	(276)	(289)	(304)	—
Incremental Operating Cash Flow		$ 818	$9,134	$11,096	$10,476	$10,163	$10,581	$11,021	$10,587	$10,182	$11,010
Residual Value—After Tax											$ 3,000
Working Capital Recovery											6,383
Total Cash Flow	$(54,800)	$ 818	$9,134	$11,096	$10,476	$10,163	$10,581	$11,021	$10,587	$10,182	$20,393
Present Value 10.0%	$(54,800)	$ 744	$7,549	$ 8,336	$ 7,155	$ 6,310	$ 5,973	$ 5,656	$ 4,939	$ 4,318	$ 7,862
				Gross present value (PV - cash flow years 1–10)							
Net present value	$ 4,042										
		$58,842									
*MACRS Depreciation Rate		14.29%	24.49%	17.49%	12.49%	8.93%	8.93%	8.93%	4.45%	0.00%	0.00%

257

TABLE 9.20

New Product, Sensitivity Analysis ($000)

	Original Assumption	Revised Assumption	Revised NPV	Change in NPV
Purchase Price of New Equipment	$(50,000)	$(55,000)	$485	$(3,557)
Working Capital (% of Incremental Sales)	8.0%	9.0%	3,651	(391)
Initial Sales	$60,000	$55,000	(188)	(4,230)
Sales Growth	−10% / 5%	−11% / 4%	2,071	(1,971)
Cost of Sales (Excluding Depreciation—% of Sales)	62.0%	63.0%	1,699	(2,343)
Operating Costs (% of Sales)	15.0%	14.0%	1,699	(2,343)
Additional Product Launch Expense, Year 1	$18,000	$20,000	2,951	(1,091)
Tax Rate	40.0%	41.0%	3,690	(352)
Residual Value	$5,000	$4,000	3,810	(232)
Cost of Capital	10.0%	11.0%	1,117	(2,925)
The original net present value for this new product			$4,042	

TABLE 9.21

New Product, Scenario Analysis ($000)

	Original Assumptions	Cost Cutting	Growth	Aggressive Growth
Purchase Price of New Equipment	$(50,000)	$(45,000)	$(55,000)	$(55,000)
Working Capital (% of Incremental Sales)	8.0%	8.0%	9.0%	9.0%
Initial Sales	$60,000	$50,000	60,000	66,000
Sales Growth	−10% / 5%	−15% / 3%	−5% / 6%	0% / 8%
Cost of Sales (Excluding Depreciation—% of Sales)	62.0%	61.0%	63.0%	63.0%
Operating Costs (% of Sales)	15.0%	12.0%	16.0%	17.5%
Additional Product Launch Expense, Year 1	$18,000	$15,000	$20,000	$22,000
Tax Rate	40.0%	40.0%	40.0%	40.0%
Residual Value	$5,000	—	—	—
Cost of Capital	10.0%	10.0%	10.0%	10.0%
Gross Present Value (PV - CF Years 1–10)	$58,842	$51,290	$57,234	$63,134
Initial Investment	54,800	49,000	60,400	60,940
Net Present Value	4,042	2,290	(3,166)	2,194
Change from Original Case	n/a	(1,752)	(7,208)	(1,848)

ness models. The original case is documented, along with a cost-cutting scenario and two growth scenarios:

- The cost-cutting scenario trades reduced volumes (sales) and growth for reduced investment levels, cost of sales, and marketing expenses. Also, there is no residual value assumed for this lower-priced equipment.
- The growth scenario trades higher sales growth for additional investment in equipment, production costs, and marketing expense. Since the equipment is run to generate more product, its residual value is assumed to be zero.
- The aggressive growth trades a higher initial sales level and more substantial growth for additional investment in equipment, production costs, and marketing expense. Since the equipment is run to generate more product, its residual value is assumed to be zero.

The results indicate that the original scenario was the most economically viable scenario. The original scenario resulted in a net present value which was $1.8 million higher than either the cost-cutting or aggressive growth scenarios and a walloping $7.2 million better than the growth scenario.

ADDITIONAL KEY CONCEPTS

Now that we have discussed more comprehensive project analysis, this section reviews additional key concepts about cash flow and investment analysis.

Inflation

Should the projected cash flows be based on nominal estimates (including inflation) or should the estimates be based on "real" (excluding inflation) cash flow estimates? For a number of reasons, the cash flows should be nominal and include reasonable estimates of inflation:

- Inflation is a fact of life for most organizations.
- Deflation is also a part of life for some industries.
- Inflation affects prices and costs differently.
- Cost of capital includes a market expected general rate of inflation.
- Comparing a nominal (including inflation) cost of capital to real (excluding inflation) cash flows can lead to the rejection of economically viable projects.

- Comparing a real cost of capital to real cash flows may lead to acceptance of an inferior project and understatement of working capital investment and overstatement of the depreciation tax shield.
- Nominal cash flow projections provide a comparative basis for postcompletion audits.

One consulting client that used projections of real cash flows remarked, "Our company is not in the business of forecasting inflation." This is precisely the point! Whenever cash flow projections are made, there is an implicit assumption about inflation. If we do not explicitly address inflation, implicitly we are saying that inflation is expected to be 0.0 percent, which may be a good or a bad assumption.

Allocated Costs

To repeat from the beginning of this section, when determining cash flows, we are interested in only relevant, incremental cash flows. That is clearly the case in the previous examples of equipment replacement and new product. In the new product investment analysis, the administrative costs to hire a brand manager and an assistant were specifically included in the projected operating expenses. We did not allocate the salaries and related expenses of the marketing director, vice president of marketing, marketing department, or chief executive officer. We did not allocate floor space and related occupancy expenses. The salaries, related expenses, and occupancy expenses are not a function of the acceptance or rejection of the new product. They are not incremental, and they are not relevant to this analysis.

The words *allocate, allocated,* and *allocation* should raise a red flag. Any allocated expenses must be reviewed and their incremental nature determined. If the expenses are not incremental, they should not be included in the analysis.

Financial Costs and Financial Servicing

The two previous projects, equipment replacement and new product, illustrate the operational nature of the investment analysis cash flows. Related interest costs, debt repayment, dividends, stock repurchases, etc., are considered financing-related cash flows and are not directly considered in the investment cash flow development. Only operating cash flows are directly projected and considered for investment analysis. Financing implications are captured through the discount rate, the cost of capital.

Accounting Measures and Investment Analysis

In Chap. 7, we introduced and discussed a number of accounting performance metrics. Earlier in this chapter, we discussed the differences between accounting measures and economic measures.

While a hypothetical example, the new-product analysis in this chapter is representative of the cash flow patterns exhibited by new retail (consumer) products. Based upon almost any accounting metric, return on assets or economic value added, this project should not be accepted because it does not generate positive returns in its first few years, despite increasing shareholders' value by $4 million over its 10-year life.

While it is important to understand and anticipate the accounting ramifications of new product introductions through strategic planning, economic measures dictate the acceptance or rejection of an investment.

SUMMARY

Capital investment decisions, which involve commitments for large outlays whose benefits (or drawbacks) extend well into the future, are of the greatest significance to a firm. Decisions in these areas, therefore, have a major impact on the future well-being of the firm. This chapter focused on how capital investment decisions can be made more effective in contributing to the health and growth of a firm and enhance shareholder value. The discussion stressed the development of systematic procedures and rules throughout all four phases of capital investment. Cash flow evaluation techniques were first introduced and were followed by a discussion of the development of projects' incremental after-tax cash flows.

The chapter emphasized that one of the most crucial phases in the process is the evaluation and authorization of a proposal. Four commonly used procedures for ranking investment proposals were discussed: payback, net present value, internal rate of return, and terminal rate of return.

Payback is defined as the number of years required to return the original investment. Although the payback method is used frequently as a simple rule of thumb, it has serious conceptual weaknesses, because it ignores the facts that (1) some receipts come in beyond the payback period and (2) a dollar received today is more valuable than a dollar received in the future.

Net present value is defined as the present value of future returns, discounted at the cost of capital, minus the cost of the investment. The NPV method overcomes the conceptual flaws noted in the use of the payback method.

Internal rate of return is defined as the interest rate that equates the present value of future returns to the investment outlay. The IRR method, like the NPV method, discounts cash flows. However, the internal rate of return method assumes reinvestment at the IRR.

Terminal rate of return (or *modified internal rate of return*) is the interest rate that equates the cost of the investment with the accumulated future value of the intermediate cash flows that are assumed to be reinvested at an appropriate risk-adjusted cost of capital. The TRR explicitly incorporates an opportunity cost of capital as a reinvestment rate.

In most cases, the three discounted cash flow methods give identical answers to these questions: Which of two mutually exclusive projects should be selected? How large should the total capital budget be? However, under certain circumstances, conflicts may arise. Such conflicts are caused primarily by the fact that the IRR method makes different assumptions about the rate at which cash flows may be reinvested, or the opportunity cost of cash flows. The assumption of the NPV and TRR methods (that the opportunity cost is the cost of capital) is the correct one. While the terminal rate of return is an improvement on the internal rate of return, it may lead to an incorrect choice of mutually exclusive projects if the sizes of the investments are significantly different. Accordingly, our recommendation is to use the NPV method to make capital investment decisions.

Relevant, nominal, incremental, after-tax cash flow development is the backbone for financial investment analysis. However, just as a strong strategic planning process has strong financial considerations, which also enable managerial processes, so does a strong capital investment process and its evaluation and authorization phase. A strong evaluation and authorization phase

- Facilitates communication among the senior executives of an organization
- Sets a business direction
- Prioritizes opportunities and requirements
- Establishes business performance standards and objectives

Within this chapter, a consistent but flexible investment analysis framework is developed and applied to a variety of projects. The framework is used to illustrate how to value a replacement project and a new product proposal (complete with sensitivity and scenario analyses). This approach and framework can be extended to include major investment in information technology, research and development, administrative projects, and acquisition valuation.

QUESTIONS AND PROBLEMS

9.1   **Project Analysis.** Assume that you are evaluating the following three mutually exclusive projects:

	A	B	C
Cost	$3,400	$3,400	$3,400
Year 1	0	1,870	1,020
Year 2	0	1,870	1,700
Year 3	6,460	1,870	3,284

A.   Complete the following analyses. (For the last two lines, Terminal Value, please write in the dollar amount of the terminal value.):

	VALUES			RANK (First, Second, Third)		
	A	B	C	A	B	C
Payback period						
NPV—10%						
NPV—15%						
IRR						
TRR—10%						
TRR—15%						
Terminal value—10%						
Terminal value—15%						

B.   Compare and explain the conflicting rankings of the NPVs and TRRs versus the IRRs.

C.   Using different discount rates, is it possible to get different rankings within the NPV calculation? Why or why not?

D.   If 10 percent is the required return, which project is preferred?

E.   Which is the fairer representation of these two projects, TRR or IRR? Why?

9.2   **Postcompletion Audit.** A. Two years ago, a new product capital project was approved for $75 million based upon the cash flows listed below. Calculate the net present value for the original proposal at an 18 percent discount rate.

Year	Original proposal
0	$(75)
1	2
2	20
3	30
4	38
5	55

B.   The three-year postcompletion audit contains a financial reevaluation of this project. The postcompletion audit reflects an overrun of $2 million during the implementation of the equipment (year 0) and ongoing performance that fell $6 million short of the year 1 projection and $5 million short of the year 2 projection. Marketing assures us that the wrinkles have been worked out, and starting this year, performance will improve to the level originally projected. Recalculate the net present value.

C.   What additional questions would you want to ask Marketing regarding this new product and its forecasts for the remaining three years?

9.3   **Net Present Value Impact.** Comment on the effects that the following would have on the net present value (i.e., increase, decrease, or no effect). Provide a short explanation of your answer. Each item is independent of every other item.

A.   The discount rate is lowered.

B.   Ingredient costs increase and price increases cannot be passed on to customers.

C.   The new process would require additional working capital investment.

D.   In a machine replacement analysis, it is further learned that a complete overhaul of the old machine, which is under consideration for replacement, will be needed in year 4.

E.   The sales price decreases with no increase in the number of units sold or change in the cost structure.

9.4   **Cash Flow Determination.** Please construct the annual cash flows and calculate the net present value for a project with the following information:

Year	Sales Growth
2	40%
3	25%
4	20%
5	10%

First Year Sales:	20,000 units
Unit Price:	$50 years 1–2
	$60 years 3–5
Working Capital:	$63,000 initially (year 0 with recovery)
Variable Cost:	$45 per unit
Fixed Cost (exc. depr.):	$60,000
Initial Investment:	$750,000 (depreciate to $0)
Salvage Value:	$50,000 at the end of year 5
Tax Rate:	35%
Cost of Capital:	12%

9.5   **Incremental Cash Flow.** Which of the following cash flows should be treated as incremental cash flows when computing the net present value of an investment?

		Incremental (Inc) Nonincremental (NI)
A.	Expenditure on plant and equipment.	
B.	Cost of R&D undertaken in connection with a new product during the last 3 years.	
C.	Dividend payments.	
D.	Reduction in the sales of the company's other products.	

SOLUTIONS TO QUESTIONS AND PROBLEMS

9.1   A.

Year	A	B	C
0	$(3,400)	$(3,400)	$(3,400)
1	—	1,870	1,020
2	—	1,870	1,700
3	6,460	1,870	3,284

	Values			Rank		
Technique	A	B	C	A	B	C
Payback period	2.53	1.82	2.21	3	1	2
NPV—10%	$1,453	$1,250	$1,400	1	3	2
NPV—15%	$ 848	$ 870	$ 932	3	2	1
IRR	23.86%	29.92%	28.01%	3	1	2
TRR—10%	23.86%	22.10%	23.40%	1	3	2
TRR—15%	23.86%	24.07%	24.67%	3	2	1
Terminal value 10%	6,460	6,190	6,388	1	3	2
Terminal value 15%	6,460	6,494	6,588	3	2	1

B.   The conflicting rankings between the NPV and TRR versus the IRR are a direct result of the reinvestment assumption implied by the IRR.

C.   As demonstrated above, using different discount rates can yield different project rankings due to the impact of different cash flow patterns.

D.   At 10 percent, project C is preferred because it has the highest NPV (and TRR).

E.   The TRR (or MIRR) is a fairer representation because it avoids the implicit reinvestment assumption assumed by the IRR. That is, the IRR assumes reinvestment at the IRR.

9.2

	A Original	B Revised
Year	Proposal	Audit
0	$ (75)	$ (77)
1	2	(4)
2	20	15
3	30	30
4	38	38
5	55	55
NPV	$2.96	($7.72)
18.0%		

C. In general, there would be a series of questions. The questions would try to discover what originally "went wrong" (sales performance, margins, etc.), what corrective actions were being taken to improve performance, and what measures could be taken to further improve the project's remaining projected performance to eradicate the negative NPV. Other areas of questioning include establishing the track record of the management team and a review of the project's parameters, such as, Is 18 percent the proper discount rate? And could the life be extended for a sixth year?

9.3 A. A lower discount rate causes the NPV to increase.

B. Rising ingredient costs increase expenses. If these rising costs cannot be passed onto customers, income and cash flow decrease, which decreases the NPV of the project.

C. Additional working capital requirements cause a reduction in cash flows and NPV. Even if the working capital is fully recovered, the time value of money is lost.

D. In this case, a project is under consideration that replaces an existing piece of equipment. It is discovered that the existing piece of equipment needs a major overhaul. The old piece of equipment is less attractive, and its replacement more attractive.

E. A reduction in sales price with no increase in units sold reduces net income, cash flow, and NPV.

9.4

	Year 0	Year 1	Year 2	Year 3	Year 4	Year 5
Units		20,000	28,000	35,000	42,000	46,200
Growth			40.0%	25.0%	20.0%	10.0%
Price		$50.00	$50.00	$60.00	$60.00	$60.00
Variable cost per unit		$45.00	$45.00	$45.00	$45.00	$45.00
Sales		$1,000,000	$1,400,000	$2,100,000	$2,520,000	$2,772,000
Variable cost		900,000	1,260,000	1,575,000	1,890,000	2,079,000
Fixed cost		60,000	60,000	60,000	60,000	60,000
Depreciation		150,000	150,000	150,000	150,000	150,000
Operating income		(110,000)	(70,000)	315,000	420,000	483,000
Taxes		38,500	24,500	(110,250)	(147,000)	(169,050)
Net income		$(71,500)	$(45,500)	$204,750	$273,000	$313,950
Net income		$(71,500)	$(45,500)	$204,750	$273,000	$313,950
Depreciation		150,000	150,000	150,000	150,000	150,000
Fixed capital	$(750,000)	—	—	—	—	—
Working capital	(63,000)	—	—	—	—	63,000
Salvage value		—	—	—	—	32,500
Cash flow	$(813,000)	$78,500	$104,500	$354,750	$423,000	$559,450
12.0%	NPV	$179,171				

9.5   A.   Expenditures on plant and equipment are incremental.

B.   Cost of previous R&D is a sunk cost—not incremental.

C.   Dividend payments are not an operating cash flow. Dividends are a return of capital and, therefore, are not included in an investment analysis.

D.   Cannibalization of the company's other products is definitely an incremental impact. Cash flows net of lost sales from other company products must be considered.

CHAPTER 10

Cost of Capital, Hurdle Rates, and Financial Structure

In Chap. 9, we present numerous capital investment analysis techniques and discuss how to determine cash flows through the use of numerous project examples. Paramount to the investment evaluation is the discount rate, the cost of capital. The cost of capital is the opportunity cost of funds invested in the firm. It represents the minimum acceptable rate of return for corporate investments. In the Chap. 9 new-product example, we saw that a 1 percent change in the cost of capital (from 10 to 11 percent) had a significant impact on the net present value. The net present value fell by $2.9 million, or 72 percent.

For financial executives, determining the cost of capital is one of the most important responsibilities. Remember the inverse relationship between the discount rate and the value of the project. As the discount rate rises (falls), the value of the project falls (rises). Set the cost of capital (discount rate) too high, and the growth of the firm suffers because projects that otherwise would have a positive net present value could have a negative net present value and the firm would not invest in a "good" new project. Also, if the cost of capital is set too high, the firm operates at a disadvantage. To attain acceptable higher levels of return, the company raises prices or uses less costly (lower-quality) components. All these impact the long-term performance of the firm. On the other hand, set the cost of capital (discount rate) too low, and many projects that should be rejected for insufficient returns are now implemented because they have a positive net present value.

For the nonfinancial executive, it is critical to understand the genesis of the cost of capital to ensure that adequate returns are provided from invested capital. This understanding also facilitates the discussions between finance and operations. Some executives have already asked why they need to earn a return of 10 percent on a project when the company can borrow money at 6 percent. Understanding that debt is only one source of capital is important for any executive.

This chapter develops an estimation approach for the cost of capital, discusses the concept of financial structure and an optimal capital structure, and introduces the concept of divisional or project hurdle rates.

269

COST OF CAPITAL

A consolidated Hershey balance sheet for December 31, 1998, is presented in Table 10.1. It includes assets, operating and financial liabilities, and stockholders' equity. Accounts payable along with deferred taxes and other liabilities comprise "operating" liabilities, or liabilities that are directly based in the operations of the firm. The cash flows attributable to the rise and fall in operating liabilities are explicitly accounted for when determining cash flows, just as we did in Chap. 9. Consequently, these amounts are not considered capital.

It is the financial liabilities and the stockholders' equity that comprise capital. From Table 10.1, the book value of capital can be summarized as follows ($ millions):

Capital Component	December 1998	December 1994
Short-term debt	$ 345	$ 0
Current portion of LTD	1	8
Long-term debt	879	157
Total debt*	1225	165
Preferred stock	0	0
Common stock	1043	1441
Total stockholders' equity	1043	1441
Total capital*	$2268	$1606

*Total debt and total capital exclude "operating" liabilities, such as accounts payable and deferred taxes. Operating liabilities are the direct result of operations and consequently are accounted for directly in operating cash flows.

TABLE 10.1

Summarized Balance Sheet
December 31, 1998 ($ Millions)

Current assets	$1134	Accounts payable*	$ 469
		Short-term debt	345
		Current portion of LTD	1
Net plant, property, and equipment	1648	Long-term debt	879
Goodwill	530	Deferred taxes	321
Other assets	92	Other liabilities	346
		Stockholders' equity	1043
Total assets	$3404	Total liabilities and stockholders' equity	$3404

*Accounts payable also includes accrued liabilities.

TABLE 10.2

Summarized Balance Sheet
December 31, 1994 ($ Millions)

Current assets	$ 949	Accounts payable*	$ 788
		Short-term debt	0
		Current portion of LTD	8
Net plant, property, and equipment	1468	Long-term debt	157
Other assets	474	Other liabilities	497
		Stockholders' equity	1441
Total assets	$2891	Total liabilities and stockholders' equity	$2891

*Accounts payable also includes accrued liabilities.

Table 10.2 presents the consolidated balance sheet for Hershey Foods from 4 years earlier, December 1994. The 1994 capital structure is summarized above and demonstrates a distinctive recapitalization contrast to the 1998 capital structure. During the intervening years, Hershey Foods repurchased over $1.0 billion of its own common stock while issuing a similar amount of debt.

This case study will illustrate how the cost of capital can be estimated for a firm. Although we attempt to make the procedures specific and numerically precise, we recognize that considerable judgment must be exercised. Because of the crucial role of the cost-of-capital estimation in guiding a firm's investment decisions, and because the valuation of a firm is highly sensitive to the applicable cost of capital employed, the judgment must be arrived at with great care. The purpose of this Hershey example is to provide a framework of the main procedures that should be employed in estimating the cost of capital.

The cost of capital represents the weighted average cost of permanent financing raised by the corporation. It can be expressed as

$$K_c = w_d K_d + w_{ps} K_{ps} + w_{cs} K_{cs} \qquad (10.1)$$

where K_c, K_d, K_{ps}, K_{cs} = cost of capital, cost of debt (after-tax), cost of preferred stock, cost of common stock

w_d, w_{ps}, w_{cs} = weight in debt, weight in preferred stock, weight in common stock

TABLE 10.3

Cost of Capital Overview

	Weight	×	Cost	=	WACC*
Debt	$w_d\%$		$K_d\%$		$w_d\,K_d$
Preferred stock	$w_{ps}\%$		$K_{ps}\%$		$w_{ps}\,K_{ps}$
Common stock	$w_{cs}\%$		$K_{cs}\%$		$w_{cs}\,K_{cs}$
Total	100%				WACC

*WACC is the weighted average cost of capital.

The cost of capital and the cost of each of its components reflect the opportunity costs or minimum returns required by investors. Table 10.3 demonstrates the concept of Eq. (10.1). As we complete this section, values will be substituted into Table 10.3 to illustrate the cost of capital.

This section first explains how to calculate the cost of the individual capital components (debt, preferred stock, and common stock) and then discusses the proper weights to use to finalize the weighted average cost of capital (WACC).

In each section, the recommended technique is presented and discussed. Where the practice of estimating individual cost components or weights is divergent, alternative estimation techniques are discussed. A most useful article, "Best Practices in Estimating Cost of Capital" (*Financial Practice and Education*, Spring/Summer 1998) by Bruner, Eades, Harris, and Higgins, succinctly identifies numerous cost of capital estimation techniques that are used in practice, by major corporations and financial advisers. Results of this survey are referred to as the cost-of-capital survey. While we remain strong in our recommendations, we also feel compelled to expose the reader to common alternative techniques.

Capital Component Costs

This section discusses the cost of each component of capital in turn:

- Cost of debt
- Cost of preferred stock
- Cost of common equity

Each component is evaluated on an after-tax basis, although this only has a meaningful effect on the cost of debt. Of the three primary capital sources, only the cost of debt (interest expense) is recognized as a tax-deductible expense. An after-tax cost of capital is developed because a project's operating cash flows (used in investment analysis—see Chap. 9) are on an after-tax basis.

Cost of Debt

Simply put, the cost of debt is interest expense. In the United States, interest expense is tax-deductible, and consequently the cost of debt is reduced by the amount of the tax savings.

The cost of debt is stated on an after-tax basis as follows:

$$K_d = I(1 - T) \tag{10.2}$$

where K_d = cost of debt (after tax)
   I = interest rate (before tax)
   T = marginal tax rate

To illustrate, in Table 10.4, two companies, A and B, are in the same industry, manufacturing, selling, and delivering the same product. Both companies sell the same amount of goods ($1000) with the same cost of goods sold ($800) and the same $200 of operating income or earnings before interest and taxes (EBIT).

TABLE 10.4

Cost of Debt

After-tax cost of debt = Before tax cost of debt × (1 − Tax rate)

	Financial Structures	
	A	**B**
Debt	$ 1000	$ 0
Interest rate	10%	10%
Interest	$ 100	$ 0
Sales	$ 1000	$ 1000
Cost of goods sold	800	800
Operating income	200	200
Interest expense	100	0
Pretax income	100	200
Income taxes	40	80
Net income	$ 60	$ 120
Pretax cost of debt	$ 100	
After-tax cost of debt	60	

After-tax cost of debt = 10% × (1 − 40%) = 6%

The only difference is that company A has $1000 of debt in its capital base (or capital structure) while company B has no debt. Company A pays 10 percent interest on its debt. So company A has another expense ($100 of interest expense) and reports $100 less in pretax income. Since both companies pay the same 40 percent tax rate, company A has a reduced tax expense due to the lower pretax income. Net after taxes, the $100 of added interest expense results in net income that is lower by only $60.

The cost of debt in this example is:

$$K_d = I(1 - T)$$
$$K_d = 10\%(1 - 40\%)$$
$$K_d = 6\%$$

The tax deductibility is a unique characteristic of debt. Preferred stock and common stock do not share this favorable consideration. As illustrated above and in practice, debt has a significant cost advantage due, in part, to its tax deductibility.

Estimating the Interest Rate

The applicable interest rate is the current market rate. The current market cost of debt reflects the opportunity cost for the bond investor, and consequently the cost for the borrower. The current market cost of debt also reflects the rate at which the corporation could refinance its current debt portfolio.

But which cost of debt—the cost of short-term debt or the cost of long-term debt? As we described the composition of the yield curve in Chap. 6, long-term interest rates reflect an amalgamation of current and future expectations of interest rates. That is, long-term interest rates include this year's one-year interest rate and the expectation of next year's one-year interest rate and the one-year interest rate expectation for the year after that, and so on. The long-term cost of a short-term "rollover" strategy (annual borrowing and refinancing) is thus captured in today's long-term interest rate.

The recommended approach to calculating the cost of debt is to calculate the tax effect of the current market cost of long-term debt. But how do you estimate the corporation's current cost of debt? Three approaches are discussed below:

- Specific bond evaluation (when bonds are traded)
- General interest rates (market indices)
- Discussions with lenders or investment bankers

Specific Bond Evaluation   If the corporation's debt frequently trades, market interest rates are determined from current market prices. From the tools developed in Chap. 3, The Time Value of Money, we can calculate the market interest rate. Say, for example, a 30-year corporate bond was issued 3 years ago. The bond pays an annual 7.0 percent coupon (or stated) interest rate and has a maturity value of $1000. Today, this 27-year bond sells for 92, or $920 ($1000 × 0.92). The current market rate is 7.71 percent, as depicted in Table 10.5. This is calculated in a similar, iterative process as the internal rate of return was calculated in Chap. 9 (see Table 9.9b). In this case, we will use trial-and-error to find the interest rate that equates the present values of a 26-year annuity of $70 and a lump sum of $1070 (in year 27) with the current market price of the bond, $920. The interest rate of 7.71 percent equates the two. Said differently, a person who buys this bond today pays $920 for a 27-year bond that pays $70 per year and returns the principal of $1000 (in 27 years). The bond investor earns 7.71 percent, which is this company's pretax cost of debt. On an after-tax basis, assuming a 40 percent tax rate, the after-tax cost of debt is 4.63 percent.

General Interest Rates   Often, debt is privately placed or does not trade on a routine basis. In those cases, the current market rate can be estimated by using the corporation's credit rating and the Merrill Lynch Bond Index, as reported in *The Wall Street Journal*. Table 10.6 includes the yield comparisons listing from *The Wall Street Journal* (August 29, 2000).

Independent rating agencies, such as Moody's, Standard & Poor's, and Fitch Investor Services, assess the liquidity risk and default risk of a corporation. They also review the contractual provisions of specific indentures. Based upon their assessment, bonds are rated. AAA is the

TABLE 10.5

Current Market Cost of Debt

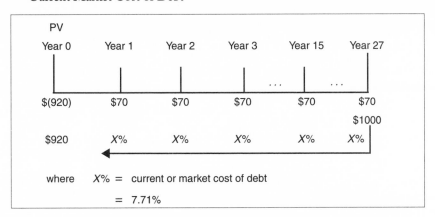

TABLE 10.6

Current Market Interest Rates

			52 Week	
Yield Comparisons Based on Merrill Lynch Bond Indexes, priced as of midafternoon Eastern time.				
	8/28	8/25	High	Low
Corp.-Govt. Master	6.78%	6.74%	7.43%	6.32%
Treasury 1–10 yr	6.21	6.17	6.90	5.67
10+ yr	6.01	5.96	6.93	5.96
Agencies 1–10 yr	6.93	6.89	7.65	6.30
10+ yr	6.73	6.69	7.35	6.59
Corporate				
1–10 yr High Qlty	7.22	7.18	7.89	6.55
Med Qlty	7.77	7.72	8.43	7.10
10+ yr High Qlty	7.72	7.67	8.24	7.26
Med Qlty	8.17	8.11	8.76	7.73
Yankee bonds (1)	7.45	7.42	8.10	7.16
Current-coupon mortgages (2)				
GNMA 7.50%	7.58	7.55	8.15	7.24
FNMA 7.50%	7.66	7.63	8.39	7.23
FHLMC 7.50%	7.67	7.64	8.41	7.26
High-yield corporates	12.06	12.07	12.50	10.50
Tax-exempt bonds				
7–12 yr G.O. (AA)	4.70	4.70	5.50	4.70
12–22 yr G.O. (AA)	5.41	5.40	6.14	5.40
22+ yr revenue (A)	5.65	5.64	6.35	5.64

Note: High quality rated AAA-AA; medium quality A-BBB/Baa; high yield, BB/Ba-C.
(1) Dollar-denominated, SEC-registered bonds of foreign issuers sold in the U.S. (2) Reflects the 52-week high and low of mortgage-backed securities indexes rather than the individual securities shown.

highest quality which commands the lowest interest rate, AA is the next-highest quality level with a slightly higher interest premium, etc.

Corporate bonds are broken down to include an average market rate for bonds with a maturity of 1 to 10 years and those greater than 10 years. (See boxed lines.) Also, each maturity is categorized by high quality (credit rating of AAA-AA) and medium quality (credit rating of A-BBB). For bonds with a credit rating of BB or lower, the line "High-yield corporates" provides an estimate of the current market rates. At this moment in time, shorter-term bonds of high-quality firms pay 7.22 percent while medium-quality firms pay 7.77 percent for their funds, or a 0.55 percent (55 basis points) higher cost.

With a marginal tax rate of 40 percent, that is, 35 percent statutory federal tax rate plus a 5 percent state and local tax rate (net of federal tax benefits), the cost of debt is estimated below:

| | Cost of Debt | |
10+ Year Maturity at Credit Rating	Before Tax	After Tax (40%)
High quality	7.72%	4.63%
Medium quality	8.17%	4.90%
High yield	12.06%	7.24%

The chart shows the cost of debt for long-term (greater than 10 years) debt.

Discussions with Lenders or Investment Bankers   A third technique for estimating the current market cost of debt is to actively engage in talks with potential lenders. This can be done either directly with a lending institution or indirectly with an investment banker. Although this approach can provide the most accurate and committed cost of debt, it may be premature, involve too much time, and put strains on future banking relationships without significantly improving the quality of the estimated cost of debt.

While there may be different approaches to estimating the current cost of debt, the current market cost of debt remains our recommendation. An alternative technique, the current cost of existing debt, is discussed below.

Cost of Debt—Alternative Technique

In the best practices survey, the authors note that the current market cost of debt, as recommended above, is the number one technique used to estimate the cost of debt, by corporations, financial advisers, and textbooks. The current cost of existing debt is the next most common technique. Thirty-seven percent of the corporations and 40 percent of the financial advisers use the current cost of existing debt to estimate the cost of debt. The current cost of existing debt looks at the debt that the corporation currently has outstanding and calculates the weighted average cost of that debt.

Table 10.7 presents the many debt instruments that were outstanding in December 1998 for Hershey Foods Corporation. At that time, Hershey's capital structure included $1225 million of debt. As we saw in Table 10.1, this debt included $346 million of short-term debt and $879 million of long-term debt. The details of Table 10.7 are found

TABLE 10.7

Hershey's Cost of Debt ($ Millions)

	Balance 12/31/98	Weight	Interest Rate	Weighted Cost
Short-term debt	$ 346	28.2%	5.2%	1.47
Debentures				
Due 2021	100	8.2	8.8%	0.72
Due 2027	250	20.4	7.2%	1.47
Notes				
Due 2005	200	16.3	6.7%	1.09
Due 2007	150	12.2	7.0%	0.85
Due 2012	150	12.2	7.0%	0.85
Other	29	2.5	6.8%	0.17
Total	$1225	100.0%		6.62%
		× (1 – Tax rate)		61.2%
		After-tax cost of debt		4.05%

in the footnotes to the financial statements within its annual report, as discussed in Chap. 2. To illustrate, Hershey has an outstanding debenture (unsecured debt) that matures in the year 2027. At $250 million, this debenture comprises 20.4 percent of Hershey's outstanding debt and carries a pretax interest rate of 7.20 percent.

The next step is to calculate a weighted-average interest rate. Continuing the example, the 2027 debenture had a weighted interest rate of 1.47 percent (20.4 × 7.20 percent). The individual weighted interest rates carry little significance. However, when the weighted interest rates are added together, they yield a weighted average interest rate on Hershey's total $1225 million outstanding debt of 6.62 percent. With a 1998 tax rate of 38.8 percent (combined all in federal, state, and local income tax rates), the cost of Hershey's existing debt is 4.05 percent.

A slight modification to this approach blends the cost of the existing debt with the cost of any anticipated new debt. That is, this modification maintains the framework from Table 10.7 and adds a line to it for new debt to be issued, dollar amount, and estimated interest rate. That new debt is combined with the current debt, weights are recalculated, and a modified cost of debt is calculated. In this way, limited current market conditions are introduced into the calculation.

In summary, the recommended technique—the current market cost of debt—estimates Hershey's after-tax cost of debt at 4.75 percent (or within a range of 4.63 to 4.90 percent). This is 0.70 percent (70 basis points) higher than Hershey's historical cost of debt. This also reflects the interest rate increases of 1999 and 2000. To reflect the opportunity cost of debt, we remain steadfast in our recommendation to use the current market cost of debt (4.75 percent).

Cost of Preferred Stock

Preferred stock is a hybrid security. It is a hybrid in the sense that although it is classified as equity, preferred stockholders do not partici-pate in the successful growth of the corporation. A preferred stock-holder receives a contractually set dividend. This dividend does not change over time as a common stock dividend. Because the dividend does not change, the cost of preferred stock behaves similarly to the cost of debt. Since preferred stock has no maturity date, the cost also behaves as a perpetual bond. The ultimate maturity value is not in question—only the value of the dividends.

The cost of preferred stock is calculated as

$$K_{ps} = D_{ps} / P_{ps} \qquad (10.3)$$

where K_{ps} = cost of preferred stock
D_{ps} = preferred stock dividend
P_{ps} = price of preferred stock

For example, if a company has preferred stock with a dividend of $6.25 and the current price of that stock is $62.50, then the cost of the pre-ferred stock is 10 percent, as follows:

$$
\begin{aligned}
K_{ps} &= D_{ps} / P_{ps} \\
&= \$6.25 / \$62.50 \\
&= 10.0\%
\end{aligned}
$$

Table 10.8 illustrates the cash flows to a preferred stockholder. Each year the preferred stockholder receives $6.25. Although Table 10.8 stops at year 100, preferred stock dividends are perpetual. By equating that stream of dividends to the $62.50 cost of the preferred stock, the resulting return on the investment is 10 percent. Said differently, by discounting the perpetual stream of dividends at an investor's required rate of return (that is, 10 percent), that investor would be willing to pay $62.50 for the preferred stock. Once again, this technique incorporates the current stock price and the current opportunity cost of preferred stocks. The current market cost is our recommended approach to cal-culating the cost of preferred stock.

Notice, there are no related tax deductions for the firm that has outstanding preferred stock and pays preferred stock dividends. Since dividends are not tax-deductible in the United States, the after-tax cost

TABLE 10.8

Cost of Preferred Stock

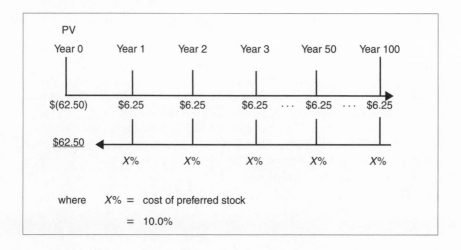

where $X\%$ = cost of preferred stock

= 10.0%

of preferred stock is the same cost as the pretax cost of preferred stock. Consequently, most manufacturing firms have little to no preferred stock outstanding.

On the other hand, utilities make broad use of preferred stock because it bolsters the equity base of the utility without diluting the common stock ownership. This larger equity base allows a utility to take on additional borrowing. The cost of the preferred stock is passed on to consumers of the utility's services in the rate base.

Cost of Preferred Stock—Alternative Technique

Similar to the historical cost of debt discussed above, some firms consider a historical cost of preferred stock. When preferred stock is issued, it is issued with a dividend rate tied to the stated par value of the stock. This rate is the historical cost of preferred stock. In this example, if the preferred stock sold for $50 and had a $50 par value, the resulting historical cost of preferred stock is 12.5 percent:

$$K_{ps} = D_{ps} / P_{ps}$$
$$= \$6.25 / \$50.00$$
$$= 12.5\%$$

Over time, the market price of the stock fluctuates, and the resulting cost rises or falls in reaction to the underlying preferred stock price movement. By using today's stock price, a more current cost of preferred stock is attained and reflects the opportunity cost of preferred stock funds. Preferred stock is not a common form of financing for most manufacturing firms. Common stock or debt generally provide the largest proportion of financing for most corporations.

Cost of Common Equity

Common equity represents a major component of a corporation's balance sheet. The most common captions from the balance sheet include

- Common stock at par value
- Additional capital paid in excess of par
- Treasury stock
- Retained earnings
- Numerous accounting adjustments

The first two items, common stock at par and additional capital paid in excess of par, represent the original amounts for which the common stock was issued. Treasury stock reflects amounts paid to repurchase shares of stock that no longer are outstanding, but remain available for issuance. Retained earnings include cumulative earnings in the corporation that were retained (i.e., not paid out as dividends) in the corporation. The numerous accounting adjustments include such things as cumulative foreign translation adjustments, certain employee compensation involving shares of stock, and other more recently adopted accounting conventions that recognize the equity impact of certain quasi-income or expense items without requiring those items to be recorded through net income.

The cost of equity encompasses all aspects of the common equity section.

Calculating the Cost of Common Equity

When calculating the cost of debt, the contractual obligations of interest and the repayment of principal make determining the cost of debt a straightforward and explicit exercise. Common equity has no explicit return obligations. Instead, implicit investor expectations determine stock prices which in turn drive the cost of common equity. The cost of equity represents the opportunity cost of equity capital. To accomplish this estimate, we attempt to understand what reasonable investors should expect when they make an investment in the equity of a particular firm.

We will review three different approaches to calculating the cost of common equity:

- Dividend growth model
- Capital asset pricing model
- Arbitrage pricing theory

The dividend growth model (DGM) is an internally focused, company-specific measure. The capital asset pricing model (CAPM) and the arbitrage pricing theory (APT) are externally focused, company-specific measures. The CAPM considers the stock's return relationship to the stock market's return as a whole, while APT focuses on the stock's return relationship to many economywide variables.

All three techniques are presented and discussed in turn below. The strengths and weaknesses of all three are highlighted. Although carrying its own shortcomings, the CAPM is the recommended approach for estimating the cost of common equity.

Dividend Growth Model

Most corporations have little activity in the common equity market. Their activity is limited to issuing (selling) common stock and repurchasing stock if the corporation has an ongoing share repurchase program. The stock market's primary purpose is to facilitate secondary trading or trading between individuals (or between their institutions).

If a company chooses to pay dividends, those dividends are generally the only ongoing cash flow contact that a company has with its common equity holder. As a common equity stockholder, the investor also participates in the growth of the corporation. The growth in increased sales, profits, and cash flow is forwarded to the common equity investor through higher dividends, which result in higher share prices.

The dividend growth model compares today's stock price with the anticipated level of dividend payments and estimates the cost of equity as follows:

$$K_{cs} = \frac{D_{cs1}}{P_{cs}} + G \qquad (10.4)$$

where K_{cs} = cost of common stock
D_{cs1} = common stock dividend for year 1
P_{cs} = price of common stock
G = growth rate

To apply this to the Hershey Foods case, Hershey raised its dividend to $0.24 per quarter or $0.96 per year, for the coming year. The stock price at the end of 1998 was $62.19, and the estimated growth rate is 10 percent. Hershey's cost of common equity capital is 11.5 percent as follows:

$$K_{cs} = \frac{\$0.96}{\$62.19} + 10.0\%$$

$$= 1.5\% + 10.0\%$$

$$= 11.5\%$$

The 11.5 percent cost of equity is comprised of a 1.5 percent dividend yield and 10.0 percent expected growth. The dividend, stock price, and resulting dividend yield can be observed while the growth rate must be estimated.

Table 10.9 illustrates the concept behind the dividend growth model. The share of stock pays a $0.96 dividend at the end of year 1. After the assumed 10 percent growth, the year 2 dividend is $1.06, and that of year 3 is $1.16. By year 50, the dividend per share has grown to $102.45, assuming a 10 percent growth rate. By year 100, the dividend has grown to more than $12,000 per share and is still growing into perpetuity.

The dividend growth model finds the discount rate that equates the future projected dividends (which are projected to infinity) to today's stock price. This process is similar to finding an internal rate of return. Although it sounds as if the mathematics should be more complicated, Eq. (10.4) provides the discount rate.

The estimated growth rate is a major component when applying the dividend growth model. As illustrated, the estimated growth rate represents the future growth in dividends. However, the future growth in dividends is a function of the underlying growth of the business. That is, the dividend growth rate is tied to the growth exhibited in sales, income, cash flow, etc.

There are at least three different approaches to estimating the long-term growth rate. This growth rate can be estimated by calculating an internal growth rate, calculating historical growth rates, or

TABLE 10.9

Interpretation of Dividend Growth Model

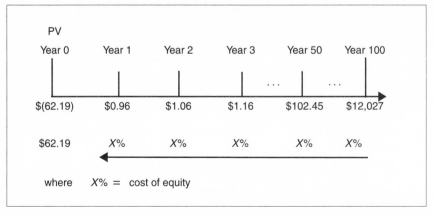

Note: Dividends are assumed to grow at 10 percent annually. This is *our assumption for illustrative purposes.* Do not buy stock in Hershey based upon this illustrative growth rate. The stock price in December 1998 was $62.19.

observing management's stated growth objective if it is publicly disclosed via the annual report or other public statements.

The internal growth rate is a financial ratio that is an extension of return on retained earnings. The return on retained earnings is similar to the return on equity except the distortive effects of stock issuance and repurchases as well as the effects of accounting adjustments have been eliminated. The internal growth rate considers a firm's profitability, tax rate, asset efficiency, capital structure, and dividend policy. The internal growth rate assumes that all the underlying relationships (profitability, etc.) remain constant or have minimal fluctuation. The internal growth rate is calculated as

$$G = \text{RORE}(1 - \text{DPR})\qquad\qquad(10.5)$$

where G = internal growth rate
       RORE = return on retained earnings
       = (net income/retained earnings)
       DPR = dividend payout ratio
       = (dividends per share/EPS)

Return on retained earnings is calculated as 1998 net income divided by the 1998 retained earnings. The dividend payout ratio is calculated as 1998 dividends paid per common share divided by 1998 earnings per common share.

In Hershey's case the 1998 internal growth rate is ($ millions, except per-share values)

$$\begin{aligned}
G &= \text{RORE}(1 - \text{DPR}) \\
&= \left(\frac{\$341}{\$2190}\right)\left(1 - \frac{\$0.92}{\$2.38}\right) \\
&= 15.6\%(1 - 0.387) \\
&= 9.6\%
\end{aligned}$$

This internal growth rate approximates the historical growth rate of earnings (EPS) and dividends (DPS) per share:

	Growth Rates	
	EPS	DPS
1998 Annual growth rate	5.8%	9.5%
1993 to 1998 Compound annual growth rate	10.7%	10.0%
1988 to 1998 Compound annual growth rate	11.5%	10.8%

The historical growth of earnings and dividends is similar to the publicly discussed objective of 10 percent (double-digit) growth.

The dividend growth model approach to estimating the cost of equity has some appeal to management as it directly links the strategic plan, goals, and objectives to the cost of capital, and it is simple to calculate. However, if a company does not pay a dividend or has an erratic or uncertain growth rate, the dividend growth model cannot be used. Alternative approaches must be employed in those cases.

Capital Asset Pricing Model (CAPM)

The CAPM approach to estimating the cost of equity compares the shareholder return (stock price appreciation plus dividends) to the return of the market (i.e., Standard & Poor's 500). From the cost of capital survey, 81 percent of the companies use CAPM to estimate their cost of equity. It is our recommended approach as well.

The cost of common stock K_{cs}, or the cost of equity, via the CAPM approach can be represented as

$$K_{cs} = R_f + \beta(K_m - R_f) \tag{10.6}$$

where

R_f = risk-free rate of return

β = beta (statistical relationship discussed below)

$K_m - R_f$ = market's return in excess of risk-free rate

By using the capital asset pricing model, the cost of equity is estimated from a "risk-free" base level and adjusted for risk relative to the stock market.

Table 10.10 graphically illustrates the first step in the process of calculating beta. Point A is a hypothetical point that corresponds to the following set of assumptions:

	Market	Stock
Capital appreciation	10%	22%
Dividend yield	2%	1%
Less: risk-free rate of return	(6)%	(6)%
Total excess return	6%	17%

In this case, point A in Table 10.10 shows a solid return for the market and an even stronger return for the stock. In addition, the market paid a 2 percent dividend yield while the stock paid only a 1 percent dividend. The risk-free rate was 6 percent. For the market, the excess return was 6 percent; for the stock, a 17 percent excess return. In fact, each point in Table 10.10 was theoretically calculated using the same process. When Value Line (an investment advisory service that pub-

TABLE 10.10

Capital Asset Pricing Model Graphical Overview

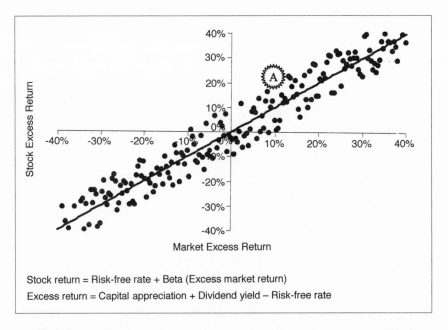

Stock return = Risk-free rate + Beta (Excess market return)

Excess return = Capital appreciation + Dividend yield − Risk-free rate

lishes beta) calculates beta, it uses excess returns of the past 5 years and plots 260 weekly data points.

Next, draw a regression line through the plotted data. The slope of this line is the beta. It is based on the statistical relationship between the individual stock's return and the stock market's return.

Each stock has its own unique beta, as illustrated by Table 10.11. A beta of 1.0 (stock Y) indicates that the stock has the same amount of risk as the general stock market. If a stock has a beta of 1.0 and the stock market has an excess return of 10 percent, the stock is expected to have an excess return of 10 percent. If the stock's beta is greater (less) than 1, the risk of that stock is greater (less) than the market. If the stock's beta is 2.0 (stock X, Table 10.11) and the stock market has an excess return of 10 percent, the stock is expected to have a 20 percent excess return. Conversely, if the stock's beta is 0.5 (stock Z) and the market has a 10 percent excess return, the stock is expected to have a 5 percent excess return. Reliable betas can be found in Value Line.

Since 1926, the market has had, on average, an excess return of 5.63 percent more than the long-term bond rate. The risk-free rate is the current risk-free long-term government bond rate. To illustrate the use of the CAPM for Hershey Foods Corporation:

$$K_{cs} = R_f + \beta(K_m - R_f)$$

where $\quad R_f = 6.00\%$ (June 1999)

$\beta = 0.90$ (Value Line, May 1999)

$K_m - R_f = 5.63\%$ (trend since 1926)

so

$$K_{cs} = 6.00\% + 0.90(5.63\%)$$
$$= 11.07\%$$

From the capital asset pricing model, the cost of equity capital is estimated at 11.07 percent.

Issues Related to the Capital Asset Pricing Model

Estimating the cost of equity via the capital asset pricing model has some appeal because it employs an independent, statistical relationship between the individual stock and the stock market. CAPM alleviates the need to estimate a long-term growth rate for the firm.

TABLE 10.11

CAPM: Three Different Stocks

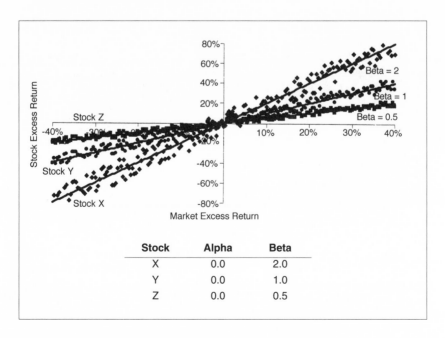

Stock	Alpha	Beta
X	0.0	2.0
Y	0.0	1.0
Z	0.0	0.5

Companies can use CAPM whether or not they have a dividend or a steady, stable growth in that dividend.

However, CAPM has some issues:

- Risk-free rate
- Beta calculation
- Excess return of the market
- Correlation between one stock and the market
- Conceptual issues

Each one of these issues is addressed below. Although the CAPM approach remains the recommended estimation technique, anyone employing CAPM should be aware of these issues.

Risk-Free Rate   Many choices are faced when selecting the risk-free rate. Should the rate be based on short-term U.S. Treasury Bills, long-term U.S. Treasury bonds, or some other measure of a risk-free return? We advocate that the risk-free rate be measured via the long-term U.S. Treasury bonds. Long-term government bonds incorporate the market's expectations about expected short-term (Treasury Bill) interest rates and are more indicative of a risk-free rate of return with a similar "long-term maturity" time frame as a share of stock or the underlying life of the investment. Consequently, our recommendation is to use the long-term U.S. Treasury bond rate as the risk-free rate.

The cost-of-capital survey found a wide dispersion of the risk-free rate. One-third of the companies base the risk-free rate on 10-year U.S. Treasury bonds, another one-third use 10- to 30-year U.S. Treasury bonds, while the remainder use a number of other measures. The 30-year U.S. Treasury bond risk-free rate was the most common (40 percent) used by the financial advisers.

Beta Calculation   Numerous variations are used to calculate the specific returns that underlie the beta calculation. For example, the number of years (3 years versus 5 years), the period of return (weekly versus monthly), and the style of return (annual versus annualized) all affect the specific value of beta. In the cost-of-capital survey, the authors compared betas from Value Line, Bloomberg, and S&P. All three services calculate betas slightly differently. The cost-of-capital survey found the range of estimated betas over these three sources differed by 0.42 on average for the 27 corporations included in the study.

Excess Return of the Market   Excess return measures the amount by which the market's return exceeds the risk-free rate of return. In the CAPM, it is intended to be a forward looking measure based on an expected excess return.   However, many companies approximate an expected excess return by looking at the historical excess returns. Again, it matters whether the risk-free rate is a short-term Treasury Bill, long-term U.S. Treasury bond, or some other rate. It also matters if the return is the average of annual returns or whether it is a compound annual growth rate (CAGR) as calculated in Chap. 3, Time Value of Money. Finally, it also depends on the time period used to develop historical excess returns.

The Center for Research in Security Prices (CRSP) database with data back to 1926 is an excellent source for stock market returns as well as the risk-free returns from U.S. Treasury Bills or U.S. Treasury bonds. The CRSP database includes security prices from which annual returns can be calculated and averaged.   The annual returns include capital appreciation (depreciation) and any interest or dividends paid throughout the year.

The following shows the outcome of investing $1 in large company stocks, long-term government bonds, and U.S. Treasury Bills in 1925. Over the full span (until 1996), the $1 investment is worth:

Investment	Value in 1996
Large company stocks	$1371.07
Long-term Treasury bonds	33.73
U.S. Treasury Bills	13.54

A $1 investment (present value) in 1925 grew to reach $1371.07 (future value), 71 years later in 1996, yielding a CAGR of 10.71 percent. The following represents the 1925 to 1996 CAGRs for each investment and the resulting excess returns:

Investment	CAGR	Excess Return
Large company stocks	10.71%	N/A
Long-term Treasury bonds	5.08%	5.63%
U.S. Treasury Bills	3.74%	6.97%

The excess returns were calculated by subtracting the CAGRs of the bonds and bills from the CAGR of the stocks.

Some argue that the period of 1925 to 1996 is irrelevant for today. Those same people advocate a shorter time frame. The following summarizes these excess returns by the two methods of calculating returns (average annual return and compound annual growth rate) for various time periods:

**EXCESS RETURNS (LARGE COMPANY STOCKS
LESS BONDS OR BILLS)**

	Bonds		Bills	
	Average	*CAGR*	*Average*	*CAGR*
1925–1996	8.89%	5.63%	10.03%	6.97%
1986–1996	4.96%	5.89%	10.72%	9.82%
1976–1996	5.10%	5.01%	8.52%	7.27%
1966–1996	3.39%	4.09%	0.52%	5.11%

Historical excess returns vary between 0.52 and 10.72 percent depending on the specific viewpoint of the best way to derive them.

Our recommendation for the excess return premium is based on the compound annual growth rate of large company stocks and long-term U.S. Treasury bonds from 1926 to the most recent year. The CAGR of the long-term government bonds is subtracted from the CAGR of large company stocks to yield an excess return of 5.63 percent. This return is an appropriate proxy for future expectations of an excess return. The market's excess return based on a shorter time period becomes arbitrary. The past 71 years have seen many different economic events, from the depression to the recent boom. For consistency with our prior recommendation, long-term government bonds should be used as the risk-free rate. Extending the "maturity" time frame argument, the excess returns as measured by the compound annual growth rate provide long-term growth rates to match the long-term aspects of stocks. The difference between using the suggested (1925–1996) CAGR versus the average annual return is 3.26 percent. The technique/assumption of choice will greatly impact the resulting cost of equity and cost of capital.

From the cost-of-capital survey, most corporations (37 percent) use an excess market return between 5 and 6 percent. Again, the responses were widely disparate, ranging from 4 to 7.5 percent to "long-term arithmetic average (8.9 percent)."

Correlation Between One Stock and the Market   The graphical presentation of the capital asset pricing model as depicted in Table 10.10 illustrates a relationship between the excess return of a stock and the excess return of the market. A straight line was statistically fit through the data and revealed a relationship between the excess return of the market and the excess return of the stock, which was measured as the stock's beta or the slope of this regression line. As previously discussed, the higher the stock's beta, the more sensitive the stock's excess return is to market's excess return.

Another statistical relationship is measured by correlation or the goodness of fit between the two variables. Correlation ranges between 0.00 and 1.00 with a measure of 1.00 indicating an exact relationship between the two variables. As Table 10.10 was constructed, the correlation is approximately 0.90, which is an indication of a relatively significant relationship between the variables. Table 10.10 was created for illustrative purposes to present the concept of CAPM.

Table 10.12 presents actual data between the excess returns of Hershey Foods Corporation and the excess returns of the stock market as measured by the Standard & Poor's 500. Table 10.12 was constructed by comparing annualized weekly excess returns over a 3-year period. Because the returns were calculated on a weekly basis and then annualized, some observations produced large (positive and negative) annualized returns.

Table 10.12 continues to illustrate a positive relationship between the excess return of Hershey Food's stock and the stock market. However, that relationship is more dispersed than illustrated in Table 10.10, and its correlation is significantly lower. The graph in Table 10.12 has a weak correlation of only 0.20. This is not unique to Hershey Foods. Few individual stocks have a correlation greater than 0.30. There are many variables that affect a stock's value and returns. The general movement of the stock market is only a portion of that relationship.

TABLE 10.12

CAPM Reality
Hershey Foods versus Market

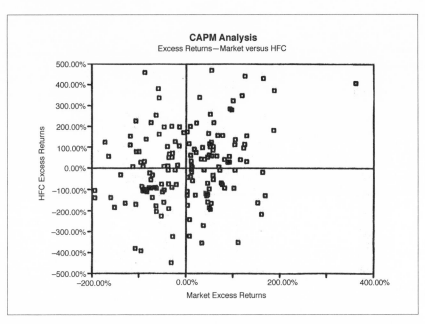

Conceptual Issues   The capital asset pricing model remains a conceptually useful framework and an approach that is easy to apply for estimating the cost of equity.   There are some conceptual issues with CAPM. CAPM assumes that all markets are efficient with all investors having access to the same information with the same expectations. It also assumes that all investors are risk-averse, are rational, and view securities in the same way. It also assumes that there are no transaction costs or taxes and that there are no restrictions on securities.

Numerous studies have called into question the validity of CAPM. Two issues have been raised that, from a theoretical view, invalidate CAPM. First, for CAPM to be true, the regression line must always pass through the origin. That implies that when the market's excess return is zero, so is the stock's excess return.   Studies have found that the intercept term is significantly different from zero, which invalidates CAPM.

Second, for CAPM to be true, no other factors can explain a security's return. Evidence shows that firm size, dividend yield, price/earnings ratios, and seasonality can explain much of the security's return that is unexplained by CAPM.   This also invalidates CAPM. In June 1992, Eugene Fama and Kenneth R. French published "The Cross-Section of Expected Stock Returns" (*Journal of Finance*, pp. 427–465).   The study tested more than 2000 stocks and failed to find a significant relationship between the historic betas and historic returns during the period from 1963 to 1990.   Although this study called into question the historical results of CAPM, it did not comment about the validity of CAPM as an expectational model.

The arbitrage pricing theory is an approach that has been more recently popularized in the financial literature and may someday replace CAPM as the recommended approach to estimate the cost of equity.

Arbitrage Pricing Theory (APT)

APT is a multiple regression model based on macroeconomic variables. Additional research needs to be conducted on the APT.   After the research and simplification, APT may be the recommended tool for estimating the cost of equity.   However, until then, the recommended approach for calculating the cost of equity remains CAPM.

Cost of Equity: Summary

The cost of debt is an explicit cost, while the cost of equity is implicit. In the previous sections, we reviewed three common techniques for estimating the cost of common stock or equity capital. Each technique has certain limitations and interpretations of required assumptions, which render it less than perfectly applicable. To summarize:

Dividend growth model: Most applicable to firms that pay dividends with a steady, stable growth rate underlying those dividends. Subject to wide variations in expected growth rate assumptions.

Capital asset pricing model: Subject to wide interpretations and calculation of major components such as the risk-free rate, beta, and market risk premium.

Arbitrage pricing model: Requires additional research, refinement, and simplification before wide application.

Our recommendation remains: estimate the cost of equity via the capital asset pricing model.

Cost of New Debt and Equity

For new debt, preferred stock and common stock, issuance costs must be considered and will slightly increase the cost of each capital source.

For debt, new debt is typically issued at par value or the maturity value of $1000. The stated interest rate is the pretax cost of debt. For example, a 10-year bond that is issued at $1000 and pays $100 of interest each year before returning its $1000 of principal costs 10 percent (pretax) and 6 percent after-tax assuming a 40 percent tax rate. If there is a 3 percent issuance fee, the proceeds are only $970 (instead of $1000). The cost of debt is recalculated based upon this lower initial value, resulting in a pretax cost of debt of 10.50 percent, and 6.30 percent after-tax assuming a 40 percent tax rate.

For preferred stock and common stock, the price per share is reduced by the issuance cost per share. Equation (10.3) (for preferred stock) and Eq. (10.4) (for common stock) are adjusted to reflect the price of a share of stock less the issuance cost per share:

Preferred stock $$K_{ps} = \left(\frac{D_{ps}}{P_{ps} - C_{ps}} \right)$$

where K_{ps} = cost of preferred stock
D_{ps} = dividend
P_{ps} = price of preferred stock
C_{ps} = cost per share to issue preferred stock

Common stock $$K_{cs} = \left(\frac{D_{cs1}}{P_{cs} - C_{cs}} + G \right)$$

where K_{cs} = cost of common stock
D_{cs1} = dividend for year 1
P_{cs} = price of common stock
C_{cs} = cost per share to issue common stock
G = growth rate

To illustrate using preferred stock, if a company issues 4 million preferred shares to raise approximately $250 million, the company may pay 2 to 3 percent issuance costs. The final specific issuance fee would be a negotiation point. At a 3 percent issuance cost, this would be $7.5 million of issuance costs, or $1.875 per share. The adjusted cost of the preferred stock would be

$$
\begin{aligned}
K_{ps} &= \left(\frac{D_{ps}}{P_{ps} - C_{ps}} \right) \\
&= \left(\frac{\$6.25}{\$62.50 - \$1.875} \right) \\
&= 10.31\%
\end{aligned}
$$

This refinement provides a better estimate of newly issued preferred stock.

Capital Component Costs—Summary

In the preceding pages, we discussed the cost of debt, preferred stock, and common stock. We also discussed common alternatives used in practice. To summarize our recommendations:

- Cost of debt: current market cost of debt, after-tax
- Preferred stock: cost based on current market value of preferred stock
- Common stock: capital asset pricing model

The next section discusses the appropriate weights to use to find the weighted average cost of capital (WACC).

WEIGHTING THE CAPITAL COMPONENTS

At this point, the individual costs of each capital component, debt, preferred stock, and common stock were addressed individually. The final step in estimating the cost of capital is to weight each component and calculate the weighted average cost of capital. There are a few customary methods or weighting techniques: (1) book value weights and (2) market value weights.

Book value weights are based on the capital structure represented by the balance sheet. For Hershey Foods as of December 31, 1998, the balance sheet included debt of $1225 million (short-term debt, current portion of long-term debt, and long-term debt) and equity of $1043 million for a total capital pool of $2268 million. Hershey has no outstanding preferred stock. Consequently, debt represents 54.0 percent of the capital structure, and equity represents 46.0 percent.

Book value equity is an accounting concept that primarily keeps track of earnings retained in the business over the years along with the original level of equity capital injected into the firm net of any stock repurchase. Most of Hershey's equity capital was injected in the 1920s with a small issue in 1984. However, in 1995 and 1997, Hershey bought back more than $1 billion of its stock on the open market. As we saw, the stockholders' equity section of Hershey Foods actually decreased between 1994 and 1998 due to the stock repurchases offset by the additional earnings retained in the business. The book value of equity is subject to numerous accounting adjustments. The basis for market value weights, the market value of debt and equity, is not subject to the mechanics of accounting. The market value of equity is determined by the total capitalization of the outstanding shares of stock. In this case, Hershey Foods has 141.0 million shares of stock outstanding at $58 per share, or a market value of $8178 million compared to the book value of $1043 million. A current stockholder of Hershey Foods demands that Hershey earn the cost of equity (11.07 percent—CAPM) on the current investment value of $58, not on the $7.40 book value per share ($1043 million book value of equity divided by 141.0 million shares outstanding).

The major difference between book- and market-based weights is the value of equity. In the case of Hershey Foods:

HERSHEY FOODS CAPITAL STRUCTURE WEIGHTS ($ Millions)

	Book Weights		Market Weights	
	Amount	*Percent*	*Amount*	*Percent*
Debt	$1225	54.0	$1200	12.8
Equity	1043	46.0	8178	87.2
Total	$2268	100.0	$9378	100.0

In this example, the market value of the debt is similar to the book value of debt. The majority of Hershey's debt is privately held. Obtaining the current market value of that debt would be almost impossible. The impact of using market or book values for the debt is inconsequential. Therefore, two simplifying approaches may be reasonable and not materially distorting: (1) Extrapolate market value to book value relationships of traded debt to the privately placed debt, or (2) simply assume that the market value of private debt is similar to the book value of private debt. Our recommendation remains: Use current market values where available.

Additionally, most corporations have a long-term strategic plan that includes projected financial statements. A corporation may also have, as a part of the strategic plan (or separate from it), a long-term financing plan that may include debt issuance, debt repayment, equity issuance, equity repurchase, etc. A corporation may establish some long-term goals or objectives surrounding its capital structure. This is called a target capital structure and should be based on the future market values as opposed to the future book values. That is, a corporation such as Hershey Foods may set an internal objective of establishing a capital structure of 15 percent debt and 85 percent equity, market value. If this is a corporate objective that the corporation is diligently working toward and if this is stated based upon a goal founded in capital structure based on future estimated market weights, then this target capital structure should be used as the appropriate weighting structure. (*Note*: This target capital structure is hypothetical for illustrative purposes and does not reflect an objective that Hershey Foods may or may not have.)

Said differently, the future will be the venue for the cost of capital. The cost of capital as anticipated by the future capital structure is what demands management attention in determining the cost of capital.

In summary, the three potential weighting structures indicate the following capital structures:

HERSHEY FOODS
CAPITAL STRUCTURE WEIGHTS

	Book	Market	Target
Debt	54%	13%	15%
Equity	46%	87%	85%

Our recommendation is to use a target capital structure if that target is based on targeted market values. If the target capital structure is based on book weights or does not exist, then the current market-based capital structure weights should be used.

COST OF CAPITAL APPLICATION

The weighted average cost of capital (or simply, cost of capital) brings together the individual costs of each capital source. The individual costs are weighted by the capital structure techniques discussed in the previous section.

Table 10.13a illustrates Hershey's capital structure on a book weight basis, i.e., a total capital structure of $2268 million with 54 percent in debt and 46 percent in equity. Hershey's debt on an after-tax basis costs 4.75 percent (current market) while equity, using the CAPM, costs 11.07 percent. The resulting cost of capital is 7.66 percent. Tables 10.13b and c illustrate the cost of capital calculation based on market weights and target weights, respectively. If Hershey Foods had preferred stock, that would be inserted and considered in a similar fashion.

TABLE 10.13a

Hershey's Cost of Capital—Historical Book Basis Weights

	Percent of Total	After-Tax Cost	Weighted Cost
Debt $1225	54.0%	4.75%	2.57%
Equity $1043	46.0%	11.07%	5.09%
Total	100.0%		7.66%

Hershey's cost of capital = 7.66%

TABLE 10.13b

Hershey's Cost of Capital—Market Basis Weights

	Percent of Total	After-Tax Cost	Weighted Cost
Debt $1200	12.8%	4.75%	0.61%
Equity* $8178	87.2%	11.07%	9.65%
Total	100.0%		10.26%

Hershey's cost of capital = 10.26%

*The market value of the equity is calculated as $58 (price per share, July 1999) times 141.0 million shares outstanding.

TABLE 10.13c

Hershey's Cost of Capital—Target Basis Weights

	Percent of Total	After-Tax Cost	Weighted Cost
Debt 15%	15%	4.75%	0.71%
Equity 85%	85%	11.07%	9.41%
Total	100.0%		10.12%

Hershey's cost of capital = 10.12%

Note: This target capital structure is hypothetical for illustrative purposes and does not reflect an objective that Hershey Foods may or may not have.

To summarize Tables 10.13a through c:

HERSHEY FOODS' COST OF CAPITAL (COC)						
	Book Weights		Market Weights		Target Weights	
	Weight	*COC*	*Weight*	*COC*	*Weight*	*COC*
Debt (4.75%)	54%	2.57%	12.8%	0.61%	15%	0.71%
Equity (11.07%)	46%	5.09%	87.2%	9.65%	85%	9.41%
Total	100%	7.66%	100%	10.26%	100%	10.12%

Hershey's recommended cost of capital is 10.12 percent. In calculating the cost of capital, it is easy to get carried away with a false sense of precision. Given all the assumptions about the capital structure, future growth rates, beta, the market's excess return, etc., as well as the ever-changing nature of the precise capital structure and stock price, the degree of precision must be carefully weighed. Once again, judgment must enter into the final recommendation.

FINANCIAL STRUCTURE

This section develops an overview of financial structure. Financial structure indicates the amount of debt and equity used in financing a firm. For any financial structure, debt is always a less expensive form of capital than equity, since the cost of debt is tax-deductible and in case of bankruptcy, debt holders have priority over equity holders. However, debt also comes with fixed, explicit costs. Every dollar of debt increases the risk of the firm and the cost of all financing. With too much debt and wavering business conditions, a firm may be forced into bankruptcy.

Without going into many of the theoretical details underlying financial structure theory, we illustrate the traditional financial structure in Table 10.14. The x axis shows debt as a percent of the capital (debt + equity) structure. The y axis lists the after-tax cost as a percentage. The graph itself contains three lines: the cost of debt (the lowest line), the cost of equity (the highest line), and the resulting cost of capital (the middle line). Each is discussed in turn.

The cost of debt for a corporation is similar to the cost of personal debt. The more debt you have, the riskier you are and the higher the cost of debt. For an individual, the least expensive form of debt is a mortgage. It is a form of secured debt collateralized by the house, and it is tax-deductible. However, a mortgage can only be used to borrow a limited percentage of the house's fair market value. Personally, it is the least expensive financing source. After the mortgage, the next least-expensive debt financing is available through a home equity loan. The home equity loan is collateralized by additional fair market value of equity left in the house beyond the primary mortgage. Once again, a home equity loan has a significant advantage since the interest payments are generally tax-deductible. After the home equity loan, educational loans may provide the next least costly form of debt financing. Automobile loans secured by the automobile, unsecured personal loans, and credit card loans are additional sources of personal borrowing, all with increasing costs and no tax deductions. If an individual needs to borrow beyond this level, a visit may be necessary to secondary and tertiary lenders at dramatically higher interest costs.

TABLE 10.14

Financial Structure
Traditional Approach

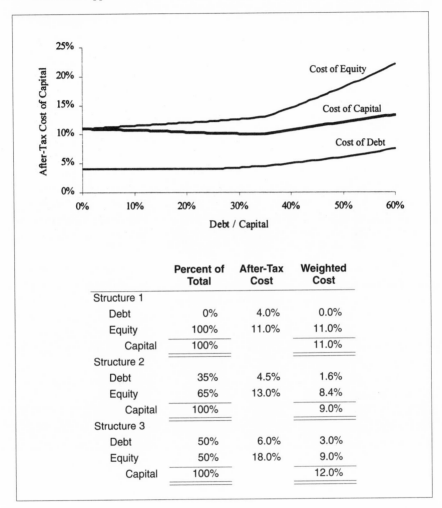

	Percent of Total	After-Tax Cost	Weighted Cost
Structure 1			
Debt	0%	4.0%	0.0%
Equity	100%	11.0%	11.0%
Capital	100%		11.0%
Structure 2			
Debt	35%	4.5%	1.6%
Equity	65%	13.0%	8.4%
Capital	100%		9.0%
Structure 3			
Debt	50%	6.0%	3.0%
Equity	50%	18.0%	9.0%
Capital	100%		12.0%

This same process occurs in concept for a firm and is depicted for a corporation by the cost of debt line in Table 10.14. However, any interest expense is generally tax-deductible for a corporation. Up to some point, the cost of debt is relatively flat for a corporation. As it is presented, somewhere between 25 and 30 percent capital structure, debt begins to cost slightly more. As the corporation takes on more debt, its marginal cost continues to increase.

The cost of equity begins with a slight upward trend. The first dollar of debt and each subsequent dollar make the corporation a bit riskier. This added risk is reflected as a higher cost of equity. Notice, for all capital structures the cost of debt is always less than the cost of equity for any given financial structure.

The cost of capital line is a mathematical representation of the individual cost of debt and cost of equity appropriately weighted for the total capital structure. To illustrate the cost of capital line, we review the three financial structures:

> Financial structure 1: The first financial structure is for an all-equity firm. This firm uses no debt, and consequently its cost of capital is equal to the cost of equity, or 11.0 percent. The cost of debt is at its lowest level, but there is no debt outstanding.
>
> Financial structure 2: At the second financial structure, the firm has 35 percent debt and 65 percent equity. Notice the debt and equity both cost more under this structure than under the first structure. However, by moving to this financial structure from the first financial structure, the corporation substitutes less expensive debt (4.5 percent—this structure) for more expensive equity (11.0 percent—in the first structure). Weighting the individual cost results in a 9.0 percent cost of capital. The second capital structure takes advantage of the less expensive cost of debt and results in a lower cost of capital.
>
> Financial structure 3: At the third financial structure, the firm's financial structure is evenly split, 50 percent debt and 50 percent equity. Notice that debt and equity both cost more under this structure than under the second structure. Unfortunately, due to the higher cost of both debt and equity, the resulting cost of capital is 12.0 percent, which is higher than either of the previous structures.

This suggests that there is an optimum financial structure that minimizes the cost of capital.

In today's cost reduction environment, businesses press to do more with less. Corporations seek to develop supplier relationships throughout the supply chain to reduce and eliminate costs. We "beat up" other suppliers and play off relationships to save one-quarter of one cent on envelopes or other office supplies. While it is important to reduce all explicit costs within an organization, the most widely used commodity in any organization is capital. It is the responsibility of the chief financial officer to minimize the cost of capital. The impact is major!

Factors Affecting Financial Structure

Each firm and each industry have numerous influences that lead to its capital structure decision:

- Growth rate of sales
- Cash flow stability
- Industry characteristics
- Asset structure
- Management attitudes
- Lender attitudes

Each is discussed below.

Growth Rate of Sales
The future growth rate of sales is a measure of the extent to which the earnings per share of a firm is likely to be magnified by leverage.   If sales and earnings grow at a rate of 8 to 10 percent a year, for example, financing by debt with limited fixed charges should magnify the returns to owners of the stock.   However, the common stock of a firm whose sales and earnings are growing at favorable rates commands a high price; this favors equity financing. The firm must weigh the benefits of using leverage against the opportunity of broadening its equity base when its common stock prices are high.

Cash Flow Stability
Cash flow stability and debt ratios are directly related. With greater stability in sales and operating earnings, a firm can incur the fixed charges of debt with less risk than when its sales and earnings are subject to substantial declines. When operating cash flow is low, the firm may have difficulty meeting its fixed interest obligations.

Industry Characteristics
Debt-servicing ability is dependent on the profitability, as well as the volume, of sales. Hence, the stability of profit margins is as important as the stability of sales. The ease with which new firms can enter the industry and the ability of competing firms to expand capacity both influence profit margins. A growth industry promises higher profit margins, but such margins are likely to narrow if the industry is one in which the number of firms can be easily increased through additional entry. For example, the franchised fast-service food companies were a very profitable industry in the early 1960s, but it was relatively easy for new firms to enter the business and compete with the older firms. As the industry matured during the late 1960s and early 1970s, the capacity of the old and the new firms grew at an increased rate. As a consequence, profit margins declined.

Asset Structure
Asset structure influences the sources of financing in several ways. Firms with long-lived fixed assets, especially when demand for their

output is relatively assured (e.g., public utilities), use long-term mortgage debt extensively. Firms that have their assets mostly in receivables and in inventories whose value is dependent on the continued profitability of the individual firm (e.g., those in wholesale and retail trade) rely less on long-term debt financing and more on short-term financing.

Management Attitudes

The management attitudes that most directly influence the choice of financing are those concerning control of the enterprise and risk. Large corporations whose stock is widely owned may choose additional sales of common stock because such sales will have little influence on the control of the company.

In contrast, the owners of small firms may prefer to avoid issuing common stock in order to ensure continued control. Because they generally have confidence in the prospects of their companies and because they can see the large potential gains to themselves resulting from leverage, managers of such firms are often willing to incur high debt ratios. The converse can, of course, also hold; the owner-manager of a small firm may be more conservative than the manager of a large company. If the net worth of the small firm is, say, $1 million, and if it all belongs to the owner-manager, that individual may well decide to limit the use of debt, which increases the risk of losing a substantial portion of his or her wealth.

Lender Attitudes

Regardless of managements' views, lenders' attitudes determine financial structures. The corporation discusses its financial structure with lenders and gives much weight to their advice. But if management seeks to use leverage beyond norms for the industry, lenders may be unwilling to accept such debt increases. They emphasize that excessive debt reduces the credit standing of the borrower and the credit rating of the securities previously issued. The lenders' point of view has been expressed by a borrower (a financial vice president), who stated, "Our policy is to determine how much debt we can carry and still maintain an Aa bond rating, then use that amount less a small margin for safety."

INDUSTRY GROUP ANALYSIS APPLICATION: FOOD INDUSTRY

The food industry is characterized by moderate sales growth, stable cash flows, and balanced investment in current and long-term assets. The industry is viewed favorably by lenders, but managers have varying impressions of leverage. Companies such as Wrigley and Tootsie

Roll employ little to no debt, while companies such as General Mills and Quaker Oats have more than 80 percent of the book value of their capital in debt. Table 10.15 traces the history of Hershey Foods Corporation against the history of the food process industry. The metric—capitalization ratio—calculates debt (both short-term and long-term) as a percent of capital (debt and equity) on a book basis. As exhibited, the year 1995 was a watermark year as the management team began a major recapitalization effort. By 1997, Hershey repurchased more than $1.0 billion of its shares and financed most of the purchases with debt. Thus, it experienced a double dose of leverage—a reduction in equity accompanied by an increase in debt. Hershey approximated the industry average.

Table 10.16 presents the capitalization ratios for 12 food companies that comprise the food processing industry. There is a wide dispersion of the use of leverage within the industry. Once again these are book-based weights.

TABLE 10.15

Capitalization Ratio*

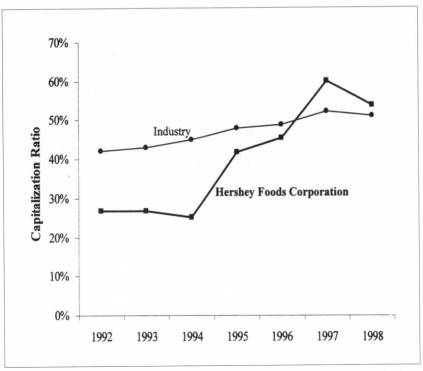

*This capitalization ratio is calculated as the book values of: (Short-term debt + Long-term debt)/(Short-term debt + Long-term debt + Equity).

Table 10.17 estimates the cost of capital for each of these 12 firms. In Table 10.17, the *x* axis presents debt (short-term and long-term) as a percentage of capital (debt and equity) based on market values of debt and equity. A different story is presented for the industry, as even the most leveraged firms have market value of less than 20 percent of their capital in debt.

The top graph shows the cost of debt (black squares), the estimated cost of equity using CAPM (open squares), and resulting cost of capital (black dots). The lower graph focuses on only the cost of capital by narrowing the *y* axis range. From the lower graph, a downward slope in the cost of capital is casually noted, which suggests there is still room for the industry to become more leveraged and reduce its cost of capital further.

TABLE 10.16

Food Industry Capitalization Ratio,* 1998

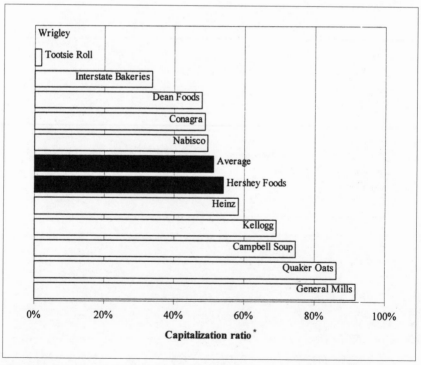

*This capitalization ratio is calculated as the book values of: (Short-term debt + Long-term debt)/(Short-term debt + Long-term debt + Equity).

TABLE 10.17

Food Industry: Cost of Capital Market Weights

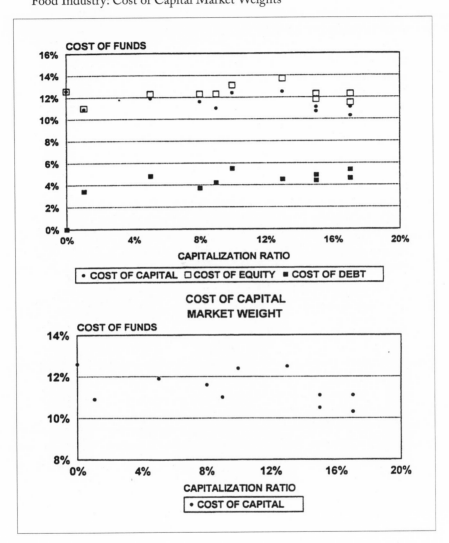

DIVISION OR PROJECT HURDLE RATES

Most corporations are complex entities comprised of numerous divisions or separate businesses. For example, in the early 1990s, Pepsico was comprised of three separate businesses: soft drinks (Pepsi brands), snack foods (Frito-Lay), and fast food restaurants (Pizza Hut, Taco Bell, and Kentucky Fried Chicken). Each of these businesses had its own set of competitors, business issues, and business risks. Additionally, sales growth rates, cash flow stability, and asset structure (current versus long-term) differed for each division.

Divisional hurdle rates examine each division as if it were a stand-alone business. For example, industry betas and industry financial structures are estimated for the soft drink, snack food, and fast food restaurant industries. Fast food restaurants, typically, have minimal current assets, because they have little (if any) accounts receivable and thin levels of inventories, and heavy long-term asset investment in land and building. This asset composition is conducive to higher levels of debt and a lower cost of capital.

After estimating the industry betas and financial structure, a cost of capital can be calculated as discussed above for each division. Each division will have its own estimated cost of capital, which is the minimal acceptable rate of return for that division. Consequentially, a 10 percent returning project may be acceptable in one division, but not another division, just as a 10 percent returning project might be acceptable in one industry (company) and not another.

Some companies "drill" the divisional cost of capital concept to a deeper level—project cost of capital. Although there is limited financial theory that is directly applicable in practice, the conceptual attraction of project hurdle rates is well founded in theory—added risk requires added return. Companies often develop project categories, such as cost reduction, cost avoidance, capacity expansion, new product line extension, and brand new product. Often the project categories also include regulatory (or environmental) capital, R&D capital, and administrative capital. While most companies limit their project categories to three to seven categories, one major Fortune 500 firm has 26 individual project categories.

Although a company may not be able to exactly quantify the cost of capital requirement for a new product, the management recognizes that a new product is riskier than capacity expansion for existing products, which is riskier than investment in a cost savings project. Some companies arbitrarily extend this argument and require higher returns for capacity expansion projects than for cost savings projects and even higher returns for new products than for capacity expansion projects.

SUMMARY

The cost of capital is the opportunity cost of funds that is required to compensate investors for their investment in the organization. Because investors generally dislike risk, the required rate of return is higher on riskier securities. As a class, bonds are less risky than preferred stocks; and preferred stocks, in turn, are less risky than common stocks. The result is that the required rate of return is lowest for bonds, higher for preferred stocks, and highest for common stocks.

Within each of these security classes there are variations among the issuing firms' risks; hence, required rates of return vary among firms.

The cost of debt is defined as the required yield to maturity on new increments of debt capital, K_d, multiplied by (1 – tax rate). The cost of preferred stock with no maturity date is the required yield. It is found as the annual expected preferred dividend divided by the preferred stock price. The cost of common equity is the return required to prevent the price of the common stock from declining from its current levels. The cost of common equity may be calculated by at least three methods. The recommended approach is the capital asset pricing model—the risk-free rate plus the product of the market risk premium and the firm's beta.

Increasing the leverage ratio in a firm will make the debt and equity riskier because it increases the probability of bankruptcy. If bankruptcy costs are substantial, then with increasing leverage the value of the firm will rise, reach a peak, and then fall. The maximum point on this curve indicates a target debt or leverage ratio.

The first step in calculating the weighted cost of capital K is to determine the cost of the individual capital components. The next step is to establish the proper set of weights to be used in the averaging process. The basic issues are whether to use the actual historical financing costs of the firm and whether to use book or market value in calculating the proportions or weights of each source of financing. Financing costs must represent current opportunity costs, so the actual historical financing costs (reflected in the books) are not relevant. With regard to weights or proportions of each source of financing, theory calls for the use of target capital structure. However, current market values may not represent the target equilibrium values, so we do not necessarily apply the market values that we observe at a particular time. We should use those proportions or weights that represent the debt capacity of the firm appropriate for use in formulating the firm's target leverage proportions. A wide range of factors would have to be considered by a firm's management in formulating its target leverage ratio.

QUESTIONS AND PROBLEMS

10.1 **Cost of debt.** An outstanding bond has a $1000 face value, a 9.5 percent annual coupon, and 10 more years until it matures. The bond currently sells for $1153. What are the *historical after-tax cost of debt* and the *current after-tax cost of debt*? Assume a 40 percent tax rate.

10.2 **Capital asset pricing model.** What is the expected return on asset X if it has a beta of 0.85, the expected market return is 11.50 percent, and the risk-free rate is 5.75 percent?

10.3   **Cost of capital.** A. Calculate the cost of each financing source for Keyboard, Inc. The tax rate is 40 percent:

Financial Source		Cost
Debt	Twelve-year bond, 6.75% annual coupon, current price of $960.81	
Preferred stock	Dividend $5.50, current price of $63.75	
Common stock	Beta of 1.45, excess market return of 5.63%, risk-free rate of 6.05%	

  B.   Currently, there are 121 million shares of common stock outstanding at $48 per share and 4 million shares of preferred stock outstanding. Also there is currently $956 million of debt outstanding. Calculate the weighted average cost of capital, using current market weights.

  C.   The company is targeting a capital structure of 25 percent debt, 5 percent preferred stock, and 70 percent common equity. Recalculate the cost of capital based on target weights. Compare your answer to part B.

10.4   **Hurdle rates.** Assume that Hershey Foods has a policy that cost savings projects must earn a 16 percent hurdle rate and that new products must earn a 25 percent hurdle rate. The hurdle rate is a result of historical analysis and the perceived risk associated with both project types. I have funding requests for two projects, project A, which is a cost savings project with a 16.5 percent rate of return and project B, which is a higher-returning, new product and has a 22 percent rate of return. If I can fund only one of them, which project should I recommend and why?

10.5   **Cost of capital and products.** How could the cost-of-capital structure influence a product's price or a product's quality?

10.6   **Net present value and cost of capital.** HT Inc. is considering a new process to speed production and reduce costs. The project will last 7 years and have an initial investment of $1,400,000. The after-tax cash flows are estimated at $315,000 per year. The firm has a targeted debt-to-equity ratio of 1.5. Its pretax cost of equity is 14 percent, and its pretax cost of debt is 8 percent. The tax rate is 40 percent. What is the NPV of this project?

SOLUTIONS TO QUESTIONS AND PROBLEMS

10.1

				Book	**Market**
N	=	10			
Pmt =	$95		Pretax	9.50%	7.29%
FV	= $1000		Posttax	5.70%	4.37%
PV	= $1153			Historical = Book	

$i\%$ = 7.29% pretax cost of debt

$$\text{After-tax cost of debt} = (7.29\%)(1 - 0.40)$$
$$= 4.37\%$$

10.2

$$\text{Risk-free + beta (market - risk-free)} = \text{expected return of } A$$
$$5.75\% + 0.85(11.50\% - 5.75\%) = 10.6375\%$$

10.3   A.

N = 12
Pmt = $67.50
FV   = $1000
PV   = $960.81
$i\%$ = 7.25% pretax cost of debt
After-tax cost of debt = (7.25%)(1 – 0.40)
= 4.35%

Cost of preferred stock
Dividend / Price = $5.50 / $63.75 = 8.63%

Cost of common stock
Risk-free + beta (market – risk-free) = expected return of stock
6.05% + 1.45(5.63%) = 14.21%

B.

	Shares (Millions)	Price per Share	Weights Amount ($ Millions)	Weight	Cost	Weighted Cost
Debt			$956	13.6%	4.35%	0.59%
Preferred stock	4.0	$63.75	255	3.6%	8.63%	0.31%
Common stock	121.0	$48.00	5808	82.8%	14.21%	11.77%
Total			$7019	100.0%		12.67%

C.

	Target Weight	Cost	Weighted Cost
Debt	25%	4.35%	1.09%
Preferred stock	5%	8.63%	0.43%
Common stock	70%	14.21%	9.95%
Total	100%		11.47%

10.4 Assuming that the hurdle rate structure incorporates an estimate of the riskiness of a new product versus a cost savings project, Hershey should accept the cost savings project. The cost savings project's expected return exceeds its risk-adjusted hurdle rate. Although the new product's expected return is 5.5 percent higher than the cost savings project, the new product is not expected to have a return that exceeds its hurdle rate. In fact the new product falls short of the required return by 3 percent.

10.5 If the cost of capital is estimated too high, the only way to justify the project's investment is to raise prices or to reduce the product's costs. A cost reduction may be accompanied by reduced quality.

10.6 The following table includes a debt-to-equity ratio of 1.5:

	Weights			
	Amount ($ Millions)	Weight	Cost	Weighted Cost
Debt	1.50	60.0%	4.80%	2.88%
Equity	1.00	40.0%	14.00%	5.60%
Total	2.50	100.0%		8.48%

	Project	
Year	$000	PV
0	($1400)	$(1400)
1	315	290
2	315	268
3	315	247
4	315	227
5	315	210
6	315	193
7	315	178
	NPV	$ 213

CHAPTER 11

Long-Term Financing

This chapter discusses long-term financing: sources of long-term financing, procedures for obtaining long-term financing, and specific forms of long-term financing. The common forms of long-term financing include long-term debt, preferred stock, common stock, and leasing. Each is presented, in turn, below.

The chief financial officer or the treasurer of an organization is responsible for making recommendations to the board of directors and chief executive officer. These recommendations carefully weigh the advantages and disadvantages of each financial instrument. Once the decision is made, the chief financial officer or the treasurer is responsible for obtaining the long-term financing for the organization.

For other executives of the corporation, a basic understanding of the process and available financing alternatives acquaints the executive with specific terms and concepts, broadens the executive's understanding of financial markets, and enhances the knowledge about why specific financing decisions are made within the organization.

SOURCES OF LONG-TERM FINANCING

Through the stages of a firm's development, an organization faces different sources of available financing. See Table 11.1. During the first phase, the start-up, a firm avails itself of financing from personal savings, personal loans, and government agencies such as the Small Business Administration (SBA) or Small Business Investment Corporations (SBIC). The SBA and SBIC are federal agencies. State governments may also have "incubator" funds available to encourage rural or inner city development, or to attract various start-up businesses.

During rapid growth, the second phase, a firm finances itself through internal sources or direct financing. The firm can obtain direct financing in the form of a loan from a commercial bank, insurance company, or pension fund. In addition, a firm can obtain funds from venture capitalists. These sources are discussed in detail below.

TABLE 11.1

Financing Sources through a Firm's Development

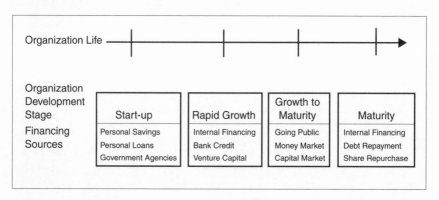

The third phase, growth to maturity, is financed by going public and through money and capital markets. An investment bank is generally involved in this process. Investment banking is discussed below along with the common forms of long-term financing: long-term debt (including lease alternatives), preferred stock, and common stock.

During the firm's final phase, maturity and industry decline, a firm finances through internal sources while repaying its debt or repurchasing its shares.

DIRECT FINANCING

Venture capital financing is a form of direct financing and is discussed later. This section concentrates on obtaining direct debt financing (loans). Direct long-term financing includes (1) term lending by commercial banks and insurance companies and (2) private placement of securities with insurance companies and pension funds. Term loans are direct business loans with a maturity of more than 1 year but less than 15 years, with provisions for systematic repayment (amortization during the life of the loan). Private placements are direct business loans with a maturity of more than 15 years. The distinction is, of course, arbitrary. Private placement differs from the term loan only in its arbitrary maturity length; this distinction becomes even fuzzier when we discover that some private placements call for repayment of a substantial portion of the principal within 5 to 10 years. Thus, term loans and private placements represent about the same kind of financing arrangements.

Characteristics of Term Loans and Private Placements

Most term loans are repayable on an amortized basis. The purpose of amortization, of course, is to have the loan repaid gradually over its life rather than all due at maturity. This protects both the lender and the borrower against the possibility that the borrower will not make adequate provisions for retirement of the loan during its life. Amortization is especially important for a loan used to purchase a specific item of equipment; here, the schedule of repayment will be geared to the productive life of the equipment, and payments will be made from cash flows resulting from use of the equipment. The mechanics of preparing an amortization schedule are illustrated in Table 11.2 and discussed below.

A loan amortization schedule segregates loan payments into interest and principal over the life of a loan. A portion of each payment pays interest for that period while the remainder of the payment reduces the principal amount. Table 11.2 illustrates a $10,000, 12 percent five-year loan that requires only annual payments. The payments are calculated at $2774.10 per year, using the annuity tools discussed in Chap. 3, Time Value of Money.

To illustrate, the $10,000 principal amount was outstanding for the full year (assuming the payment is received at the end of the year). The interest on $10,000 at a rate of l2 percent accrues to $1,200 for the year. The remaining $1574.10 ($2774.10 payment less $1200 interest) reduces the outstanding principal to a value of $8425.90 to begin the second year. This process continues until the loan is fully paid back in year 5.

Evaluation of Direct Financing

From the standpoint of the borrower, the advantages of direct financing are that

TABLE 11.2

Loan Amortization Table
(5 year; $10,000; 12%)

Year	Beginning balance	Payment	12.0% interest	Principal	Ending balance
1	$10,000.00	$2,774.10	$1,200.00	$1,574.10	$8,425.90
2	8,425.90	2,774.10	1,011.11	1,762.99	6,662.91
3	6,662.91	2,774.10	799.55	1,974.55	4,688.36
4	4,688.36	2,774.10	562.60	2,211.50	2,476.86
5	2,476.86	2,774.10	297.22	2,476.88	0.00

1. Much seasonal short-term borrowing can be dispensed with, thereby reducing the danger of nonrenewal of loans.
2. The borrower avoids the expenses of Securities and Exchange Commission (SEC) registration and investment bankers' distribution.
3. Less time is required to complete arrangements for obtaining a loan than is involved in a bond issue.
4. Since only one lender is involved, rather than many bondholders, it is possible to modify the loan indenture.

The disadvantages to a borrower of direct financing are that

1. The interest rate may be higher on a term loan than on a short-term loan because the lender is tying up money for a longer period and, therefore, does not have the opportunity to review the borrower's status periodically (as is done whenever short-term loans are renewed).
2. The cash drain is large. Since the loans provide for regular amortization or sinking fund payments, the company experiences a continuous cash drain. From this standpoint, direct loans are less advantageous than equity funds (which never have to be repaid), a preferred stock without maturity, or even a bond issue without a sinking fund requirement.
3. Since the loan is a long-term commitment, the lender employs high credit standards, insisting that the borrower be in a strong financial position and have a good current ratio, a low debt-equity ratio, good activity ratios, and good profitability ratios.
4. Because of the long-term exposure of the lender, the loan agreement has restrictions that are not found in a 90-day note.
5. Investigation costs may be high. The lender stays with the company for a longer period. Therefore, the longer-term outlook for the company must be reviewed, and the lender makes a more elaborate investigation than would be done for a short-term note. For this reason, the lender may set a minimum on any loan (for example, $50,000 in order to recover the costs of investigating the applicant).

In addition, there are some advantages to the public distribution of securities that are not achieved by term loans or private placement:

1. The firm establishes its credit and achieves publicity by having its securities publicly and widely distributed. Because of this, it will be able to engage in future financing at lower rates.

2. The wide distribution of debt or equity may enable its repurchase on favorable terms at some subsequent date if the market price of the securities falls.

Thus, direct long-term financing has both advantages and limitations. Its use continues through the rapid growth stage and into the growth to maturity stage as a firm assesses and makes tradeoffs with other forms of financing.

VENTURE CAPITALISTS

Firms that have growth potential face greater risks than almost any other type of business, and their higher risks require special types of financing. This led to the development of specialized venture capital financing sources. Some venture capital companies are organized as partnerships; others are more formal corporations termed investment development companies.

Investment banking firms and commercial banks have also established venture capital subsidiaries. Related to these are some venture capital investments by firms whose owners often have had prior investment banking or commercial banking experience. Some venture capital firms represent investment activities by wealthy individuals. Another longtime source of venture capital is represented by large, well-established business firms. A number of large corporations have invested both money and various types of know-how to start or to help develop small business firms. The owner of the small firm is usually a specialist, frequently a technically oriented person who needs both money and help in such administrative services as accounting, finance, production, and marketing. The small firm's owner contributes entrepreneurship, special talents, a taste for risk taking, and a passion to see the successful development and commercialization of an idea. A number of major corporations have found that there is a mutual advantage for this form of venture capital investment.

When a new business makes an application for financial assistance from a venture capital firm, it receives a rigorous examination. Some development companies use their own staffs for this investigation, while others depend on a board of advisers acting in a consultative capacity. A high percentage of applications is rejected, but if the application is approved, funds are provided. Venture capital companies generally take an equity position in the firms they finance, but they may also extend debt capital. However, when loans are made, they generally involve convertibles or warrants or are tied in with the purchase of stock by the investment company. Often the venture capital firm will take convertible preferred stock for its investment. This avoids burdening the new capital-hungry firm with a requirement to pay interest on debt or technically be in default. The convertible preferred stock also provides the venture capital firm with a prior position in liquidation and the opportunity to obtain a substantial equity position if the venture turns out well.

Another technique is the use of a staged capital commitment. In staged capital commitment (SCC), the venture capitalist agrees to provide capital in various stages in the venture as opposed to providing all expected capital requirements up front. Also, the venture capitalist typically reserves the option to abandon, revalue, or increase his or her capital commitment to the project at each future round of financing.

SCC reduces the perceived risk to the venture capitalist, since the venture capitalist receives a wealth of information about the company (e.g., how has the company performed relative to its initial business plan, whether the management team works well together, whether the market research reveals adequate demand, whether new competition has surfaced) before the next round of financing arrives. This new information reduces the uncertainty of the value of the company and aids in the venture capitalist's decision as to how to proceed.

Also, the knowledge that the company is scheduled to run out of cash is a powerful motivator for management to focus its energies on creating value from its limited resources.

INVESTMENT BANKING

In the U.S. economy, saving is done by one group of persons and investing by another. (Investing is used here in the sense of actually putting money into plant, equipment, and inventory and not in the sense of buying securities.) Savings are placed with financial intermediaries, who, in turn, make the funds available to firms wishing to acquire plants and equipment and to hold inventories.

One of the major institutions performing this channeling role is the investment banking institution. The term investment banker is somewhat misleading, since investment bankers are neither investors nor bankers. That is, they do not invest their own funds permanently, nor are they repositories for individuals' funds, as are commercial banks or savings banks. What, then, is the nature of investment banking?

The many activities of investment bankers can be described first in general terms and then with respect to specific functions. The traditional function of the investment banker has been to act as the middleman in channeling individuals' savings and funds into the purchase of business securities. The investment banker does this by purchasing and distributing the new securities of individual companies while performing the functions of underwriting, distribution of securities, and advice and counsel.

Underwriting

Underwriting is the insurance function of bearing the risks of adverse price fluctuations during the period in which a new issue of securities is being distributed. The nature of the investment banker's underwriting function can best be conveyed by example. A business firm needs $400 million. It selects an investment banker, holds conferences, and decides to issue $400 million of bonds. An underwriting agreement is drawn up. On a specific day, the investment banker presents the company with a check for $400 million (less commission). In return, the investment banker receives bonds in denominations of $1000 each to sell to the public.

The company receives the $400 million before the investment banker has sold the bonds. Between the time the firm is paid the $400 million and the time the bonds are sold, the investment banker bears all the risk of market price fluctuations in the bonds. Conceivably, it can take the investment banker days, months, or longer to sell the bonds. If the bond market deteriorates in the interim, the investment banker carries the risk of loss on the sale of the bonds.

One fundamental economic function of the investment banker, then, is to underwrite the risk of a decline in the market price between the time the money is transmitted to the firm and the time the bonds are placed in the hands of their ultimate buyers. For this reason, investment bankers are often called underwriters; they underwrite risk during the distribution period.

Distribution

The second function of the investment banker is to market new issues of securities. The investment banker is a specialist with a staff and organization to distribute securities and, therefore, the capacity to perform the physical distribution function more efficiently and more economically than an individual corporation can. A corporation that wished to sell an issue of securities would find it necessary to establish a marketing or selling organization—a very expensive and ineffective method of selling securities. The investment banker has a permanent, trained staff and dealer organization available to distribute securities. In addition, the investment banker's reputation for selecting good companies and pricing securities fairly builds up a broad clientele over time, and this further increases the efficiency with which securities can be sold.

Advice and Counsel

The investment banker engaged in the origination and sale of securities through experience becomes an expert adviser about terms and characteristics of securities that will appeal to investors. This advice and guidance is valuable. Furthermore, the firm's reputation as a seller of securities depends on the subsequent performance of the securities. Therefore, investment bankers often sit on the boards of firms whose securities they have sold. In this way, they can provide continuing financial counsel.

GOING PUBLIC AND IPOs

We have described how firms may be aided during the early stages of their growth by sources such as venture capital. We have also described the nature of investment banking in bringing seasoned issues of debt and equity to the market. We can draw on this background to discuss going public and initial public offerings.

Going public represents a fundamental change in lifestyle in at least four respects: (1) The firm moves from informal, personal control to a system of formal controls; (2) information must be reported on a timely basis to the outside investors, even though the founders may continue to have majority control; (3) the firm must have breadth of management in all the business functions if it is to operate its expanded business effectively; and (4) the publicly owned firm typically draws on a board of directors, which should include representatives of the public owners and other external interest groups, to help formulate sound plans and policies.

The timing of the decision to go public is especially important, because small firms are more affected by variations in money market conditions than larger companies are. During periods of tight money and high interest rates, financial institutions, especially commercial banks, find that the quantity of funds demanded exceeds the supply available at legally permissible and conventionally acceptable rates. One important method employed to ration credit is to raise credit standards. During tight money periods, both a stronger balance sheet record and a longer and more stable record of profitability are required to qualify for bank credit. Since financial ratios for small and growing firms tend to be less strong, such firms bear the brunt of credit restraint. Obviously, the small firm that goes public and raises equity capital before a money squeeze is in a better position to ride it out. This firm has already raised some of its needed capital, and its equity cushion enables it to present a stronger picture to the banks, thus helping it to obtain additional capital in the form of debt.

In a firm-commitment cash offer, the investment banker agrees to underwrite and distribute the issue at an agreed upon price for a specified number of shares to be bought by the underwriters. The issuer still bears some risk with regard to both price and number of shares sold. These are subject to revision by the investment banker between the date a preliminary agreement is signed and the actual issue date after SEC clearance and other procedures have been completed. Typically, a day before the actual issue date in a conference between the investment banker, lawyers, accountants, and the issuer, the number of shares to be sold may be adjusted downward (depending on the strength of the market) and an issue price is set.

A best-efforts offering is subject to the additional risk that if a minimum number of shares is not sold, the investment banker withdraws the offering. Best-efforts offerings generally involve smaller issuers and smaller size of issue. They also involve industries or activities where future performance of the firm is difficult to predict. The volatility of price movements in the market after issue is likely to be greater. Thus the investment banker may find it difficult to make a good estimate of the potential market. In a best-efforts offering, the issuer has no assurance that the offer will succeed.

The Decision to Go Public

With all the foregoing as background, what are the pros and cons of a firm's going public?

A number of advantages can be stated:

1. Obviously, additional funds are raised.
2. The disclosure and outside monitoring may make it easier to raise additional funds in the future.
3. A public price is established, and its subsequent behavior is a test of the performance of the firm.
4. It is often useful to have public prices, which establish values for tax purposes.
5. Increased liquidity is provided because of the market that may develop in the stock.

A number of potential disadvantages of going public must be considered:

1. Some loss of control is involved in sharing ownership.
2. The activities of the firm are now more fully disclosed.
3. More formal reporting to public agencies is required. This can be costly.
4. If the firm's shares do not attract a following, the market for them may be relatively inactive, thereby losing the potential benefits of performance evaluation and aligning incentives.
5. Outside investors may push for short-term performance results to an excessive degree.

6. A public firm must publish information that may disclose vital and competitively sensitive information to rival firms.

7. Stockholders' servicing costs and other related expenses may also be a consideration for smaller firms.

8. An advantage of not going public is that major programs do not have to be justified by detailed studies and reports to the board of directors. Action can be taken more speedily, and sometimes getting a new investment program underway early is critical for its success.

Generalization is not possible. The going-public decision depends on the circumstances of the firm and the preferences of its major owners. The advantages and disadvantages of going public may be so closely balanced that the decision may be reversed as time, circumstances, and preferences change.

The following sections discuss critical terms and concepts about long-term debt, preferred stock, and common stock. Each discussion concludes with advantages and disadvantages to issuers of each form of capital.

LONG-TERM DEBT FINANCING

An understanding of long-term forms of financing requires some familiarity with technical terminology. The discussion of long-term debt begins with an explanation of several important instruments and terms.

Instruments of Long-Term Debt Financing

Most people have had some experience with promises to pay. A bond is simply a long-term promissory note. A mortgage represents a pledge of designated property for a loan. Under a mortgage bond, a corporation pledges certain real assets as security for the bond. The pledge is a condition of the loan. A mortgage bond, therefore, is secured by real property, which is defined as real estate land and building. On a personal basis, a personal mortgage is exemplified by the primary mortgage of your home or a home equity loan. Nonpayment of a mortgage leads to foreclosure on the pledged property and loss of that property. A chattel mortgage is secured by personal property (any other kind of property, including equipment, inventories, and furniture); but this is generally an intermediate-term instrument. An automobile loan is a personal example of a chattel mortgage.

A debenture is a long-term bond that is not secured by a pledge of any specific property. However, like other general creditors, it has a claim on any property not otherwise pledged. Again, on a personal level, borrowing on a credit card is similar to a debenture. It is unsecured borrowing.

Indenture

The long-term relationship between the borrower and the lender of a long-term promissory note is established in a document called an *indenture*. In the case of an ordinary 60- or 90-day promissory note, few developments that will endanger repayment are likely to occur in the life or affairs of the borrower. The lender looks closely at the borrower's current position, because current assets are the main source of repayment. A bond, however, is a long-term contractual relationship between the bond issuer and the bondholder; over this extended period, the bondholder has cause to worry that the issuing firm's position may change materially.

The bond indenture can be a document of several hundred pages that discusses a large number of factors important to the contracting parties, such as (1) the form of the bond and the instrument, (2) a complete description of property pledged, (3) the authorized amount of the bond issue, (4) detailed protective clauses, or covenants, (5) a minimum current ratio requirement, and (6) provisions for redemption or call privileges. Bond covenants can be divided into four broad categories: (1) those restricting the issuance of new debt, (2) those with restrictions on dividend payments, (3) those with restrictions on merger activity, and (4) those with restrictions on the disposition of the firm's assets.

Bond covenants that restrict subsequent financing are by far the most common type. The covenant provisions are usually stated in terms of accounting numbers and consequently are easy to monitor. The issuance of debt may carry restrictions that require all new debt to be subordinated or prohibit the creation of new debt with a higher priority unless existing bonds are upgraded to have an equal priority. All these restrictions are designed to prevent the firm from increasing the riskiness of outstanding debt by issuing new debt with a superior or equal claim on the firm's assets. Alternate restrictions may prohibit the issuance of new debt unless the firm maintains minimum prescribed financial ratios related to the firm's capitalization or liquidity.

Bond covenants that restrict dividend payments are necessary if for no other reason than to prohibit the extreme case of shareholders voting to pay themselves a liquidating dividend that would leave the bondholders holding an empty corporate shell. The dividend covenant does not prohibit dividends per se; rather, it restricts the financing of the payment of dividends with new debt or by sale of the firm's existing assets. Bond covenants may also restrict merger activity and restrict production or investment policies.

Call Provision

A call provision gives the issuing corporation the right to call in the bond for redemption. The provision generally states that the company must pay an amount greater than the par value of the bond; this additional sum is defined as the call premium. A callable bond typically has a grace period in which the bond is noncallable. After this grace period the bond is callable each year with a declining premium over some time period. For example, a callable 20-year bond is issued in 2000. The bond's call provision includes a 5-year grace period, during which the bond is not callable. The callable premium may then be described that any bond called in the sixth year is callable at 105 (or $1050 on a $1000 par value bond); in the seventh year, the bond is callable at 104 ($1040); in the eighth year at 103 ($1030); in the ninth year at 102 ($1020); in the tenth year at 101 ($1010); and thereafter at 100 or par value of $1000.

The call privilege is valuable to the firm but potentially detrimental to the investor, especially if the bond is issued in a period when interest rates are thought to be cyclically high. The problem for investors is that the call privilege enables the issuing corporation to substitute bonds paying lower interest rates for bonds paying higher ones.

Sinking Fund

A sinking fund is a provision that facilitates the orderly retirement of a bond issue (or, in some cases, preferred stock issue). Typically, it requires the firm to buy and retire a portion of the bond issue each year. Sometimes, the stipulated sinking fund payment is tied to the current year's sales or earnings, but usually it is a mandatory fixed amount. If it is mandatory, a failure to meet the payment causes the bond issue to be thrown into default and can lead the company into bankruptcy. Obviously, then, a sinking fund can constitute a serious cash drain on the firm. In most cases, the firm is given the right to handle the sinking fund in either of two ways: (1) calling the bonds at a predetermined price or (2) buying the bonds on the open market.

Secured Bonds

Secured long-term debt can be classified according to (1) the priority of claims, (2) the right to issue additional securities, and (3) the scope of the lien.

Priority of Claims

A senior mortgage has prior claims on assets and earnings. Senior railroad mortgages, e.g., have been called the "mortgages next to the rail," implying that they have the first claim on the land and assets of the rail-road corporations. A junior mortgage is a subordinate lien, such as a second or third mortgage. It is a lien or claim junior to others.

Right to Issue Additional Securities

Mortgage bonds can also be classified with respect to the right to issue additional obligations pledging already encumbered property. In the case of a closed-end mortgage, a company cannot sell additional bonds (beyond those already issued) secured by the property specified in the mortgage. If the bond indenture is silent on this point, then the mortgage is called open-ended and additional mortgages can be issued on the same property, up to a point.

Scope of the Lien

Bonds can also be classified with respect to the scope of their lien. A lien is granted on certain specified property. When a specific lien exists, the security for a first or second mortgage is a specifically desig-nated property. On the other hand, a blanket mortgage pledges all real property currently owned by the company. Real property includes only land and those things affixed to it; thus, a blanket mortgage is not on cash, accounts receivable, or inventories, which are items of per-sonal property. A blanket mortgage gives greater protection to the bondholder than does a specific mortgage because it provides a claim on all real property owned by the company.

Unsecured Bonds

Debentures

The reasons for a firm's use of unsecured debt are diverse. Paradoxi-cally, the extremes of financial strength and weakness may give rise to its use. Also, tax considerations and great uncertainty about the level of the firm's future earnings have given rise to special forms of unse-cured financing. A debenture is an unsecured bond and, as such, pro-vides no lien on specific property as security for the obligation. Debenture holders, therefore, are general creditors whose claim is pro-tected by property not otherwise pledged. The advantage of deben-tures from the issuer's standpoint is that the property is left unencumbered for subsequent financing. However, in practice, the use of debentures depends on the nature of the firm's assets and its general credit strength.

A firm whose credit position is exceptionally strong can issue debentures; it simply does not need specific security. However, the credit position of a company may be so weak that it has no alternative to the use of debentures; all its property may already be encumbered.

Subordinated Debentures

The term *subordinate* means below or inferior. Thus, subordinated debt has claims on assets after unsubordinated debt in the event of liquidation. Debentures can be subordinated to designated notes payable—usually bank loans—or to any or all other debt. In the event of liquidation or reorganization, the debentures cannot be paid until senior debt as named in the indenture has been paid.

The reasons for the use of subordinated debentures are clear. They offer a tax advantage over preferred stock; yet, they do not restrict the borrower's ability to obtain senior debt, as would be the case if all debt sources were on an equal basis. The use of subordinated debentures is further stimulated by periods of tight money, when commercial banks tend to require a greater equity base for short-term financing.

Income Bonds

Income bonds provide that interest be paid only if the earnings of the firm are sufficient to meet the interest obligations. The principal, however, must be paid when due. Thus, the interest itself is not a fixed charge. Income bonds, historically, have been issued because a firm has been in financial difficulties and its history suggests that it may be unable to meet a substantial level of fixed charges in the future. More generally, however, income bonds simply provide flexibility to the firm in the event that earnings do not cover the amount of interest that would otherwise have to be paid.

Floating-Rate Notes

When inflation forces interest rates to high levels, borrowers are reluctant to commit themselves to long-term debt. Yield curves are typically inverted at such times, with short-term interest rates higher than long-term. One factor is that borrowers would rather pay a premium for short-term funds than lock themselves into high long-term rates for two or three decades.

The floating-rate note (FRN) was developed to decrease the risks of interest rate volatility at high levels. In an FRN, the coupon rate varies at a given percentage above prevailing short- or long-term Treasury debt yields. The FRN rate is typically either fixed or guaranteed to exceed a stated minimum for an initial period and then adjusted at specified intervals to movements in the Treasury rates.

Floating-rate notes provide another illustration of the flexibility of financial markets and instruments. The increased volatility of fluctuations in interest rates has brought forth debt instruments with new types of provisions. Additional new efforts by lenders to achieve protection against inflation include a provision that the principal will also float—that it will be tied to the value of real assets such as oil or silver.

Other inflation hedges by lenders include debt that is convertible to shares of the company's common stock; or add-on contingent interest fees based on some measure of company performance such as sales or income. Such hedges are added to a fixed interest rate that will be lower than it would otherwise have to be to provide protection against uncertain inflation. Thus, the lender trades off some inflation protection against some near-term interest income.

PREFERRED STOCK FINANCING

Preferred stock has claims and rights ahead of common stock but behind all bonds. The preference may be a prior claim on earnings, a prior claim on assets in the event of liquidation, and/or a preferential position with regard to both earnings and assets.

The hybrid nature of preferred stock becomes apparent when we try to classify it in relation to bonds and common stock. The priority feature and the (generally) fixed dividend indicate that preferred stock is similar to bonds. Payments to preferred stockholders are limited in amount, so that common stockholders receive the advantages (or disadvantages) of leverage. However, if the preferred dividends are not earned, the company can forgo paying them without danger of bankruptcy. In this characteristic, preferred stock is similar to common stock. Moreover, failure to pay the stipulated dividend does not cause default of the obligation, as does failure to pay bond interest.

Evaluation of Preferred Stock as a Source of Long-Term Financing

There are both advantages and disadvantages to selling preferred stock. Among the advantages are that

1. In contrast to bonds, the obligation to make committed interest payments is avoided.
2. A firm wishing to expand because its earning power is high can obtain higher earnings for the original owners by selling preferred stock with a limited return than by selling common stock.
3. By selling preferred stock, the financial manager avoids the provision of equal participation in earnings that the sale of additional common stock would require.
4. Preferred stock also permits a company to avoid sharing control through participation in voting.
5. In contrast to bonds, it enables the firm to conserve mortgageable assets.
6. Since preferred stock typically has no maturity and no sinking fund, it is more flexible than bonds.

Among the disadvantages are that

1. Characteristically, preferred stock must be sold on a higher yield basis than that for bonds.
2. Preferred stock dividends are not deductible as a tax expense, which is a characteristic that makes their cost differential very great in comparison with that of bonds.
3. As shown in Chap. 10, the after-tax cost or debt is approximately 60 to 65 percent of the stated coupon rate for profitable firms. The after-tax cost of preferred, however, is generally the full percentage amount of the preferred dividend.

In fashioning securities, the financial manager needs to consider the investor's point of view. Frequently, it is asserted that preferred stocks have so many disadvantages to both the issuer and the investor that they should never be issued. Nevertheless, preferred stock is issued in substantial amounts. Preferred stock provides the following advantages to the investor:

1. It provides reasonably steady income.
2. Preferred stockholders have a preference over common stockholders in liquidation.
3. Many corporations (e.g., insurance companies) like to hold preferred stocks as investments because 70 or 80 percent of the dividends received on these shares is not taxable.

Preferred stock also has some disadvantages to investors:

1. Although the holders of preferred stock bear a substantial portion of ownership risk, their returns are limited.
2. Price fluctuations in preferred stock may be greater than those in bonds.
3. The stockholders have no legally enforceable right to dividends.
4. Accrued dividend arrearages are seldom settled in cash comparable to the amount of the obligation that has been incurred.

Basically, preferred stock enables a firm to use leverage without fixed charges. For corporate investors at least 70 percent of the dividends can be excluded from taxable income, so that the 35 percent tax rate becomes only 10.5 percent. Generally, preferred stocks had been sold mostly by utility companies for whom the nondeductibility of dividends as an expense for tax purposes is less of a disadvantage because of the nature of the regulatory ratemaking process, which essentially treats taxes paid as an expense to be considered in setting allowable rates of return.

COMMON STOCK FINANCING

Two important positive considerations are involved in equity ownership: income and control. The right to income carries the risk of loss. Control also involves responsibility and liability.

Through the right to vote, holders of common stock have legal control of the corporation. As a practical matter, however, in many corporations, the principal officers constitute all, or a majority of, the members of the board of directors. In this circumstance, the board may be controlled by the management rather than by the owners. However, numerous examples demonstrate that stockholders can reassert their control if they are dissatisfied with the corporation's policies. In recent years, proxy battles with the aim of altering corporate policies have occurred with increasing frequency, and firms whose managers are unresponsive to stockholders' desires are subject to takeover bids by other firms.

Another consideration involved in equity ownership is risk. On liquidation, holders of common stock are last in the priority of claims. Therefore, the portion of capital they contribute provides a cushion for creditors, if losses occur on dissolution. The equity-to-total-assets ratio indicates the percentage by which assets may shrink in value on liquidation before creditors will incur losses.

Rights of Common Stockholders

The rights of holders of common stock in a business corporation are established by the laws of the state in which the corporation is chartered and by the terms of the charter granted by the state. Charters are relatively uniform on many matters, including collective and specific rights. Certain collective rights are usually given to the holders of common stock: (1) the right to amend the charter with the approval of the appropriate officials in the state of incorporation, (2) the right to adopt and amend bylaws, (3) the right to elect the directors of the corporation, (4) the right to authorize the sale of fixed assets, (5) the right to enter into mergers, (6) the right to change the amount of authorized common stock, and (7) the right to issue preferred stock, debentures, bonds, and other securities. Holders of common stock also have specific rights as individual owners: (1) the right to vote in the manner prescribed by the corporate charter, (2) the right to sell their stock certificates (their evidence of ownership) and, in this way, to transfer their ownership interest to other persons, (3) the right to inspect the corporate books, and (4) the right to share residual assets of the corporation on dissolution. (However, the holders of common stock are last among the claimants to the assets of the corporation.)

Nature of Voting Rights and Proxy Contests

For each share of common stock owned, the holder has the right to cast one vote at the annual meeting of stockholders or at such special meetings as may be called.

Proxy

Provision is made for the temporary transfer of the right to vote by an instrument known as a proxy. The transfer is limited in its duration; typically, it applies only to a specific occasion, such as the annual meeting of stockholders. The SEC supervises the use of the proxy machinery and frequently issues rules and regulations to improve its administration.

Cumulative Voting

A method of voting that has come into increased prominence is cumulative voting. Cumulative voting for directors is required in 22 states, including California, Illinois, Michigan, Ohio, and Pennsylvania. It is permissible in 18, including Delaware, New Jersey, and New York. Ten states make no provision for it.

Cumulative voting permits multiple votes for a single director. For example, suppose six directors are to be elected. Without cumulative voting, the owner of 100 shares can cast 100 votes for each of the six openings. When cumulative voting is permitted, the stockholder can accumulate the votes and cast all for one director, instead of 100 each for six directors. Cumulative voting is designed to enable a minority group of stockholders to obtain some voice in the control of the company by electing at least one director to the board.

Preemptive Right

The preemptive right gives holders of common stock the first option to purchase additional issues of common stock. In some states, the right is made part of every corporate charter; in others, the right must be specifically inserted in the charter.

The purpose of the preemptive right is twofold. First, it protects the power of control for present stockholders. If it were not for this safeguard, the management of a corporation could issue new common stock to new stockholders in an attempt to wrest control from current stockholders.

The second, and by far the more important, protection that the preemptive right affords stockholders concerns dilution of value. Selling new common stock at below market value enables new shareholders to buy stock on terms more favorable than those that had been extended to the old shareholders. The preemptive right prevents such occurrences.

Evaluation of Common Stock as a
Source of Long-Term Financing

The advantages of financing with common stock include these:

1. Common stock does not entail fixed charges. If the company generates the earnings, it can pay common stock dividends. In contrast to bond interest, however, there is no legal obligation to pay dividends.

2. Common stock carries no fixed maturity date.

3. Since common stock provides a cushion against losses of creditors, the sale of common stock increases the creditworthiness of the firm.

4. Common stock can, at times, be sold more easily than debt. It appeals to certain investor groups because (a) it typically carries a higher expected return than does preferred stock or debt and (b) since it represents the ownership of the firm, it provides the investor with a better hedge against inflation than does straight preferred stock or bonds. Ordinarily, common stock increases in value when the value of real assets rises during an inflationary period.

5. Returns from common stock in the form of capital gains may be subject to a lower personal income tax rate on capital gains. Hence, the effective personal income tax rates on returns from common stock may be lower than the effective tax rates on the interest on debt or preferred stock dividends.

   Disadvantages to the issuer of common stock include the following:

1. The sale of common stock may extend voting rights or control to the additional stockowners who are brought into the company. For this reason, among others, additional equity financing is often avoided by small and new firms, whose owner-managers may be unwilling to share control of their companies with outsiders.

2. The use of debt may enable the firm to utilize funds at a fixed low cost, whereas common stock gives equal rights to new stockholders to share in the future net profits of the firm.

3. The costs of underwriting and distributing common stock are usually higher than those for underwriting and distributing preferred stock or debt.

4. As we saw in Chap. 10, if the firm has more equity or less debt than is called for in the optimum capital structure, the average cost of capital will be higher than necessary.

5. Common stock dividends are not deductible as an expense for calculating the corporation's income subject to the federal income tax, but bond interest is deductible. The impact of this factor is reflected in the relative cost of equity capital vis-à-vis debt capital.

LEASE FINANCING

It is important to remember that lease financing is a substitute for debt. Leases take several different forms, the most important of which are sale and leaseback, service or operating leases, and straight financial leases. These three major types of lease are described below.

Sale and Leaseback

Under a sale and leaseback arrangement, a firm owning land, buildings, or equipment sells the property to a financial institution and simultaneously executes an agreement to lease the property back for a certain period under specific terms.

Note that the seller, or lessee, immediately receives the purchase price put up by the buyer, or lessor. At the same time, the seller-lessee retains the use of the property. This parallel is carried over to the lease payment schedule. Under a mortgage loan arrangement, the financial institution receives a series of equal payments just sufficient to amortize the loan and to provide the lender with a specified rate of return on investment. Under a sale and leaseback arrangement, the lease payments are set up in the same manner. The payments are sufficient to return the full purchase price to the financial institution in addition to providing it with some return on its investment.

Operating Leases

Operating, or service, leases include both financing and maintenance services. IBM is one of the pioneers of the service lease contract. Computers and office copying machines, together with automobiles and trucks, are the primary types of equipment covered by operating leases. The leases ordinarily call for the lessor to maintain and service the leased equipment, and the costs of this maintenance are either built into the lease payments or contracted for separately. Another important characteristic of the operating lease is that, frequently, it is not fully amortized. In other words, the payments required under the lease contract are not sufficient to recover the full cost of the equipment. Obviously, however, the lease contract is written for considerably less than the expected life of the leased equipment, and the lessor expects to recover the cost either in subsequent renewal payments or on disposal of the equipment. A final feature of the operating lease is that, frequently, it contains a cancellation clause, giving the lessee the right to cancel the lease and return the equipment before the expiration of the basic agreement. This is a put option that allows return of the equipment if technological developments render it obsolete or if it simply is no longer needed, which is an important consideration for the lessee.

Financial Leases

A strict financial lease is one that does not provide for maintenance services, is not cancelable, and is fully amortized (i.e., the lessor contracts for rental payments equal to the full price of the leased equipment). The typical arrangement involves the following steps:

1. The firm that will use the equipment selects the specific items it requires and negotiates the price and delivery terms with the manufacturer or distributor.
2. The user firm arranges with a bank or leasing company for the latter to buy the equipment from the manufacturer or distributor, simultaneously executing an agreement to lease the equipment from the financial institution. The terms call for full amortization of the financial institution's cost, plus a return on the lessor's investment. The lessee generally has the option to renew the lease at a reduced rental on expiration of the basic lease, but does not have the right to cancel the basic lease without completely paying off the financial institution.

Financial leases are almost the same as sale and leaseback arrangements, the main difference being that the leased equipment is new and the lessor buys it from a manufacturer or a distributor instead of from the user-lessee. A sale and leaseback can thus be thought of as a special type of financial lease.

Influences on the Leasing versus Owning Decision

In the absence of major tax advantages and other "market imperfections," there should be no advantage to either leasing or owning. However, there are wide ranges of factors that may influence the economic viability of leasing. These possible influences include differences in financing costs, tax differences, differences in maintenance costs, asset acquisition cost differences, differences in obsolescence and residual values, and differences in the contractual positions in leasing versus other forms and sources of financing. Whether these other factors will actually give an advantage or disadvantage to leasing depends on the facts and circumstances of each transaction analyzed.

As an example, a university may consider leasing its transportation fleet because a lessor may have the following advantages that could be shared with the university through reduced lease payments:

1. A lessor may be in a better credit position (lower cost of financing).
2. The lessor may be in a high tax bracket and pass on the depreciation tax shield to the university, which pays no income tax.
3. A lessor may be able to maintain the auto fleet in a more cost-effective manner.
4. The lessor may have a large national purchasing power (buys more than 100,000 vehicles per year) and thus acquires the vehicles at greatly reduced costs.
5. The lessor may have better disposal capabilities at the end of the lease, which results in higher residual values.

Again, the lessor can share all these savings with the lessee in the form of reduced lease payments. In this way, the lease decision may be more attractive than the buy decision.

SUMMARY

Venture capital financing has taken on increased importance in recent years. Venture capital firms typically use convertible preferred stock in staged financing as the good performance of the recipient firm is demonstrated. Venture capital is a form of direct financing. Two other major forms of direct financing are term lending by commercial banks and the private placement of securities with insurance companies and pension funds. Term loans and private placements represent similar financing arrangements.

The investment banker provides middleman services to both the seller and the buyer of new securities, helping plan the issue, underwriting it, and handling the job of selling the issue to the ultimate investor. The investment banker must also look to the interests of the brokerage customers; if these investors are not satisfied with the banker's products, they will deal elsewhere. Thus the investment banker performs a certification role for the issuer.

Going public and initial public offerings represent a fundamental change in the lifestyle of business firms. Costs of flotation are higher for initial public offerings than for seasoned issues. Flotation costs are higher for best-efforts offerings than for firm commitments. Best-efforts offerings typically involve smaller firms whose share prices exhibit greater volatility in the aftermarket.

A bond is a long-term promissory note. A mortgage bond is secured by real property. An indenture is an agreement between the firm issuing the bond and the numerous bondholders. Secured long-term debt differs with respect to (1) the priority of claims, (2) the right to issue additional securities, and (3) the scope of the lien provided. These characteristics determine the amount of protection provided to the bondholder.

While the characteristics of preferred stock vary, some patterns persist. Preferred stocks usually have priority over common stocks with respect to earnings and claims on assets in liquidation. Preferred stocks are perpetual (no maturity) but are sometimes callable. They are typically nonparticipating and offer only contingent voting rights. Preferred stock dividends are usually cumulative.

Common stock involves the balancing of risk, income, and control. We analyzed various dimensions of the rights of common stockholders. We discussed voting rights, cumulative voting, the proxy mechanism, and preemptive rights.

The most important forms of lease financing are (1) sale and leaseback, in which a firm owning land, buildings, or equipment sells the property and simultaneously executes an agreement to lease it for a certain period under specific terms; (2) service leases or operating leases, which include both financing and maintenance services and are often cancelable and call for payments under the lease contract that may not fully recover the cost or the equipment; and (3) financial leases, which do not provide for maintenance services, are not cancelable, and do fully amortize the cost of the leased asset during the basic lease contract period.

For the issuer, each form of long-term financing has both advantages and disadvantages that change over time. These advantages and disadvantages must be carefully balanced and considered when making any financing decision.

QUESTIONS AND PROBLEMS

11.1 **Venture capital.** Why are convertible preferred stock and a staged capital commitment employed by venture capitalists?

11.2 **Preferred stock.** If the corporate income tax were abolished, would this raise or lower the amount of new preferred stock issued?

11.3 **Term loan.** A firm is seeking a term loan from a bank. Under what conditions would it want a fixed interest rate, and under what conditions would it want the rate to fluctuate with the prime rate?

11.4   **Lease advantages.** Hershey Foods Corporation is a high marginal taxpayer and a high creditworthy firm. Explain when it might make sense for Hershey to lease an asset. Under what conditions should Hershey lease its computer systems?

11.5   **Security "sweeteners."** For each of the terms below, indicate if the term represents a sweetener for the issuer or buyer of a security. Provide a short explanation.

A. Convertibility   C. Covenants   E. Voting rights
B. Callable   D. Sinking fund   F. Cumulative dividends

SOLUTIONS TO QUESTIONS AND PROBLEMS

11.1   Preferred stock is less risky than common stock due to the order of bankruptcy if the company should not survive. The convertibility feature allows participation as the company grows and succeeds. Staged capital commitment permits the venture capitalist to fund the company in stages. After the first stage has been successfully completed and management demonstrates its abilities, a second round of financing is provided. Both of these techniques are aimed at reducing risk.

11.2   If the corporate income tax were abolished, the tax deductibility of interest would be rendered a moot point. Thus, one of the major advantages of debt would be neutralized, and more preferred stock would likely be issued.

11.3   A fixed interest loan eliminates all interest rate risk due to fluctuating market rates. If a company believes rates will fall in the future, it may want to take advantage of a floating rate debt instrument.

11.4   Hershey is a highly creditworthy firm and a high marginal taxpayer. As a result, it is unlikely that a lessor would be able to offer Hershey a lower implicit interest rate or share in more tax savings. However, in the case of computer equipment, many leasing companies (including computer manufacturers) can purchase the hardware at a reduced cost and pass along the savings in the form of lower lease payments. In addition, computer leasing companies generally have better access to the secondary (used) market which could result in a higher anticipated salvage value. The higher anticipated salvage value could also be passed along in the form of reduced lease payments.

11.5

Item	Sweetener for	Explanation
A. Convertibility	Buyer	Allows conversion (participation) to common stock.
B. Callable	Issuer	Allows the issuer to call the bond early if rates fall.
C. Covenants	Buyer	Protects the buyer from subsequent actions of the issuer.
D. Sinking Fund	Buyer	Protects the buyer by requiring the issuer to accumulate funds to payoff the principal.
E. Voting Rights	Buyer	Allows participation in the management of the firm.
F. Cumulative Dividends	Buyer	Protects the buyer if management decides to suspend dividends.

APPENDIX
Interest Tables

TABLE A.1

Future Value of $1 at the End of n Periods: $\text{FVIF}_{r,n} = (1 + r)^n$

Period	1%	2%	3%	4%	5%	6%	7%	8%	9%	10%	12%	14%	15%	16%	18%	20%	24%	28%	32%	36%
1	1.0100	1.0200	1.0300	1.0400	1.0500	1.0600	1.0700	1.0800	1.0900	1.1000	1.1200	1.1400	1.1500	1.1600	1.1800	1.2000	1.2400	1.2800	1.3200	1.3600
2	1.0201	1.0404	1.0609	1.0816	1.1025	1.1236	1.1449	1.1664	1.1881	1.2100	1.2544	1.2996	1.3225	1.3456	1.3924	1.4400	1.5376	1.6384	1.7424	1.8496
3	1.0303	1.0612	1.0927	1.1249	1.1576	1.1910	1.2250	1.2597	1.2950	1.3310	1.4049	1.4815	1.5209	1.5609	1.6430	1.7280	1.9066	2.0972	2.3000	2.5155
4	1.0406	1.0824	1.1255	1.1699	1.2155	1.2625	1.3108	1.3605	1.4116	1.4641	1.5735	1.6890	1.7490	1.8106	1.9388	2.0736	2.3642	2.6844	3.0360	3.4210
5	1.0510	1.1041	1.1593	1.2167	1.2763	1.3382	1.4026	1.4693	1.5386	1.6105	1.7623	1.9254	2.0114	2.1003	2.2878	2.4883	2.9316	3.4360	4.0075	4.6526
6	1.0615	1.1262	1.1941	1.2653	1.3401	1.4185	1.5007	1.5869	1.6771	1.7716	1.9738	2.1950	2.3131	2.4364	2.6996	2.9860	3.6352	4.3980	5.2899	6.3275
7	1.0721	1.1487	1.2299	1.3159	1.4071	1.5036	1.6058	1.7138	1.8280	1.9487	2.2107	2.5023	2.6600	2.8262	3.1855	3.5832	4.5077	5.6295	6.9826	8.6054
8	1.0829	1.1717	1.2668	1.3686	1.4775	1.5938	1.7182	1.8509	1.9926	2.1436	2.4760	2.8526	3.0590	3.2784	3.7589	4.2998	5.5895	7.2058	9.2170	11.703
9	1.0937	1.1951	1.3048	1.4233	1.5513	1.6895	1.8385	1.9990	2.1719	2.3579	2.7731	3.2519	3.5179	3.8030	4.4355	5.1598	6.9310	9.2234	12.166	15.917
10	1.1046	1.2190	1.3439	1.4802	1.6289	1.7908	1.9672	2.1589	2.3674	2.5937	3.1058	3.7072	4.0456	4.4114	5.2338	6.1917	8.5944	11.806	16.060	21.647
11	1.1157	1.2434	1.3842	1.5395	1.7103	1.8983	2.1049	2.3316	2.5804	2.8531	3.4785	4.2262	4.6524	5.1173	6.1759	7.4301	10.657	15.112	21.199	29.439
12	1.1268	1.2682	1.4258	1.6010	1.7959	2.0122	2.2522	2.5182	2.8127	3.1384	3.8960	4.8179	5.3503	5.9360	7.2876	8.9161	13.215	19.343	27.983	40.037
13	1.1381	1.2936	1.4685	1.6651	1.8856	2.1329	2.4098	2.7196	3.0658	3.4523	4.3635	5.4924	6.1528	6.8858	8.5994	10.699	16.386	24.759	36.937	54.451
14	1.1495	1.3195	1.5126	1.7317	1.9799	2.2609	2.5785	2.9372	3.3417	3.7975	4.8871	6.2613	7.0757	7.9875	10.147	12.839	20.319	31.691	48.757	74.053
15	1.1610	1.3459	1.5580	1.8009	2.0789	2.3966	2.7590	3.1722	3.6425	4.1772	5.4736	7.1379	8.1371	9.2655	11.974	15.407	25.196	40.565	64.359	100.71
16	1.1726	1.3728	1.6047	1.8730	2.1829	2.5404	2.9522	3.4259	3.9703	4.5950	6.1304	8.1372	9.3576	10.748	14.129	18.488	31.243	51.923	84.954	136.97
17	1.1843	1.4002	1.6528	1.9479	2.2920	2.6928	3.1588	3.7000	4.3276	5.0545	6.8660	9.2765	10.761	12.468	16.672	22.186	38.741	66.461	112.14	186.28
18	1.1961	1.4282	1.7024	2.0258	2.4066	2.8543	3.3799	3.9960	4.7171	5.5599	7.6900	10.575	12.375	14.463	19.673	26.623	48.039	85.071	148.02	253.34
19	1.2081	1.4568	1.7535	2.1068	2.5270	3.0256	3.6165	4.3157	5.1417	6.1159	8.6128	12.056	14.232	16.777	23.214	31.948	59.568	108.89	195.39	344.54
20	1.2202	1.4859	1.8061	2.1911	2.6533	3.2071	3.8697	4.6610	5.6044	6.7275	9.6463	13.743	16.367	19.461	27.393	38.338	73.864	139.38	257.92	468.57
21	1.2324	1.5157	1.8603	2.2788	2.7860	3.3996	4.1406	5.0338	6.1088	7.4002	10.804	15.668	18.822	22.574	32.324	46.005	91.592	178.41	340.45	637.26
22	1.2447	1.5460	1.9161	2.3699	2.9253	3.6035	4.4304	5.4365	6.6586	8.1403	12.100	17.861	21.645	26.186	38.142	55.206	113.57	228.36	449.39	866.67
23	1.2572	1.5769	1.9736	2.4647	3.0715	3.8197	4.7405	5.8715	7.2579	8.9543	13.552	20.362	24.891	30.376	45.008	66.247	140.83	292.30	593.20	1178.7
24	1.2697	1.6084	2.0328	2.5633	3.2251	4.0489	5.0724	6.3412	7.9111	9.8497	15.179	23.212	28.625	35.236	53.109	79.497	174.63	374.14	783.02	1603.0
25	1.2824	1.6406	2.0938	2.6658	3.3864	4.2919	5.4274	6.8485	8.6231	10.835	17.000	26.462	32.919	40.874	62.669	95.396	216.54	478.90	1033.6	2180.1
26	1.2953	1.6734	2.1566	2.7725	3.5557	4.5494	5.8074	7.3964	9.3992	11.918	19.040	30.167	37.857	47.414	73.949	114.48	268.51	613.00	1364.3	2964.9
27	1.3082	1.7069	2.2213	2.8834	3.7335	4.8223	6.2139	7.9881	10.245	13.110	21.325	34.390	43.535	55.000	87.260	137.37	332.95	784.64	1800.9	4032.3
28	1.3213	1.7410	2.2879	2.9987	3.9201	5.1117	6.6488	8.6271	11.167	14.421	23.884	39.204	50.066	63.800	102.97	164.84	412.86	1004.3	2377.2	5483.9
29	1.3345	1.7758	2.3566	3.1187	4.1161	5.4184	7.1143	9.3173	12.172	15.863	26.750	44.693	57.575	74.009	121.50	197.81	511.95	1285.6	3137.9	7458.1
30	1.3478	1.8114	2.4273	3.2434	4.3219	5.7435	7.6123	10.063	13.268	17.449	29.960	50.950	66.212	85.850	143.37	237.38	634.82	1645.5	4142.1	10143
40	1.4889	2.2080	3.2620	4.8010	7.0400	10.286	14.974	21.725	31.409	45.259	93.051	188.88	267.86	378.72	750.38	1469.8	5455.9	19427	66521	*
50	1.6446	2.6916	4.3839	7.1067	11.467	18.420	29.457	46.902	74.358	117.39	289.00	700.23	1083.7	1670.7	3927.4	9100.4	46890	*	*	*
60	1.8167	3.2810	5.8916	10.520	18.679	32.988	57.946	101.26	176.03	304.48	897.60	2595.9	4384.0	7370.2	20555	56348	*	*	*	*

*FVIF > 99,999.

TABLE A.2

Present Value of $1 Received at the End of n Periods: $PVIF_{r,\,n} = 1/(1+r)^n = (1+r)^{-n}$

Period	1%	2%	3%	4%	5%	6%	7%	8%	9%	10%	12%	14%	15%	16%	18%	20%	24%	28%	32%	36%
1	.9901	.9804	.9709	.9615	.9524	.9434	.9346	.9259	.9174	.9091	.8929	.8772	.8696	.8621	.8475	.8333	.8065	.7813	.7576	.7353
2	.9803	.9612	.9426	.9246	.9070	.8900	.8734	.8573	.8417	.8264	.7972	.7695	.7561	.7432	.7182	.6944	.6504	.6104	.5739	.5407
3	.9706	.9423	.9151	.8890	.8638	.8396	.8163	.7938	.7722	.7513	.7118	.6750	.6575	.6407	.6086	.5787	.5245	.4768	.4348	.3975
4	.9610	.9238	.8885	.8548	.8227	.7921	.7629	.7350	.7084	.6830	.6355	.5921	.5718	.5523	.5158	.4823	.4230	.3725	.3294	.2923
5	.9515	.9057	.8626	.8219	.7835	.7473	.7130	.6806	.6499	.6209	.5674	.5194	.4972	.4761	.4371	.4019	.3411	.2910	.2495	.2149
6	.9420	.8880	.8375	.7903	.7462	.7050	.6663	.6302	.5963	.5645	.5066	.4556	.4323	.4104	.3704	.3349	.2751	.2274	.1890	.1580
7	.9327	.8706	.8131	.7599	.7107	.6651	.6227	.5835	.5470	.5132	.4523	.3996	.3759	.3538	.3139	.2791	.2218	.1776	.1432	.1162
8	.9235	.8535	.7894	.7307	.6768	.6274	.5820	.5403	.5019	.4665	.4039	.3506	.3269	.3050	.2660	.2326	.1789	.1388	.1085	.0854
9	.9143	.8368	.7664	.7026	.6446	.5919	.5439	.5002	.4604	.4241	.3606	.3075	.2843	.2630	.2255	.1938	.1443	.1084	.0822	.0628
10	.9053	.8203	.7441	.6756	.6139	.5584	.5083	.4632	.4224	.3855	.3220	.2697	.2472	.2267	.1911	.1615	.1164	.0847	.0623	.0462
11	.8963	.8043	.7224	.6496	.5847	.5268	.4751	.4289	.3875	.3505	.2875	.2366	.2149	.1954	.1619	.1346	.0938	.0662	.0472	.0340
12	.8874	.7885	.7014	.6246	.5568	.4970	.4440	.3971	.3555	.3186	.2567	.2076	.1869	.1685	.1372	.1122	.0757	.0517	.0357	.0250
13	.8787	.7730	.6810	.6006	.5303	.4688	.4150	.3677	.3262	.2897	.2292	.1821	.1625	.1452	.1163	.0935	.0610	.0404	.0271	.0184
14	.8700	.7579	.6611	.5775	.5051	.4423	.3878	.3405	.2992	.2633	.2046	.1597	.1413	.1252	.0985	.0779	.0492	.0316	.0205	.0135
15	.8613	.7430	.6419	.5553	.4810	.4173	.3624	.3152	.2745	.2394	.1827	.1401	.1229	.1079	.0835	.0649	.0397	.0247	.0155	.0099
16	.8528	.7284	.6232	.5339	.4581	.3936	.3387	.2919	.2519	.2176	.1631	.1229	.1069	.0930	.0708	.0541	.0320	.0193	.0118	.0073
17	.8444	.7142	.6050	.5134	.4363	.3714	.3166	.2703	.2311	.1978	.1456	.1078	.0929	.0802	.0600	.0451	.0258	.0150	.0089	.0054
18	.8360	.7002	.5874	.4936	.4155	.3503	.2959	.2502	.2120	.1799	.1300	.0946	.0808	.0691	.0508	.0376	.0208	.0118	.0068	.0039
19	.8277	.6864	.5703	.4746	.3957	.3305	.2765	.2317	.1945	.1635	.1161	.0829	.0703	.0596	.0431	.0313	.0168	.0092	.0051	.0029
20	.8195	.6730	.5537	.4564	.3769	.3118	.2584	.2145	.1784	.1486	.1037	.0728	.0611	.0514	.0365	.0261	.0135	.0072	.0039	.0021
21	.8114	.6598	.5375	.4388	.3589	.2942	.2415	.1987	.1637	.1351	.0926	.0638	.0531	.0443	.0309	.0217	.0109	.0056	.0029	.0016
22	.8034	.6468	.5219	.4220	.3418	.2775	.2257	.1839	.1502	.1228	.0826	.0560	.0462	.0382	.0262	.0181	.0088	.0044	.0022	.0012
23	.7954	.6342	.5067	.4057	.3256	.2618	.2109	.1703	.1378	.1117	.0738	.0491	.0402	.0329	.0222	.0151	.0071	.0034	.0017	.0008
24	.7876	.6217	.4919	.3901	.3101	.2470	.1971	.1577	.1264	.1015	.0659	.0431	.0349	.0284	.0188	.0126	.0057	.0027	.0013	.0006
25	.7798	.6095	.4776	.3751	.2953	.2330	.1842	.1460	.1160	.0923	.0588	.0378	.0304	.0245	.0160	.0105	.0046	.0021	.0010	.0005
26	.7720	.5976	.4637	.3607	.2812	.2198	.1722	.1352	.1064	.0839	.0525	.0331	.0264	.0211	.0135	.0087	.0037	.0016	.0007	.0003
27	.7644	.5859	.4502	.3468	.2678	.2074	.1609	.1252	.0976	.0763	.0469	.0291	.0230	.0182	.0115	.0073	.0030	.0013	.0006	.0002
28	.7568	.5744	.4371	.3335	.2551	.1956	.1504	.1159	.0895	.0693	.0419	.0255	.0200	.0157	.0097	.0061	.0024	.0010	.0004	.0002
29	.7493	.5631	.4243	.3207	.2429	.1846	.1406	.1073	.0822	.0630	.0374	.0224	.0174	.0135	.0082	.0051	.0020	.0008	.0003	.0001
30	.7419	.5521	.4120	.3083	.2314	.1741	.1314	.0994	.0754	.0573	.0334	.0196	.0151	.0116	.0070	.0042	.0016	.0006	.0002	.0001
35	.7059	.5000	.3554	.2534	.1813	.1301	.0937	.0676	.0490	.0356	.0189	.0102	.0075	.0055	.0030	.0017	.0005	.0002	.0001	*
40	.6717	.4529	.3066	.2083	.1420	.0972	.0668	.0460	.0318	.0221	.0107	.0053	.0037	.0026	.0013	.0007	.0002	.0001	*	*
45	.6391	.4102	.2644	.1712	.1113	.0727	.0476	.0313	.0207	.0137	.0061	.0027	.0019	.0013	.0006	.0003	.0001	*	*	*
50	.6080	.3715	.2281	.1407	.0872	.0543	.0339	.0213	.0134	.0085	.0035	.0014	.0009	.0006	.0003	.0001	*	*	*	*
55	.5785	.3365	.1968	.1157	.0683	.0406	.0242	.0145	.0087	.0053	.0020	.0007	.0005	.0003	.0001	*	*	*	*	*

*The factor is zero to four decimal places.

TABLE A.3

Sum on an Annuity of $1 Per Period for n Periods: $FVIFA_{r,t} = \sum_{t=1}^{n}(1+r)^{t-1} = \dfrac{(1+r)^n - 1}{r}$

Number of Periods	1%	2%	3%	4%	5%	6%	7%	8%	9%	10%	12%	14%	15%	16%	18%	20%	24%	28%	32%	36%
1	1.0000	1.0000	1.0000	1.0000	1.0000	1.0000	1.0000	1.0000	1.0000	1.0000	1.0000	1.0000	1.0000	1.0000	1.0000	1.0000	1.0000	1.0000	1.0000	1.0000
2	2.0100	2.0200	2.0300	2.0400	2.0500	2.0600	2.0700	2.0800	2.0900	2.1000	2.1200	2.1400	2.1500	2.1600	2.1800	2.2000	2.2400	2.2800	2.3200	2.3600
3	3.0301	3.0604	3.0909	3.1216	3.1525	3.1836	3.2149	3.2464	3.2781	3.3100	3.3744	3.4396	3.4725	3.5056	3.5724	3.6400	3.7776	3.9184	4.0624	4.2096
4	4.0604	4.1216	4.1836	4.2465	4.3101	4.3746	4.4399	4.5061	4.5731	4.6410	4.7793	4.9211	4.9934	5.0665	5.2154	5.3680	5.6842	6.0156	6.3624	6.7251
5	5.1010	5.2040	5.3091	5.4163	5.5256	5.6371	5.7507	5.8666	5.9847	6.1051	6.3528	6.6101	6.7424	6.8771	7.1542	7.4416	8.0484	8.6999	9.3983	10.146
6	6.1520	6.3081	6.4684	6.6330	6.8019	6.9753	7.1533	7.3359	7.5233	7.7156	8.1152	8.5355	8.7537	8.9775	9.4420	9.9299	10.980	12.136	13.406	14.799
7	7.2135	7.4343	7.6625	7.8983	8.1420	8.3938	8.6540	8.9228	9.2004	9.4872	10.089	10.730	11.067	11.414	12.142	12.916	14.615	16.534	18.696	21.126
8	8.2857	8.5830	8.8923	9.2142	9.5491	9.8975	10.260	10.637	11.028	11.436	12.300	13.233	13.727	14.240	15.327	16.499	19.123	22.163	25.678	29.732
9	9.3685	9.7546	10.159	10.583	11.027	11.491	11.978	12.488	13.021	13.579	14.776	16.085	16.786	17.519	19.086	20.799	24.712	29.369	34.895	41.435
10	10.462	10.950	11.464	12.006	12.578	13.181	13.816	14.487	15.193	15.937	17.549	19.337	20.304	21.321	23.521	25.959	31.643	38.593	47.062	57.352
11	11.567	12.169	12.808	13.486	14.207	14.972	15.784	16.645	17.560	18.531	20.655	23.045	24.349	25.733	28.755	32.150	40.238	50.398	63.122	78.998
12	12.683	13.412	14.192	15.026	15.917	16.870	17.888	18.977	20.141	21.384	24.133	27.271	29.002	30.850	34.931	39.581	50.895	65.510	84.320	108.44
13	13.809	14.680	15.618	16.627	17.713	18.882	20.141	21.495	22.953	24.523	28.029	32.089	34.352	36.786	42.219	48.497	64.110	84.853	112.30	148.47
14	14.947	15.974	17.086	18.292	19.599	21.015	22.550	24.215	26.019	27.975	32.393	37.581	40.505	43.672	50.818	59.196	80.496	109.61	149.24	202.93
15	16.097	17.293	18.599	20.024	21.579	23.276	25.129	27.152	29.361	31.772	37.280	43.842	47.580	51.660	60.965	72.035	100.82	141.30	198.00	276.98
16	17.258	18.639	20.157	21.825	23.657	25.673	27.888	30.324	33.003	35.950	42.753	50.980	55.717	60.925	72.939	87.442	126.01	181.87	262.36	377.69
17	18.430	20.012	21.762	23.698	25.840	28.213	30.840	33.750	36.974	40.545	48.884	59.118	65.075	71.673	87.068	105.93	157.25	233.79	347.31	514.66
18	19.615	21.412	23.414	25.645	28.132	30.906	33.999	37.450	41.301	45.599	55.750	68.394	75.836	84.141	103.74	128.12	195.99	300.25	459.45	700.94
19	20.811	22.841	25.117	27.671	30.539	33.760	37.379	41.446	46.018	51.159	63.440	78.969	88.212	98.603	123.41	154.74	244.03	385.32	607.47	954.28
20	22.019	24.297	26.870	29.778	33.006	36.786	40.995	45.762	51.160	57.275	72.052	91.025	102.44	115.38	146.63	186.69	303.60	494.21	802.86	1298.8
21	23.239	25.783	28.676	31.969	35.719	39.993	44.865	50.423	56.765	64.002	81.699	104.77	118.81	134.84	174.02	225.03	377.46	633.59	1060.8	1767.4
22	24.472	27.299	30.537	34.248	38.505	43.392	49.006	55.457	62.873	71.403	92.503	120.44	137.63	157.41	206.34	271.03	469.06	812.00	1401.2	2404.7
23	25.716	28.845	32.453	36.618	41.430	46.996	53.436	60.893	69.532	79.543	104.60	138.30	159.28	183.60	244.49	326.24	582.63	1040.4	1850.6	3271.3
24	26.973	30.422	34.426	39.083	44.502	50.816	58.177	66.765	76.790	88.497	118.16	158.66	184.17	213.98	289.49	392.48	723.46	1332.7	2443.8	4450.0
25	28.243	32.030	36.459	41.646	47.727	54.865	63.249	73.106	84.701	98.347	133.33	181.87	212.79	249.21	342.60	471.98	898.09	1706.8	3226.8	6053.0
26	29.526	33.671	38.553	44.312	51.113	59.156	68.676	79.954	93.324	109.18	150.33	208.33	245.71	290.09	405.27	567.38	1114.6	2185.7	4260.4	8233.1
27	30.821	35.344	40.710	47.084	54.669	63.706	74.484	87.351	102.72	121.10	169.37	238.50	283.57	337.50	479.22	681.85	1383.1	2798.7	5624.8	11198.0
28	32.129	37.051	42.931	49.968	58.403	68.528	80.698	95.339	112.97	134.21	190.70	272.89	327.10	392.50	566.48	819.22	1716.1	3583.3	7425.7	15230.3
29	33.450	38.792	45.219	52.966	62.323	73.640	87.347	103.97	124.14	148.63	214.58	312.09	377.17	456.30	669.45	984.07	2129.0	4587.7	9802.9	20714.2
30	34.785	40.568	47.575	56.085	66.439	79.058	94.461	113.28	136.31	164.49	241.33	356.79	434.75	530.31	790.95	1181.9	2640.9	5873.2	12941	28172.3
40	48.886	60.402	75.401	95.026	120.80	154.76	199.64	259.06	337.88	442.59	767.09	1342.0	1779.1	2360.8	4163.2	7343.9	22729	69377	*	*
50	64.463	84.579	112.80	152.67	209.35	290.34	406.53	573.77	815.08	1163.9	2400.0	4994.5	7217.7	10436	21813	45497	*	*	*	*
60	81.670	114.05	163.05	237.99	353.58	533.13	813.52	1253.2	1944.8	3034.8	7471.6	18535	29220	46058	*	*	*	*	*	*

*FVIFA > 99,999.

TABLE A.4

Present Value of an Annuity of \$1 Per Period for n Periods: $\text{PVIFA}_{r,\,t} = \displaystyle\sum_{t=1}^{n} \frac{1}{(1+r)^{t}} = \frac{1 - 1/(1+r)^{n}}{r}$

Number of Periods	1%	2%	3%	4%	5%	6%	7%	8%	9%	10%	12%	14%	15%	16%	18%	20%	24%	28%	32%
1	0.9901	0.9804	0.9709	0.9615	0.9524	0.9434	0.9346	0.9259	0.9174	0.9091	0.8929	0.8772	0.8696	0.8621	0.8475	0.8333	0.8065	0.7813	0.7576
2	1.9704	1.9416	1.9135	1.8861	1.8594	1.8334	1.8080	1.7833	1.7591	1.7355	1.6901	1.6467	1.6257	1.6052	1.5656	1.5278	1.4568	1.3916	1.3315
3	2.9410	2.8839	2.8286	2.7751	2.7232	2.6730	2.6243	2.5771	2.5313	2.4869	2.4018	2.3216	2.2832	2.2459	2.1743	2.1065	1.9813	1.8684	1.7663
4	3.9020	3.8077	3.7171	3.6299	3.5460	3.4651	3.3872	3.3121	3.2397	3.1699	3.0373	2.9137	2.8550	2.7982	2.6901	2.5887	2.4043	2.2410	2.0957
5	4.8534	4.7135	4.5797	4.4518	4.3295	4.2124	4.1002	3.9927	3.8897	3.7908	3.6048	3.4331	3.3522	3.2743	3.1272	2.9906	2.7454	2.5320	2.3452
6	5.7955	5.6014	5.4172	5.2421	5.0757	4.9173	4.7665	4.6229	4.4859	4.3553	4.1114	3.8887	3.7845	3.6847	3.4976	3.3255	3.0205	2.7594	2.5342
7	6.7282	6.4720	6.2303	6.0021	5.7864	5.5824	5.3893	5.2064	5.0330	4.8684	4.5638	4.2883	4.1604	4.0386	3.8115	3.6046	3.2423	2.9370	2.6775
8	7.6517	7.3255	7.0197	6.7327	6.4632	6.2098	5.9713	5.7466	5.5348	5.3349	4.9676	4.6389	4.4873	4.3436	4.0776	3.8372	3.4212	3.0758	2.7860
9	8.5660	8.1622	7.7861	7.4353	7.1078	6.8017	6.5152	6.2469	5.9952	5.7590	5.3282	4.9464	4.7716	4.6065	4.3030	4.0310	3.5655	3.1842	2.8681
10	9.4713	8.9826	8.5302	8.1109	7.7217	7.3601	7.0236	6.7101	6.4177	6.1446	5.6502	5.2161	5.0188	4.8332	4.4941	4.1925	3.6819	3.2689	2.9304
11	10.3676	9.7868	9.2526	8.7605	8.3064	7.8869	7.4987	7.1390	6.8052	6.4951	5.9377	5.4527	5.2337	5.0286	4.6560	4.3271	3.7757	3.3351	2.9776
12	11.2551	10.5753	9.9540	9.3851	8.8633	8.3838	7.9427	7.5361	7.1607	6.8137	6.1944	5.6603	5.4206	5.1971	4.7932	4.4392	3.8514	3.3868	3.0133
13	12.1337	11.3484	10.6350	9.9856	9.3936	8.8527	8.3577	7.9038	7.4869	7.1034	6.4235	5.8424	5.5831	5.3423	4.9095	4.5327	3.9124	3.4272	3.0404
14	13.0037	12.1062	11.2961	10.5631	9.8986	9.2950	8.7455	8.2442	7.7862	7.3667	6.6282	6.0021	5.7245	5.4675	5.0081	4.6106	3.9616	3.4587	3.0609
15	13.8651	12.8493	11.9379	11.1184	10.3797	9.7122	9.1079	8.5595	8.0607	7.6061	6.8109	6.1422	5.8474	5.5755	5.0916	4.6755	4.0013	3.4834	3.0764
16	14.7179	13.5777	12.5611	11.6523	10.8378	10.1059	9.4466	8.8514	8.3126	7.8237	6.9740	6.2651	5.9542	5.6685	5.1624	4.7296	4.0333	3.5026	3.0882
17	15.5623	14.2919	13.1661	12.1657	11.2741	10.4773	9.7632	9.1216	8.5436	8.0216	7.1196	6.3729	6.0472	5.7487	5.2223	4.7746	4.0591	3.5177	3.0971
18	16.3983	14.9920	13.7535	12.6593	11.6896	10.8276	10.0591	9.3719	8.7556	8.2014	7.2497	6.4674	6.1280	5.8178	5.2732	4.8122	4.0799	3.5294	3.1039
19	17.2260	15.6785	14.3238	13.1339	12.0853	11.1581	10.3356	9.6036	8.9501	8.3649	7.3658	6.5504	6.1982	5.8775	5.3162	4.8435	4.0967	3.5386	3.1090
20	18.0456	16.3514	14.8775	13.5903	12.4622	11.4699	10.5940	9.8181	9.1285	8.5136	7.4694	6.6231	6.2593	5.9288	5.3527	4.8696	4.1103	3.5458	3.1129
21	18.8570	17.0112	15.4150	14.0292	12.8212	11.7641	10.8355	10.0168	9.2922	8.6487	7.5620	6.6870	6.3125	5.9731	5.3837	4.8913	4.1212	3.5514	3.1158
22	19.6604	17.6580	15.9369	14.4511	13.1630	12.0416	11.0612	10.2007	9.4424	8.7715	7.6446	6.7429	6.3587	6.0113	5.4099	4.9094	4.1300	3.5558	3.1180
23	20.4558	18.2922	16.4436	14.8568	13.4886	12.3034	11.2722	10.3711	9.5802	8.8832	7.7184	6.7921	6.3988	6.0442	5.4321	4.9245	4.1371	3.5592	3.1197
24	21.2434	18.9139	16.9355	15.2470	13.7986	12.5504	11.4693	10.5288	9.7066	8.9847	7.7843	6.8351	6.4338	6.0726	5.4509	4.9371	4.1428	3.5619	3.1210
25	22.0232	19.5235	17.4131	15.6221	14.0939	12.7834	11.6536	10.6748	9.8226	9.0770	7.8431	6.8729	6.4641	6.0971	5.4669	4.9476	4.1474	3.5640	3.1220
26	22.7952	20.1210	17.8768	15.9828	14.3752	13.0032	11.8258	10.8100	9.9290	9.1609	7.8957	6.9061	6.4906	6.1182	5.4804	4.9563	4.1511	3.5656	3.1227
27	23.5596	20.7069	18.3270	16.3296	14.6430	13.2105	11.9867	10.9352	10.0266	9.2372	7.9426	6.9352	6.5135	6.1364	5.4919	4.9636	4.1542	3.5669	3.1233
28	24.3164	21.2813	18.7641	16.6631	14.8981	13.4062	12.1371	11.0511	10.1161	9.3066	7.9844	6.9607	6.5335	6.1520	5.5016	4.9697	4.1566	3.5679	3.1237
29	25.0658	21.8444	19.1885	16.9837	15.1411	13.5907	12.2777	11.1584	10.1983	9.3696	8.0218	6.9830	6.5509	6.1656	5.5098	4.9747	4.1585	3.5687	3.1240
30	25.8077	22.3965	19.6004	17.2920	15.3725	13.7648	12.4090	11.2578	10.2737	9.4269	8.0552	7.0027	6.5660	6.1772	5.5168	4.9789	4.1601	3.5693	3.1242
35	29.4086	24.9986	21.4872	18.6646	16.3742	14.4982	12.9477	11.6546	10.5668	9.6442	8.1755	7.0700	6.6166	6.2153	5.5386	4.9915	4.1644	3.5708	3.1248
40	32.8347	27.3555	23.1148	19.7928	17.1591	15.0463	13.3317	11.9246	10.7574	9.7791	8.2438	7.1050	6.6418	6.2335	5.5482	4.9966	4.1659	3.5712	3.1250
45	36.0945	29.4902	24.5187	20.7200	17.7741	15.4558	13.6055	12.1084	10.8812	9.8628	8.2825	7.1232	6.6543	6.2421	5.5523	4.9986	4.1664	3.5714	3.1250
50	39.1961	31.4236	25.7298	21.4822	18.2559	15.7619	13.8007	12.2335	10.9617	9.9148	8.3045	7.1327	6.6605	6.2463	5.5541	4.9995	4.1666	3.5714	3.1250
55	42.1472	33.1748	26.7744	22.1086	18.6335	15.9905	13.9399	12.3186	11.0140	9.9471	8.3170	7.1376	6.6636	6.2482	5.5549	4.9998	4.1666	3.5714	3.1250

INDEX

ABOUT THE AUTHORS

Samuel C. Weaver, Ph.D., is associate processor of finance at Lehigh University, where he formerly served as the Theodore A. Lauer Adjunct Professor of Finance. He spent 20 years as an executive with Hershey Chocolate USA, serving in various capacities, including director, financial planning, and analysis. Dr. Weaver serves on the Board of Trustees of the Finacial Management Association and is on the Board of Editors of *Financial Practice and Education* and *Financial Management Collection.*

J. Fred Weston, Ph.D., is Professor Emeritus Recalled of Managerial Economics and Finance at the John E. Anderson Graduate School of Management at UCLA, where, since 1968, he has been Director of the UCLA Research Program on Takeovers and Restructuring. He received his Ph.D. degree from the University of Chicago in 1948. Dr. Weston has served as president of the American Finance Association, president of the Western Economic Association, president of the Financial Management Association, and member of the American Economic U.S. Census Advisory Committee. He has been selected as a fellow of the American Finance Association, of the Financial Management Association, and of the National Association of Business Economists, and published 147 journal articles and 31 books, including *Managerial Finance, Public Policy Toward Mergers* and *The Art of M&A Financing and Refinancing.*